VOLUME I

Research on Sentencing: The Search for Reform

Alfred Blumstein, Jacqueline Cohen, Susan E. Martin, and Michael H. Tonry, *Editors*

Panel on Sentencing Research

Committee on Research on Law Enforcement and the Administration of Justice

Commission on Behavioral and Social Sciences and Education

National Research Council

NATIONAL ACADEMY PRESS
Washington, D.C.   1983

Library of Congress Cataloging in Publication Data
Main entry under title:

Research on sentencing.

Bibliography: v. 1, p.
1. Sentences (Criminal procedure)—United States.
2. Sentences (Criminal procedure)—United States—
States. I. Blumstein, Alfred. II. National Research
Council (U.S.). Panel on Sentencing Research.
KF9685.R38 1983   345.73'0772   83–4048
                        347.305772
International Standard Book Number 0–309–03347–0

Available from

NATIONAL ACADEMY PRESS
2101 Constitution Avenue, NW
Washington, DC 20418

Printed in the United States of America

iii

iv

Contents

v

Tables and Figures

FIGURES

Contents
Volume II

Preface

The Panel on Sentencing Research is an outgrowth of the ferment that significantly affected sentencing practice in the 1970s. That ferment is reflected in a variety of sentencing "reforms," many of which had their roots in research, much of which involved technical questions of some complexity.

The Panel on Sentencing Research was established in September 1980 to review that research on sentencing and its impact. The panel was created in response to a request from the National Institute of Justice to the National Academy of Sciences as a panel of the Committee on Research on Law Enforcement and the Administration of Justice of the Commission on Behavioral and Social Sciences and Education of the National Research Council. The panel's task was to assess the quality of the available research, to indicate how the application of research techniques could be improved, and to suggest directions for future research, especially that supported by the National Institute of Justice. To address this range of issues, the panel was composed of specialists representing a variety of academic disciplines, methodological approaches, and operational expertise in the criminal justice system (see Appendix B for biographical sketches of panel members and staff).

The issue of sentencing is very broad, and so the panel very early had to limit the scope of its work. Much of the public concern over sentencing relates to its effects on crime, but those effects were explicitly excluded from the panel's efforts because two other panels of the Committee on Research on Law Enforcement and the Administration of Justice—the

Panel on Research on Rehabilitative Techniques and the Panel on Research on Deterrent and Incapacitative Effects—had recently reviewed the research in their respective areas and identified directions for future research.

Sentencing also involves many complex philosophical questions relating to the role of punishment in society, to the appropriate form of punishment, and to the symbolic qualities of punishment. The panel inquired into these areas to provide a background perspective for its work but viewed their resolution to involve predominantly normative, nonempirical considerations and thus to fall outside the panel's research-related mandate. There are also many important issues surrounding the question of the sentencing of juveniles; however, since most of the recent sentencing research and reform has been directed at the adult criminal justice system, that has been the focus of the panel's attention.

In addressing its task, the panel directed its major attention to those issues on which a reasonable body of research already existed or for which new research held promise of making important new contributions. The panel commissioned several papers to synthesize the research in some areas that were particularly extensive, to explicate important methodological issues that limited the validity of existing research, and to identify particularly promising future research possibilities. These papers were presented at a conference the panel organized at Woods Hole, Massachusetts, on July 27–29, 1981 (see Appendix A for a list of participants). The discussion of those papers provided an important contribution to the panel's deliberations, and a number of the commissioned papers, revised in response to the panel's suggestions, are contained in Volume II. Those papers, which represent the views of the individual authors rather than the panel, are published because the panel believes they make a valuable contribution to the literature on sentencing research.

The report of the panel is presented in this volume. It is the result of vigorous debates and some compromises. Although some members of the panel would have preferred greater emphasis given to certain issues or arguments, the report represents the collective views of the panel.

The panel appreciates the constructive criticism and review the report has received from others. A draft of the panel's report was sent for review to all participants at the Woods Hole conference and to all members of the Committee on Research on Law Enforcement and the Administration of Justice.

The panel would like to express its deep appreciation for the extensive contributions by its staff. Susan Martin of the National Research Council served as study director and, as such, managed the affairs of the panel and addressed many of the sociological issues involved in the work of the panel. As a consultant, Jacqueline Cohen of Carnegie-Mellon University had a primary responsibility for addressing the analytical issues in the research reviewed, but her skills and commitment resulted in many important contributions throughout the report. Michael Tonry of the University of Maryland School of Law, also as a consultant, contributed valuable perspectives on the many legal and philosophical considerations involved throughout the work of the panel. A final editing of the panel's report and the papers in Volume II was undertaken by Eugenia Grohman and Christine McShane, respectively, of the Commission on Behavioral and Social Sciences and Education, and their editorial skills are much appreciated. Diane Goldman at the National Research Council provided major administrative and secretarial support throughout the work of the panel, and her dedication was notable. Jane Beltz provided comparable support at Carnegie-Mellon University.

We would also like to express our appreciation to the National Institute of Justice. Robert Burkhart and Cheryl Martorana of the institute attended most of the meetings of the panel and were most helpful in providing advice and information on the institute's program on sentencing research.

ALFRED BLUMSTEIN, *Chair*
Panel on Sentencing Research

Research on Sentencing: The Search for Reform

Summary

INTRODUCTION

The sentencing decision is the symbolic keystone of the criminal justice system: in it, the conflicts between the goals of equal justice under the law and individualized justice with punishment tailored to the offender are played out, and society's moral principles and highest values—life and liberty—are interpreted and applied. Therefore, it is not surprising that as crime increased and questions about the criminal justice system's fairness and effectiveness grew pressing in the early 1970s, reformers began reexamining the courts and their sentencing practices.

BACKGROUND

The decade of the 1970s was characterized by a variety of efforts to modify sentencing practices, to establish more detailed criteria for sentencing, and to establish new sentencing institutions and procedures. These reforms have included:

- Abolition of plea bargaining
- Plea-bargaining rules and guidelines
- Mandatory minimum sentences
- Statutory determinate sentencing
- Voluntary/descriptive sentencing guidelines
- Presumptive/prescriptive sentencing guidelines

1

- Sentencing councils
- Requiring judges to provide reasons for sentences
- Parole guidelines
- Abolition of parole
- Adoption or modification of good time procedures
- Appellate review of sentences

Most states have given serious consideration to at least one of these reforms, and many have adopted one or more of them.

The rapid alteration of American sentencing laws and practices during the 1970s followed a fairly long period of relative inactivity on sentencing policy. Indeterminate sentencing systems were in widespread use until the 1970s and had not changed materially for 50 years: plea negotiation was the predominant but little acknowledged mode of disposition of criminal cases; statutes set upper limits on the sentences to be imposed for each offense, but judges rarely invoked those limits and had no other guidance when setting sentences; most sentences were indeterminate; and the decisions of parole boards were immune from review or appeal.

By 1982, however, most jurisdictions had made dramatic changes in their sentencing practices and institutions. Parole release had been abolished for the majority of prisoners in as many as 10 states, and parole guidelines had been established in at least 8 others. Determinate sentencing statutes, under which prisoners could predict their release dates at the time of sentencing assuming good behavior in prison, were in effect in more than 10 states, and mandatory minimum sentence laws were in effect for some offenses in more than 30 states. Several states had adopted statewide sentencing guidelines, and local sentencing guidelines had been established in more than 50 jurisdictions.

This period of rapid change was associated with widespread dissatisfaction with indeterminate sentences, precipitated by six major factors:

1. *Prison uprisings*. The prison uprisings (e.g., at Attica in New York, the Tombs in New York City, and at other prisons in California, Florida, and Indiana) of the late 1960s demonstrated that prisoners were deeply discontented and that "rehabilitation" was little more than rhetoric in many prisons.

2. *Concern about individual rights and the control of discretion*. Utilitarian practices and their effectiveness were questioned by those concerned with individual rights and with arbitrary uses of discretion. Immune from review, judges and parole boards had broad discretion to decide who went to prison and how long they stayed there, and both became the objects of reform proposals.

3. *Demand for accountability*. Throughout the legal system there was a movement for increased accountability in official decision making. Courts began to require public officials to indicate the bases of their decisions and to give the individuals affected by them the opportunity to dispute material allegations and present evidence, and prisons began to be required to publish their disciplinary rules and to give prisoners an opportunity to defend themselves against charges of rule violation.

4. *Disillusionment with rehabilitation*. After dominating thinking in corrections for more than a century, the rehabilitative ideal was challenged on both empirical and ideological grounds. This challenge undermined the credibility of the argument for indeterminate sentences that permitted release of prisoners when they had been rehabilitated.

5. *Disparity and discrimination*. A number of statistical and experimental studies of judicial sentencing suggested that sentencing displayed substantial disparity and racial and class discrimination. Findings of widespread inconsistencies both within and between jurisdictions contributed to a belief that sentencing practices were unfair.

6. *Crime control*. Official rates of reported crime had increased almost steadily since the early 1960s, and political candidates, public officials, and others were repeatedly expressing frustration at the criminal justice system's inability to control crime. Among the targets of public frustration were "lenient" judges and parole boards that were said to release dangerous people into the community without adequate concern for public safety.

These factors, among others, coalesced into a compelling case against indeterminate sentencing. The indeterminate sentencing system that was all but universally supported in the 1950s had few defenders by the late 1970s. A remarkable consensus emerged among left and right, law enforcement officials and prisoners' groups, reformers and bureaucrats that the indeterminate sentencing era was at its end. Rather less clear was what should replace it.

The Sentencing Reform Movement

A substantial number of structural innovations were proposed and adopted in various jurisdictions. Some attempted to provide unambiguous guidance on sentencing in critical cases (e.g., mandatory minimum sentence laws for drug, firearms, and repeated violent offenses). Some attempted to create decision rules for cases involving relatively harsh sentences (e.g., parole guidelines that set standards for prison release decisions— but necessarily left untouched judges' decisions about whom to imprison). Still others attempted to set standards for prison sentences (e.g., determinate sentencing laws and presumptive sentencing guidelines), to abolish or regulate plea bargaining, or to eliminate the power of parole boards to set release dates for the majority of prisoners.

Several efforts to alter sentencing systems have resulted in shifting—rather than reducing—discretionary decision making. Maine abolished its parole board but did nothing to give guidance to judges or prosecutors. California's detailed statutory determinate sentencing law shifted power from the parole authority, which was abolished, to the judge and to the prosecutor, whose discretion over decisions about what charges to bring increased in importance. Illinois's new law shifted power over release decisions from the parole board, which was abolished, to prison authorities, who control the large amount of "good time" available.

Changes in sentencing policies have coincided with both substantial increases in rates of reported crime and growing prison populations. The latter has been attributed both to more severe sentences and to demographic trends that have substantially increased the number of people in the age group with the highest imprisonment rates. The resulting prison congestion has forced attention to the connection between sentencing practice and corrections institutions and prompted concern for possible undesirable consequences that may follow if sentencing changes generate more prisoners than prisons can accommodate.

Goals of Sentencing

The variety of reforms reflects in part the heterogeneous goals of punishment. The primary goals of punishment include the utilitarian ones of crime control (the rehabilitation of offenders, the incapacitation of people likely to commit future crimes, and the deterrence of the sentenced offender as well as others from further offenses) and the general retributive one of imposing deserved punishment. These diverse goals can conflict and, depending on their relative priority in any particular case, may present conflicting arguments for choosing a sentence in that case.

A concern for utilitarian goals involves looking forward to the effects of sentences on the offender and on future crimes by the offender or others. Utilitarian sentences are generally justified on the bases of predictions of future crime and rehabilitative potential, and individualized sentencing is accepted, although it can result in different treatments for similar cases. In contrast, concern for retributive or "just deserts" goals involves looking backward to the defendant's personal culpability, to the nature of the criminal act, and perhaps to the harm it caused. Emphasis is on the punishment *deserved* by the offender rather than on the crime-prevention effects of alternative punishments. This emphasis raises concern about the inequity associated with different treatments for similar cases.

The preceding characterization oversimplifies. Legislatures in establishing penal codes, judges in deciding cases, and parole boards in setting release dates are rarely purely utilitarian or purely retributive, and there are numerous forms of utilitarianism and retribution. Decision makers are influenced by mixtures of personal values and opinions that, like the purposes of punishment, often conflict. The shift away from a wide acceptance of rehabilitation as a goal of punishment has been replaced by an environment in which there is much more disagreement over the goals of sentencing and over which goals are appropriate in individual cases.

SCOPE OF THE STUDY

Sentencing reforms have invoked social science research in several ways. In a number of sentencing guidelines projects, the design of new sentencing standards depended upon research results, notably the statistical analyses of prior sentencing practice. Social science research has also been used in assessing the impact of various sentencing reforms. In at least one reform, the formulation of the Minnesota sentencing guidelines, design and impact issues have been directly linked: estimates of effects on prison populations were used explicitly in designing the new sentencing standards.

The Panel on Sentencing Research was convened to review this growing body of research, to assess the quality of the research and the validity of the approaches used, and to suggest substantive and methodological priorities for future research on sentencing.

The panel adopted a broad view of "sentencing." In ordinary usage the term refers narrowly to decisions by judges. However, to restrict attention only to what judges do would fail to acknowledge other processes and participants that influence whether convicted offenders go to prison and how long they stay there. Witnesses and victims do or do not cooperate with authorities. Police officers decide whether to arrest and book, and for what offense. Prosecutors decide whether to prosecute and for what charge and often negotiate with the defense counsels about charge dismissals and sentencing concessions in exchange for guilty pleas. In some cases a judge or a jury determines guilt; more often a judge accepts a guilty plea. After conviction the judge announces the sentence. Prison officials decide whether an individual prisoner will be awarded "good time," and parole boards decide when and under what conditions an individual will be released and when parole status will be revoked. Most of these actors operate independently from the others, sometimes within the guidelines and policies of separate organizations, sometimes influenced and constrained by laws. Consideration of "sentencing" thus requires consideration of more than the decisions of judges. The panel's focus is on decision making in the court—including plea bargaining as well as the sentences imposed by judges—and on decisions by corrections and parole authorities.

The conflicting goals of the sentencing process involve moral and philosophical issues that far exceed the panel's mandate or competence to resolve. We have attempted, however, to be sensitive to these issues and to suggest how different philosophical premises might differentially affect the formulation of sentencing policy, yield different sentencing structures, and imply different sentences in individual cases.

In this report we focus primarily on statistical studies of sentencing that have used quantitative data on case attributes and decision-process variables. Much research on criminal sentencing has used other research strategies. Among the most common have been observation of the behavior of criminal court participants and interviews with them. Such research is particularly useful in identifying variations in case processing across jurisdictions and in suggesting the key determinants and processes leading to sentence outcomes. Another body of research investigates sentencing and its impact through use of experimental simulations. The careful controls possible in experimental research provide the opportunity for isolating subtle effects. They also facilitate disentangling the effects of variables that are often interrelated in natural settings.

Our emphasis on statistical studies is due to the large number of studies that use these methods and the technical questions they raise. However, this ought not be taken to imply that this approach is the only one of value. Indeed, we believe that statistical analysis of quantitative data about sentencing should be but one part of an overall research strategy that also includes experiments, interviews, and observation.

The need to limit the scope of the panel's review led us to exclude from intensive examination some subjects that a broad conception of sentencing might properly encompass. We focus on adult courts, and we do not examine research or policy initiatives concerning the sentencing of juveniles. And we do not consider the fiscal costs of implementing various sentencing policies. Perhaps the most salient exclusion is that we do not address the crime control effects of sentences; these involve rehabilitation programs and their effects and the deterrent and incapacitative effects of sentences. These subjects have recently been reviewed by other panels of the Committee on Research on Law Enforcement and the Administration of Justice of the National Research Council.

In this report the panel focuses on research in four areas:

• The determinants of sentencing, particularly those associated with discrimination and disparity, and the methodological problems that plague this research.
• The various methods used to structure sentencing decisions, especially sentencing guidelines, and the role and validity of such methods.
• The effects on sentencing outcomes and system operations of attempts to structure the sentencing process and sentencing decisions.
• The connections between sentencing policy and the corrections system, particularly prison populations.

We review the principal research findings in each area, comment on major methodological problems and their implications for the validity of those findings, and offer proposals for improving the quality of the findings and for answering questions that have not yet been adequately addressed. The recommendations for future research are necessarily limited by the nature of the sentencing process. Future research, like existing research, must operate within a complex environment of organizational, legal, and political constraints. We do not attempt to offer policy recommendations; rather, we have sought to illuminate the uses and limits of research in shaping sentencing policy. With that information those responsible for establishing sentencing policy should be in a better position to make more informed policy choices.

DETERMINANTS OF SENTENCES

The volume and complexity of research into the determinants of judicial sentences increased enormously in the 1960s and 1970s. Underlying much of this research has been a fundamental concern with accounting for the diversity of sentence outcomes observed in courts in order to answer the important questions about the presence and extent of disparity and discrimination in sentencing. That concern has led to attempts to identify the variety of variables, and the interrelationships among those variables, that combine to influence observed sentence outcomes. To date, however, the general state of knowledge about the factors influencing sentence outcomes still remains largely fragmented. Indeed, research on sentencing derives from a variety of different theoretical and disciplinary perspectives.

INTRODUCTION: DISCRIMINATION AND DISPARITY

Motivated by charges that sentencing is unfair, much sentencing research has investigated the extent of unwarranted variation in sentences, particularly the validity of claims of widespread discrimination against minority and poor defendants and of wholesale disparities in sentences. While widely used, "discrimination" and "disparity" are rarely defined consistently. For the purposes of this report, they are distinguished in terms of the *legitimacy* of the criteria for determining sentences and the *consistency* with which those criteria are applied to similar cases.

Discrimination exists when some case attribute that is objectionable—typically on moral or legal grounds—can be shown to be associated with sentence outcomes after all other relevant variables are adequately controlled.[1] Such an association may be regarded as presumptive evidence of the existence and extent of deliberate discrimination. Race is the clearest example of an illegitimate criterion; it is a "suspect classification" from a legal perspective and is widely viewed as inappropriate on moral grounds. The range of potentially illegitimate variables is viewed broadly here and may include case-processing variables, like bail status or type of attorney, in addition to the personal attributes, like race, sex, and class, that are conventionally cited as bases of discrimination.

Disparity exists when "like cases" with respect to case attributes—regardless of their legitimacy—are sentenced differently. For example, this might occur when different judges place different weights on the various case attributes or use different attributes altogether in their sentencing decisions. Disparity refers to the influence in sentence outcomes of factors in the decision-making process. The most commonly cited examples include disparity across judges within the same jurisdiction or across entire jurisdictions.

By these definitions discrimination and disparity are distinct behaviors (see Table S–1). If all decision makers behaved similarly and used race or bail status in the same way as a factor in sentences, it would be possible (even if unlikely) to have discrimination without disparity. If all decision makers held shared values about legitimate case attributes

---

[1] As a policy matter, concern with discrimination has been primarily involved with deliberate behavior that is discriminatory in intent. Research on discrimination, however, rests on outcomes; it does not and cannot distinguish purposive discriminatory behavior from behavior that is discriminatory in effect. As a result, research findings of discrimination refer to findings of discriminatory outcomes that may or may not result from discriminatory intent or be evidence of purposive behavior.

TABLE S–1 Sentence Outcomes Characterized in Terms of Disparity and Discrimination

Legitimacy of Sentencing Criteria	Application of Sentencing Criteria	
	Consistent	Inconsistent
Legitimate	No disparity and no discrimination	Disparity
Illegitimate	Discrimination	Disparity and discrimination

but placed different weights on them, the result would be disparity without discrimination. If some decision makers gave weight to race in their sentencing decisions and some did not (or gave race less weight), sentences would exhibit both disparity and discrimination.

Evaluating the extent of discrimination or of unwarranted disparity requires important normative judgments about how much and what types of variation are unwarranted. Concern with discrimination focuses largely on the invidious role of certain personal attributes of the offender, particularly race and socioeconomic status, and the use of various case-processing variables. Concern for disparity, in contrast, centers on the organizational and structural contexts in which sentencing decisions are made and on the attributes and goals of individual decision makers.

THE RANGE OF VARIABLES CONSIDERED AND THEIR EXPLANATORY POWER

Determination of the nature and extent of disparity and discrimination requires identification of the role, relative importance, and interactions among all the variables that affect sentencing. The variables that have been considered to be determinants of sentences fall broadly into two main classes: variables that characterize the *case* and variables related to the decision-making *process*.

The case variables include attributes of the offense, principally offense seriousness (e.g., crime type(s) charged or convicted and victim harm) and quality of evidence (e.g., number of witnesses and existence of tangible evidence); attributes of the offender (e.g., prior criminal record and demographic attributes such as age and race); and case-processing factors (e.g., charge reductions or dismissals and method of case disposition).

The process variables include structural-context factors (e.g., community attitudes toward crime and statutory or administrative regulations governing sentencing); individual decision-maker factors (e.g., demographic attributes and general political/ideological orientations of judges, probation officers, and others); and procedural variables (e.g., the role of the judge in plea bargaining).

Studies of the determinants of sentences have been characterized by the steady increase in the number and complexity of variables considered as influences on sentence and by growing methodological sophistication in the statistical analyses. The earliest studies often involved simple bivariate contingency tables examining the relationship of a single variable to sentence outcomes (e.g., the number of people sentenced to prison for each race). More recent studies use multivariate techniques that permit simultaneous statistical controls for the variety of factors hypothesized to affect sentences.

> *Despite the number and diversity of factors investigated as determinants of sentences, two-thirds or more of the variance in sentence outcomes remains unexplained.*

The validity of statistical inferences about the determinants of sentences depends crucially on the methodological rigor with which the effects are estimated. Thus, our findings and conclusions are weighed in light of serious methodological shortcomings in the research.

One methodological concern affecting most research on the determinants of sentencing is the treatment of the outcome variable—sentence imposed. A sentencing decision involves a choice among a number of qualitatively different options, including suspended sentences, supervised probation, fines, and incarceration, as well as a choice on the amount of the chosen sentence. Two different approaches have been used to reconcile the different qualitative and quantitative dimensions of sentences. Some researchers focus on the variations in the magnitude of only one sentence type—typically the length of prison terms for incarcerated offenders. Other studies collapse different sentence types into a single arbitrary scale of sentence severity.

Analyses that attempt to estimate the effects of variables on the magnitude of a single sentence type are vulnerable to two forms of error. Focusing on only one sentence type by assigning values of zero to all other sentence outcomes in ordinary least-squares regression results in biased estimates of the effects. Trying to avoid these biases by restricting the analysis to only those cases of a single sentence type (e.g., only those cases sentenced to prison) can introduce selection bias effects.

Correcting for these potential biases requires that the analysis be extended to include the choice among sentence types.

Statistical analyses that use a single, arbitrary scale that combines different sentence types as the outcome variable are particularly vulnerable to serious problems in interpreting findings. The arbitrariness of the scale makes it difficult to assess the magnitude of the impact of determinants on the various sentence types: the impact of a change in a determinant can be interpreted only as an increment in the arbitrary scale units and not in terms of additional years in prison or dollars of fine. Also, since factors can be expected to affect individual sentence types differently, the effects associated with a single arbitrary scale may not be relevant to any of the individual sentence types. A factor like unemployment, for example, might affect the decision to incarcerate but not the length of prison terms. These different effects will both be measured with error when a single scale of sentence outcomes is used in statistical analyses.

These problems pervade much of existing sentencing research, affecting both the comparability of results across different studies and the strength of conclusions drawn from that research. A more desirable approach is to partition the sentence outcome into two related outcomes involving: (1) a choice among different sentence types and (2) a choice on the magnitude of the selected type. Statistical techniques (e.g., PROBIT, LOGIT) are available for analysis of the choice of sentence type; then, taking account of the bound at zero in the analysis of magnitude, these separate aspects of sentence outcome can and should be estimated simultaneously.

THE PRIMARY DETERMINANTS OF SENTENCES

Using a variety of different indicators, offense seriousness and offender's prior record emerge consistently as the key determinants of sentences.

The more serious the offense and the worse the offender's prior record, the more severe the sentence. The strength of this conclusion persists despite the potentially severe problems of pervasive biases arising from the difficulty of measuring—or even precisely defining—either of these complex variables. This finding is supported by a wide variety of studies using data of varying quality in different jurisdictions and with a diversity of measures of offense seriousness and prior record.

Offense seriousness measures are usually limited to the use of the legally defined offense types or the statutory maximum penalties for each offense type. Elements of the offense related to offender culpability (e.g., excessive harm to the victim, weapon use, offender/victim relationship and victim provocation, and the offender's role as a principal or accessory) are often not available to researchers using summary court records. The potential elements of "prior record" are generally more visible to the researcher, including items like the number, recency, and seriousness of prior arrests, prior convictions, and prior incarcerations. These record data, however, are often incomplete and may not accurately reflect the data available to the judge. Even when the necessary data elements are available, it is not clear how the variables should be combined to develop measures of offense seriousness or prior record that reflect their effects on sentence outcomes. These factors contribute to measurement error in the offense seriousness and prior record variables.

The bias in the estimated effects of offense seriousness depends on the nature of the error in measuring seriousness. Measurement error that is independent of the level of seriousness yields underestimates (i.e., the estimated effect is in the same direction as the true effect but smaller in magnitude). If, however, the error due to unmeasured elements varies systematically with observed seriousness, the effects of seriousness on sentence outcomes may be underestimated or overestimated.

For example, the existence of a prior relationship between offender and victim or victim provocation are elements of seriousness usually unobserved by researchers that are likely to mitigate offense seriousness. Without observation of these elements, measured seriousness will overstate seriousness as viewed by judges (i.e., measured seriousness is positively related to its measurement error) and underestimate the effect of seriousness on sentence. Other unobserved elements of seriousness, such as injury to a victim, weapon use, or economic loss, by contrast, are likely to increase seriousness above its measured values and so overestimate the true effect of seriousness on sentence outcomes.

Variations in the quality of the data used in the assessment of offense seriousness leave some studies more vulnerable to underestimates and others more vulnerable to overestimates of the effect of offense seriousness. The measurement errors in prior record are likely to result in underestimates of the effect of record on sentences. Despite these biases, offense seriousness and prior record are consistently found to have strong effects on sentences. The consistency of these results under a variety of different biasing conditions increases confidence in the validity of the conclusion that offense seriousness and prior record are the primary determinants of sentence outcomes.

DISCRIMINATION BY RACE

There are two types of evidence often cited in support of the assertion that there is racial discrimination in sentencing. The first is the important fact that blacks are incarcerated in numbers disproportionate to their representation in the population: in 1979, blacks were 10.1 percent of the U.S. adult male population, but they were 48.0 percent of inmates of state prisons. The second appears in studies—there are now more than 70—that attempt to find a statistical association between the race of defendants and the sentences they receive in criminal courts: some of these studies find an association that has been interpreted as evidence of racial discrimination in sentencing.

> *The available research suggests that factors other than racial discrimination in sentencing account for most of the disproportionate representation of blacks in U.S. prisons, although racial discrimination in sentencing may play a more important role in some regions or jurisdictions, for some crime types, or in the decisions of individual participants.*

We must stress, however, that even a small amount of racial discrimination is a very serious matter, both on general normative grounds and because small effects in aggregate can imply unacceptable deprivations for large numbers of people. Thus, even though the effect of race may be small compared with other factors, such differences are still important.

Prison Populations

The overrepresentation of blacks in prison is clear evidence that some interaction of individual behavior patterns and societal response leads to the imposition of severe punishments on one group of people at rates that are disproportionate to their numbers in the population; however, it is *not* by itself evidence of racial discrimination at the sentencing stage in criminal courts.

The disproportionate rate of imprisonment of blacks may be the product of a wide variety of behaviors and processes. One source of the disproportion may be differences in the types and amounts of illegal behavior across the races. These behavioral differences may interact with patterns in the deployment of law enforcement resources and differing rates of apprehension, conviction, and imprisonment for various crime types to affect the racial composition of prisons. Racial discrimination may occur in the arrest process, the charging process, or the sentencing decision; or decisions by parole authorities may result in longer stays in prison for blacks. Some or all of these processes could be at work and could contribute to the disproportionate number of black prison inmates. Only some might involve racial discrimination.

The evidence about differential offense rates across races is scanty, and we cannot say with confidence whether the proportion of blacks arrested is the same as the proportion actually involved in illegal activities. It is possible to investigate, as has been done using victimization studies, the racial identities of offenders as reported by their victims. One set of studies reports a fairly close correspondence between the proportion of robbers and assaulters who are reported by victims to be black and the proportion of persons arrested for robbery and aggravated assault who are black. However, on the basis of available evidence for crimes more generally, we can conclude little about the degree to which blacks are arrested in true proportion to their offense rates by crime.

Focusing only on the *postarrest* phases of the criminal justice system, one approach to assessing the extent of racial discrimination is to examine data on the correspondence between racial proportions at arrest and in prison. In 1979, 35 percent of the adults arrested for index offenses[2] were black. For the crimes most likely to result in prison terms—murder and robbery—53 percent of the adults arrested were black. These data are consistent with the assertion that blacks are overrepresented in prison populations primarily because of their overrepresentation in arrests for more serious crime types, an argument counter to the assertion that overrepresentation results largely from discrimination at postarrest stages of the criminal justice system.

One problem in generalizing from such data is the difficulty in accurately characterizing racial discrimination through global statements about the criminal justice system in the United States as a whole. If and when it occurs in the criminal justice system, discrimination on the basis of race is likely to vary across jurisdictions, regions, crime types, and individual participants. Use of highly aggregated national data could mask racial differences in sentencing at more disaggregated levels. Race may be taken into account in ways that either advantage or disadvantage defendants who are black. We cannot say how much of the similarity in the proportion of blacks arrested and blacks imprisoned reflects racial neutrality and how much of it reflects the net result of offsetting effects

---

[2] Index offenses are murder, nonnegligent manslaughter, forcible rape, robbery, aggravated assault, burglary, larceny-theft, motor vehicle theft, and arson.

across jurisdictions, regions, crime types, or across the intervening case-processing points between arrest and prison. Aggregate data cannot reveal such differences. The variety of possibilities of offsetting relationships that might be obscured by aggregate data underscores the need for careful, disaggregated research on racial effects for individual crime types at different stages of the criminal justice system and within individual jurisdictions.

Whatever the cause, however, the disproportion of blacks in U.S. prisons is a matter of significant concern. When, on any day in this country, more than 3 percent of all black males in their twenties are in state prisons and another approximately 1.5 percent are in federal prisons and local jails, there is a serious social problem that cannot be ignored. The existence of the disproportion has raised serious questions about the legitimacy of criminal justice institutions; correctly identifying the sources of the disproportionality is crucial to the quest for effective solutions.

The Sentencing Process

The second type of evidence derives from studies of the process of sentencing itself. The studies on race and sentencing are vulnerable in varying degrees to a variety of statistical problems. Many early studies of sentencing—including those of capital punishment—found substantial racial discrimination, with blacks apparently being sentenced more harshly than whites. These studies were seriously flawed by statistical biases in the estimates of discrimination arising from failure to control for prior record, offense seriousness, and other important variables that affect case disposition. To the extent that race is associated with offense seriousness or prior record, with blacks committing more serious offenses or having worse prior records, the variable of race would have picked up some of the effect of the omitted variables and produced overestimates of the discrimination effect.

It is doubtful, however, that the large magnitude of the effect found in these early studies would be completely eliminated by the introduction of appropriate controls. Some portion of the estimated race effect found by these studies may indeed reflect discrimination in sentencing in those areas extensively studied, particularly capital punishment in the South in the 1940s, 1950s, and 1960s.

More recent studies that control for more variables have yielded varied results. Some find evidence of racial discrimination, and others do not. The introduction of controls for offense seriousness and prior record, especially in studies using pre-1969 data, reduces the widespread finding of racial discrimination in sentencing. Discrimination, nevertheless, continues to be found by more recent studies, particularly in rural courts, for selected crime types, when the victim is white, or only for some judges in a jurisdiction. Even in these contexts, however, offense seriousness and prior record remain the dominant variables in sentence outcomes.

Despite the substantial improvements in addressing the problem of omitted variables, recent studies are still subject to potential biases arising from measurement error and sample selection. Use of incomplete measures of offense seriousness and of prior record bias the effects of these variables on sentences and contaminate the estimated effects of correlated variables like race that are generally measured more accurately. The direction of the bias in a correctly measured variable depends on the bias in the incorrectly measured variable and the nature of the correlation between these variables. When, for example, blacks commit more serious offenses, there are opposite biases in seriousness and race; if the effect of seriousness is underestimated, the discrimination effect is overestimated, and vice versa.

The direction of bias in the estimated race effect arising from measurement errors in offense seriousness and prior record may be affected by sample selection, where the cases ultimately available for sentencing are a selected sample, including only a portion of the population of "similar" offenses originally committed. Aside from challenges to the generalizability of results, sample selection can pose serious threats to the validity of statistical results even within the selected sample. In sentencing research, these internal selection biases can arise when unobserved (and thus unmeasured) factors are common to both the selection and sentence processes, thereby inducing (or altering) correlations in the selected samples between the unmeasured variables and other included variables like race that are also common to both selection and sentencing. Depending on the nature of the resulting correlation, use of selected samples could result in either overestimates or underestimates of the effect of race on sentencing.

The possibility of nontrivial correlations of race with poorly measured but key variables like offense seriousness and prior record raises the possibility of serious measurement error biases in the estimates of discrimination effects. Further complications are introduced by the possibility that the correlations vary with the selection process and by crime type or jurisdiction. If so, the statistical biases attributable to measurement error may be trivial in some cases but critical in others. The biases may even work in opposite directions in different studies. Measurement error bias, operating either directly or through sample selection, could thus substantially obscure the true incidence of discrimination in sentencing.

DISCRIMINATION BY SOCIOECONOMIC STATUS

> *The evidence of discrimination on grounds of social and economic status is uncertain.*

The relevant research is characterized by inconsistent findings that are subject not only to the methodological uncertainties that apply to race but also to additional difficulties in measuring social and economic status. Furthermore, there is substantial debate about the legitimacy of reliance on some socioeconomic status (SES) variables in sentencing. Employment and education, for example, may be valuable as predictors of criminal recidivism and thus may be considered by some to be legitimate determinants of sentences. Alternatively, the strong association of these SES variables with race and wealth, which are more unequivocally illegitimate, raises questions about the legitimacy of sentencing that is based in part on variables that are associated with illegitimate variables. Even if the empirical questions regarding the influence of SES variables on sentences were resolved, conclusions about the discriminatory nature of these variables would depend on resolution of the normative dilemmas that they present.

DISCRIMINATION BY SEX

> *The evidence on the role of sex in sentencing is only preliminary.*

Despite the disproportionately low number of women arrested and imprisoned (in 1979, although women constituted 52 percent of the adult population, they accounted for only 20.5 percent of all adults arrested for index crimes, 8.7 percent of adults arrested for murder and robbery, and 4 percent of adults in state prisons), sex differences in sentencing—and differences in the criminal activity of men and women offenders more generally—have not generated a large volume of research. A review of the limited available research findings suggests that differences by sex of defendant are found in the pretrial release decision and in the sentence decision, especially for less severe sentence outcomes. The strength of the conclusions drawn from the existing body of research, like those on race and socioeconomic status, must be moderated by the potential biases arising from errors in measuring seriousness and prior record and from possible selection effects resulting from the differential filtering of cases to the sentencing stage.

CASE-PROCESSING VARIABLES

Three case-processing variables have frequently been cited as potential factors that influence sentence outcomes: mode of disposition (guilty plea, bench trial, or jury trial); pretrial release status (free on bail, released on own recognizance, or detained); and type of attorney (none, court appointed, or privately retained). The evidence varies in quality and in the consistency of findings for each of these factors. The evidence indicating that guilty pleas result in less severe sentences is most convincing. Pretrial detention is commonly found to be associated with more severe sentences, but this result is particularly vulnerable to biased estimates and hence is best viewed cautiously. The evidence on the role of attorney type is mixed and does not support a conclusion that attorney type is independently related to sentence outcome.

> *The strongest and most persistently found effect of case-processing variables is the role of guilty pleas in producing less severe sentences.*

It appears that defendants convicted at trial receive harsher sentences in many jurisdictions than do similarly situated defendants who plead guilty. Such a sentence differential is sometimes thought to be an essential element of the process by which large numbers of defendants are induced to plead guilty. Evidence for this differential comes both from interviews with court participants and from statistical analyses of case records in a large number of jurisdictions. While the statistical evidence on the guilty plea "discount" is subject to possible biases arising from measurement error and sample selection, the existence of independent evidence of a guilty plea discount suggests that these biases are not likely to be large relative to the true effect.

Defendants held in pretrial detention are often found to receive substantially harsher sentences than do defendants who are free while awaiting trial. A variety of factors has been suggested that may disadvantage the detained defendant, including: a reduced ability to wage a successful defense, incentives to plead guilty to avoid lengthy stays in local jails, and a labeling process by which detained defendants are presumed—because they are detained—to be more dangerous or to have committed more serious crimes. It is possible, however, that the apparent relationship between pretrial detention and harsher sentences may be at least partially spurious. The association of pretrial detention with poorly measured variables like offense seriousness or prior record raises the possibility of biases in either direction in the estimated effect of pretrial detention on sentence severity. While there appears to be both empirical evidence and theoretical reasons to support the view that pretrial detention exercises an independent influence on sentence outcome, further research is needed to establish the existence and magnitude of such a relationship.

The results of research on type of counsel and sentences are mixed and do not support a general conclusion that attorney type is independently related to sentence. Anecdotal evidence suggests that defendants represented by public defenders or appointed counsel receive harsher sentences than do those represented by privately retained counsel. This difference has been attributed to heavier workloads or less criminal court experience for public or appointed attorneys, which contributes to less adequate legal defense and increased pressure to dispose of cases through plea negotiations. The spirit of cooperation and compromise that characterizes court regulars is another factor that might jeopardize the positions of defendants represented by overworked or inexperienced counsel. Relations among judges, prosecutors, and various kinds of defense counsel, however, vary substantially among courts, as do the competence, resources, and credibility of various kinds of counsel. It thus would be surprising if type of counsel had a consistent effect across jurisdictions on sentencing outcomes. Attorney type is also likely to vary with offense type and with the prior criminal record of the defendant. Statistical analyses of the effects of attorney type have generally failed to control adequately for these other determinants of sentences.

DISPARITY

While substantial disparities in sentencing probably exist, the relative magnitude of disparity is not known. Furthermore, both normative disagreements and measurement problems make it difficult to determine how much of the disparity is unwarranted.

Numerous statistical studies of case records and court observations report substantial variation in the sentences imposed by judges serving in a single court jurisdiction. The validity of the statistical results, however, is often jeopardized by inadequate controls for other important determinants of sentences that distinguish the cases before different judges or before a single judge. Some experimental simulation studies in which subjects "sentence" identical cases also report extensive sentencing variation among judges. The experimental studies face challenges to their validity because of the artificial and often contrived character of the experiments and because of the use of limited case information, which leaves considerable room for judicial interpretation and imputation of relevant but missing information.

Nevertheless, in at least one carefully controlled study in which judges made real decisions in identical cases, interjudge variation was extensive. Similarly, although some statistical studies have added as many as 30 explanatory variables on case attributes, about two-thirds of the variation in sentencing within single jurisdictions still remains unexplained.

There is little doubt that substantial unexplained variation in sentences does exist. Some of this variation, however, may only give the appearance of disparity when cases seem alike to an outside observer but differ materially in the case attributes observed by the judge(s). Some of this apparent disparity could probably be reduced if better models of sentencing using richer data sets were developed. Sentence decisions are typically modeled as a simple additive model in which the factors determining sentences are all considered simultaneously and always enter the decision in the same way. Sentence decisions, however, may be hierarchical, following a branching structure in which the weight given some factors depends on the presence or absence of other factors. In a particularly heinous crime, for example, the viciousness of the crime alone may be enough to lead to incarceration. In less vicious crimes, a wide variety of factors, including the defendant's prior criminal record and general community ties, may enter the decision whether to imprison. If better models were used, some of the currently unexplained variation might be reduced. It is difficult to estimate just how much of the apparent disparity in sentences might be accounted for by systematic application of identifiable factors.

The principal normative objections to disparity relate to variations in sentences emanating from inconsistencies among judges and even in the decisions of a single judge over time. Inconsistencies among judges in different jurisdictions may arise from differences in court organization and work load and differences in local community attitudes toward crime and punishment. The variations in sentences within a court are more likely to be associated with differences in individual judicial attitudes and reasoning processes and with alternative resolutions of the basic conflict over the different goals of punishment. Presentence recommendations reflecting the attitudes and sentencing goals of prosecutors or probation officers may also be a factor in differences across and even within judges.

The extent to which this disparity is regarded as unwarranted remains an important policy question that depends on the resolution of important competing values. There is agreement that sentences should result from the evenhanded application of general sentencing principles, and there is also recognition that there are often legitimate social, cultural, and philosophical differences over what those principles should be, as reflected, for example, in conflicting interpretations of the goals of sentencing. Resolution of this policy issue would benefit from continued efforts to clarify and articulate the principles that currently do and those that ought to underlie sentence decisions.

STRUCTURING SENTENCING DECISIONS

A substantial body of knowledge has accumulated in recent years about the design, implementation, and enforcement of new sentencing practices. These changes include policy innovations variously affecting prosecutors, judges, and parole administrators. Sentencing guidelines are but one of these new practices; because they are the most richly developed methodologically, they are used in this report to illustrate methodological and policy problems that are characteristic of many reforms.

POLICY AND TECHNICAL CHOICES

The first empirically based sentencing standards, the U.S. Parole Commission's guidelines, were developed in the early 1970s by the Parole Decision Making Project to make explicit the policies of the commission and systematize parole decision making. The successful implementation of the parole guidelines led to a test of the feasibility of developing similar empirically based guidelines for sentencing.

Development of such "descriptive"[3] sentencing guidelines involved several steps: first, data collection on a sample of cases sentenced in the

---

[3] Terminological confusion in characterizing sentencing guidelines arises because they vary on two important dimensions—their legal authority and the role of empirical research in their conception and development. Depending on their use of empirical data on past sentencing practices and on whether the underlying goal is to codify existing practices or to establish new sentencing policies, guidelines have been characterized as "descriptive" and "prescriptive." Neither of these terms is literally accurate: all guidelines are statements of policy or normative choices and to date most have used empirical data on existing practices in their development.

At the same time, guidelines have either presumptive legal authority—meaning that judges are expected to impose the sentence recommended by the guideline in ordinary cases and provide reasons for sentences that do not adhere to the guidelines—or have only voluntary legal force—thereby creating no defendants' rights to appeal. (Guidelines could theoretically have mandatory legal force, but they were developed to provide a less court for which the guidelines were being devised; second, a multivariate analysis of these case data and the development of a statistical model of past sentencing practices aimed at identifying the combination of variables that explained the greatest proportion of variation in sentencing outcomes; third, transformation of the model of past practices into sentencing guidelines for application by judges.

> *Statistical models of past judicial sentencing practices are valuable aids, but they are insufficient as the sole bases for formulating sentencing policy.*

The assumptions and methodology underlying such "descriptive" sentencing guidelines have led to a number of challenges. First, there is a debate about the extent to which a model based on aggregate data of past case dispositions represents an "implicit policy" that is collectively shared by the judges in that court. While prior record and offense seriousness have been found to be the primary determinants of sentences for virtually all judges, research also suggests that judges give different weights to these common factors, emphasize different aspects of offense seriousness and prior record, and consider different additional variables in sentencing. In instances in which the sentencing patterns of the judges in a jurisdiction vary widely across judges, a model may provide a statistical average of their sentences, but it does not necessarily represent an "implicit policy" with which any of the judges would agree.

Second, models designed to characterize past sentencing practice must overcome the methodological problems already noted generally for research on the determinants of sentencing: errors arising from omitted variables, measurement and scaling problems, and selection biases. The degree to which any model represents actual court practice depends on the skills of the modeler in incorporating the complexity of the considerations that enter the sentencing decisions. When a model is fully

---

rigid alternative to mandatory sentencing laws, as connoted by the term "guideline.")

Given these options, four types of guidelines are possible: descriptive/voluntary, descriptive/presumptive, prescriptive/voluntary, and prescriptive/presumptive. In practice, however, only descriptive/voluntary and prescriptive/presumptive guidelines have been established. The former type is illustrated by those in Denver, Philadelphia, Massachusetts, and New Jersey; the latter by those in Minnesota and Pennsylvania.

When we focus on one particular dimension, largely in abstraction, we refer to guidelines in terms of that dimension (e.g., descriptive guidelines or presumptive guidelines); however, when considering specific examples, it is necessary to keep in mind that both dimensions are actually present.

specified and the variables are completely measured, that model can provide useful information in the development of sentencing policy.

Reasonably representative models of existing sentencing practices are useful in providing information that can serve as a basis for comparing a new standard with traditional patterns, educating policy makers about the general operation of the system, and serving as a data base for projecting the impacts of alternate proposed policies. However, in several instances in the development of "descriptive" sentencing guidelines, the models were fundamentally flawed by the elimination of ethically unacceptable variables, such as race and guilty plea, from the model in an effort to eliminate their effects in the guidelines. The consequence of omitting these variables, particularly when they are correlated with variables that are included in the model, is that the model will be misestimated and the guidelines may inadvertently incorporate effects of the omitted ethically unacceptable variables.

> *Ethical decisions must be made in moving from a model of past practice to guidelines; there is no value-free solution to the estimation problem.*

One cannot simply delete an ethically objectionable variable from the equation being estimated to eliminate its effect. Rather, the model must be formulated and estimated with the objectionable variable included; then, a discrimination-free sentencing guideline could be created by using that fully estimated model with the objectionable variable suppressed. This requires a choice: one must decide how *all* offenders should be treated. For example, to eliminate racial discrimination, if it is found, one must decide whether to adopt the existing standard for sentencing blacks, adopt that used for sentencing whites, or choose a new standard to be applied uniformly to everyone.

Other important policy choices cannot be avoided in translating data on past sentencing practices into sentencing standards; even adoption of "descriptive" sentencing criteria that involve no explicit alterations from the estimated model of past practices entails policy judgments on issues that have traditionally been hidden. Among the necessary decisions are the following:

1. Whether to base new sentences on conviction offenses, thereby tying sentences to the outcomes of counsels' negotiations over charges, or on actual offense behavior as determined at a sentencing hearing.

2. Whether to establish explicit sentence concessions for guilty pleas.

3. Whether to exclude from consideration in new sentencing standards variables that are ethically or normatively suspect: e.g., prior

arrests may explain some variation in sentencing practices independently of other prior record factors, yet punishment for prior alleged conduct not resulting in conviction offends important legal values.

4. Whether to authorize intercourt disparity within the same jurisdiction: e.g., the differences between rural and urban regions within a state might be perpetuated by providing local courts with a sufficiently broad range of sentences to choose from or suppressed by trying to force them all into a more narrow range.

> *Resolving technical questions concerning the design and presentation of new sentencing schedules also necessarily involves important policy decisions.*

The normative aspects of ostensibly technical matters arise from the inherent tension between the aim of making criteria in sentencing standards rich and detailed, thereby providing guidance on subtle sentencing choices, and the aim of making them few in number and uncomplicated to use, thereby diminishing the likely incidence of errors in their application.

The following technical choices entail implicit policy choices.

1. Should new sentence schedules be expressed as a two-axis grid (one representing an offense seriousness scale and the other axis representing an offender scale) on which applicable sentences are easily located (e.g., Minnesota's sentencing guideline grid), or should more complicated approaches be used that require more complex calculations for each sentence (e.g., New Jersey's sentencing guidelines)? The former approach minimizes the likelihood of administrative errors in determining the prescribed sentence; the latter permits specification of more detailed sentencing criteria.

2. Should sentencing standards use different bases or the same bases for decisions concerning the type and the amount of punishment (e.g., distinguishing the decision to imprison from the length of imprisonment)? Research efforts have consistently found that different factors influence consideration of the two choices, but the two-stage approach makes calculating the guideline sentence considerably more complex and thus more vulnerable to error.

3. Should easily calculated, additive point systems be used to categorize offenses and offenders, or should guidelines use more elaborate but less easily calculated scoring systems that take account of particular combinations of variables and reflect contingent patterns of decision making?

4. Should there be one set of generic sentencing criteria for all offenses (e.g., only one sentencing matrix for all offenses as in Minnesota) or should there be more offense-specific criteria based on statutory felony class (as in Denver), generic offense type (as in Arizona, where all burglaries are treated together regardless of felony class), or on some other basis?

All of these illustrative technical matters present choices between simplicity and ease of application but less specific policy guidance, and greater policy differentiation among offenses and offenders but with greater complexity and its associated risk of application errors, loss of credibility among officials, and rejection of the entire scheme.

> *Projections of the likely impact of alternative sentencing criteria are indispensible to formulation of sound sentencing policy.*

Existing methodological and statistical techniques can be used in impact projections to inform policy making.

Development of sentencing standards may be a wholly normative process or include empirically informed efforts. A wholly normative process is one in which policy choices are made without regard to past practices or to their projected impact. Most statutory determinate and mandatory minimum sentence laws have been developed in this way. Empirically informed policies make use of knowledge of past policies, practice, or both and project the impact of new practices. Sound public policy formulation, whether by statute or by administrative regulation, requires the consideration of information about the likely consequences of alternative policy proposals. What might be the impact of a 2-year mandatory minimum sentence for robbery, for example, on court resources and on prison populations and corrections costs? Efforts to answer such questions necessitate attempts to project the anticipated effects of changes from past practices as a vital part of any sentencing policy change.

DEVELOPING, IMPLEMENTING, AND ENFORCING NEW SENTENCING POLICIES

> *Sentencing is a complex process involving discretionary decisions by many people. Attempts to promulgate new sentencing policies that have included extensive efforts to gain the understanding and support of the affected individuals and organizations and to anticipate the im-*

*pact of changes on their institutional and personal in-
terests appear to have been more successful in gaining
legislative approval when needed and to have achieved
higher rates of compliance when implemented.*

Some empirical research and many anecdotes illustrate the ease with
which policy initiatives can be frustrated by officials' manipulation or
accommodation. Prosecutors can circumvent plea-bargaining bans and
rules by shifting to new forms of bargaining. Lawyers and judges can
frustrate parole guidelines by negotiating sentences that will expire before the offender is subject to applicable guidelines. Mandatory sentence
laws can be frustrated by prosecutors who fail to charge the predicate
offense or by judges who make "findings of fact" that essential elements
of the predicate offense have not been proven.

Under sentencing guidelines and statutory determinate sentencing
laws with presumptive authority and under mandatory sentencing laws,
prosecutors and defense attorneys may be able to circumvent applicable
standards through charge bargains. Tactical solutions to counterbalance
such circumvention include:

• real offense sentence standards that offset charge bargains by basing
sentences on actual offense behavior rather than on the conviction offense;

• charge reduction guidelines and guilty plea discounts that structure
adaptive responses by providing approved means to satisfy institutional
pressures for circumvention;

• parole guidelines in which release decisions are based on actual
offense behavior and that effectively constitute an administrative review
of sentences resulting from the exercise of prosecutorial and judicial
discretion; and

• various forms of appellate review that provide incentives to appeal
sentences that are inconsistent with stated policy.

If new sentencing policies are to be effective, their purposes must be
specified clearly and stated in terms that are credible to key participants.
Policy formulation must also include consideration of likely patterns of
adaptation and manipulation and must include features designed to offset anticipated evasions and, where sentence calculations are required,
provide statistical or other data necessary to correctly determine a guideline sentence. In addition, reformers can increase compliance by involving interest groups in the policy development process so that they
perceive themselves as having a stake in the successful implementation
of the new policy.

Sentencing initiatives that include credible enforcement mechanisms are more likely to attain compliance by affected decision makers.

The credibility of a policy depends in part on its legal authority and on the existence of enforcement mechanisms. Thus far, sentencing policy initiatives have possessed three levels of legal authority. Voluntary sentencing guidelines (like those in Denver) typically have only moral or collegial authority, and the credibility of the policy itself is critical. The only major evaluation of the impact of voluntary sentencing guidelines concluded that they had no discernible impact. Whether this is because they were voluntary, because they were insufficiently promoted, because they were not credible in the eyes of judges, or for some other reason is not known. Presumptive sentencing guidelines (like Minnesota's) or statutory determinate sentences (like California's) have presumptive legal authority; the decision maker may disregard the standards, but must provide reasons for doing so that are subject to review. The monitoring and enforcement system established by the Minnesota Sentencing Guidelines Commission, together with appellate sentence review, appears to have resulted in much higher rates of formal compliance (both in imposing sentences that fall within the guidelines and in providing reasons for deviating from guideline sentences) than those found in jurisdictions with voluntary guidelines. Mandatory sentencing laws have prescriptive legal authority that formally requires a decision maker to make a particular disposition.

Legal authority by itself is not necessarily predictive of substantive compliance with sentencing rules: judges and others can always ignore the guidelines or statute. A rule's legal authority does become meaningful, however, in the presence of credible enforcement mechanisms. Presumptive and mandatory standards, for example, are more likely to be observed if there is a realistic likelihood that a judge's failure to comply will be challenged.

Enforcement mechanisms can be formal or informal. The primary formal enforcement mechanisms are various types of appellate review (e.g., Minnesota), administrative review of sentences (e.g., California), and review of prison sentences by parole boards (e.g., U.S. Parole Commission). The bureaucratic nature of criminal court decision making, however, can present serious practical obstacles to effective formal enforcement of sentencing criteria. A prosecutor, for example, is unlikely to appeal a lenient sentence that resulted from plea negotiations to which he was a party. Informal enforcement mechanisms include such things as maintaining and sustaining case-by-case monitoring and facilitating media attention to sentencing decision making.

The obstacles to credible enforcement of sentencing criteria are formidable, but not insurmountable. Like effective political bridge building on behalf of new guidelines, informal enforcement programs require careful attention by legislatures and agencies attempting to ensure change in sentencing patterns.

ASSESSMENT OF THE EFFECTS OF NEW SENTENCING POLICIES

In assessing the effects of sentencing innovations, one must consider adaptive behavior by personnel in the criminal justice system, changes in patterns of case flow, and their effects on sentence severity and disparity. Our analysis thus concentrates on how innovations have affected the behavior of judges and other key participants and on what happens to defendants.

We have reviewed the results of evaluations of reform efforts directed at eliminating or controlling plea bargaining, structuring judicial sentencing decisions through mandatory or determinate sentence provisions or sentencing guidelines, and eliminating or structuring parole release decisions.

THE RESULTS OF REFORMS

Compliance with procedural requirements of sentencing innovations has been widespread, but such behavioral changes have often represented compliance in form rather than in substance.

Prosecutors have refrained from proscribed forms of plea bargaining, judges have imposed mandated sentences on convicted offenders, and parole boards have released prisoners according to guideline requirements. However, substantial modifications in case-processing procedures, counteracting the stated intent of innovations, have been observed throughout the criminal justice system. These changes typically involve increases in early disposition of cases, such as increased case screening, that may serve to limit application of new laws and rules to increase sentence severity.

The elimination of plea bargaining in Alaska was followed by an increase in the proportion of felony arrest cases screened out, but it did not lead to either a decrease in the proportion of offenders pleading guilty or to a large increase in the number of trials. In Michigan, a mandatory minimum sentencing law for gun offenses was accompanied by earlier dispositions for moderately serious cases and a rise in the rates of acquittals and dismissals. Under a mandatory sentence law for firearm offenses in Massachusetts, there were increases in early dispositions and acquittals in gun-carrying cases of moderate severity. Another effect of both New York's mandatory sentencing law for drug offenses and the Massachusetts gun law was a dramatic increase in case-processing time and in the number of appeals.

The most sweeping effort to restructure sentencing behavior was the adoption in California of a determinate sentencing law to replace the indeterminate sentences that had prevailed for more than half a century. Immediately after the new law took effect, the rates of early guilty pleas increased, as did the proportion of cases disposed of in the lower courts. There are also indications that prosecutors frequently dropped charged enhancements in the final disposition of a case to avoid appeals and to accelerate guilty pleas.

> *The extent of compliance with reforms has varied with: (a) the level of organizational or political support for the reform; (b) the existence of statutory or administrative authority supporting the procedural requirement; and (c) the existence of credible monitoring and enforcement mechanisms.*

High levels of substantive compliance appear to have been achieved when those charged with carrying out the new policy approved of it and were not seriously inconvenienced by it and when decision makers were subject to credible administrative controls or to formal or informal enforcement mechanisms. For example, high rates of substantive compliance with efforts to control plea bargaining have occurred when prosecutors have established administrative procedures to monitor the behavior of assistant prosecutors and when those assistants have shared organizational goals that they perceive as better served by complying with imposed controls on plea bargaining. Similarly, parole board members and examiners in several jurisdictions appear to have adhered to administratively imposed parole guidelines.

In contrast to prosecutors and parole board members, judges are seldom subject to effective organizational controls. With voluntary guidelines, studies have found no evidence of systematic judicial compliance; with changes directly mandated by statute, as in the cases of mandatory minimum and determinate sentencing laws, studies have found formal (but not necessarily substantive) judicial compliance. However, under Minnesota's presumptive sentencing guidelines, the presence of effective external enforcement mechanisms, in the form of appellate review of sentences and close monitoring by the Guidelines Commission, has resulted in generally high rates of substantive compliance with guidelines by judges in that state.

> *There have been modest changes in sentencing outcomes, particularly some increases in prison use, in jurisdictions that have adopted sentencing reforms. These increases in sentence severity were typically found in previously marginal prison cases—cases that might or might not have resulted in short prison terms in the past. Less ambiguous cases, including both more serious cases for which prison terms were fairly certain outcomes and less serious cases for which prison terms were relatively rare, have experienced little change in sentencing outcomes.*

Mandatory minimum sentencing laws in Michigan, for example, resulted in little change in the likelihood of incarceration for defendants indicted on felony charges. The severity of prison sentences imposed for each offense category, however, did increase slightly. In New York, the risk of incarceration for the small numbers of drug offense defendants who were convicted increased substantially, but steady declines in the numbers and rates of arrest, indictment, and conviction offset this increase. The terms for those drug offenders sentenced to prison, however, increased markedly.

In California, there is some evidence of increasing representation of less serious cases among prison commitments. A comparison of the proportions of people sent to prison for robbery and burglary indicates a trend toward increased proportions of burglary cases (the less serious of the two offenses) among prison commitments. This increase in the proportion of imprisoned burglars is not accounted for by a shift to more serious types of burglary by offenders, suggesting the emergence of a new, lower threshold of seriousness for imposition of prison sentences. However, the trend has been gradual and predates implementation of the determinate sentencing law and so may not be due entirely to the new law.

Changes in sentencing outcomes resulting from sentencing guidelines present a mixed picture. The voluntary guidelines adopted in Denver and Philadelphia were designed to codify rather than to alter existing policy. Predictably, they were found to have had no significant impact either on the level of prison commitment at sentencing or on the amount of variation among sentences. The presumptive sentencing guidelines in Minnesota were designed explicitly to depart from previous sentencing practices and in particular to increase prison commitments for those who commit offenses against persons, even if they have limited criminal histories, while decreasing prison commitments for property offenders regardless of their criminal records. On the basis of the commission's preliminary monitoring data, the presumptive guidelines appear to have significantly altered sentencing in Minnesota in the intended directions.

> *The substantial increases in prison populations in jurisdictions that have adopted sentencing reforms continue preexisting trends in sentencing and do not appear to be substantially caused by these sentencing reforms.*

While research evidence is limited, two findings support this conclusion. First, prison population increases have occurred in states that have not systematically altered sentencing laws and practices as well as in those states that have done so. Second, in the one instance in which long-term data on prison populations were examined as part of an evaluation of the impact of sentencing law changes, California's determinate sentencing law appears to have continued a trend that was under way prior to adoption of that law. Thus, sentencing reform efforts, rather than stimulating prison population increases, may themselves reflect a broader shift in public sentiment regarding criminal justice system policies.

THE METHODOLOGY OF IMPACT STUDIES

> *While changes in system operations and sentence outcomes have been observed, almost all the impact studies suffer from methodological problems that limit our ability to attribute these changes to the sentencing reforms. Inadequate observation periods mar many of the impact studies.*

The typical design involves only two periods, with observations limited to the 6-month or 1-year periods before and after implementation. Such short observation periods preclude identifying preexisting trends and do not allow sufficient time to realize the full effect of a change. Limited observation periods are especially common in impact studies of plea-bargaining bans and mandatory sentencing laws.

> *The validity of impact studies is seriously jeopardized if they fail to investigate the considerable opportunities for differential filtering of cases before and after the implementation of new rules or procedures. To date, impact studies have been too narrowly focused, examining changes*

only in those parts of the process directly affected by a
sentencing reform.

This narrow focus makes it difficult to detect the potentially important
influence of a change on earlier processing decisions that determine
which cases are available for sentencing and on subsequent decisions
that affect actual discharge from a sentence.

The validity of the conclusions of many impact studies
is limited because of their failure to control adequately
for changes in the mix of cases before and after the
change takes effect.

A variety of factors, including measures of the seriousness or harm
involved in offenses and the prior record of offenders, affect sentencing
outcomes independently of any sentencing reform. The impact studies
reviewed in this report involved few controls for case-mix variation
beyond statutory crime-type categories.

SENTENCING POLICIES AND PRISON POPULATIONS

Sentencing policies affect the size of prison populations through their
influence on the numbers of commitments, the lengths of sentences
imposed, and the times actually served. Statutory changes in sentencing
policies and changes in sentencing and related processing decisions by
judges, prosecutors, and police all affect the number of commitments
to prison and the sentence lengths imposed. Actual time served is importantly affected by corrections officials in awarding, revoking, and
calculating good-time credits and in granting furloughs and prerelease
privileges and by parole authorities in establishing parole release dates
and revoking parole.

Changes in sentencing policy may affect prison populations, and, if
they result in overcrowding, may undermine realization of the goals of
the policy makers. The panel examined the relationship between sentencing policy and prison populations with particular focus on recent
increases in prison populations and their possible impact on prison life.
The panel explored alternative techniques for projecting future prison
populations and considered some possible responses to the problem of
prison populations exceeding limited prison capacity.

Prison populations increased steadily in the 1970s, and
further increases are projected throughout the 1980s. This
growth in prison populations appears to continue preex-

isting trends and is only marginally related to recent sentencing reforms.

Between the end of 1972 and the end of 1981, the total number of persons confined in state and federal prisons grew from 196,183 to 352,476 for an enormous 9-year increase of 80 percent. This increase far exceeded the growth in the civilian population: the rate of incarceration in state and federal prisons climbed from 95 per 100,000 population in 1972 to 154 per 100,000 in 1981. The increase is associated with demographic shifts as the post-World War II baby boom generation reached the age of highest imprisonment rates and also with a possible trend toward increased punitiveness, reflected symbolically by widespread enactment of mandatory minimum sentencing laws. We note again that increases in prison population are found both in states that have adopted reforms and those that have not.

Prison populations have increased more rapidly than has available prison capacity. Many institutions are crowded, and little immediate relief from population pressures is in sight.

Prison administrators can administratively affect rated prison capacity by changing the standards by which capacity is calculated. But even the addition of 23,000 beds to rated capacity between 1972 and 1977 was far below the increase of 92,528 prison inmates over the same period. As of March 1982, single institutions or the entire corrections systems in 28 states were under court order to reduce overcrowding or eliminate other unconstitutional conditions of confinement; many of these court orders had been in effect for several years. Similar court challenges were pending in 19 other states.

Various projections of future prison populations, despite different assumptions, all anticipate further growth in the number of inmates in state custody throughout the 1980s. Because expansion of facilities appears to be occurring more slowly than the increase of prisoners in many states, population pressures will continue for the next several years.

Studies of the effects of crowding and of determinate sentencing systems on prison life are few and preliminary, suggesting several avenues for further research. Corrections officials suggest that crowding, by increasing stress for both inmates and staff, has deleterious effects on both the management of corrections institutions and on the health and safety of inmates and staff. Studies of the effects of crowding on human behavior under varied circumstances have yielded inconclusive findings; research on the effects of institutional size and prison housing arrangements on physical and mental health and on inmate behavior are still preliminary and are often confounded by the difficulty of separating the effects of crowding from other unpleasant aspects of prison life.

Examinations of the effects of determinate sentencing on the availability of rehabilitation programs, on inmates' participation in them, and on inmate behavior and disciplinary mechanisms suggest less effect than either supporters or detractors of change anticipated. Preliminary findings from California, Oregon, and the federal prison system indicate little change in programs available to inmates, slight decreases in participation in them, and little direct connection between inmate misconduct and sentencing policy.

> *Responsible formulation of sentencing policy requires baseline projections of the size and composition of prison populations with no policy changes, as well as estimates of the impact of various policy options. Analytical techniques for this purpose, although still crude, can be applied to estimate the effects of proposed policy changes, thereby making the value choices explicit.*

Because construction of new prison facilities is slow and costly, projections of the future size and composition of prison populations under current or proposed sentencing policies are desirable in considering whether to build new facilities. Accurate estimation has proven very difficult because of uncertainties in predicting the behavior of the many participants involved in sentencing decisions and in understanding the basic causal links among the decisions that contribute to the determination of prison populations. However, various techniques have been developed to provide estimates of future populations under various assumptions. And these techniques can be used to estimate the effects of particular policy proposals. This approach would provide legislatures and the public with the opportunity to consider explicitly the trade-offs between a desired level of punitiveness and its costs. Such consideration may ensure a balance between the severity of sentencing policies or laws and the availability of prison capacity. Without that balance, prison populations could exceed capacity, leading to unintended adaptive responses and systematic evasion of the policies or laws by judges and prosecutors.

The long-term effects of changes in sentencing policy on prison populations can be estimated through demographic-specific and crime-type-specific flow models and through microsimulation modeling techniques. Disaggregated flow models that treat the criminal justice system as a sequence of stages that process defendants as "units of flow" often cannot incorporate important behavioral responses to changing input conditions. By projecting prison populations under the assumption of a continuation of current policies, the models can provide a warning that a system would be approaching capacity, highlighting the need for some policy response. In microsimulation models, the basis of projections is a sample of individual simulated offenders, each characterized by relevant case attributes, possibly generated from actual case records. Alternative sentencing policies are then applied to this sample and the expected prison population associated with each policy is estimated. The Minnesota Sentencing Guidelines Commission fruitfully made use of such a model in developing its guidelines. Projection techniques are still in relatively early stages of development and are limited by the uncertainty of behavioral responses within the criminal justice system and by limitations on available data.

Increased prison populations and projections of further population growth have stimulated a search for alternative mechanisms for handling larger numbers of offenders in the face of limited capacity. Three general types of alternative strategies are available: direct regulation of prison population through controls on prisoner intake and release; construction to expand the supply of prison capacity; and reduction of the demand for prison space through use of alternatives to incarceration. The choices among these alternatives can be informed by research findings on the relative cost, impact, and effectiveness of each approach.

> *A continuation of the current rate of prison admissions, in the absence of some new prison population "safety-valve" mechanisms, is likely to result in a dramatic rise in prison populations.*

Mechanisms to control prison populations that are now in use in different jurisdictions include sentencing policies designed to limit prison commitments, parole release, increased early release for good behavior, executive clemency, and emergency powers acts.

There is an ongoing debate about the relationship between prison construction and prison populations. A reactive or population model suggests that the construction of new prison facilities occurs as a direct response to increases in prisoner populations. A capacity model hypothesizes that prison construction is itself a stimulus to prison population growth, so that more prison capacity results in the sentencing of more prisoners to fill that capacity, leading to further construction. A recent and widely cited study tested these alternative models and reported significant support for the capacity model, concluding that additions to rated capacity were filled within 2 years of their opening.

However, a reanalysis of those data shows that the calculations were in error and thus that the reported results are not empirically supported.

During the 1970s a variety of alternatives to incarceration were developed and implemented. They include pretrial diversion, intensified community supervision in lieu of secure 24-hour custody, community corrections acts designed to retain offenders under local supervision, restitution or community service programs, and prerelease programs for incarcerated offenders.

> *Evidence from evaluations of these programs suggests that these alternatives have been used more frequently as a supplement to existing nonincarcerative sanctions for use with offenders who would have remained in the community rather than as an alternative sanction for offenders who would otherwise have been incarcerated.*

Although few studies have adequately measured the extent to which offenders placed in the alternative programs would otherwise have been incarcerated, a large proportion of alternative program participants are minor offenders, including persons convicted of traffic violations who have been given a fine or probation. Prerelease programs for incarcerated offenders have permitted limited numbers of otherwise incarcerated offenders to be assigned to lower security facilities several months prior to parole or conditional release, but prison populations in secure facilities have continued to rise, and high rates of technical violation by those in prerelease programs may have resulted in an increase in the total length of their incarceration.

RESEARCH AGENDA

The issues involved in sentencing reform are such that it is not reasonable to anticipate that research will soon provide the "solution" to any jurisdiction's sentencing problems nor suggest a single "optimum" sentencing policy. Choices among alternate sentencing policies inherently involve value choices and will inevitably reflect political considerations within a jurisdiction. Nevertheless, those choices can be clarified and informed by research that illuminates the nature and bases of current sentencing practice and the potential consequences when changes are introduced.

SENTENCING PRACTICE AND BEHAVIOR

One important role for research, and one that should be pursued by jurisdictions considering changes in their sentencing policies, is careful exploration of the determinants of sentences. This research should emphasize approaches that will reduce the risk of selection bias that often arises when one examines only cases involving a sentencing decision. The research should begin examining the handling of cases as early as possible in the criminal justice process, and certainly no later than indictment. Research intended to measure racial discrimination should emphasize the treatment of less serious offenses, which offer greater room for discretion and greater opportunity for discrimination. Researchers, in selecting jurisdictions, should examine in detail the various stages between arrest and imprisonment to discern the degree to which discrimination may be introduced at some of these intermediate stages but fail to be detected in the aggregate because of possibly offsetting effects. Research designed to determine the extent of disparity in a jurisdiction should emphasize investigation of the role of frequently neglected variables that affect the decision-making process at various stages in the criminal justice system, particularly those factors related to assessments of offender culpability.

The federal government can assist in this process by supporting the development of improved methods for pursuing such research and by serving as an active repository for completed studies on these issues. A primary function for that repository would be to facilitate interjurisdiction comparisons on a continuing basis, both to improve the methodological quality and technique of such studies and to identify patterns that are consistent across jurisdictions.

ESTIMATING THE EFFECTS OF CHANGES IN SENTENCING POLICY

A second primary role of research is to improve the ability of a jurisdiction to anticipate the consequences of a change in sentencing policy. In recent years, there has been some improvement in the ability to estimate those effects on prison populations, and, in view of the current and anticipated crowding in U.S. prisons, improvement in the ability to develop reliable estimates of that effect is very important. As such capability to estimate impact becomes available to legislatures and sentencing commissions, they can reasonably be expected to take those effects into account in establishing their sentencing policies.

Most sentencing policy changes are likely to result in only partial compliance by justice system personnel. It is necessary to understand better the extent, nature, and sources of variation in the responses of practitioners, including the development of estimates of the effects of different forms of legal authority, monitoring practices, and enforcement mechanisms in effecting a policy change.

NATURAL EXPERIMENTS TO STUDY THE EFFECTS OF SENTENCING CHANGES

A third role for research is examination of the impact of changes in sentencing policy and practice. Often valuable research opportunities arise from natural experiments associated with the many changes in sentencing policies, including adoption of determinate sentencing laws, mandatory-minimum laws, sentencing guidelines, the abolition of parole boards, and promulgation of new administrative policies by parole authorities, prosecutors, and corrections officials. Each of these changes represents an opportunity to discern how the various actors involved in the sentencing process react to the change and how the change affects their practices. Such knowledge is valuable in providing feedback both to the jurisdiction making the change and to other jurisdictions considering similar policies. In choosing among the possible research opportunities available for these purposes, one must look to jurisdictions where a change is likely to generate compliance; where adequate "before" data are available that characterize practice prior to the introduction of the change; and where there is—or can be developed with some technical assistance—a valid research design, so that the direct and indirect consequences of the change can be adequately estimated.

We recommend the establishment of a continuing center to identify such targets of opportunity and to aid researchers in the formulation and execution of study designs.

1

Introduction: Sentencing Practices and the Sentencing Reform Movement

The sentencing decision is the symbolic keystone of the criminal justice system. It is here that conflicts between the goals of equal justice under the law and individualized justice with punishment tailored to the offender are played out and here that the criminal law is interpreted and applied. So it is not surprising that, as crime increased and questions about the fairness and effectiveness of the criminal justice system grew more and more pressing in the United States in the early 1970s, reformers turned to the courts and their sentencing practices, which one federal judge characterized as "lawless" (Frankel, 1972).

Increased awareness of the pivotal role of sentencing in linking the criminal law and criminal sanctions has recently focused reform efforts on sentencing. These developments followed 50 years in which there had been little change in sentencing practices and institutions. When the National Commission on Reform of Federal Criminal Laws reported to Congress in 1970, its sentencing proposals to rationalize and simplify the then-ubiquitous systems of indeterminate sentencing differed little from those of the Model Penal Code developed in the 1950s. When the commission reported, "determinate," "presumptive," and "flat-time" sentencing had not yet been proposed. The U.S. Parole Commission's parole guidelines were several years away. With minor exceptions, sentencing was not on state legislative agendas. Sentencing guidelines were beyond the horizon.

Since 1975, however, substantial changes have been introduced. Parole has been abolished in at least 10 jurisdictions, while parole guidelines have been established in at least 9 others. More than 30 states have passed mandatory minimum sentencing laws for selected offenses. By 1982, statewide sentencing guidelines were in effect or in advanced stages of development in 6 states, and local sentencing guidelines had been developed in more than 50 jurisdictions. In Alaska, plea bargaining has been abolished by the attorney general, and many local prosecutors have banned some or all forms of plea bargaining or have regulated it closely.

The sentencing reform movement has forced a reconsideration of the sentencing process and the goals of criminal sanctions. For many years the term "sentencing" produced civics-book images of high-ceilinged courtrooms, robed judges, and abashed defendants. The existence of plea negotiations was usually not acknowledged, and so defendants were often required to pretend at sentencing that their confessions had resulted only from remorse or contrition. The hypocrisy was blatant: everyone in the courtroom knew that most guilty pleas were induced by prosecutorial concessions or assurances, but the illusion of autonomous judicial decision making was maintained. Similarly, questions about the conflicts between utilitarian and retributive sentencing goals and the tensions between an individualized offender-oriented approach and uniform treatment of similar offenses were ignored. The claims of supporters of the system that the indeterminate sentence simultaneously was just and effective in incapacitating, rehabilitating, and deterring would-be offenders meshed neatly with the interests of criminal justice system personnel to maintain the status quo. By the late 1970s it was generally acknowledged that negotiated justice is the norm in most criminal courts, and there was a growing sense that neither fairness nor crime control had resulted from existing practices. And it was also recognized that "sentencing" encompasses a variety of participants, processes, and conflicting goals that influence a judge's sentence.

Sentencing is now understood as the allocation of punishment, and among the allocators are legislators, victims, police officers, prosecutors, defense counsel, judges (and occasionally juries), parole boards and examiners, and prison administrators. The decisions of criminal justice officials at arrest, prosecution, conviction, sentencing, and parole affect the nature and amount of punishment suffered by an offender. Additional choices by criminal justice system officials also can affect the punishment of an offender: the bail-release decision; assignment to a diversion program; assignment to a particular prison; loss or award of "good time"—time off a sentence for good behavior—by prison authorities; and revocation of probation or parole. At any point in the process the decisions of victims, police officers, prosecutors, and judges can terminate official proceedings or affect the decisions of others at a subsequent stage. Each of those decisions takes place in the context provided by the legislature through the criminal laws that prohibit certain behaviors and establish minimum and maximum punishments for them. And throughout this process, the decisions are affected by the conflicting normative goals and institutional interests that characterize the system.

In this chapter we first describe the variety of decision processes that, together, determine whether an offender is formally punished and, if so, how much. We next survey the origins of the processes described and the purposes they serve and review some of the philosophical controversies involved in the sentencing decision. We conclude with a brief survey of the origins, chronology, and manifestations of the current movement to change sentencing rules and institutions.

THE PROCESSES THAT CONSTITUTE SENTENCING

Any effort to "reform" or even to understand sentencing must take into account the existence of the many participants and decisions that together constitute "sentencing" and the conflicting values, perspectives, and interests among them. This very complexity, however, frustrates efforts to change the criminal justice process in America.

VICTIMS AND WITNESSES

Victims initiate criminal justice action when they decide to complain to the police. They also, subsequently, affect the likelihood of conviction and punishment through their ability and willingness to cooperate with the prosecution. Victim and witness noncooperation is a major cause of charge dismissals in the United States (Institute for Law and Social Research, 1981; Vera Institute of Justice, 1977). According to the National Crime Survey, 56 percent of violent crimes went unreported in 1978 (including 35 percent of robberies with injury), as did 75 percent of personal crimes of theft and 64 percent of household crimes (U.S. Department of Justice, 1980b). In general, the more serious the crime and the greater the likelihood that reporting the crime will produce some result, the higher the rate of reporting, and the more likely a victim is to cooperate with the prosecution.

Victims have little direct effect on the actual sentences received by convicted offenders, because they rarely are consulted by the judge or the prosecutor during plea negotiations, at trial, or during a sentencing hearing. However, their role in activating the criminal justice system is very important, and the growing awareness of the frustration and neglect of victims of crime has contributed to increased attention to their concerns.

POLICE

Police decide whom to notice, to stop, to arrest, to book, and (in some jurisdictions) to charge. Police officers have the primary authority to decide who will *not* be pursued by the criminal justice system. Most police patrol work involves officers in "keeping the peace" or handling threats to public order (Bittner, 1970; Wilson, 1973). For perpetrators of minor offenses involving public disorder, family violence, and small-scale drug trafficking, Feeley (1979) asserts that "the process [of going through misdemeanor court] is the punishment" (also see Alfini, 1981; Ryan, 1980/1981). The exercise of discretion in the police decision to arrest largely dictates the outcome in these cases. The police also possess substantial autonomy in handling serious crimes of violence and investigating organized illegal activities and large property loss or damage (see Manning, 1980; Rubenstein, 1974). Police are relatively free to decide which complaints to follow up, with what diligence and resources, and to select their means of investigation, using informants, surveillance, undercover, and "sting" operations. Police decisions to file criminal charges are subject to review by prosecutors and judges, but police decisions to disregard crimes or to pursue only informal remedies are not subject to any further review.

PROSECUTORS

Prosecutors establish priorities and determine the vigor with which various kinds of cases will be pursued. In the 1970s, for example, many prosecutors ceased prosecuting marijuana possession cases; in effect, those prosecutors decriminalized marijuana use in their jurisdictions.

Prosecutors also exercise substantial discretion over individual cases. Prosecutors decide what charges to file or, if the police file charges, what to dismiss. Like the decisions of police officers, prosecutors' decisions to release without arrest, or to arrest on only minor charges, are final. Charge dismissals or unilateral reductions are not subject to independent review. Prosecutors also decide whether, when, and what to negotiate and whether to recommend a particular sentence to a judge or agree to a recommendation by defense counsel. The large majority of convictions result from guilty pleas, most of which are the result of negotiations.

Plea bargaining takes diverse forms. In *horizontal charge bargains*, a prosecutor agrees to drop several charges for an offense type if the defendant pleads guilty to the remaining charges (e.g., three burglary charges are dropped when the defendant pleads guilty to a fourth). In *vertical charge bargains*, a prosecutor agrees to drop the highest charge if the defendant pleads guilty to a less serious charge (e.g., a narcotics trafficking charge is dropped if the defendant pleads guilty to a narcotics possession charge, or a charge of armed robbery is dropped if the defendant pleads guilty to a charge of robbery). In *sentence bargains*, a prosecutor agrees that the defendant will receive a specific sentence in return for a guilty plea. In *fact bargains*, a prosecutor agrees not to introduce evidence of specific aggravating circumstances. Other plea bargaining variants involve prosecutorial agreements to recommend or not to oppose particular sentences or to dismiss charges in consideration of the defendant's cooperation in other prosecutions or investigations. Whatever form plea bargaining takes, the prosecutor and to a lesser extent the defense counsel often stand supreme. The judge sometimes has little choice but to ratify their decisions, and, constitutionally, prosecutors' plea-bargaining tactics are virtually immune from judicial review (*Bordenkircher* v. *Hayes*, 434 U.S. 357 [1978]).

The criteria by which prosecutors screen and evaluate cases and allocate their offices' limited resources are rarely the subject of public debate, but they pose difficult questions regarding priorities, policies, and goals. Should uniform policies or rules regulating plea bargaining be adopted? What should they be? How should such policies or rules balance considerations of the seriousness of the offense, the characteristics of the offender, the strength of evidence or the likelihood of winning a case, and its possible political repercussions? Should an office concentrate its resources on, and recommend incarceration for, chronic property offenders who may pose little physical danger to other people but who are likely to continue offending; on white-collar offenders or corrupt public officials whose nonviolent property offenses may involve large dollar losses to the public or affect confidence in the integrity of their government; or on violent offenders, particularly those who may have short prior records and who may be unlikely to repeat their offenses? Should considerations of whether an individual is likely to be deterred from further offending, incapacitated by incarceration, or rehabilitated by a particular sanction affect prosecutors' recommendations, or should there be a uniform standard of punishment based on only the seriousness of the offense? If the latter, how should a uniform standard be devised?

JUDGES

Judges impose sentences. They decide who goes to prison and who does not; they set the terms of nonincarcerative sentences; and (depending on whether there is a parole board and on the rules governing parole eligibility) they set minimum, maximum, or actual lengths of jail and prison terms. Where there is a parole release agency, the judge's critical decisions are who goes to prison and for what minimum and maximum terms; where there is no such agency, the judge's decision also determines the actual amount of time served.

Judges' decisions are affected by the diverse goals they pursue in sentencing in general and in any particular sentence. How might a judge sentence a person who is a chronic property offender compared with an offender convicted for the first time of assault? A judge who has utilitarian goals might be more inclined to incarcerate the property offender on the basis of crime prevention concerns. Such a judge might ask whether a period of incarceration is likely to deter or rehabilitate either offender and assess the chances of recidivism in terms of the offender's prior record and personal characteristics. Or the judge might consider how many similar offenses might be averted by incarceration and weigh the cost of incapacitation against the cost of the crimes and the danger to public safety posed by the offender. A judge who has retributive goals would focus on the amount of harm done by the criminal acts and the offender's personal culpability in deciding on the sentence that is "deserved." Such a judge might give the assaulter a heavier sentence on the basis of offense seriousness.

Judges' powers, however, are informally but importantly affected by the work of other court personnel. First, in jurisdictions in which sentence bargaining is common, often a judge's choice is whether to ratify the negotiated sentence. Second, where charge bargaining is prevalent, a judge usually accedes to proposed charge dismissals and may impose a sentence only within the constraints set by any statutory sentence provisions. Third, probation officers devote more time to investigation of the offender's circumstances and to consideration of the case than judges possibly can, and so they control the flow of information to judges. Probation officers are attached to most modern felony courts; presentence reports containing their recommendations are commonly provided to judges, and these recommendations are usually followed (Carter and Wilkins, 1967; Townsend et al., 1978).

PAROLE BOARDS

Although parole boards have been abolished in some jurisdictions—and in others they have lost their authority to determine release dates—in the majority of states they retain control over parole release. Judges often set maximum sentences (and in some states minimums as well), but the maximum is often very long; parole boards decide who and when to release prior to sentence expiration; the conditions to which a parolee will be subject while on parole; when and why parole can be revoked; and when after revocation, if at all, an offender can be rereleased prior to the end of the maximum sentence. Parole revocation receives little attention from researchers or reformers, yet one of every five paroled prisoners is recommitted or otherwise returned to prison for violation of parole conditions within 3 years after an initial parole (Criminal Justice Research Center, 1980:668, hereafter cited as *Sourcebook*, 1980).

Parole boards traditionally make individualized release decisions, taking account of a wide variety of offender characteristics. In establishing uniform criteria for releasing offenders, they, too, face the basic dilemma in criminal justice: How much emphasis should be placed on the seriousness of the conviction offense in attempting to follow the injunction to "treat like cases alike" and how much on the characteristics of the defendant, including prior record and employment status, in predicting whether the release constitutes a danger to the community?

CORRECTIONS ADMINISTRATORS

Corrections administrators affect the duration of imprisonment by the award, withdrawal, or denial of time off for good behavior and by their recommendations and reports to parole boards when a prisoner is being considered for early release. Corrections administrators also influence the quality of a prisoner's confinement through decisions about institutional assignments and participation in various kinds of furlough programs. Whether an inmate spends time in a maximum security prison, in a less restrictive minimum security facility, or in a group home in his or her hometown is almost entirely in the hands of corrections authorities. Admission to a work, educational, or terminal furlough program is often akin to release from prison.

EXECUTIVE CLEMENCY: COMMUTATIONS AND PARDONS

Although pardons and similar executive release mechanisms once played a major part in prison releases (see Barnes and Teeters, 1959; Messinger, 1979), these ad hoc powers are no longer extensively used in most states.

LEGISLATURES

Legislative influence in sentencing is first and last: it is first because a legislature constructs and can always alter the basic statutory framework that other officials are charged to carry out; it is last because most punishments prescribed by law are not self-executing but can be realized only through other officials. If those officials behave inconsistently with the law, there is little a legislature can do. Even such seemingly authoritative laws as those calling for mandatory minimum sentences can be effected only through others; if prosecutors and judges choose to circumvent the law, mandatory terms will not be imposed. Sometimes a legislature's punishment decisions are definitive: for example, if incarceration is eliminated from the sanctions available for marijuana possession, the remaining punishment decisions are of less consequence than before; if marijuana use were legalized, punishment would no longer be applicable. Sometimes statutes are drafted so broadly that they provide little guidance in individual cases. For example, the maximum prison terms authorized for most offenses—5 or 10 or 25 years— are so much longer than the sentences typically imposed or served that the legislative decision has little significance for the operation of the system.

THE SYSTEM AS A WHOLE

The operations of this complex system of criminal justice, with its network of multiple, overlapping, and interconnecting discretions and conflicting goals, are not easily altered; like the operation of any complex system, they are influenced by powerful forces of tradition, institutional convenience, scarcity of resources, and self-interest. Officials who wish to circumvent or undermine a new law can usually find ways to do so; legislative changes are impositions from outside and are often resisted. A mandatory minimum sentence law, for example, can easily be avoided if the prosecutor dismisses or never files charges. A determinate sentencing law or sentencing guidelines can be evaded by artful charge bargaining. Parole guidelines can be evaded by lawyers who regard the applicable parole release date as an upper limit and arrange for the defendant to plead guilty to an offense bearing a maximum sentence less than that specified in the guidelines.

Such reactions are foreseeable. The staffs of prosecutors' offices and the courts have institutional goals and personal interests to serve and limited resources to expend. Sometimes their personal views of justice and injustice may not easily accept legislative solutions to the crime problem. Since new laws are seldom accompanied by appropriation of funds sufficient to permit literal and wholehearted compliance with them, something must give, and that something is often compliance.

The complexity of the system also often confounds reform initiatives by merely shifting the locus of decision-making power from one agency to another. The California determinate sentencing law, for instance, eliminated parole release decisions for most prisoners, but in doing so it simply shifted power over release from the parole agency to the judge and beyond the judge to the prosecutor. Although there is no evidence that prosecutors are better situated or qualified than judges or parole boards to make sentencing decisions, the greater predictability of sentences under the new law afforded prosecutors increased influence on sentences by means of their charging and charge dismissal decisions. Illinois's determinate sentencing law abolished parole release and allowed day-for-day credits for good behavior, but the prisoner receives no vested right to earned good time. And since good time can be withdrawn for misconduct, it is prison guards and officials, not the parole board, the judge, or the legislature, who effectively determine when prisoners are released.

The criminal justice system's complexity makes it difficult to predict the effects of change. In later chapters, we discuss the implications of this complexity for conducting research on the determinants of sentencing (Chapter 2), for thinking about how to structure and implement new sentencing strategies (Chapter 3), for evaluating the impact of new sentencing systems (Chapter 4), and for anticipating and structuring the effect of changes in sentencing on prisons (Chapter 5). In the rest of this chapter, we explore the often-conflicting goals of criminal justice sanctions; we briefly review the evolution of present American sentencing institutions, comparing them with their European counterparts; and we use that as background for describing the origins of the sentencing reform movement.

THE GOALS OF CRIMINAL SANCTIONS

Sentencing in general or the methods and consequences of change in specific sentencing practices cannot be considered without regard for the purposes and goals of the sanctioning process. Whether the allocation of punishment is efficient, just, or effective cannot be assessed without specifying the criteria by which to judge the outcomes. The criteria might include the expeditious disposition of cases, the reduction of crime, and the rendering of morally perfect justice, however measured. Such issues have moral and philosophical implications far beyond the panel's mandate or competence. While we have made no effort to resolve differences about the philosophy of punishment, we have attempted to be sensitive to those differences. We also suggest how various philosophical premises might differentially affect sentencing structures and the formulation of sentencing policy. The goals and purposes of punishment that are most often asserted are of two sorts: normative and functional.

NORMATIVE GOALS

It is often stated that the normative goals of punishment are the utilitarian ones of rehabilitation, incapacitation, and deterrence and the retributive one of imposing deserved punishment as an end in itself. Rehabilitation refers to the reform of the offender, and it can include special deterrence, which is the inhibiting effect of the sanction on the future behavior of the offender. Incapacitation refers to the effect of isolating identified offenders from society, thereby preventing them from committing further crimes. Deterrence refers primarily to general deterrence, which is the inhibiting effect of sanctions on others. To state these goals, however, obscures more than it enlightens. These diverse goals often conflict and, depending on their relative priority, may argue for different dispositions in particular cases.

The English philosopher H. L. A. Hart (1968) provides a useful framework for consideration of the normative goals of punishment. Observing that debates about the philosophy of punishment are often unnecessarily confused, he proposed that debaters devote separate attention to the three distinct questions:

- The general justifying aim—What is the general justification of the social institution of punishment?
- The question of liability—Who is to be punished?
- The question of amount—How much?

Hart's framework usefully isolates issues for discussion and demonstrates the potential coherence of punishment philosophies that have more than one purpose. For example, one can reasonably claim the utilitarian goal of crime prevention as the general justification of punishment and still insist that retributive considerations require that punishment be limited to conscious offenders and that the amount of punishment be closely proportioned to the offender's moral culpability.

Thus one can consistently accept utilitarian prevention as the social justification of punishment and at the same time argue that moral considerations forbid the imposition of exemplary punishments. Alternatively, one can invoke retributive considerations to argue that liability to punishment should depend on an individual's conscious offending while the amount of punishment need not be closely proportioned to culpability but can instead be adjusted to reflect rehabilitative needs, deterrent and incapacitative considerations, and so on.

Developments in philosophy over the last 20 years have importantly influenced the criminal law and sentencing. In both moral and political philosophy there has been a resurgence of interest in contractarian theories, often called "rights theories" (e.g., Dworkin, 1977; Gewirth, 1978; Nozick, 1973; Rawls, 1971), which pose several questions as their central concerns: What rights do individuals have? What is the source of those rights? When and under what circumstances may rights be disregarded or overridden? This new interest in rights conflicts with the older utilitarian premises of the substantive criminal law and the institutions of the criminal justice system. A punishment philosophy based primarily on concern for rights is what Hart called "backward-looking," interested primarily in the moral quality of the offender's acts and the punishment that the offender deserves for them; a utilitarian punishment philosophy is "forward-looking," primarily concerned with the effects of punishment.

In Hart's terms, indeterminate sentencing and its institutions are decidedly forward-looking. Thus, one rationale of parole is that people will remain incarcerated until they are rehabilitated. Parole release policies have typically been influenced by recidivism rates and the aim of keeping in prison longer those offenders who are expected to commit additional crimes. Criminal codes commonly provide maximum sentences that are designed to permit substantial scope for their discretionary reduction by the parole board and to permit judges to individualize sentences. Both the Model Penal Code (American Law Institute, 1962) and the *Study Draft* of the National Commission on Reform of Federal Criminal Laws (1970) are avowedly rehabilitative in their premises. Few of these practices or premises follow from a backward-looking punishment philosophy.

One influential manifestation of the development of rights theories is the just deserts theory articulated by Andrew von Hirsch, who argues that the justification of punishment in individual cases rests on the offender's moral culpability and that the amount of punishment must be proportional to that culpability rather than being determined by utili-

tarian considerations. One important corollary of a punishment jurisprudence that emphasizes desert is that equality in sentences imposed
becomes a concern of the highest priority. Utilitarian considerations
such as deterrent or incapacitative effects or the defendant's alleged
need for rehabilitation cannot be invoked to justify unequal sentences
in individual cases (see Coffee, 1978; Singer, 1979; von Hirsch, 1981).
From this perspective, sentencing "disparity," a term implying the absence of uniformity, proportionality, or both, came to be seen as a
primary source of injustice. While some supporters of the retributive
goals of sentencing, including von Hirsch, have advocated uniform sentences that would generally decrease the severity of punishment and
reserve the use of prison as a sanction largely for violent offenders, a
retributive perspective does not necessarily imply any particular level
of sanction severity. Indeed, other advocates of sentencing based on
retributive goals believe that, for offenders to receive just sanctions
proportionate to their crimes, sentences should be more severe and
certain as well as more consistent.

These are not simply theoretical arguments. Debates about the goals
of sanctions and the problem of disparity have echoed throughout legislative chambers and judicial conferences across the country. Legislators and public officials have adopted policies that express support for
punishment regimes premised on just deserts and similar notions. Section 1170 of the California Penal Code, for example, begins: "The Legislature finds and declares that the purpose of imprisonment for crime
is punishment." Section 2 of the act authorizing the establishment of
the Oregon parole guidelines provides that the ranges of prison sentences
contained in the parole guidelines (1977:Ch. 372, Sec. 2):

> shall be designed to achieve the following objectives:
> (a) Punishment which is commensurate with the seriousness of
> the prisoner's criminal conduct; and
> (b) to the extent not inconsistent with paragraph (a) of this sub-
> section [deterrence and incapacitation].

Thus Oregon law explicitly subordinates utilitarian considerations of
crime prevention to the achievement of commensurate punishment. The
Minnesota Sentencing Guidelines Commission (which was established
in 1978 by the legislature to design sentencing guidelines to structure
judges' decisions) considered various options—labeled just deserts,
modified just deserts, incapacitation, and modified incapacitation—in
deciding which types of cases should go to prison. The commission

adopted the modified just deserts option. Illinois's determinate sentencing law seeks to achieve greater proportionality between an offender's culpability and the sanction by increasing certain sentences through a separate schedule of "extended terms" for crimes involving "exceptionally brutal or heinous behavior indicative of wanton cruelty" (Illinois Revised Statutes, 1977:Ch. 38, Sec. 1005-8-1). In addition, many states have adopted mandatory minimum sentencing laws that reflect, in part, concern with ensuring more certain and severe sanctions for certain serious offenses. Thus concern with equality, proportionality, and the reduction of disparity in sentencing has animated many reform efforts and has significantly affected policy debate and decisions in many jurisdictions.

FUNCTIONAL GOALS

David Rothman's (1980) book on the development of various criminal justice and mental health institutions in this century is entitled *Conscience and Convenience*: conscience because the creation and dispersion of these institutions resulted in part from the efforts of benevolent reformers; convenience because the reformers' individual treatment ethos legitimated administrators' possession and exercise of enormous, seldom-reviewed powers over their patients, prisoners, and clients. Rothman's thesis is that these "progressive" institutions survived and retained their credibility for so long because of this congruence between reformers' visions and administrators' needs.

One need not be a cynic to accept Rothman's broad thesis. It requires no conspiracy theories to recognize that the day-to-day operation of institutions is often substantially determined by the needs of the people who manage them. Individuals operating inside institutions are motivated by diverse mixtures of personal, institutional, professional, and altruistic considerations. Efforts to change institutions and their operations are likely to founder unless one considers the functional goals of the people who operate them.

A substantial literature on the operations of criminal courts has come into being in the last 15 years (e.g., Eisenstein and Jacob, 1977; Levin, 1977), and it suggests some of the functional goals that motivate the lawyers, judges, and others who operate the courts: to achieve just results—by the participants' standards—in individual cases; to maintain an acceptable guilty-plea rate in order to process cases expeditiously; to maintain amicable relations with the other participants in the process;

to operate efficiently within material and personnel restraints.[1] The sentencing reforms of the last decade have challenged the long-standing equilibrium between the formal goals of punishment and the functional goals of those who operate the criminal justice system. The tensions between normative goals and institutional interests have been resolved in various ways in other countries and at other times in the United States.

AMERICAN SENTENCING IN COMPARATIVE AND HISTORICAL PERSPECTIVE

CONTEMPORARY AMERICAN SENTENCING

The characteristic of the modern American criminal justice system that distinguishes it from earlier times and from other countries today is the existence of three independent centers of sentencing authority—prosecutors, trial judges, and parole boards. The plea-bargained guilty plea—which results from prosecutors' offices—is the most usual outcome of criminal cases in America; in many jurisdictions even a judge's influence over plea bargaining is limited. At the next stage of the process, judges have sole authority to decide who goes to prison (or jail), subject to negotiated guilty-plea constraints and mandatory sentencing laws and for all convictions following trials. Then, within the constraints of maximum and minimum sentences set by the judge, parole boards (in those jurisdictions that retain parole release) have authority to decide when prisoners are released. By law and tradition, each of these three decision makers is organizationally and politically separate. Appellate courts, the independent forum for review of administrative and judicial decisions in other contexts, have traditionally deferred to the decisions of prosecutors, trial judges, and parole boards.

The U.S. Supreme Court has affirmed that most prosecutorial charging and plea-bargaining decisions are not subject to judicial review (*Bordenkircher* v. *Hayes*, 434 U.S. 357 [1978]) and that the U.S. Parole Commission's release decisions do not present judicially cognizable sub-

---

[1]Some historians and social theorists offer various hypotheses about the latent social functions of punishment. Specifically, these theorists argue that changes in the forms of social control, including the penal system, are influenced by changes in the social structure, such as: shifts in labor market conditions; the need to avoid disruptions caused by unemployed, underemployed, and unemployable people; and the need to channel workers' discontent and maintain existing power relations. These issues go far beyond our focus on the criminal justice system and are not considered in this report.

stantive issues (*U.S.* v. *Addonizio*, 442 U.S. 178 [1979]). Although practical considerations and deference to administrative expertise are sometimes invoked as reasons for this hands-off approach, the fundamental explanation is rooted in the basic concept of separation of powers: prosecutors and parole boards are in the executive branch of government and hence not subject to certain kinds of judicial review. (Of course, that both are executive branch agencies does not mean that their processes or policies are coordinated: the two agencies have different origins, different rationales, and different constituencies.)

Prosecutors

Public prosecution in the United States is locally organized and highly political. Since chief prosecutors (or district attorneys) are usually elected local officials and are often ambitious politicians anxious for higher office or judgeships, their political terms of reference are primarily local and largely insulated from external controls. Serving political as well as managerial functions, chief prosecutors are in a position to affect policy through internal administrative procedures. Chief prosecutors can establish supervisory, monitoring, and record-keeping systems to ensure that assistant prosecutors comply with their policies. This is possible because prosecutors' offices are usually small organizations; even in the largest cities, the professional staffs number in the few hundreds. Furthermore, assistant prosecutors are often young lawyers who view their entry-level, low-paying jobs as temporary apprenticeships on the way to private practice or political careers. Hence, they are anxious to demonstrate that they are team players and gain favorable recommendations from the chief prosecutor. Efforts to achieve more uniform statewide sentencing practices must win the support of chief prosecutors, accept the fact that local chief prosecutors can defy state policies when they wish to do so, or develop other means to restrict the prosecutors' powers.

Parole Boards

Parole boards are state agencies; their members are typically appointed by the governor (or, at the federal level, the President), sometimes with the advice and consent of the legislature. The relevant political constituencies are at the state level, notably the governor, the legislature, and the press. Although local controversies occasionally reverberate in state capitals, a parole board, much more than a prosecutor's office, can distance itself from day-to-day politics. Parole boards set policies that apply to all state prisoners. Because hearing examiners are dependent on their superiors for assignments, performance evaluations, and promotions, parole boards are in a position to establish criteria for release decisions and to establish administrative systems to monitor compliance by hearing examiners.

Trial Judges

As a formal matter, a trial judge's sentencing decisions are constrained only by conscience and by the usually wide range of sentences authorized by the applicable criminal statutes. Trial judges, unlike parole hearing examiners and assistant prosecutors, are almost immune from organizational controls: their salaries are fixed by law; their terms are usually long; impeachment is a difficult and rarely invoked procedure. Only in periods immediately preceding a campaign for reelection or retention need judges pay particular heed to public opinion or to the political ramifications of their decisions. In the United States, judges value their independence and are not easily regulated.

No general right of sentence appeal exists under federal law, and there is reason to doubt whether meaningful review is available in those states that have established systems of appellate sentence review (Samuelson, 1977; Zeisel and Diamond, 1977). The Eighth Amendment of the U.S. Constitution, as currently interpreted, does not empower appellate judges in most cases to decide whether lawful sentences imposed by trial judges are excessively severe (*Estelle* v. *Rummel*, 445 U.S. 263 [1980]; *Hutto* v. *Davis*, 445 U.S. 947 [1980]). Consequently, appellate review of sentences is available only when a legislature, state supreme court, or state constitution has expressly established such a system.

As a practical matter, judges are subject to organizational constraints. Judges in administrative positions can place some pressures on their colleagues by threatening to assign them to unpopular courts or dockets. Trial judges may be constrained by bargains negotiated by counsel. Charge bargains may reduce the maximum sentence allowable to a level below that which the judge believes appropriate. (In most jurisdictions, for example, a negotiated misdemeanor plea to a felony charge will make a state prison sentence impossible.) Sentence bargains require that a judge accept the sentence negotiated or let the defendant withdraw a guilty plea; although a judge is not required to accept sentence bargains, a proposal that both the prosecutor and the defense counsel believe to be appropriate is unlikely to be rejected. And, although a trial judge's sentencing decisions are seldom subject to meaningful review by appellate judges, the intended length of a prison sentence is subject to reconsideration by the parole board.

An additional practical consideration for judges, particularly when sentencing an offender convicted of a heinous crime, is the increased public pressure that results from the judge's heightened visibility through media coverage. The indirect effect on judicial behavior of both peer pressure and prevailing community standards of justice can be seen in differences in the sentences imposed for similar offenses by judges who ride a circuit and sentence cases in more than one district (Gibson, 1978b).

EUROPEAN SENTENCING SYSTEMS

The U.S. criminal justice system is the product of U.S. history. Despite diversity among European criminal justice systems, three features of the U.S. sentencing process distinguish it from many of those in Europe: the importance of plea bargaining and the prominence of the prosecutor; the inflation of prison sentence lengths in anticipation of their later reduction by parole boards; and the absence of meaningful appellate sentence review. A common theme in all these features is the relatively greater detachment from politics in European sentencing.

Plea Bargaining

In comparison with U.S. practice, plea bargaining is not as important a feature of the criminal process in England, France, the Scandinavian countries, or West Germany (Andenaes, 1983; Jackson, 1972; Thomas, 1979; Weigend, 1980).[2] Defendants who plead guilty receive leniency in some of these countries, but this leniency is available to all who plead guilty, is modest in amount, and does not result from the negotiations of lawyers.

Although the organization of public prosecution varies from country to country, a common feature is that public prosecutors in Western Europe are not elected officials. In France and West Germany, for example, public prosecutors are appointed officials and are career civil servants. In England, there are no public prosecutors except for the Director of Public Prosecutions (a central government official) and his

---

[2]There have in recent years been assertions that something akin to plea bargaining exists in several European criminal justice systems (see, for example, Baldwin and McConville [1977] concerning England and Goldstein and Marcus [1977] concerning France, Italy, and West Germany). To the extent that plea-bargaining analogues exist in those countries, they are substantially less visible than in the United States.

small staff, who prosecute the few most serious cases; the function of public prosecution is largely performed by police solicitors and private lawyers who are appointed on a case-by-case basis to represent the Crown.

It is uncertain why plea bargaining is of limited importance in Western European legal systems. Smaller case loads, stronger professional norms against negotiation, removal of the prosecutor from local politics, and the organizational structure of prosecutors' offices have been suggested as contributing factors.

Parole

By 1930 every U.S. state had created a parole board (Rothman, 1980), and parole subsequently became the primary form of prison release. In 1976, for example, more than 70 percent of persons released from U.S. prisons were released on parole (*Sourcebook*, 1980:661). By contrast, release on parole remains the exception, not the norm, in most European countries. The English Parole Board, for example, was not created until 1967, and most prisoners in England are not released on parole, because sentences imposed are much shorter than in America (seldom longer than 2–3 years); remission of sentence (time off for good behavior) reduces maximum sentences by a third; and prisoners are not eligible for parole until they have served one-third of the term imposed (Jackson, 1972). In Norway, prisoners are eligible for parole only after serving one-half the sentence imposed, and sentences seldom exceed 2 years. For a 2-year sentence, remission shortens the time served by 8 months, and so parole release would reduce that sentence by at most another 4 months (Andenaes, 1983). In West Germany, where local panels of judges have authority to release prisoners early, the scope of parole release is similarly narrow (Weigend, 1983).

The lesser reliance on parole authorities to determine the lengths of prison sentences and to shorten the nominal sentences declared by judges has at least two important consequences in Europe: the judge is much more the central figure in sentencing, and sentences that are imposed are very close to the sentences actually served. European judges are seldom presented with negotiated proposals for disposition of cases, and they are not as constrained as American judges by personal, institutional, and work-group considerations to delegate or share their power. Moreover, they have no need to increase the sentences they impose to offset the amounts by which parole boards will routinely shorten them. Thus the sentences imposed in Europe are shorter than those in the

United States; however, there is conflicting literature on whether prison sentences actually served in various European countries are shorter than those actually served in the United States (see Advisory Council on the Penal System, 1978:Appendix C).

Appellate Sentence Review

Appellate review of sentences, which is rare in America, is common in Europe. In England and Norway, appellate judges have established case law standards for sentences, and aggrieved defendants can seek review of the appropriateness of their sentences. This establishes meaningful constraints on trial judges' decisions and provides a mechanism for reducing the incidence and extent of unwanted disparities in sentences.

It is possible that the failure of appellate sentence review to take hold in the United States resulted in part from the widespread adoption of parole. When parole boards exercised authority over release, judges' sentences were of secondary importance: if parole boards could release a prisoner when they saw fit, case law standards for nominal sentences would have little real meaning. Moreover, if sentences were too severe, parole boards could rectify matters. Thus, in a sense, parole boards became mechanisms for review of sentences in the United States and appellate courts did not. Plea bargaining also has provided a practical impediment to appellate sentence review. Defendants who plead guilty in connection with a *sentence* bargain are not well situated later to object to the sentence received. Although *charge* bargains need not severely limit judges' sentencing options, the perception that the defendant has voluntarily pled guilty knowing that he is vulnerable to any lawful sentence may also have impeded the development of appellate sentence review.

THE DEVLOPMENT OF AMERICAN SENTENCING STRUCTURES AND EFFORTS TO REFORM THEM

The ideological bases and institutional structures of sentencing in America have changed substantially since colonial days. These changes reflect and parallel a series of reforms throughout the criminal justice system that have contributed to its contemporary form. The main characteristics of sentencing goals and practices in several periods are briefly noted here to illustrate the relatively recent origin of current sentencing practices.

Colonial America

Prior to the American revolution, American criminal justice practices resembled those in Britain. The criminal law was harsh. In a society with limited communications, no police (only a voluntary nightwatch system), few jails, and rudimentary record-keeping, crime control efforts were designed principally to deter would-be offenders by imposing punishments so terrible that few would dare break the law. More than 350 offenses were punishable by capital punishment (Hartung, 1952), and less serious offenses were subject to sentences of corporal punishment, fines, or banishment. Penal incarceration was a rarely applied sanction, although sometimes offenders were held in jail to prevent flight pending trial or until their execution.

1790–1820: Reform of the Law

The founding of the republic and the era of political ferment that followed it led to major reforms in American sentencing ideas and practices that increasingly diverged from those in Europe. The principal one was a movement away from capital punishment to imprisonment—a measured time of exclusion from society for criminal offenses. This change had both ideological and practical support. The number of capital crimes was greatly reduced, in part because such harsh punishment had failed to deter crime and had resulted, instead, in juries that more and more frequently refused to convict. At the same time, Enlightenment ideas, particularly those of the philosopher Beccaria, gained favor. He argued that greater certainty of punishment, rather than an emphasis on severity, would more effectively deter crime. Many legislatures came to the conclusion that wholesale reliance on capital punishment was self-defeating. More lenient codes prescribing fixed periods of imprisonment were recognized as both more humane and appropriate for a new nation with a populist government. They also represented a more promising form of crime control, since they offered the prospect of reforming criminals, not merely punishing them.

By 1820 many state legislatures had drafted new criminal codes that prescribed fixed sentences to match the seriousness of the offense. Sentences were long: 40 years for murder, 20 years for arson, and 10 years for burglary were common (Rothman, 1981). Yet, in contrast to capital punishment, imprisonment seemed more humane and more certain, and therefore more effective.

1820–1900: Emphasis on Prisons

Although reformers at the beginning of the nineteenth century had hoped to find an answer to the crime problem through sentencing reform and criminal codes, for much of the rest of the century attention was shifted from sentences and the likelihood of their imposition to the penitentiary—as nineteenth century prisons were called—and the experience of punishment as the critical mechanism of crime control.

By midcentury penitentiaries had been built in many states. The reasons for and significance of this development have been variously interpreted. It has been argued that they signified the triumph of Enlightenment ideals and the rejection of inhumane forms of corporal and capital punishment (McKelvey, 1977); an indictment of a disordered society by Jacksonian reformers nostalgic for a stable but vanished colonial society (Rothman, 1971); and a precursor, or metaphor, for a surveillant disciplinary society (Foucault, 1978). Whatever their origins, prisons were built and prisoners were sentenced to long terms of incarceration fixed by judges.

Faith in the rehabilitative potential of the penitentiary affected sentencing procedures in several ways. Initially it reinforced the legitimacy of uniform fixed dispositions based exclusively on the crime itself: the penitentiary was viewed as a panacea for all types of deviant behavior. In addition, the promise of offender reform led to a shift in emphasis from the traditional principles of deterrence and retribution to concern with rehabilitation. Reformers expected imprisonment not only to dissuade would-be and sentenced offenders from pursuing criminal acts, but also to alter the offenders themselves. Until about 1850 there was no sense of conflict among the purposes of sentencing, since reformers viewed the penitentiary and its regimen as simultaneously deterring offenders from further criminality, incapacitating them, and rehabilitating them through fixed sentences of long duration. All agreed that sentences should be lengthy: for the conservatives, to deter offenders; for reformers, to allow time for rehabilitation to occur.

By the 1860s, when penitentiaries were only a few decades old, their defects had become clear, and a new wave of reformers set out to improve the institutions and save prisoners from them (Rothman, 1980). To cope with the crowding, brutality, and disorder of prisons, "good time" was introduced, giving wardens a mechanism of control other than corporal punishment; the use of governors' pardoning powers greatly increased; and probation programs first appeared, to keep minor offenders out of institutions. More important, from the standpoint of sentencing, was the arrival of indeterminate sentences—under which corrections officials could decide when prisoners would be released based on their rehabilitation—initiated at New York State's Elmira Reformatory when that institution opened in 1877.

1900–1970: The Rehabilitative Model

Among the accomplishments of the Progressive era reformers between 1900 and 1930 was the all-but-universal adoption of indeterminate sentencing based on rehabilitation of the offender and the creation of parole boards with discretion over release decisions. Reformers asserted that the causes of criminal behavior were different for each offender, and therefore they sought to individualize criminal justice procedures. The medical model prevailed as the offender came to be viewed as sick—or in need of treatment—and the prescription had to be tailored to each offender's illness. Thus the determinants of sentences were shifted away from the offense to the offender—from what he had done to who he was. And a decision about the offender's "cure" could only be made by a professional after treatment, not at the time of commitment.[3]

Just as historians differ in their accounts of the origins of the prisons, they also disagree on the reasons for the creation of the rehabilitative penal system with its vast discretions and minimal accountability. Rothman (1980) believes modern institutions resulted from a congruence between the humanitarian impulses of benevolent reformers and the instrumental convenience that rehabilitative discretions afforded officials; other historians disagree with this explanation (see, e.g., Mennel, 1973; Platt, 1977; Walker, 1979, 1980). There is agreement, however, that modern American criminal justice practices are of very recent origin.

Between 1930 and 1970 there were changes in criminal law and procedure, but these had little impact on the ways criminal offenders were handled. The American Law Institute worked on the Model Penal Code throughout the 1950s and completed its work in 1962; in the following years many state legislatures adopted derivative criminal codes. The Model Penal Code and the proposed criminal code of the National Commission on Reform of Federal Criminal Laws (1970) exemplify the stability of the attitudes of the legal establishment toward the criminal justice system between 1930 and 1970. Both codes had avowedly rehabilitative outlooks; both perpetuated the indeterminate sentence and

---

[3] During this period, too, juvenile courts were established with an even stronger emphasis on rehabilitation, and the scope and claims of probation were expanded.

the parole board; both granted immense discretion to judges and parole boards. Although the Model Penal Code also dealt with some matters of criminal procedure, the major procedural changes of the 1960s emanated from the Warren Court, which issued a series of opinions that applied to the states most of the criminal procedure provisions the Bill of Rights imposed on the federal system.

THE CURRENT SENTENCING REFORM MOVEMENT

Since 1970 numerous sweeping reforms of the criminal justice system have been undertaken. After nearly 40 years of stability, the indeterminate sentencing system has been abruptly rejected in state after state. Between 1975 and January 1982, 11 states abolished parole release for the majority of offenders,[4] 17 states established administrative rules for release decisions (e.g., parole guidelines),[5] more than 30 states passed mandatory minimum sentence laws, and, in almost every state, judges experimented with guidelines to structure their own sentencing decisions.

The history of sentencing reform in the 1970s is yet to be written; time must pass before historians will be able to understand this frenzy of activity. However, we note several recent developments that either influenced recent sentencing initiatives or were themselves symptomatic of the same social forces that caused those initiatives.

Prison Uprisings and the Civil Rights Movement

Prison uprisings in the late 1960s, at the Tombs in New York City and state prisons in Florida, Indiana, New York (Attica), and elsewhere, demonstrated several things: prisoners were deeply discontented; they were disproportionately black and brown; rehabilitation rhetoric was, in many prisons, no more than rhetoric. The civil rights movement had reached inside prison walls by the mid-1960s. A large number of successful prisoners' rights cases in the federal courts gave prisoners an opportunity to be heard outside the prison, and they were listened to. The first influential book calling for rejection of the indeterminate sen-

[4]Alaska, Arizona, California, Colorado, Connecticut, Illinois, Indiana, Maine (which was first), Minnesota, New Mexico, and North Carolina.

[5]Florida, Georgia, Hawaii, Louisiana, Maryland, Michigan, Minnesota, New York, Ohio, Oregon, Rhode Island, South Carolina, Washington, West Virginia, and Wisconsin (*Uniform Parole Reports*, 1980).

tencing system, *Struggle for Justice* (American Friends Service Committee, 1971), began by quoting the demands of a group of prisoners in the Tombs. Prisoners, their complaints, and what goes on inside prisons were major catalysts of modern sentencing reform (see, for example, Zimring, 1983).

The Philosophy of Rights and Control of Discretion

Modern criminal law and the indeterminate sentencing system took shape in an era when utilitarianism was the philosophical perspective most commonly brought to bear on public policy matters. The Model Penal Code and the more than 30 state codes emulating it were avowedly utilitarian in premises and outlook. Retribution was expressly denounced, and rehabilitation was endorsed as the primary goal of punishment. Williams in England (e.g., 1961) and Wechsler in the United States, among the foremost scholars of the criminal law, were both utilitarians primarily concerned with crime prevention as the foremost goal of the criminal law. The indeterminate sentencing system overtly focused primarily on offenders and their amenability to treatment rather than on their offenses. Until the 1960s few principled objections were raised to indeterminacy, to the rehabilitative ideal, and to the primacy of utilitarianism in the philosophy of punishment (but see Allen, 1959; Hart, 1968).

Although it was anticipated by Hart's *Punishment and Responsibility* (1968), the recent challenge to utilitarianism was exemplified by Rawls's *A Theory of Justice* (1971), which was followed by a series of powerful antiutilitarian books (e.g., Dworkin, 1978; Gewirth, 1978; Nozick, 1974). Grossly oversimplified, the primary complaint of antiutilitarians was that utilitarianism does not adequately address justice for individuals. The advocates of rights theories are primarily concerned with the rights of individuals and the constraints that those rights place on the assertion of state power. These theories require that criminal responsibility should be predicated on moral culpability (which is not necessarily a requirement of a utilitarian jurisprudence) and that punishment should be primarily retributive in aim and proportional in amount to an offender's culpability.

Parallel trends appeared in writings on sentencing reforms. Von Hirsch's *Doing Justice* (1976) endorsed retribution, or just deserts, and proposed that sentencing be guided by detailed sentencing criteria relating largely to a defendant's moral culpability (see also The Twentieth Century Fund, 1976). The indeterminate sentencing system with its vast range of discretion conflicted with rights theories. The principal theoretical rival of retribution, the modified utilitarianism of Norval Morris (1974) and the American Bar Association Criminal Justice Standards Project (1980), gives greater weight to crime preventive strategies in sentencing while still insisting that retributive concerns establish meaningful limits on the amount of punishment that can be imposed in individual cases. These philosophical developments, along with the distrust for authority characteristic of the 1960s and 1970s, gave important support to proposals for changing the extensive discretion of judges and parole administrators in deciding who went to prison and how long they stayed there.

Demand for Accountability

Throughout the legal system in the 1960s and 1970s, there was a movement for increased accountability in official decision making. Judicial decisions in many contexts required that public officials indicate reasons for decisions and give adversely affected individuals an opportunity to defend themselves and to dispute material allegations or evidence. Prison administrators, for example, began to be required to publish their disciplinary rules and to give prisoners an opportunity to defend themselves against rule violation charges (*Wolff* v. *McDonnell*, 418 U.S. 539 [1974]). Other cases established procedural requirements to be observed before offenders could have probation revoked (*Gagnon* v. *Scarpelli*, 411 U.S. 778 [1973]), have parole revoked (*Morrissey* v. *Brewer*, 408 U.S. 471 [1972]), or, in some states, be denied parole (*Greenholtz* v. *Inmates*, 442 U.S. 1 [1979]).

Parole came under vigorous attack on the grounds that parole release decisions lacked standards and, hence, accountability (Davis, 1969, 1976). These attacks, coupled with the general movement for increased accountability in official decision making, led to studies of whether parole boards followed implicit criteria in parole release decisions and whether those criteria could be expressed in decision rules. A major long-term project demonstrated the feasibility of detailed published criteria for parole release decisions (Gottfredson et al., 1978). The U.S. Parole Commission adopted parole guidelines based on that research in 1974, and several state parole boards soon followed. The research team that had developed the first parole guidelines later explored the feasibility of using that same method to develop sentencing guidelines for judges (Wilkins et al., 1978). Empirically derived sentencing guidelines projects have since been undertaken in more than 50 jurisdictions.

Rejection of Rehabilitation

After three-quarters of a century of intellectual hegemony, the rehabilitative ideal began to crumble in the 1960s (see, e.g., Allen, 1959) and collapsed in the 1970s, primarily because of two objections. First, there was substantial evidence that rehabilitative programs do not demonstrably and substantially reduce the later criminality of their clients (Brody, 1976; Greenberg, 1975; Lipton et al., 1975; Robison and Smith, 1971). In reviewing the most comprehensive of the reviews, by Lipton et al., a National Research Council panel concluded that the authors were "reasonably accurate and fair in their appraisal of the rehabilitation literature," but it noted two significant limitations (Sechrest et al., 1979:5-6):

> . . . first, inferences about the integrity of the treatments analyzed were uncertain and the interventions involved were generally weak; second, there are suggestions to be found concerning successful rehabilitation efforts that qualify the [Lipton et al.] conclusion that "nothing works."

Nonetheless, the uncritical support that rehabilitative programs received before 1970 has been displaced by a deep skepticism. If rehabilitative programs didn't "work," the claim that prisoners could be released when they were rehabilitated lost much of its credibility.

Second, there were objections to the rehabilitative ideal because the extensive discretion characterizing sentencing and corrections programs were often abused. This was a powerful criticism in a period of widespread distrust of authority and acute sensitivity to the reality—or even to the appearance—of racial discrimination and arbitrary decisions.

Disparity and Discrimination

No doubt influenced by prison uprisings, rights theories, increasing emphasis on accountability, and decreasing emphasis on rehabilitation (as well as by the widespread availability of computers for social science research, which made elaborate multivariate analyses possible), researchers undertook many statistical simulation studies to determine whether there was substantial evidence of disparity and racial and class discrimination in sentencing. The findings on discrimination were mixed (see Hagan, 1974; Hagan and Bumiller, Volume II), but on disparity they were striking: the research could account for only a small amount of the variation in sentences imposed by judges (Diamond and Zeisel, 1975; Institute for Law and Social Research, 1981; Partridge and Eldridge, 1974; Rich et al., 1981; Tiffany et al., 1975). While such disparities were not particularly troublesome when the rehabilitative ideal pre-scribed sentence variation based on offender characteristics, without that justification the evidence of substantial, unexplained, and often apparently unwarranted disparities in sentencing became a primary ra-tionale for proposals to structure, confine, and monitor the discretion of trial judges and parole boards.

Crime Control

Official rates of reported and recorded crime have increased almost steadily since the early 1960s, and there have been numerous criticisms of the effectiveness of the criminal justice system (van den Haag, 1975; Wilson, 1975). Accordingly, increased attention and federal research funding were given to nonrehabilitative sentencing strategies like in-capacitation and deterrence and to projects concerned with "career criminals." (Federal funds were used to establish "career criminal" pros-ecution units across the United States.) With this heightened emphasis on crime control, people on the political right joined people on the political left, concerned about discrimination, disparity, and accounta-bility, in a combined assault on the institutions of the indeterminate sentencing system.

The indeterminate sentencing system that had been all-but-universally supported through most of the 1960s had few defenders left by the late 1970s. By then, a broad consensus in favor of change had formed among the political left and right, law enforcement agencies and prisoners' groups, and reformers and criminal justice systems officials. There was rather less agreement on what should replace indeterminate sentencing. Unlike previous waves of reform, the current movement is characterized by a cacophony of voices disagreeing over the purposes and justification for determinate sentences and over whose discretion should be curtailed.

The Role of Social Science Research in Sentencing Changes

Social science research tends to percolate into the policy arena and subtly alter the ways policy makers and citizens think about issues. The results of sentencing research have followed this pattern. Sentencing policy changes have been influenced by social science research findings and have themselves precipitated a substantial body of research (see Weiss, 1981).

On the subject of rehabilitation, research pulling together the many assessments of rehabilitation programs tended to confirm what some observers had suspected about those programs and removed the basic justifications for indeterminate sentencing policies. While research was not the driving force behind the effort to reduce unwarranted disparity in sentencing, the availability of data confirming the impression of widespread disparities and suggesting the existence of discrimination by race and socioeconomic status contributed to the quest for policies to limit judicial discretion. Similarly, as the goals of sentencing shifted toward deterrence and incapacitation, researchers sought to assess the magnitude of the deterrent and incapacitative effects of various sanctioning policies on crime rates, as well as to assess the career criminal programs designed to implement those goals.

The effect of research on the development of sentencing guidelines has been direct and instrumental. The tradition of research on predictors of parole success, which dates back to the 1920s, was stimulated in the 1960s by the availability of multivariate statistical techniques facilitating better identification of the predictors of success. Corrections authorities and researchers worked cooperatively to develop improved prediction instruments to help parole authorities structure discretionary release procedures. After successfully demonstrating the feasibility of the U.S. Parole Commission's guidelines, researchers applied the same techniques to modeling the factors associated with judicial sentencing decisions. At a time when judicial decision making was under strong attack, "descriptive" guidelines that would articulate and rationalize existing sentencing policies had an appeal that led to their widespread dissemination and adoption. More recently, social science modeling methods and data on past sentencing practice were used by the Minnesota Sentencing Guidelines Commission in developing "prescriptive" guidelines that explicitly altered existing policies and practices.

In sum, research on sentencing has contributed to the general discussion of sentencing policy in several ways: it challenged prevailing doctrines and assumptions; documented emerging beliefs and thereby gave them added impetus; specified the nature and extent of bias in the system; strengthened the case for change; provided a technology for individual decision making; legitimated alternative rationales for punishment; encouraged the search for alternative policies while providing ammunition for a critique of these options; and provided a conceptual language for the policy discourse.

Several groups have had important roles in the diffusion of research into the policy arena. Legal scholars, blue-ribbon commissions, and crusading or popular authors have all drawn on social science research to support policy recommendations. Federal agencies, particularly the Law Enforcement Assistance Administration and the National Institute of Justice (NIJ), have supported empirical research on sentencing. In the late 1970s, NIJ made sentencing a priority area for research funding. It has both funded and disseminated the results of some policy-relevant research and evaluation studies, which include the development and testing of various kinds of descriptive sentencing guidelines and assessments of the impact of determinate sentencing laws.

SCOPE OF THIS REPORT

The policy and research developments in sentencing in the past decade; the variety of proposals for changing sentencing practices that are pending in Congress, state legislatures, and administrative agencies; and the newly emerging data on the impact of recently adopted policy innovations suggested the need for an interim review of empirical findings about what may be termed the sentencing reform movement. This report is designed to meet that need. It reviews the findings and methodologies of several bodies of sentencing research, points to the ways social science research has informed policy making, and suggests future avenues of inquiry and improved methods for research and for formulating sentencing policy.

The historical, comparative, and descriptive review presented in this chapter provides some perspective for what follows. Chapter 2 reviews the methods and findings of empirical research on the determinants of sentences, with particular attention to research on discrimination and disparity. Chapter 3 considers the development and formulation of sentencing policy. It reviews the variety of approaches taken to develop systems of structured discretion for greater evenhandedness in sentencing decisions. Chapter 4 reviews the evaluation literature that has attempted to determine the effects of various innovations on sentencing outcomes and officials' behavior. Chapter 5 considers the relationship between sentencing policies and prison populations. It examines the implications of changes in sentencing practices on the size, conditions, and management of prison populations, as well as the problems of projecting and controlling the size of those populations. Chapter 6 sets out directions for future research.

It is important to make clear what is not included in this volume and the reasons for these omissions. Although we recognize the importance of the crime control effects of sentencing, we do not attempt to account for the effects of sentencing on offender rehabilitation or on deterrence and incapacitation; these subjects have recently been considered by other National Research Council panels (Blumstein et al., 1978; Martin et al., 1981; Sechrest et al., 1979). Limitations of time and expertise and the absence of appropriate research led us to exclude several other subjects from its broad conception of sentencing. For example, we did not examine police arrest and charging practices, bail-setting and pretrial release policies, or the role of public opinion in the establishment of sentencing policies. Nor did we examine research or policy concerning the sentencing of juveniles, even though young offenders are disproportionately arrested for serious offenses against persons. We determined that despite the overlap of the juvenile and criminal justice systems, legal and organizational issues raised by an inquiry into the former system would detract from a more intensive focus on the latter. Finally, although we did devote some attention to programs that provide alternatives to incarceration, we have not surveyed those programs or exhaustively reviewed the relevant evaluation literature.

2

Determinants of Sentences

ISSUES

A diverse body of research exists on the determinants of sentences. This subject has been pursued from widely varying perspectives exploring the roles of normative premises and conceptions of justice, social structure, organizations, conflict, and politics in influencing sentence outcomes. Underlying much of this research has been a fundamental concern with accounting for the diversity of sentence outcomes observed in courts. This has involved attempts to identify the variety of variables, and the interrelationships among those variables, that combine to influence observed sentence outcomes.

The increasing complexity of variables considered as factors influencing sentences has been accompanied by increasing methodological sophistication of the statistical analyses of sentencing. The earliest studies often involved no more than simple bivariate contingency tables examining the relationship of a single variable to sentences (e.g., the number sentenced to prison for each race). More recent studies use assorted multivariate techniques, usually applied to linear models, that permit simultaneous statistical controls for the variety of factors thought to affect sentences.

To date, the general state of knowledge about the factors influencing sentence outcomes remains largely fragmented, and there is no widely accepted theory on the determinants of sentences. Indeed, research on sentencing derives from a variety of different theoretical and disciplinary perspectives.

The Range of Variables Considered as Determinants of Sentences

Research on sentencing has considered both the role of *case attributes* at the time of sentencing and the role of various aspects of the sentence *decision-making process*. The principal variable measures that are used in sentencing research are listed below.

I. Case Attributes
  1. Offense Attributes
    a. Offense Seriousness: crime type(s) charged or convicted; number of charges; statutory maximum sentence; injury or threat of injury to victim; weapon use; value of property stolen or damaged; number of accomplices; role of offender as principal or accessory in offense; victim vulnerability; victim provocation; nature of offender/victim relationship; intent
    b. Quality of Evidence: number of witnesses; cooperation of witnesses; existence of tangible evidence; strength of defendant's alibi
  2. Offender Attributes
    a. Prior Criminal Record: number of arrests, convictions, or incarcerations; types of offenses; recency of prior events; liberty status at time of offense—release on bail, probation, or parole at time of offense
    b. Demographic Attributes: age; race; sex
    c. Socioeconomic Status: occupational prestige; income; education
    d. Social Stability: employment history; marital status; living arrangements; history of drug or alcohol abuse
  3. Case-Processing Variables
    Charge reductions or dismissals; pretrial release status—on bail or detained; attorney type—none, court-appointed, or privately retained; method of case disposition—guilty plea, bench or jury trial; time of guilty plea; presentence recommendations by probation officer, prosecutor, and defense counsel

II. Attributes of Decision-Making Process
  1. Structural Variables ("Where")
    Community attitudes toward crime and punishment; publicity surrounding this case or other similar cases; selection process of

judges—elected or appointed; timing of next election of court officials; stability of courtroom workgroups; processing time; historical time period
2. Individual Decision-Maker Variables ("Who")
Individual identifiers of key decision makers in each case; demographic attributes of key decision makers; general political/ ideological orientation of decision makers—conservative or liberal; decision maker's philosophy of sentencing—relative importance placed on retributive, rehabilitative, deterrent, or incapacitative goals; decision maker's "special hang-ups" (e.g., being especially harsh on drug offenses or weapons offenses)
3. Procedural Variables ("How")
Local legal practices in criminal cases; role of judge in plea bargaining; plea bargaining over charges and/or sentencing options; statutory (e.g., criminal code) or administrative regulations governing sentencing; richness of variables maintained for each case; accuracy of those variables (data sources and validity checks); accessibility of data (e.g., manual or machine-readable files)

Variables on case attributes include attributes characterizing the offender and the offense, particularly variables that function as indicators of criminal culpability and the potential rehabilitative/deterrent/incapacitative effect of imprisoning the offender. These variables include various factors in offense seriousness and characteristics of the offender, such as prior criminal record, employment, age, and sex. Also among the case attributes at the time of sentencing are the outcomes of earlier decisions in case processing, like charging and bail decisions, mode of case disposition, and attorney type.

The variables characterizing the sentence decision-making process relate to where the decision is made, who makes the decision, and how the decision is made. The "where" variables refer to the social context in which the decision is made (e.g., jurisdiction or region) and are meant to reflect differences in community attitudes toward crime and punishment and differences in system attributes (e.g., case load, backlogs, elected or appointed judges). The "who" variables refer to decision-maker attributes, particularly attributes of judges and perhaps of probation officers, prosecutors, and defense counsel if they have contributed to the sentence outcome. These variables might include indicators of primary cultural reference groups, political orientation, and philosophy of sentencing for individual decision makers. The "how" variables refer to procedural differences, such as whether or not there is a formal pretrial conference, whether that conference involves the judge, and whether the conference is limited to consideration of charges or also explicitly includes sentence options.

DISCRIMINATION AND DISPARITY

Exploration of the determinants of sentences is often framed in the context of important policy questions. Motivated by charges that sentencing is unfair, a major concern in sentencing research has been the extent of unwarranted variation in criminal sentences, particularly the validity of claims of widespread discrimination against black and poor defendants, and of large disparities in sentences. While widely used, the concepts of "discrimination" and "disparity" are rarely defined consistently. In this report they are distinguished in terms of the legitimacy of the criteria for determining sentences and the consistency with which those criteria are applied to similar cases.

Discrimination exists when some case attribute that is objectionable (typically on moral or legal grounds) can be shown to be associated with sentence outcomes after all other relevant variables are adequately controlled.[1] Such an association is taken as presumptive evidence of the existence and extent of deliberate discrimination. Race is the clearest example of an illegitimate criterion; it is a "suspect classification" from a legal perspective and is widely viewed as inappropriate on moral grounds. The range of potentially illegitimate variables is viewed broadly in this report and may include case-processing variables, like bail status or type of attorney, in addition to the personal attributes that are conventionally cited as bases of discrimination (see list above).

Disparity exists when "like cases" with respect to case attributes— regardless of their legitimacy—are sentenced differently. For example, this might occur when judges place different weights on the various case attributes or use different attributes in their sentencing decisions. Disparity refers to the influence in sentence outcomes of factors that characterize the decision-making process. The most commonly cited examples of disparity are differences among judges within the same jurisdiction or in different jurisdictions.

---

[1] As a policy matter, concern with discrimination has been primarily concerned with deliberate behavior that is discriminatory in intent. Research on discrimination, however, rests on outcomes and cannot distinguish purposive discriminatory behavior from behavior that is discriminatory in effect. As a result, research findings of discrimination refer to findings of discriminatory outcomes that may or may not result from discriminatory intent.

By these definitions discrimination and disparity are quite distinct behaviors (see Table 2–1). If all decision makers behaved similarly, and used race or bail status as a factor in sentences, for example, it would be possible (though unlikely) to have discrimination without disparity. If all decison makers held shared values about legitimate case attributes, but placed different weights on them, the result would be disparity without discrimination. If some decision makers gave weight to race in their sentencing decisions and some did not (or gave race less weight), sentences would exhibit both disparity and discrimination.

Evaluating the extent of discrimination or of unwarranted disparity requires important normative judgments about how much and what types of variation are unwarranted. Concern with discrimination focuses largely on the invidious role of certain personal attributes of the offender, particularly race and socioeconomic status, and the use of various case-processing variables. Concern for disparity, on the other hand, centers on the role of the organizational or structural context in which sentencing decisions are made and on the attributes of individual decision makers.

Discrimination

A finding of discrimination first requires evaluation of the legitimacy of the potential factors associated with sentencing outcomes. This assessment is likely to be highly subjective, involving disagreement over the goals of sentencing and a balancing of those goals with whatever constraints on sentencing may prevail in a particular society at a given time.

Consider, for example, the ambiguous status of variables like age and employment. The use of such variables in sentencing is often explicitly justified by statute, as in special sentencing provisions for juvenile and young adult offenders and in revisions to the Federal Criminal Code recently proposed in the U.S. Senate (S. 1722, 1980). Youthfulness can

TABLE 2–1 Characterizing Sentence Outcomes in Terms of Disparity and Discrimination

Legitimacy of Sentencing Criteria	Application of Sentencing Criteria	
	Consistent	Inconsistent
Legitimate	No disparity and no discrimination	Disparity
Illegitimate	Discrimination	Disparity and discrimination

be considered a mitigating factor based on the presumed diminished culpability of young offenders. Use of unemployment can be justified on grounds that it is an indicator of greater risk of further crime for offenders placed under supervision in the community. But arguments can also be offered that these variables are not legitimate sentencing criteria. It might be argued, for example, that the intensity of offending is high among the young and that they thus pose a serious threat of continued offending. On grounds of deterrence or incapacitation, then, youthfulness would not be a legitimate basis for being sentenced leniently (Boland and Wilson, 1978; Kennedy, 1978; Wolfgang, 1978). Likewise it might be argued that employment status is highly associated with race; to the extent that race is an illegitimate variable for sentencing, employment should be similarly suspect. For these reasons employment was recently removed as a factor in the Maryland statewide sentencing guidelines (Sentencing Guidelines Project, 1981). Similarly, because of considerations of legitimacy, education no longer appears in the federal parole guidelines (Hoffman et al., 1978).

The legitimacy of a variable for sentencing may also vary with the type of sentencing decision. Because of differences in the probabilities of recidivism, it could be argued that employment status is legitimate for determining whether to incarcerate or not, but that employment status should be immaterial to the length of a prison term. In this case, use of employment status would be nondiscriminatory (i.e., legitimate) in the prison/no prison decision, but discriminatory (i.e., illegitimate) in the decision on length of incarceration.

Discrimination can also exist when an otherwise legitimate variable is given an illegitimately large weight in the sentencing decision. For example, it might be widely accepted that pleading guilty warrants a discount in sentence; the amount of that discount, however, would likely be unacceptable if type of plea were used to determine whether or not the prosecutor seeks the death penalty. Here discrimination occurs when the impact of an otherwise legitimate variable exceeds (or falls short of) some acceptable margin.

Disparity

When considering the extent of unwarranted disparity, it is useful to distinguish four types of disparity. These different forms of disparity cannot be evaluated equivalently; they may or may not be justified, and some may even be desirable.

First, there may only be the appearance of disparity. This occurs when cases seem alike to an outside observer but differ materially in case attributes observed by the judge. For example, if the facts in two cases are identical but one defendant exhibits remorse and the other does not, they might receive different sentences. What appears to be disparity to a researcher working only from case records could be explained by the variables evident to the judge but not available in the records. Improved observations of independent variables like offender culpability, including such subtle considerations as remorse, may reduce the amount of this seeming disparity.

Second, there may be planned disparity or disparity that is deliberately introduced as a matter of social policy, such as use of exemplary sentences (Morris, 1982). Consider, for example, several tax evaders who have been tried and convicted and who are thus all vulnerable to incarceration. If it has previously been decided that it is sufficient to incarcerate only one of these offenders to achieve the desired general deterrent effect and thereby reduce the social costs associated with punishment, singling out the one offender among many for such punishment would represent planned disparity. Planned disparity might also arise if "like" offenders are entitled only to an *equal opportunity* of receiving a particular sentence, which might be imposed through means of a lottery, for example. Under both these schemes, justice is served when all like offenders are vulnerable to some range of acceptable sentences by virtue of conviction. They are, however, not all sentenced equally harshly. Instead, particular sanctions are allocated with reference to other social ends, such as crime prevention through deterrence or incapacitation and minimizing the social costs of punishment. A deliberate social policy of planned disparity would be warranted to the extent that the interests of justice can be responsibly limited to concern for an offender's vulnerability to a range of acceptable (i.e., not unjust) sentences. If, however, one's concept of justice requires equal treatment for like offenders, planned disparity in forms like exemplary sentences or equal opportunities to sanctions would be unwarranted.

The third type of disparity involves interjurisdictional disparity such as that found between urban and rural courts in the same state. Such jurisdictional differences may reflect differences in community standards of offense seriousness or punitiveness, or it might reflect local organizational conditions like court overcrowding. Whether these jurisdictional differences are warranted or not depends on the resolution of competing values, such as concern for evenhandedness or uniformity of standards versus the value of preserving local community control. In either case, however, jurisdictional differences arising from application of discriminatory (illegitimate) sentencing criteria would remain unwarranted.

The last type of disparity relates to individual judges.[2] This type of disparity can arise from fundamental philosophical differences regarding the goals of sentences, which may not be shared universally, or, even if they are, cannot be applied consistently. These differences may reflect differences in the experiences, training, and background of individual judges (or of court personnel making sentence recommendations to the judge) and would show themselves in use of different sentencing criteria or the application of different weights to the various criteria. The interjudge or intrajudge disparity that results may or may not be warranted.

On one side, it could be argued that some variation in sentences is to be expected and even tolerated in order to accommodate reasonable differences of opinion in the application of legitimate sentencing standards. As long as vulnerability to a particular judicial perspective does not vary systematically with defendant or case attributes (e.g., defendants charged with offenses involving gun use are no more likely to appear before judges favoring strong gun control than are any other defendants), the differences among judges in sentencing similar cases may be regarded as an acceptable or tolerable reflection of variation in the legitimate standards held within a community and so be warranted. (From this perspective, however, differences between jurisdictions or judges that arise from use of discriminatory (illegitimate) sentencing criteria by some judges or jurisdictions would remain unwarranted.)

Alternatively, it might be argued that the application of different legal standards to identical defendants is inconsistent with the rule of law. Normally, the U.S. legal system operates through appellate review and legislative change to eliminate conflicting legal rules, particularly when individual liberty is at issue, and does not tolerate the degree of inconsistency that may today characterize the sentencing behavior of different judges. If sentencing is to be similarly constrained by legal rules (as some proponents of reform urge), philosophical differences among judges would have to be significantly reduced or eliminated, perhaps through some compromise among judges or through the selection of a preferred sentencing rule by some democratically accountable body. Under this perspective, convergence of sentencing standards is preferable to con-

---

[2] While judges are the decision makers typically identified in discussions of disparity, disparity in sentence outcomes can also arise from differences among prosecutors or other criminal justice decision makers.

tinued toleration of disparity. Some proponents of change also argue that significant variations among judges based on different philosophies are also unwarranted, because many operational consequences of that variation—like "judge shopping" by both defense and prosecuting attorneys, and perceptions of arbitrariness in sentences—contribute to a sense of impropriety and injustice that undermines confidence in the legitimacy of the courts and the entire criminal justice system.

ALTERNATE METHODOLOGICAL APPROACHES TO ANALYSES OF SENTENCING

In this chapter we focus primarily on statistical studies of sentencing that have used quantitative data on case attributes and decision-process variables; in Volume II, Garber et al. and Klepper et al. discuss the possibility of developing more sophisticated formal models of the sentencing process as a basis for improved statistical analyses.

However, much work on criminal sentencing has used quite different research methods. Among the most common have been observation of the behavior of criminal court participants and interviews with them. Some of this work has used the paradigm of anthropological study of a new culture; some has used concepts from organization theory as the basis for data gathering and analysis; and some of this work has been primarily descriptive.

Another body of research uses experimental simulations in which subjects are asked to "sentence" experimental cases. A major concern in this experimental research is the process of attribution of factors, like offender culpability and victim provocation, by decision makers. While the processes involved in forming these judgments are not fully understood, several factors have been suggested as potentially relevant. These include the individual's ability to carry out the act, the effort expended, the degree of planning involved, the level of psychological functioning, and the type of motivation.[3] Experimental manipulation is particularly well suited for exploring the impact of these subtle and often unmeasured factors.

Our focus on one research approach is due to the large number of

---

[3] Research examining elements of attribution in the context of sentencing includes: Harvey and Engle (1978), Hogarth (1971), Hood (1972), Joseph et al. (1976), Kapardis and Farrington (1982), Monahan and Hood (1976), Sebba (1980), Thomas (1979), Walster (1966), and Wheeler et al. (1981). More general treatments of attribution theory are available in Heider (1958) and Weiner (1974).

studies and the technical questions that they raise; it should not be taken to imply that this approach is the only one of value. Indeed, we believe that statistical analysis of quantitative data about sentencing or attempts to model the process should include consideration of the particular court-house cultures in which the behavior is embedded. Such consideration requires gathering information from participants themselves. In addition, the careful controls possible in experimental research provide the opportunity for isolating the potentially subtle effects of variables, like defendant demeanor, that are difficult if not impossible to measure in aggregate statistical analyses.

Studies of criminal courts have repeatedly demonstrated that jurisdictions vary substantially in terms of norms of appropriate sentencing policy (e.g., levels of harshness) as well as in standard operating procedures (e.g., use of trial versus guilty plea and the implications of selection of one mode of disposition for ultimate sentence outcome). These norms are crucial to explanations of why different sentence outcomes occur but are typically unmeasured by generally available statistical data. In some jurisdictions, for example, bench trials are the equivalent of "slow pleas" and are appropriately coded as guilty pleas rather than trials; in others, they are quite real trials. Thus, a decision to treat bench trials as trials or as guilty pleas for purposes of statistical analysis cannot sensibly be made without knowledge of the operating norm within the particular jurisdiction. Furthermore, the potential differences in processing cases across jurisdictions, and sometimes even between courts within a jurisdiction, raise important questions about the appropriateness of cross-sectional analyses that assume a single homogeneous process in different settings.

Observation and Interviews

In our discussion of the use of variables measuring crime seriousness and prior record, we note that problems of measurement error present a difficult obstacle. Interviews with court personnel may be useful in identifying the key dimensions of case seriousness (degree of harm actually done? risk of injury? offender culpability? victim provocation?) and the important aspects of prior record (arrests? convictions? jail or prison terms? recency versus severity of prior arrests or sentences?), as well as in alerting a researcher to differences among jurisdictions that may be obscured in multijurisdictional comparisons that use only one set of measures.

Formal modeling of justice system operations can be considerably improved by field work attempting to assess accurately the actual goals and behavior of participants. Do prosecutors attempt to maximize conviction rates or sentence severity? Interviews are essential to develop sensible models. By the same token, models that use realistically different utility functions for different types of attorneys (e.g., public defenders versus marginal private practitioners versus well-established criminal lawyers) could be developed on the basis of interviewing participants.

Research based on observations or interviews faces real issues of the validity and reliability of often qualitative and subjective judgments made by investigators. Moreover, whether using quantitative or qualitative techniques, research from a single jurisdiction must confront issues of generalizability.

Experiments

Experimental manipulation of a small number of variables permits isolating the independent contribution of variables that covary or interact with other independent variables in natural settings (e.g., age and criminal record). It also provides an opportunity to explore the impact of the full range of variation in variables whose effect in natural settings is difficult to measure because of their limited variation in those settings (e.g., sex or conviction type—guilty plea or trial). Small effects of some variables that may be obscured by the much larger effects of other variables in aggregate statistical analyses can also be highlighted in experiments. This is particularly important in considerations of variables that, despite their small effect in aggregate data, are nevertheless important for conceptual or policy reasons (e.g., racial discrimination).

Experimental studies face challenges to the external validity of results arising from the artificial and often contrived character of the experimental situation. These studies, for example, often use inappropriate decision makers, drawing from jury pools or college students who are markedly different from and lack the experience of typical sentencers. Recognizing the problems of having inexperienced respondents assign sentences, the studies often ask respondents to assign levels of responsibility or blameworthiness, factors that no doubt affect sentences but are not the sole determinants. Furthermore, the use of often limited case information leaves considerable room for respondent interpretation and imputation of relevant but missing information, which jeopardizes the validity of experimental controls. Experimental research is also vulnerable to response biases when respondents, aware that they are the subjects of research, give the socially desirable or expected response.[4]

Statistical and Combined Approaches

Research on sentencing based strictly on available or uniformly coded quantitative data from several jurisdictions is likely to miss the influence of subtle and typically unmeasured factors as well as to obscure important differences that may exist across jurisdictions. Furthermore, most attempts to characterize the process quantitatively have been limited to simple linear models in which sentences are posed as functions of simple weighted sums of the independent explanatory variables. More complex characterizations of the process, which are likely to reflect the reality of sentencing decisions more closely and yet still be tractable to analysis, are possible. These models might include, for example, interactions among explanatory variables and hierarchical decision structures, in which some variables are determining factors of sentences when they are present, while in their absence a different set of variables prevails. Standard statistical techniques are available for estimating both simple linear models and more complex models.

An overall research strategy that combines interviews, observation, and the familiarity with courthouse cultures that such approaches afford; experiments with their potential for isolating otherwise subtle effects; and statistical analyses of aggregate quantitative data on case attributes and decision-process variables is likely to be most useful in developing knowledge about the determinants of sentences.

FINDINGS

Despite the growing diversity of factors considered and the increasing methodological sophistication of statistical analyses of sentencing, large portions—two-thirds or more—of variance in sentence outcomes remain unexplained. For the portion that is explained, we have reviewed the findings relating to the role of offense seriousness, prior record, race, socioeconomic status, gender, and various case-processing variables. The validity of statistical inferences about the determinants of sentences

---

[4] This type of response bias can be reduced by having the research focus on variables that are not highly charged (as race is) and for which there is no consensus on their use and weight. Use of experienced respondents (i.e., real judges) is also likely to reduce respondent susceptibility to social influence.

depends crucially on the methodological rigor with which the effects were estimated. Thus, the findings presented here are weighed in light of potentially serious methodological flaws in the research.

METHODOLOGICAL CONCERNS

One methodological concern affecting most research on the determinants of sentences is the treatment of the outcome variable—sentence imposed. The sentences available to judges typically include choices among a number of qualitatively different options, including suspended sentences, supervised probation, fines, and incarceration, as well as choices on the magnitude of any particular sentence type. Two different approaches have been used to reconcile the different qualitative and quantitative dimensions of sentences. Some researchers focus on the variations in the magnitude of only one sentence type—typically the length of prison terms for incarcerated offenders. Other studies collapse different sentence types into a single, arbitrary scale of sentence severity.

Analyses that attempt to estimate the effect of variables on the magnitude of a single sentence type are vulnerable to a number of different kinds of error. To begin with, it is not obvious that the addition of one month to incarceration or probation terms (or one dollar to fines or restitution sentences) should always be treated in the same way. For short sentences (or small fines) one additional unit may represent an important increase in sentence severity, while for longer sentences (or higher fines) each additional unit may be less important. Simple linear models in which the independent variables enter additively cannot capture such decreases in the marginal severity of the sentence units. Focusing on only one sentence type by assigning values of zero to all other sentence outcomes in ordinary least-squares regression will result in biased estimates of the effects (Hausman and Wise, 1977; Tobin, 1958). Trying to avoid these biases by restricting the analysis to only those cases of a single sentence type (e.g., only those cases considered for a prison sentence) could introduce selection bias effects. (The sources and nature of these selection biases are discussed in detail below in the context of findings on racial discrimination.) Statistical techniques are available to adequately address nonlinearities in sentence outcomes while still limiting the analysis to a single sentence type. Correcting for the potential biases arising from variables truncated at zero and selected samples, however, requires that the analysis be extended to include choices among sentence types.

The alternative approach of using a single scale to represent several different sentence types inevitably raises serious questions of commensurability across the different sentence types that affect the accuracy of both the order and proportionality of the single scale. Most attempts to order the different sentence types into a single scale arbitrarily impose a ranking intended to reflect differences in severity with no empirical substantiation. One commonly used scale is that devised by the Federal Administrative Office of Courts (as reported in Hindelang et al., 1975). Use of such an arbitrary scale raises serious problems in ordering the different sentence outcomes: for example, there may be disagreement on whether 3 or more years on probation is necessarily more onerous than 6 months of incarceration. Similarly, problems of proportionality arise from the use of arbitrary numerical scores like "two" for probation terms of 13 to 36 months, "seven" for prison terms of 13 to 24 months, and "fourteen" for prison terms of 49 to 60 months. Furthermore, it is not yet empirically established that, for example, prison terms of 54 months are twice as severe as prison terms of 18 months or that prison terms of 18 months are 3.5 times as severe as probation for 24 months.

Estimates of effects obtained from statistical analyses that use a single scale presumed to measure sentence severity as the outcome variable are also vulnerable to several kinds of statistical errors. First, the scale introduces errors in the sentence outcome variable, with an associated loss of precision in estimates of the effects of the determinants of sentences. The arbitrariness of the scale also makes it difficult to interpret the magnitude of the measured effects of explanatory variables on different sentence types: the impact of a change in a determinant can be interpreted only as an increment in the arbitrary scale units and not in terms of additional years in prison or dollars of fine. Furthermore, since determinants can be expected to affect individual sentence types differently, the effects associated with the single arbitrary scale may not be relevant to any of the individual sentence types. In single-scale analyses, for example, the same model (i.e., the same factors and the same weights on those factors) is assumed to influence both the choice of the sentence type and the choice of the amount of that sentence. Such a model cannot capture a situation in which unemployment, for example, might affect the decision to imprison an offender but would have no effect on the length of the prison term. Furthermore, the choices among different levels of each sentence type (e.g., how long a prison term or how large a fine) are assumed to be determined by the same factors with the same weights on those factors. This would not accurately reflect a situation in which income, for example, does affect the choice of fine amount but has no bearing on the length of prison terms.

These problems are pervasive in research on sentencing, affecting both the comparability of results across different studies and the strength of conclusions drawn from that research. A more desirable approach would be to partition the sentence outcome into two related outcomes involving (1) a choice among different sentence types and (2) a choice on the magnitude of the selected type. Statistical techniques are available for analyzing the choice of sentence (e.g., PROBIT, LOGIT) type; then, taking account of the bound at zero in the analysis of magnitude, these separate aspects of sentence outcome could and should be estimated simultaneously. This approach would not require the use of arbitrary scales across qualitatively different sentence types. It is also more flexible, allowing for differences in the determinants of different aspects of sentences. Findings from qualitative analyses could be very useful in suggesting which variables are more likely to be factors in the different aspects of sentence outcomes. Furthermore, if scales reflecting the relative severity of sentence outcomes are desired, techniques are available for estimating scale values from existing data rather than arbitrarily imposing them (see Klepper et al., Volume II).

THE PRIMARY DETERMINANTS OF SENTENCES

Using a variety of indicators, offense seriousness and offender's prior record have emerged as the key determinants of sentences. The strength of this conclusion persists despite the potentially severe problems of bias arising from measurement error that characterize most of the empirical research.

As indicated in the list above, many different factors may influence judgments of offense seriousness and prior record; few of these are usually included in individual studies of sentencing. As a result, the effects on sentence outcomes of the included indicators of offense seriousness and prior record are particularly vulnerable to biases arising from the excluded elements.

Offense Seriousness

Typically, offense seriousness measures are limited to use of the legally defined offense types or the statutory maximum penalties for each offense type. Some elements of the offense are often unavailable to researchers using court records. These unavailable elements include excessive harm to the victim, weapon use, the role of the victim—partially reflected in the nature of the offender/victim relationship and victim provocation—and the offender's role as a principal or accessory.

Even when the necessary data elements for the different indicators reflecting offense seriousness are available, researchers do not know how the separate elements combine to influence sentence outcomes. In the most commonly used approach, the various elements reflecting seriousness are assumed to enter the decision in a simple additive fashion in which all factors affect sentence outcomes linearly.[5] In these models the different elements in offense seriousness are considered simultaneously, and they always have the same incremental impact on sentence outcomes.

These models do not adequately capture a hierarchical assessment of the elements of seriousness where the weight given some factors depends on the presence or absence of other factors. Some elements, for example, may be extremely rare, but when present they may be determining factors in sentences. In a particularly heinous crime, the brutal treatment of victims may be the only element of seriousness considered in determining sentence outcome. In less vicious crimes, a wide variety of factors reflecting different aspects of offense seriousness may enter the sentencing decision.

Offender's Prior Record

The potential elements of "prior record"—including items like the number, recency, and seriousness of prior arrests, prior convictions, and prior incarcerations—are generally more visible to researchers than elements of offense seriousness. The record data, however, are often subject to errors and incompleteness, both in the data available to decision makers and to researchers. In terms of statistically analyzing the role of record variables in sentence outcomes, data elements that are available to decision makers, but not available to researchers, are especially troublesome. This is often the case for juvenile records, which may be available either formally or informally to decision makers, but are not available to researchers as part of the case record. Much research thus focuses on the role of officially available adult prior records in sentence outcomes.

There is currently considerable debate over the extent to which juvenile records are actually used in sentencing adults and over the propriety of using those records. A recent study of the use of juvenile records in adult courts (Greenwood et al., 1980) found that, contrary to the widespread perception that juvenile records are protected against access, these records (in varying quality) are accessible and used to varying degrees in most U.S.

---

[5] A special case of this approach combines the different elements of seriousness linearly to form a single seriousness score, and this score is then posed as a factor in determining sentence outcomes.

jurisdictions. The explicit role of juvenile records in sentence outcomes in adult courts, however, remains largely unexplored.

Also, as with offense seriousness, it is not at all clear how the various elements of a record should be combined to reflect the relative impact of prior record on sentence outcomes.[6] Among the issues of concern are commensurability across types of past offenses (e.g., how many misdemeanors are equivalent to one felony?); commensurability across disposition types (e.g., should more or less weight be given to prior incarcerations compared to nonincarcerative sentences?); the form of a decay factor to accommodate diminished importance of older records; and the role of juvenile records.

Methodological Issues

Inadequate measures of important elements of offense seriousness and prior record can bias estimates of the effects of these variables on sentence outcomes. In characterizing the nature of these biases, the discussion here is simplified by treating offense seriousness and prior record as though they were single variables, each resulting from some linear combination of a variety of different elements. Under this characterization, when important elements contributing to the unidimensional measures of seriousness or prior record are not measured, there is measurement error in the main variable of interest, which results in measurement error biases in the estimated effects of these variables on sentence outcomes.[7]

The bias in the estimated effects of offense seriousness depends on the nature of the measurement error. For a linear model of the determinants of sentences, measurement error that is independent of the true level of seriousness yields *underestimates* of the effect of seriousness on sentence outcomes (i.e., the estimated effect is in the same direction as the true effect but smaller in magnitude).[8] If, however, the error in

---

[6] For prior record, as for offense seriousness, a special case involves combining the various elements of prior record, usually linearly, to form a single record score that is posed as a determinant of sentence outcomes.

[7] In a more general formulation, the different elements of offense seriousness or prior record are treated as separate measures contributing to sentence outcomes. The biases resulting from failure to include measures of important elements are called specification errors. For a linear model of the determinants of sentences, the nature and direction of the biases arising from these specification errors are similar to those described in terms of measurement error biases in unidimensional variables.

[8] This is a standard result that can be found in any text on econometrics or linear statistical estimation (e.g., Johnston, 1972; or Rao, 1973).

seriousness due to unmeasured elements varies systematically with observed levels of seriousness, the effects of seriousness on sentence outcomes can be underestimated or overestimated: a *positive* association between observed offense seriousness and its measurement error results in *underestimates*; a *negative* association between observed seriousness and its measurement error results in *overestimates*.[9]

One source of a positive association between observed seriousness and its measurement error is a negative correlation between observed and unobserved dimensions of seriousness in which high values on observed dimensions of seriousness are associated with low values on unobserved dimensions. In this case the mismeasured value of seriousness fails to include elements that offset observed dimensions of seriousness, and observed seriousness increasingly overstates true seriousness.

Victim provocation and the existence of a prior relationship between offender and victim, for example, are both elements that might serve to decrease the overall seriousness of an offense. Failure to measure either of these elements would result in underestimates of the effect of offense seriousness on sentence outcomes when more serious observed offense types (based, perhaps, on statutory classifications) are also more likely to involve victim provocation or victims previously known to the offender. Such relationships between offender and victim are likely to be more common in more serious violent offense types, which involve direct contact or confrontation between offender and victim, and less likely in theft offenses, where direct contact is less common. Both victim provocation and the involvement of victims previously known to the offender would then be unobserved factors that decrease true seriousness below its observed value. In this event, observed seriousness would increasingly overstate true seriousness (i.e., observed seriousness is positively related to its measurement error) and would result in underestimates of the effect of true seriousness on sentence outcomes.

Alternatively, observed seriousness and its measurement error might

---

[9] For error in measurement that is positively related to the observed value of seriousness, increasingly larger values of observed seriousness involve increasingly larger errors added to the true value of seriousness. The resulting relationship between the observed values of seriousness and sentence outcomes has a flatter slope, thus diminishing or underestimating the true effect of seriousness on sentence.

With a negative relationship between the error in measurement and the observed value of seriousness, increased values of observed seriousness involve increasingly larger errors subtracted from true seriousness. This results in a steeper slope for observed seriousness, thus exaggerating or overestimating the true effect of seriousness on sentence.

be negatively related and yield overestimates of the effect of seriousness if the observed and unobserved elements of seriousness are positively correlated. In this case the positive contribution to true seriousness of unobserved elements is excluded, and true seriousness is increasingly understated. This would occur, for example, if more serious observed offense types were also more likely to involve unobserved elements of seriousness such as injury to a victim, weapon use, or economic loss.

Both positive and negative associations between offense seriousness and its measurement error are likely to exist. These systematic errors in measuring seriousness would contribute to both underestimates and overestimates of the true effect of seriousness on a sentence. Any independent errors would result in underestimates.

Studies of sentencing vary in the quality of the data used, the jurisdictions examined, and the dimensions of offense seriousness included in the analysis. These variations leave some studies more vulnerable to underestimates and others more vulnerable to overestimates of the effect of offense seriousness. Despite these biases, in both directions, offense seriousness is consistently found to have a strong effect on sentences. The consistency of this result under a variety of different biasing conditions increases confidence in the validity of the conclusion that offense seriousness is an important factor in sentence outcomes.

Prior record is often measured in terms of its length—typically the number of prior contacts with the criminal justice system—without regard for the content of that record. There is some evidence to suggest that longer prior records are more likely to involve less serious offenses. Using a Sellin-Wolfgang type of scale for offense seriousness (Heller and McEwen, 1973; Sellin and Wolfgang, 1964) on the arrest records of Washington, D.C., arrestees, Moitra (1981:46) found that the more prior arrests an arrestee had, the less serious those arrests were likely to be (Figure 2–1). This might occur because of differential sanctioning by seriousness. To the extent that more serious arrests are more likely to be sanctioned and that sanctions inhibit further arrests through some combination of incapacitation, deterrence, or rehabilitation, offenders engaging in more serious prior offense types would have fewer prior arrests. Such a negative association between observed and unobserved dimensions of prior record would contribute to underestimates of the effect of prior record on sentence severity. Despite the likelihood of biases toward underestimating the effect, prior record is consistently found to have one of the strongest effects on sentence (Bernstein et al., 1977; Chiricos and Waldo, 1975; Lizotte, 1978; Lotz and Hewitt, 1977; Pope, 1975a,b).

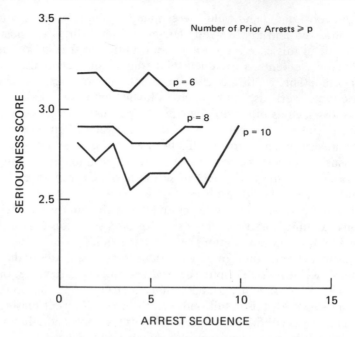

FIGURE 2–1   Average seriousness of prior arrests for arrestees with different prior-record lengths—Washington, D.C., 1973. SOURCE: Moitra (1981:Figure 2-4).

DISCRIMINATION BY RACE

There are two types of evidence often cited in support of the assertion that there is racial discrimination in sentencing. The first is the important social fact that blacks are in prisons in numbers disproportionate to their representation in the population. In 1979, blacks were 10.1 percent of the adult male population, but they comprised 48.0 percent of inmates of state prisons.[10] The second set of evidence appears in studies—there are now more than 70—that attempt to find a statistical association between the race of defendants and the sentences they receive in crimina

---

[10] The general population data for 1979 are from the U.S. Department of Commerce (1980). The data on racial distribution in state prisons are from the 1979 Survey of Inmates of State Correctional Facilities, as reported by the U.S. Department of Justice (1982b).

courts. Some of these studies find an association that has been interpreted as evidence of racial discrimination in sentencing.

Prison Populations

The overrepresentation of blacks in prison is clear evidence that *some* interaction of individual behavior patterns and societal response leads to the imposition of severe punishments on one group of people at rates out of proportion to their numbers in the population. However, it is *not* by itself evidence that this outcome is in substantial measure the result of racial discrimination at the sentencing stage in criminal courts. The disproportionate rate of imprisonment of blacks may be the product of a wide variety of behaviors and processes. One source of the disproportion may be differences in the types and amounts of illegal behavior among races. These behavioral differences may interact with patterns in the deployment of law enforcement resources and differing rates of apprehension, conviction, and imprisonment for various crime types to affect the racial composition of prisons. There might also be racial discrimination in the arrest process, the charging process, or the sentencing decision; or decisions by parole authorities may result in longer terms for black prisoners. Some or all of these processes may exist and could contribute to the disproportionate number of black prison inmates; only some might involve racial discrimination in sentencing.

The evidence about differential offense rates among races is scanty, and we cannot say with confidence whether the proportion of blacks arrested is the same as the proportion actually involved in illegal activities. It is possible to investigate, as has been done using victimization studies, the racial identities of offenders as reported by their victims. One set of studies (Hindclang, 1976, 1978; Hindelang et al., 1979) reports a fairly close correspondence between the proportion of robbers and assaulters who are reported by victims to be black and the proportion of persons arrested for robbery and aggravated assault who are black. However, on the basis of available evidence for crimes more generally, we can conclude little about the degree to which blacks are arrested in true proportion to their offense rates by crime.

Focusing only on the postarrest phases of the criminal justice system, one approach to assessing the extent of discrimination would be to examine the correspondence between racial proportions at arrest and in prison. Examination of arrest statistics as shown in Table 2–2, for example, finds a similar differential by race, with blacks accounting for 35 percent of adult arrests for index offenses nationwide in 1979. For the crime types most likely to be found in prison, namely murder and

TABLE 2–2   Distribution of Total U.S. Adult
Arrests (Over 18) by Race and Crime Type in 1979

Crime Type	Total Adult Arrests	Black Adult Arrests	Percent Black
Murder	16,534	7,942	48.0
Rape	24,427	11,339	46.4
Robbery	89,463	48,578	54.3
Aggravated assault	216,222	80,847	37.4
Burglary	238,621	74,610	31.3
Larceny	651,745	208,874	32.0
Auto theft	72,753	23,613	32.5
Violent[a]	346,646	148,706	42.9
Property[b]	972,450	309,327	31.8
Total index offenses	1,319,096	458,033	34.7

[a] Includes murder, rape, robbery, and aggravated assault.
[b] Includes burglary, larceny, and auto theft.

SOURCE: Federal Bureau of Investigation (1980: Table 35).

robbery, the differential is even larger, with blacks accounting for 53 percent of adult arrests.[11] An analysis by Blumstein (1982), exploring the consequences for prison populations of racially differential involvement in arrests, estimates that if there were *no* race-related differences in treatment by the criminal justice system after arrest, 42 percent of the prison population in 1979 would have been expected to be black, in comparison with the actual rate of 48 percent. These data are consistent with the assertion that blacks are overrepresented in prison populations primarily because of their overrepresentation in arrests for the more serious crime types, an argument counter to the assertion that overrepresentation results largely from discrimination at postarrest stages of the criminal justice system.

One problem in generalizing from such a result is the difficulty in accurately characterizing racial discrimination through global statements about the criminal justice system in the United States as a whole. If and when it occurs in criminal justice institutions, discrimination on the basis of race is likely to vary across jurisdictions, regions, crime types, and individual participants, and further research at more disaggregated levels is required to isolate those differences.

[11] Similar results are found for arrests throughout the 1970–1979 decade.

There are several possible ways that aggregate statistics can mask discrimination in the criminal justice system. Aggregate national data can conceal important differences among regions, states, or local jurisdictions. For example, rural jurisdictions (where white defendants predominate) may impose more and longer prison sentences than urban jurisdictions (where blacks predominate). The relative leniency of sentencing in urban areas could mask possible racial discrimination against blacks in both types of jurisdictions. Thus one next stage of research is a disaggregated analysis that compares sentencing patterns within local and regional units within states.

Using data that aggregate different crime types may conceal racial differences in sentencing for particular crime types. For the most serious crimes, such as murder and robbery, prison is the penalty in the great majority of cases, and prisons are predominantly filled with persons who have committed those crimes. In an aggregate analysis of prison population, racial neutrality in sentencing for these most serious offenses may obscure important racial differences in sentencing for the less serious offenses, for which prison is a possible but not an ordinary outcome. These less serious offenses leave more room for discretion in sentencing decisions and thus greater opportunity for discrimination. Future research should focus on these less serious offenses.

There can also be important differences in case processing at different points between arrest and prison, some of which may work to the advantage and some to the disadvantage of black defendants. Prosecutors, for example, may devalue the seriousness of crimes against black victims and be more likely to dismiss these cases. Since blacks are predominantly victimized by other blacks (U.S. Department of Justice, 1981a), such a practice would work to the advantage of black defendants (although it would constitute an important form of racial discrimination). Even if judges then discriminate against black defendants in sentencing, committing higher proportions of them to prison or imposing longer terms, the proportion of blacks in prison could equal the proportion at arrest. Alternatively, if prosecutors were more likely to pursue cases against black defendants, it would increase the proportion of blacks among defendants who are prosecuted and convicted. If judges then sentenced convicted blacks more leniently than convicted whites, that could also leave the proportion of convicted blacks in prison the same as at arrest.

It is also possible that the disproportionate numbers of blacks who are arrested might result from police arresting blacks on weaker evidence than they require for whites. If prosecutors dismiss the weaker cases (which would be found predominantly among black arrestees) but blacks are subject to discrimination at sentencing, the total effect of discrimination at arrest and at sentencing could still leave race-specific arrest and imprisonment rates in correspondence, thus masking both forms of discrimination. Future research on discrimination in sentencing should compare black-to-white ratios by type of crime at each of the intermediate stages of the criminal justice system between arrest and prison. Offender-based transaction statistics systems are particularly appropriate for such analysis.

It is possible that black offenders are sentenced both more severely and more leniently than white offenders and are more vulnerable to diverse racial attitudes among judges. In other words, there may be greater variation in the sentencing of minority group offenders than in that for white offenders. As a result, the black prison population could be in the same proportion as found in the arrest population by offense type, but those in prison still could have been treated disproportionately more severely than comparable white offenders, even though this effect was offset in the aggregate by the more lenient treatment given to other black defendants who received nonincarcerative sentences.

In enumerating these possibilities, we have suggested that race may be taken into account in ways that either advantage or disadvantage defendants who are black or members of other minority groups. We cannot yet say how much of the similarity in the proportion of blacks arrested and blacks imprisoned reflects racial neutrality and how much of it reflects the net result of offsetting effects. Aggregate data cannot reveal such differences. The variety of possibilities for offsetting relationships that might be obscured by aggregate data underscores the need for careful, disaggregated research on racial effects for individual crime types at different stages of the criminal justice system and within individual jurisdictions.

Our overall assessment of the available research suggests that factors other than racial discrimination in the sentencing process account for most of the disproportionate representation of black males in U.S. prisons, although discrimination in sentencing may play a more important role in some regions, jurisdictions, crime types, or the decisions of individual participants.

We also note, however, that even a small amount of racial discrimination is a matter that needs to be taken very seriously, both on general normative grounds and because small effects in the aggregate can imply unacceptable deprivations for large numbers of people. Thus even though the effect of race in sentencing may be small compared to that of other factors, such differences are important.

Whatever explains the disproportion of blacks in our prisons, the existence of this disproportion remains a significant matter of concern.

When over 3 percent of all black males in their twenties are in state prisons on any day in this country, with approximately another 1.5 percent in federal prisons and local jails (Blumstein, 1982), we face a social problem of serious proportions that cannot be ignored. The existence of the disproportion has already raised serious questions about the legitimacy of criminal justice institutions. Therefore, correctly identifying the sources of the disproportionality is crucial to the quest for effective solutions.

Studies of Sentencing

The second type of evidence on racial discrimination derives from studies of the process of sentencing itself. The role of race in sentencing has been extensively studied with uneven quality and varied results—see Table 2–3. Some studies find statistical evidence of racial discrimination; others find none. While there is no evidence of a widespread systematic pattern of discrimination in sentencing, some pockets of discrimination are found for particular judges, particular crime types, and in particular settings. The studies, however, are vulnerable in varying degrees to a variety of statistical problems that temper the strength of these conclusions.

Many early studies of sentencing—including those on capital punishment—found substantial racial discrimination, with blacks apparently being sentenced more harshly than whites (Table 2–2). These studies were seriously flawed by statistical biases in the estimates of discrimination arising from failure to control for prior record, offense seriousness, and other important variables that affect case disposition. Of the 36 studies using data on sentencing before 1969, only 12 studies have any controls for prior record and offense seriousness (see Table 2–3). The remaining 24 studies fail to control for one or both of these variables. The absence of controls is especially characteristic of studies on the use of capital punishment. All but 1 of the 15 pre-1969 capital punishment studies fail to control for prior record of the offender, a potentially important factor in choosing between life in prison and the death sentence and also in commuting death sentences. They also fail to go beyond crude controls for offense type to even distinguish between homicide cases that are eligible for capital punishment and those that are not.

To the extent that race is associated with offense seriousness or prior record, with blacks having more serious offenses or worse prior records, the race variable will pick up some of the effect of these omitted variables, resulting in overestimates of the discrimination effect. It is doubtful, however, that the large magnitude of the effect found in these early

TABLE 2–3 Distribution of Studies With Findings on Racial Discrimination by Control for Offense Seriousness and Prior Record and by Time Period Considered[a]

	Time Period					
	Pre-1969 Discrimination			1969 and Later Discrimination		
Controls for seriousness and record	No	Yes		No	Yes	
No	Ia 16.7% (n=4) [2 C.P.][b]	Ib 83.3% (n=20) [12 C.P.]	66.7% (n=24) [14 C.P.]	IIa 42.9% (n=3) [0 C.P.]	IIb 57.1% (n=4) [2 C.P.]	20.6% (n=7) [2 C.P.]
Yes	Ic 66.7% (n=8) [1 C.P.]	Id 33.3% (n=4) [0 C.P.]	33.3% (n=12) [1 C.P.]	IIc 48.1% (n=13) [0 C.P.]	IId 51.9% (n=14) [0 C.P.]	79.4% (n=27) [0 C.P.]
	33.3% (n=12) [3 C.P.]	66.7% (n=24) [12 C.P.]	(n=36) [15 C.P.]	47.1% (n=16) [0 C.P.]	52.9% (n=18) [2 C.P.]	(n=34) [2 C.P.]

Ia—Bedau (1965),[b] Bensing and Schroeder (1960),[b] Conklin (1972), Foley and Rasche (1979).

Ib—Bedau (1964),[b] Bowers (1974),[b] Bridge and Mosure (1961),[b] Bullock (1961), Cameron (1964), Florida Civil Liberties Union (1964),[b] Garfinkel (1949), Gerard and Terry (1970), Howard (1967), Jacob (1962), Johnson (1941),[b] Johnson (1951),[b] Johnson (1957),[b] Mangum (1940),[b] Martin (1934), Partington (1955),[b] Rau (1972), Wolf (1964),[b] Wolfgang et al. (1962),[b] Wolfgang and Reidel (1973)[b]

Ic—Baab and Furgeson (1968), Burke and Turk (1975), Farrell and Swigert (1978a,b), Green (1961, 1964), Judson et al. (1969),[b] Levin (1972), Mileski (1971)

Id—Lemert and Rosberg (1948), Nagel (1969), Southern Regional Council (1969), Tiffany et al. (1975)

IIa—Atkinson and Newman (1970), Greenwood et al. (1973), Perry (1977)

IIb—Bowers and Pierce (1980),[b] Cargan and Coates (1974), Uhlman (1979), Zimring et al. (1976)[b]

IIc—Bernstein et al. (1977), Chiricos and Waldo (1975), Clarke and Koch (1976), Eisenstein and Jacob (1977), Feeley (1979), Hagan et al. (1979), Hagan et al. (1980), Lotz and Hewitt (1977), McCarthy et al. (1979), Myers (1979), Pope (1975b), Shane-Dubow (1979), Sutton (1978)

IId—Clarke and Koch (1977), Gibson (1978b), Hagan and Bernstein (1979), Kelly (1976), Kulig (1975), LaFree (1980), Lizotte (1978), Pope (1975a), Rhodea (1976), Rhodes and Conly (1980), Spohn et al. (1982), Thomson and Zingraff (1981), Unnever et al. (1980), Zalman et al. (1979)

[a] The characterization of studies in this table comes primarily from Hagan and Bumiller (Volume II) and Kleck (1981), supplemented by some additional studies. The basis for a finding of discrimination is statistically significant racial differences in sentence outcomes reported in the original study.

[b] Studies of racial discrimination in the use of capital punishment.

studies would be completely eliminated by the introduction of appropriate controls, and some portion of the estimated race effect may indeed reflect discrimination in sentencing for some crimes in some areas extensively studied, particularly for capital punishment in the South in the 1940s, 1950s, and 1960s.

More recent studies using a richer set of controls have yielded varied results, with some finding evidence of racial discrimination while others do not. As indicated in Table 2–3, the introduction of controls for offense seriousness and prior record reduces the widespread finding of racial discrimination in sentencing, especially in studies using pre-1969 data. Nevertheless, discrimination continues to be found in specific contexts in more recent studies, particularly in rural courts, for selected crime types, when the victim is white, or for some judges in a jurisdiction. Even in these contexts, however, offense seriousness and prior record remain the dominant factors in sentence outcomes (Hagan and Bumiller, Volume II).

Despite substantial improvements in research in addressing the problem of omitted variables, recent studies are still subject to potential biases arising from measurement error and sample selection. These biases arise from the use of incomplete measures reflecting offense seriousness and prior record, which fail to adequately control for the role of unmeasured elements of seriousness or record in distinguishing the sentences of whites and blacks. In addition to biasing the estimates of the effects of seriousness and record on sentence, failure to adequately measure important elements of seriousness or record can also contaminate estimates of the effects of other correctly measured variables, like race. This occurs because only a portion of the true effect of seriousness, for example, is captured in the estimated effects of the included elements. Some part of the true effect is "picked up" by other correctly measured variables that are associated with the excluded elements of seriousness.[12]

Considering seriousness and record as single-score variables, each formed from a linear combination of contributing factors, the biases of interest arise from measurement errors in seriousness or record. When only one variable is measured with error, the direction of the bias in a

---

[12] The contamination or "smearing" effect is discussed in more detail in the context of measurement error in a variable in Garber et al. (Volume II) and Garber and Klepper (1980). For further treatments of the case of a single variable measured with error, see Aigner (1974), Blomqvist (1972), Chow (1957), Levi (1973), McCallum (1972), and Wickens (1972).

correctly measured variable depends on the bias in the incorrectly measured variable and the nature of the association between these variables. As illustrated in Table 2–4, when a variable like race is measured correctly and race is related to the mismeasured variable of seriousness, with blacks committing more serious offenses, there are opposite biases in seriousness and race. When the effect of seriousness is underestimated, the discrimination effect is overestimated, and vice versa. On the other hand, when whites commit more serious offenses the biases in race and seriousness are in the same direction. Similar arguments would apply to the incorrectly measured variable of prior record.

A number of studies have found associations of race with offense seriousness and prior record. For offense seriousness, blacks have been found to be substantially overrepresented in more serious offenses, particularly in violent crimes. This relationship was first noted in analyses of official data on arrests (Mulvihill et al., 1969; Wolfgang and Ferracuti, 1967; Wolfgang et al., 1972). The role of race in offense seriousness is illustrated in Table 2–5. The ratios of black to white arrest rates are highest for robbery (with black adult rates 9.80 times white adult rates) and for serious violent crimes (with black adult rates 6.12 times white adult rates) and much lower for less serious, nonindex offenses (with black adult rates only 2.38 times white adult rates). The same difference is also found in analyses of self-reported crime. While self-report measures of total criminal involvement find little difference by race, examination of self-reports disaggregated by crime type indicate progressively greater involvement of blacks as offense seriousness increases, especially in cases of violent offenses (Hindelang et al., 1979).

Direct evidence of a relationship of race with offense seriousness is also reported in studies examining sentence outcomes (Arkin, 1980; Gibson, 1978b; Spohn et al., 1982). Further indirect evidence of this relationship is found in Table 2–3: the role of race in influencing sentence severity is reduced when controls for seriousness and prior record are added to analyses, with 77 percent of the studies without controls and only 45 percent of those with controls finding discrimination in sentences. A similar reduction in effect within the same data set is reported in Burke and Turk (1975), Clarke and Koch (1976), and Spohn et al. (1982).

Evidence for a relationship between prior record and race has been reported in several studies. In accounting for the large differences in sentences of whites and blacks convicted in Philadephia, Green (1961, 1964) found that, controlling for current conviction charge, there were pronounced racial differences in prior criminal records of convicted offenders. The differences in sentences by race were consistent with

TABLE 2–4 Direction of Biases When Incorrectly and Correctly Measured Variables Are Correlated: The Case of Offense Seriousness (Incorrectly Measured) and Race (Correctly Measured)

Assumed True Effects
(1) *Seriousness*—more serious offenses result in more severe sentences

(2) *Race/discrimination*—blacks are sentenced more severly

Type of Measurement Errors in Seriousness	Direction of Bias in Seriousness Effect	Direction of Bias in Discrimination Effect	
		If Blacks Have More Serious Offenses:	If Whites Have More Serious Offenses:
1. ERROR INDEPENDENT OF SERIOUSNESS	UNDERESTIMATE	OVERESTIMATE (Because of correlation of race with seriousness, some of effect of seriousness on sentence will be picked up by blacks, exaggerating the estimated discrimination effect against blacks.)	UNDERESTIMATE (Because of correlation of race with seriousness, some of effect of seriousness on sentences will be picked up by whites, diminishing the estimated discrimination effect against blacks.)

2. SYSTEMATIC ERROR
Error Correlated With
Seriousness

a. Negative Correlation	OVERESTIMATE (Negative correlation of measurement error and seriousness whereby observed seriousness increasingly understates true seriousness.)	UNDERESTIMATE (Because of correlation of race with seriousness, some of effect of blacks on sentence was picked up by bias in seriousness. The decrease in contribution of blacks to sentence diminishes the estimated discrimination effect against blacks.)	OVERESTIMATE (Because of correlation of race with seriousness, seriousness picks up some of contribution of whites to sentences. The decrease in contribution of whites to sentence exaggerates the estimated discrimination effect against blacks.)
b. Positive Correlation	UNDERESTIMATE (Positive correlation of measurement error and seriousness whereby observed seriousness increasingly overstates true seriousness.)	OVERESTIMATE (Because of the correlation of race with seriousness, some of effect of seriousness on sentence will be picked up by blacks, exaggerating the estimated discrimination effect against blacks.)	UNDERESTIMATE (Because of the correlation of race with seriousness, some of effect of seriousness on sentence will be picked up by whites, diminishing the estimated discrimination effect against blacks.)

TABLE 2–5   Comparison of Black Arrest Rates With White Arrest Rates (Arrests per Population) by Age and Crime Type in 1970 for U.S. Cities

Crime Type	(Black Arrest Rate/ White Arrest Rate)	
	Juveniles	Adults
Serious violent	4.84	6.12
Murder	5.87	8.32
Rape	5.07	6.23
Aggravated assault	4.75	5.87
Robbery[a]	9.07	9.80
Serious property	2.46	3.65
Burglary	2.56	4.10
Larceny	2.47	3.37
Auto theft	2.27	4.43
Nonindex	1.61	2.38
Forgery, fraud, embezzlement, stolen property, arson	2.35	3.14
Simple assault, weapons, vandalism	2.46	3.84
Narcotics	.57	2.06
Prostitution, other sex offenses, gambling, liquor law violations	1.05	4.43
Other (excluding traffic and juvenile offenses)	1.62	2.11

NOTE: Arrest rates are derived from data on arrests by age, race, and crime type reported to the Federal Bureau of Investigation's uniform crime reporting program for 55 U.S. cities with populations of 250,000 or more in 1970 and from the 1970 census of populations by age and race in those cities. The arrest data for individual cities were provided by the Federal Bureau of Investigation. The ratios of black to white rates are based on the mean arrest rates for the 55 cities.

[a] Robbery is usually treated as one of the serious violent crimes, but because it is different from other violent crimes, it is treated separately in this table.

differences in prior record, with blacks generally having more serious prior records than whites. A similar difference in prior record was found in Gibson (1978b) and Spohn et al. (1982). In Burke and Turk (1975) the relationship between race and prior record involves an interaction with age. Nonwhites under age 35 were more likely to have prior incarcerations than whites in the same age group; the relationship was reversed for offenders 35 years old or over. Further indirect evidence of the relationship of prior record and race is again provided in Table

2–3: the role of race is reduced when controls for offense seriousness and prior record are included.

The observed association of race with offense seriousness might arise from differential involvement in different offense types for different races or from differential treatment through the exercise of victim or police discretion in differentially reporting offenses or in the process of investigating, arresting, and charging defendants. While not conclusive, Hindelang and associates (Hindelang, 1976, 1978; Hindelang et al., 1979) present a variety of evidence from official arrest data, self-reports of crime, and victimization surveys supporting the differential involvement hypotheses. Similarly, in the case of prior record, the association may reflect real behavioral differences in the intensity of offending or may result from differential treatment, particularly for a first offense, which then increases the likelihood of accumulating a prior record. There is some evidence to support this latter hypothesis of differential treatment resulting in differential accumulation of prior record by race (Chiricos et al., 1972; Tiffany et al., 1975). However, this may result from more serious first offenses for blacks than for whites.

Some have argued that racial discrimination in sentencing reflects a response to the combination of the offender's and victim's race. Under a presumption of racial discrimination, one might expect that offenses by blacks against white victims would be sentenced more harshly than similar offenses of whites against whites, whites against blacks, or blacks against blacks. This might occur because black victims are regarded as less important than white victims or because offenses across racial lines by blacks are viewed very seriously. When such factors have been explicitly considered in analyses, the empirical results strongly support the expected differences in sentences for various race combinations of offenders and victims.[13] Ten of 14 studies—including 7 on the use of capital punishment—find that black offenders against white victims are sentenced more harshly than other race combinations (Bowers and Pierce, 1980; Florida Civil Liberties Union, 1964; Garfinkel, 1949; Howard, 1967; Johnson, 1941; LaFree, 1980; Partington, 1965; Southern Regional Council, 1969; Wolfgang and Reidel, 1973; Zimring et al., 1976).

As noted in Kleck (1981), these studies are also subject to biases resulting from unmeasured aspects of offense seriousness. Aside from the obvious race differences, Kleck (1981) notes that interracial offenses are also more likely to involve strangers, more likely to involve other

---

[13] Because of insufficient cases, there are no studies that separately examine sentence outcomes for white offenders against black victims.

TABLE 2–6   Disposition of Felony Arrests

	Jurisdiction		
Disposition	Washington, D.C. 1973[a]	California 1979[b]	New York City 1979[c]
Felony arrests that result in felony conviction	13 percent	18 percent	12 percent
Felony arrests that result in any conviction	29 percent	20 percent[d]	Not available
Convictions sentenced to prison	32 percent	25 percent[d]	31 percent

[a] Forst et al. (1977).
[b] California Department of Justice (1980).
[c] Chambers (1981).
[d] Superior court convictions only.

felonies, and less likely to involve victim provocation. These characteristics of interracial offenses are all factors contributing to increased seriousness of the offense and presumably also to more severe sentences. Failure to measure and include these important dimensions of seriousness would lead to biased estimates of the race effect. The 10 studies finding an effect for offender and victim race either fail to include or only partially control for these dimensions of offense seriousness. Four other studies that do control for factors associated with interracial offenses do not find any effect on sentence for offender and victim race (Farrell and Swigert, 1978b; Green, 1964; Judson et al., 1969; Myers, 1979). The suppression of the estimated discrimination effect when controls for these other elements of offense seriousness are included suggests that the biases in the offender/victim race effect are likely to be dominated by overestimates.[14]

The estimated race effect may also be biased by *sample selection*. The processing of criminal cases through the various stages in the criminal justice system is like a sequence of filters, screening cases from the system according to various criteria related to case attributes. As indicated in Table 2–6, only 13 of every 100 felony arrests in Washington, D.C., in 1973 resulted in felony convictions, while another 16 resulted

[14] Unfortunately, the general lack of data for interracial offenses involving whites against black victims does not permit evaluating whether the particular race of the victim in interracial crimes is important, *independent* of other considerations like greater involvement of strangers, of other felonies, and of victim provocation in interracial crimes.

in misdemeanor convictions. Of those convicted, 32 percent were sentenced to prison. These experiences in Washington, D.C., are typical of other U.S. jurisdictions. As a result, the cases ultimately available for sentencing are a selected sample, including only a fraction of the population of "similar" offenses originally committed.

Sample selection of this sort poses problems to the generalizability of results. Offenders who are ultimately convicted or incarcerated are likely to differ in important ways from the original population of offenders. This threat to the generalizability of the results is generally well understood, and findings from studies using selected samples are usually properly restricted to an appropriately limited population.

It is less well understood, however, that sample selection can also pose serious threats to the validity of statistical results even within the selected sample. In the case of sentencing, internal selection biases can arise when unobserved and thus unmeasured factors are common to both the selection and sentence processes, thereby inducing (or altering) correlations in the selected samples between the unmeasured variables and other included variables that are also common to selection and sentencing.[15]

Examples of the process giving rise to selection biases are presented in Table 2–7. In that table, we consider separately cases in which prosecutor aggressiveness and elements of offense seriousness are unmeasured factors in both selection and sentencing. For prosecutor aggressiveness, there would be no bias in the estimated effects if there were no sample selection; the sample selection process, however, induces bias in the selected sample. For the unmeasured element of offense seriousness, on the other hand, there is already bias in the estimated effects resulting from measurement error alone; this bias, however, is reversed by sample selection.

As illustrated in the first column of Table 2–7, selection biases can arise even when there is no correlation between the unmeasured and measured variables in the original population. In this example, prosecutor aggressiveness is assumed to be an unmeasured factor both in selection and in more severe sentence outcomes. Since cases are randomly assigned to prosecutors, there is no correlation between unmeasured prosecutor aggressiveness and other measured case attributes. In

---

[15] See Klepper et al. (Volume II) for a detailed discussion of the role of sample selection biases in research on discrimination in sentencing. For more general treatments of sample selection biases, see Berk and Ray (1982), Goldberger (1981), Heckman (1976, 1979), Olsen (1980), and Tobin (1958).

TABLE 2-7 Nature of Sample Selection Biases in Estimates of the Determinants of Sentences

Assumed Underlying True Effects of Determinants on Sentence Outcomes:

Blacks
More Serious Cases } More Severe Sentence Outcomes
More Aggressive Prosecutors

How Sample Selection Operates to Result in Biased Estimates	Biases in Estimated Effect of Discrimination on Sentences		Biases in Estimated Effect of Case Seriousness on Sentences	
	Prosecutor Aggressiveness	Some Elements of Case Seriousness	Prosecutor Aggressiveness	Some Elements of Case Seriousness
Unmeasured determinants of selection and sentencing				
Prior relationship between unmeasured factor and included variable in original population	Defendant race is independent of prosecutor aggressiveness (e.g., cases are randomly assigned to prosecutors (no prior specification errors)	Blacks are likely to have more serious cases (prior specification error)	Case seriousness is independent of prosecutor aggressiveness, e.g., cases are randomly assigned to prosecutors (no prior specification errors)	More serious cases on included elements of case seriousness are likely to also be more serious on unmeasured factors (prior specifications error)

Selection process	Blacks are more likely to be selected (i.e., there is prior racial discrimination in cases processing) Cases with aggressive prosecutors are more likely to be selected	Blacks are more likely to be selected (i.e., there is prior racial discrimination in case processing) Serious cases are more likely to be selected	Serious cases are more likely to be selected Cases with aggressive prosecutors are more likely to be selected	Serious cases on measured factors more likely to be selected Serious cases on unmeasured factors are more likely to be selected
Relationship between unmeasured factor and included variable *after* selection	*Whites* that are selected are more likely to have an aggressive prosecutor	*Whites* that are selected are likely to have more serious cases	*Less serious* cases that are selected are more likely to have an aggressive prosecutor	*Less serious* cases on measured factors are likely to be more serious on unmeasured factors
Nature of bias in selected sample	*Under*estimate discrimination at sentencing (some of the effect of prosecutor aggressiveness on sentence outcome is picked up by whites in the selected sample, who are more likely to have aggressive prosecutors)	*Under*estimate discrimination at sentencing (some of the effect of seriousness on sentence outcome is picked up by whites in the selected sample, who have more serious cases)	*Under*estimate effect of seriousness on sentences (some of the effect of prosecutor aggressiveness is picked up by less serious cases in the selected sample)	*Under*estimate effect of seriousness on sentences (some of the effect of unmeasured elements of seriousness is picked up by cases in the selected sample that are less serious on observed factors)

this event, if there were *no* selection, failure to include prosecutor aggressiveness would not bias the estimates of the included determinants of sentence outcomes. The selection process, however, operates so that those cases with more aggressive prosecutors are more likely to have charges brought, less likely to be dismissed, and more likely to result in convictions and be available for sentencing. In the presence of racial discrimination, with blacks also more likely to be selected, those whites who are selected are more likely to have aggressive prosecutors than are the selected blacks. Selection thus induces a correlation between race and prosecutor aggressiveness in the selected sample. When prosecutor aggressiveness is left unmeasured, some of its effect on more severe sentence outcomes will be picked up by the selected whites, thus diminishing, or underestimating, the effect of any discrimination against blacks in sentencing.

Considering the second column in Table 2–7, there is already the potential for biased estimates of the discrimination effect arising from the correlation between the correctly measured race variable and the incorrectly measured offense seriousness variable in the original population. In this case, however, the biases arising from measurement error are confounded by sample selection. Selection occurs if more serious offenses are more likely to be prosecuted, less likely to be dismissed, and more likely to be sentenced severely. However, when offense seriousness is not measured completely, the differences in seriousness cannot be fully controlled. Despite the likely role of factors like weapon use and offender-victim relationship in assessments of seriousness by criminal justice decision makers, these factors may not be measured and included in research on sentencing.

Selection biases associated with this measurement error will arise if, in addition to considering seriousness as a basis for selection and sentencing, there is also racial discrimination throughout criminal justice processing—for example, with blacks more likely than whites to be charged, less likely to have their cases dismissed, and more likely to be sentenced severely regardless of offense seriousness. The whites who are selected, then, are likely to have committed more serious offenses than selected blacks. (Note that the selection process has reversed the original correlation found between race and seriousness.) However, because of errors in measuring seriousness, only differences in observed seriousness can be measured and included. Selected whites who are identical to selected blacks on observed seriousness are still likely to have committed more serious offenses on *unobserved* dimensions of seriousness. This correlation between correctly measured race and incorrectly measured seriousness in the selected sample results in biases in the estimated effects of both race and seriousness on sentence outcomes.

As indicated in Tables 2–4 and 2–7, independent measurement error in offense seriousness results in underestimates of the effect of seriousness on sentence. When selection operates to select more serious offenses *and* when there is prior racial discrimination, with blacks being more likely to be selected, as in the example above, whites who are selected would be likely to have committed more serious offenses. In this case, some of the unmeasured effect of seriousness on sentence would be picked up by selected whites with their more serious offenses, thus diminishing, or *underestimating*, the effect of any discrimination effect against blacks in sentencing.

Selection bias arising from measurement error in offense seriousness may also operate to exaggerate, or overstate, the actual level of discrimination against black offenders in sentencing. Consider, for example, the situation when more serious offenses are selected, but whites are now more likely to be selected. This might arise if there were discrimination against black *victims* in prosecution decisions in which victimization of blacks is treated less seriously by criminal justice decision makers, resulting in higher proportions of dismissals or charge reductions. Since blacks are overwhelmingly victimized by blacks,[16] black offenders would be less likely to be selected for further processing. Due to the greater likelihood in this situation that whites are selected regardless of seriousness, the offenses of blacks who are selected are likely to be more serious on both observed and unobserved dimensions. Once again independent measurement error in offense seriousness would lead to underestimates of the effect of seriousness on sentences. In the absence of adequate controls for unobserved differences in seriousness, some of the contribution of more serious offenses by selected blacks to sentences would mistakenly be attributed to race, thus exaggerating, or *overestimating*, the effect of discrimination against blacks in sentencing.

The exact nature of the errors in estimates of the effect of racial discrimination at sentencing, arising from any selection bias associated with measurement error in offense seriousness, depends critically on both the direction and magnitude of the contribution of seriousness and discrimination in prior selection processes. Thus, resolving the ambiguity

---

[16] The 1979 National Victimization Survey (U.S. Department of Justice, 1981a) reports that, for personal crimes of violence, 84 percent of victimizations of blacks by single offenders involved black offenders (Table 43); for black victimizations by multiple offenders, 72 percent involved all black offenders (Table 47).

about the determinants of sentences requires empirical research to identify more clearly the determinants of earlier selection in processing cases through the criminal justice system.

There is some evidence suggesting the existence of racial differences in treatment at earlier processing stages. For example, some evidence suggests that differences in sentencing outcomes may arise through racial differences associated with attorney type and employment status of the defendant, which in turn affect ability to post bail (Clarke and Koch, 1976; Farrell and Swigert, 1978a; Lizotte, 1978; Spohn et al., 1982). Each of these factors then affects the likelihood of conviction and the vulnerability to sentence. Race may also enter through its role in sentence recommendations by probation officers and prosecutors (Hagan, 1975, 1977; Hagan et al., 1979; Myers, 1979; Unnever et al., 1980). While these results are suggestive, considerably more research is required on the determinants of prior decisions affecting arrest, charges filed, dismissal, bail release, plea-bargain offers, sentence recommendations, and the like. In providing estimates of racial discrimination prior to sentencing, such results will also help to clarify the role of sample selection biases in estimates of discrimination at sentencing.

Measurement Errors and Their Consequences

Some measurement error is present in all statistical analyses of sentencing. The crucial question is how much of the estimated effect of correctly measured variables is real and how much is statistical bias. For independent errors in mismeasured variables, the bias in the estimate of an associated correctly measured variable, like race, will be larger relative to its true effect (Garber et al., Volume II; Garber and Klepper, 1980):

1. the greater the fraction of the variation in sentence outcomes attributable to incorrectly measured variables like offense seriousness and prior record;

2. the smaller the fraction of the variation in sentence outcomes attributable to the correctly measured variable, like race;

3. the greater the correlation between the correctly measured variables and the incorrectly measured variables;[17] or

---

[17] In the case of induced correlations in selected samples, the greater the fraction of variation in selection that is attributable to the correctly measured variable, race, the larger the correlation in the selected sample.

4. the greater the fraction of the independent variation in the incorrectly measured variables (after controlling for other explanatory variables) attributable to the measurement errors.

The evidence suggests a primary role for the incorrectly measured variables of offense seriousness and prior record in influencing sentence outcomes and a nontrivial relationship between these mismeasured variables and race. Conditions 1 and 2 above suggest that the bias in the effect of a presumably correctly measured offender attribute like race will be larger when race actually plays a small role in determining sentences relative to the role of the incorrectly measured variables of offense seriousness and prior record. Under condition 3, the correlation between race and the incorrectly measured variables also contributes to a larger bias. Furthermore, to the extent that these incorrectly measured variables are in fact primary determinants of sentences, conditions 1 and 4 suggest that the bias in the correctly measured variables is large when the primary determinants of sentence are measured with considerable error. Thus, the possibility of nontrivial correlations of race with other poorly measured but key variables like offense seriousness and prior record raises the threat of serious biases in the estimates of discrimination effects.

Further complications are introduced by the possibility that the correlations vary with the selection process and by crime type or jurisdiction. In this event, the statistical biases attributable to measurement error may be critical in some cases and trivial in others. The biases may even work in opposite directions in different studies. This suggests that measurement error bias, operating either directly or through sample selection, could substantially obscure the true incidence of discrimination in sentencing.

The biases in the estimates of the effects of racial discrimination in sentencing discussed above result principally from inadequate measures of key aspects of offense seriousness and prior record. One obvious remedy to this problem is to obtain improved measures of these variables in order to more fully and adequately reflect the richness of factors taken into consideration in sentencing decisions. To address the problem of selection biases more generally, analyses must be extended beyond sentencing to include examination of the selection processes as well.[18]

---

[18] Berk and Ray (1982) summarize a variety of available estimation procedures that correct for selection biases when there is no correlation between unmeasured and measured factors in the original population.

This broader approach to analyzing the determinants of sentences also has the potential of indirectly resolving the measurement error problems in key concepts like offense seriousness and prior record without requiring explicit measures of currently unavailable and difficult-to-measure variables.[19]

DISCRIMINATION BY SOCIOECONOMIC STATUS

In addition to being disproportionately black, state prison inmates are disproportionately poor and unemployed and otherwise rank low on measures of socioeconomic status. In 1979, 41 percent of state prison inmates who had been admitted to prison after November 1977[20] had either no income (22.2 percent) or incomes of less than $3,000 (19.2 percent) in the 12 months prior to arrest. Of those with incomes, the median income was $6,660—much lower than the 1979 national median income for males of $10,972.[21] The unemployment rate prior to incarceration for state prison inmates was 16.5 percent, compared to an average male unemployment rate adjusted for race and year of 7.8 percent for the decade of the 1970s.[22] In a study of prison inmates in three southern states, Chiricos and Waldo (1975) report that inmates are overwhelmingly characterized by low scores on a status measure that combines income, occupation, and education factors.

The evidence of discrimination on grounds of social or economic status is, however, equivocal. Like research on racial discrimination, this much smaller body of research is characterized by inconsistent results. Some studies find discrimination by status (Clarke and Koch, 1976; Farrell, 1971; Farrell and Swigert, 1978b; Judson et al., 1969; Lizotte, 1978;

---

[19] With a system of equations that includes common latent (i.e., unobserved) variables in several equations, the effects of the unobserved latent variables can be estimated from common movements observed in multiple outcome variables; see Garber et al. (Volume II) for a fuller discussion of this result.

[20] The inclusion only of inmates admitted after November 1977 is to avoid the inflation factor in reported incomes over time.

[21] The data on income are from the 1979 Survey of Inmates of State Correctional Facilities, as reported by the U.S. Department of Justice (1982b).

[22] Based on the data on prearrest employment available from the U.S. Department of Justice (1982b), 84.1 percent of inmates were in the labor force, resulting in an unemployment rate of 16.5 percent (13.9/84.1).

The comparable noninmate unemployment rate for males is calculated by first weighting the annual unemployment rates available from the U.S. Department of Labor (1980:62) by the racial distribution found in prison; the resulting annual rates during the 1970s are then weighted by the distribution of inmates by time served in 1979.

Thornberry, 1973), and others do not (Burke and Turk, 1975; Chiricos and Waldo, 1975; Nagel, 1969; Terry, 1967; Willick et al., 1975). Other studies report a mediating role, with status variables affecting sentence outcome indirectly through their effect on initial charge (Hagan, 1975) or on the conviction charge (Swigert and Farrell, 1977).

The research on the effects of socioeconomic status is subject to the same methodological difficulties that apply to race. In some cases important control variables are omitted entirely (Bedau, 1964, 1965); in others, incomplete measurement of important dimensions of offense seriousness and prior record contributes to possible biases in the effect of status arising from the correlation of status variables with the incorrectly measured variables.

A number of studies using official arrest data have noted an association between socioeconomic status and offense seriousness, with members of lower status groups substantially overrepresented in arrests for more serious offenses (e.g., Braithwaite, 1981; Gordon, 1976; Reiss and Rhodes, 1961; Shaw and McKay, 1942). When adequate controls for offense seriousness are taken into account, similar differences in offending are also found in studies using self-report data (Braithwaite, 1981; Elliott and Ageton, 1980; Hindelang et al., 1979). Evidence of such a relationship is also reported in studies examining sentencing outcomes (e.g., Hagan, 1975). A similar relationship is found between status and prior record, with offenders of lower status more likely to have prior convictions (Willick et al., 1975) or prior incarcerations (Burke and Turk, 1975). When such correlations are combined with errors in measuring offense seriousness or prior record, or with a failure to include these variables in the analysis, the estimates of the effect of status on sentence outcomes are vulnerable to the same serious biases that plague results on racial discrimination.

Additional problems arise from the uncertainty over how best to measure social or economic status. Socioeconomic status is a complex variable reflecting an individual's location in a social structure. Different positions are presumed to be associated with characteristic sets of beliefs, attitudes, and expected ways of behaving that not only influence the behavior of individuals in those positions, but also the expectations that others have about people of different status. Status thus links a set of attitudes or beliefs with behavior; the question is how best to characterize that link. For example, there is considerable uncertainty over the relative importance of different aspects of status, such as education, income, and occupation. It is also unclear whether status-linked behavior is principally influenced by experiences in formative years and thus by one's parents' status, or by one's own status, or by one's anticipated or desired status. This ambiguity is reflected in research on sentencing in which socioeconomic status is variously measured in terms of father's occupation (Terry, 1967), own occupation (Hagan, 1975; Judson et al., 1969; Lizotte, 1978), occupational prestige (Burke and Turk, 1975; Farrell and Swigert, 1978b; Swigert and Farrell, 1977); income (Clarke and Koch, 1976; Nagel, 1969; Thornberry, 1973); and a scale combining income, education, and occupation (Chiricos and Waldo, 1975; Willick et al., 1975). The resulting likely measurement error in the status variable contributes to biases in the estimates of the effect of a defendant's status on sentence. Moreover, research on this subject is hampered by the relative lack of variation in socioeconomic status among defendants charged with similar offenses. Research in this area is thus best pursued by focusing on those crime types with the most variation or through experimental studies of sentencing.

Even if the available estimates of the effect of status on sentence were unbiased, a finding of discrimination by status would depend on the legitimacy of specific measures of status as determinants of sentences, and at this time there is considerable debate about the legitimacy of some socioeconomic components in sentence decisions. For example, indicators like employment or education may be valuable as predictors of criminal recidivism and thus may be considered legitimate factors in determining sentences. For this reason, employment history and educational attainment were for several years explicitly included in the U.S. Parole Commission's guidelines. Alternatively, the strong association of status variables with variables like race or wealth, which are more unequivocally illegitimate, raises questions about the legitimacy of using any variables that embody race or wealth effects as factors in sentencing. For these reasons, the Minnesota sentencing guidelines explicitly exclude status variables from judicial consideration at sentencing. Reflecting similar concerns about legitimacy, educational attainment has also been removed from the federal parole guidelines. Thus, even if empirical questions regarding the influence of status on sentence were resolved, conclusions about the discriminatory nature of these variables would depend on resolution of the normative questions involved.

DISCRIMINATION BY SEX

While the disproportionality of blacks in prison is large compared to their representation in the general population, the disproportionality of men is enormous, with women accounting for 52 percent of the adult (over age 18) population but only 4 percent of state prison populations in 1979 (U.S. Department of Justice, 1982b). As with blacks, however, the disproportionality found in prison populations is mirrored in arrests. Women accounted for 20.5 percent of adult arrests for index offenses in 1979, but they accounted for only 8.7 percent of adult arrests for the violent offenses of murder and robbery that are most often found in prison. Larceny accounted for a large proportion—79 percent—of adult index arrests of women in 1979 (although women accounted for only 32.7 percent of all adult arrests for larceny).

Despite the apparently large differences in the criminal activity and imprisonment rates of men and women, sex differences in sentence outcomes have not generated a large volume of research. A recent review of this body of research found only about 20 studies since 1970 in which sex of the offender was a consideration (Nagel and Hagan, 1983). This small body of research is noteworthy for its consideration of the impact of sex differences at various stages of case processing, from pretrial release to sentence. No one study, however, considers outcomes at all stages. Based on their review of the literature, Nagel and Hagan (1983) conclude that differences in outcome by sex do exist, particularly in the pretrial release decision on type of release and in the sentence decision, especially for less severe sentence outcomes. When these differences are found, they are to the advantage of women offenders.

The strength of the conclusions drawn from the existing body of research, like those on race and socioeconomic status, must be moderated by the potential biases arising from errors in measuring seriousness and prior record and from possible selection effects resulting from the differential filtering of cases to the sentencing stage. For example, to the extent that women tend to commit less serious offenses and are also less likely to be selected for sentencing regardless of offense seriousness, those women who end up being sentenced would be likely to have committed more serious offenses. However, when there are independent measurement errors resulting from incomplete measures of seriousness, the unobserved dimensions of seriousness cannot be adequately controlled, and some of the effect of seriousness on sentence outcomes would be picked up by sentenced women with their more serious offenses. This would diminish—or understate—the true difference in sentence outcomes between men and women.

Whatever the actual effect of sex on sentence outcomes, the question of discrimination by sex depends on the legitimacy of sex differences as a determinant of sentences. This remains an unresolved legal question: sex has not been granted the status of a "suspect classification" (as has race). The fact that any sex differences that may exist are to the *advantage* of the otherwise presumed disadvantaged group also makes sex discrimination in sentencing a somewhat unique problem.

To the extent that there is discrimination in sentence outcomes by sex (or by race or by socioeconomic status), a range of "solutions" is available for eliminating that discrimination. If the objective is to equalize sentences, one can shift the outcomes of the disadvantaged group to equal those of the advantaged group, or vice versa, or one can shift both groups to achieve some average of past sentencing practices. In California's Uniform Determinate Sentencing Law, the averaging approach was used. However, since women represented such a small portion of all sentenced defendants, the effect has been to markedly increase the sentences of women, especially for violent offenses.[23]

CASE-PROCESSING VARIABLES

Three case-processing variables have frequently been cited as potential factors in differential sentence outcomes: mode of disposition (guilty plea, bench trial, or jury trial); pretrial release status (free on bail or detained); and type of attorney (none, court-appointed, or privately retained). The evidence varies in quality and in the consistency of findings for each of these factors. Of the three factors, the evidence on the role of guilty pleas in less severe sentences is most convincing. Pretrial detention is commonly found to be associated with more severe sentences, but this result is particularly vulnerable to biased estimates and hence is best viewed cautiously. The evidence on the role of attorney type is mixed and does not support a general conclusion that attorney type is independently related to sentence outcomes.

The strongest and most persistently found effect of case-processing variables is the role of guilty pleas in producing less severe sentences. It appears in some jurisdictions that defendants who exercise their right to trial receive harsher sentences than similarly situated defendants who plead guilty. Such a sentence differential is sometimes thought to be an essential element of the process by which large numbers of defendants are induced to plead guilty.

Evidence for this phenomenon comes from interviews with court participants (Alschuler, 1968, 1976; Casper, 1972; Heumann, 1978; Mather, 1974; Newman, 1956; Vetri, 1964; *Yale Law Journal*, 1956) and statis-

---

[23] This effect is discussed in greater detail in the analysis of the impact of the California Determinate Sentencing Law in Chapter 4.

tical analyses of case records in a wide variety of jurisdictions. Several statistical studies report substantial sentence differences by plea when other factors like record and charge are controlled (Brereton and Casper, 1982; Nardulli, 1978; Rhodes and Conly, 1981; Rich et al., 1981; Uhlman and Walker, 1980). One study reports sentence differences by plea in selected courtrooms but no aggregate differences in three jurisdictions (Eisenstein and Jacob, 1977), while another reports sentence differences for some crime types but not others (Rhodes, 1978).

The statistical evidence on what is called the guilty-plea discount is subject to possible biases arising from measurement error and sample selection. These potential biases are particularly troubling because they would result in *overestimates* of the effect of the discount.

Several studies have found an association between offense seriousness and mode of disposition, with more serious cases more likely to go to trial (Eisenstein and Jacob, 1977; Hagan, 1975; Klepper et al., Volume II:Table 1). This might occur because of a prosecutor's decreased willingness to accept guilty pleas to reduced charges in serious cases and a corresponding decreased willingness by a defendant to plead guilty when the risk of severe sanction is high. To the extent that offense seriousness is poorly measured, independent measurement error would contribute to underestimates of the effect of seriousness and overestimates of the effect of trial on severe sentences.

This measurement error bias will be large relative to the true effect of guilty pleas when: offense seriousness in sentence plays a large role; the role of disposition type in sentences is small; the error in measuring seriousness is large; or the correlation between seriousness and disposition type is large. Thus, measurement error bias from an association between disposition type and offense seriousness could lead to estimates of an effect of disposition type when in fact there is none. However, the interview data from court participants suggest that this statistical bias is likely to be small relative to the true effect. To begin with, the views of participants are informed by direct knowledge of the relative influence of dimensions of seriousness that may be unobservable to the researcher. Moreover, as participants in the plea negotiation process, judges, prosecutors, and defense counsel are privy to the offers made to defendants who go to trial; they thus have firsthand knowledge of the size of the guilty-plea discount reflected in the actual differences found between offers made and sentences received after trial for the same case.

Sample selection bias also may be present through differences in conviction rates, and hence different likelihoods of sentence, for trial and guilty-plea cases. Offenders who plead guilty are certain to be convicted and thus selected for sentencing, while some portion of trial cases do not result in convictions. If the strength of evidence also affects conviction rates independently of mode of disposition, stronger cases are more likely to end in a conviction. Hence it is possible that cases with the strongest evidence and those with the weakest evidence are more likely to go to trial. For the strongest cases, the prosecutor might not be willing to bargain down and accept a guilty plea to reduced charges, and there would be little advantage to the defendant to plead guilty. For the weakest cases, the defendant would have reason to hope for acquittal or dismissal in court. Among those cases going to trial, the cases with the strongest evidence would be more likely to end in conviction. On the average, then, cases that result in convictions through trial would be stronger than cases resolved by a guilty plea. Strength (or quality) of evidence may also contribute to more severe sentences, perhaps as an indicator of greater defendant culpability for the offense. In this event, controlling for other factors, the stronger evidence against offenders convicted in trials would lead to more severe sentences for those offenders than for offenders who plead guilty. However, to the extent that strength of evidence is poorly measured and thus poorly controlled in an analysis, any contribution of evidence to more severe sentences for those convicted in trials may be misinterpreted as an effect of disposition type. In this event the observed sentence differential between pleas and trials might be explained in terms of differences in the strength of evidence.

The magnitude of bias due to sample selection depends on the relative strength of the relationship between case quality and sentence severity: the smaller the role of case quality in sentence severity, the smaller the potential bias. While playing a major role in case dismissals and convictions, case quality is likely to be at most a minor factor in sentences. Certainly there is little empirical evidence supporting a claim of any major effect on sentences. Overestimates of the guilty-plea discount from sample selection are thus not likely to be large. The preponderance of evidence suggests that mode of disposition probably does exercise an independent effect on sentence outcomes.

It is a common finding that defendants held in pretrial detention receive substantially harsher sentences than those who are free awaiting trial (Clarke and Koch, 1976; Foote et al., 1954; Goldkamp, 1979; Greenwood et al., 1973; Landes, 1974; Lizotte, 1978; Morse and Beattie, 1932; Rankin, 1964; Spohn et al., 1982). This finding persists after controlling for factors like offense seriousness and prior record.

A variety of processes have been suggested as factors in the observed relationship between pretrial detention and harsher sentences. One possibility is that detained defendants are less able to assist in the preparation of their cases, both for trial and for subsequent sentence hearings. Some defendants may also lose their jobs while detained; the loss of income may affect their ability to retain private counsel, and their unemployment may be held against them in sentencing decisions. The conditions of pretrial detention may also induce detained defendants to plead guilty early and settle for less favorable outcomes. Those defendants who are free awaiting trial, on the other hand, are in a better position to delay disposition of their cases, possibly resulting in better offers from the prosecutor and decay in the strength of the prosecution case as witnesses tire of court appearances and memories fade. Finally, more severe sentences may result from a labeling process in which detained defendants are presumed to be more serious or dangerous (otherwise they would not have been detained) and hence deserving of harsher penalties.

It is also possible that the relationship between pretrial detention and harsher sentences is at least partially spurious, resulting from the role of common determinants of pretrial detention and sentence after conviction. Bail amount and subsequent release on bail, for example, have been found to be associated with the key determinants of sentences— offense seriousness and prior record (Landes, 1974; Lizotte, 1978). The more serious the offense and the worse the prior record, the more likely it is that the bail amount is set high and the defendant is detained. While most studies attempt to control for any spurious role of pretrial detention by including offense seriousness and prior record in their analyses, these variables are often poorly measured. Independent measurement error in either of these important variables will yield underestimates of the contribution of seriousness or prior record and overestimates of the contribution of pretrial detention to severe sentences. With systematic measurement errors, on the other hand, the biases might be in the opposite direction (see Table 2–4).

Sample selection biases may also distort the estimated effects of pretrial detention. The selection stage presumed to be most affected by pretrial detention is conviction, with detained defendants being more likely to be convicted. Selection biases arise when some poorly measured variable, like offense seriousness or prior record, affects both selection (in this case through conviction) and sentence severity. In the event that detained defendants are more likely to be convicted, regardless of seriousness or record, those defendants who are *not* detained but are convicted would be likely to have more serious offenses or worse records. Such a relationship would contribute to more severe sentences for defendants who are *not* detained, leading to *underestimates* of the impact of detention on sentence outcomes.

The association of pretrial detention with poorly measured variables like offense seriousness and prior record raises the possibility of biases in either direction in the estimated effect of pretrial detention on more severe sentence outcomes. While there appear to be both empirical evidence and theoretical reasons to support the view that pretrial detention has an independent influence on sentences, further research is needed to establish the existence and magnitude of such a relationship.

Anecdotal evidence suggests that defendants represented by public defenders or appointed counsel receive harsher sentences than those represented by privately retained counsel (Alschuler, 1975; Blumberg, 1964; Casper, 1972). This difference has been attributed to heavier work loads or less criminal experience for public or appointed attorneys, which contributes to less adequate defense and increased pressure to dispose of cases through plea negotiations. The spirit of cooperation and compromise that characterizes courthouse regulars is another factor that might jeopardize defendants' positions. At the same time, many privately retained counsel represent large numbers of nonaffluent clients and depend upon rapid turnover of cases to generate adequate incomes from small individual case fees. Thus, their case loads and practice styles may not be very different from those of public attorneys. Moreover, the expertise and courthouse familiarity of public defenders may work to the advantage of their clients. It should be noted that there are also likely to be important jurisdictional differences in the quality of public defense counsel.

Statistical analyses of the effects of attorney type have generally failed to control adequately for other determinants of sentences and are thus vulnerable to biases arising from measurement error and sample selection. Furthermore, the studies result in mixed conclusions, with some studies supporting the proposition of an advantage for the clients of privately retained counsel (Bing and Rosenfeld, 1970; Katz et al., 1971; Spohn et al., 1982) and others contradicting it (Beattie, 1935; Eisenstein and Jacob, 1977; Oaks and Lehman, 1968; Rhodes and Conly, 1981; Smith, 1970; Taylor et al., 1972). The evidence to date does not support the conclusion that attorney type is independently related to sentence.

DISPARITY

In studying the determinants of sentences, it is not sufficient to consider only factors relating to the offense, the offender, and case-processing variables. Although some statistical studies have included as many as 30 explanatory variables relating to case attributes, two-thirds or more of variation in sentence outcomes remains unexplained. Many researchers have looked to elements of the decision-making process, especially differences among judges, for the sources of that remaining variation.

Attempts to measure variation in judicial sentencing are not a 1970s phenomenon. As early as 1895 researchers tried to document the extent of interjudge disparity or the differences in sentencing attributable only to the identity of the judge (Francis Galton, *Nature*, 1895, cited in Banks, 1964). Early approaches were relatively straightforward; they generally compared the rates of particular sentences given by different judges. Everson (1919) found that the frequency of suspended sentences given for public intoxication by 42 magistrates in New York City varied from less than 1 percent to 83 percent. Gaudet et al. (1933) studied the sentences imposed by six New Jersey judges and showed that the rates of incarceration for their cases varied from 34 percent of all individuals sentenced by the most lenient judge to 58 percent of those sentenced by the most severe judge.

In order to conclude from these studies that judge differences accounted for the differences in sentencing patterns, it is necessary to assume that the samples of cases sentenced by each judge were comparable. Even if initial case assignment was random—a practice unlikely in most courts due to management considerations and simple carelessness—comparability of samples at the time of sentencing would probably not result. Since the judge who initially receives a case may affect its disposition by trial or guilty plea, the mix of cases ultimately available for sentencing by a judge may be a function of the judge's reputation and behavior. In order to correct for differences in the cases sentenced by different judges, some researchers have used statistical controls. The crudest of these is the matching strategy that identifies subgroups of cases sharing similar characteristics (e.g., offense, prior record) and compares the sentencing patterns of different judges for each subgroup of cases (e.g., Green, 1961). The difficulty with this approach is that a researcher can never be certain that the subgroups identified for each judge consist of strictly comparable cases; it is always possible that the cases of two judges are different on some unmeasured variable or set of variables that is crucial for the sentencing outcome.

More elaborate versions of the same type of approach use regression and related statistical techniques (e.g., PROBIT) to control for case differences across judges. Variables identifying or describing judges are then introduced in the model as independent variables in addition to case attributes, and the researcher then tests to see whether a judge variable or set of variables can explain any additional variation in sentencing. Judge variables may be in the form of individual judge identity (e.g., Rhodes, 1977; Shane-Dubow et al., 1979) or attitudinal/personality groupings (e.g., Clarke and Koch, 1977, who classified Alaskan judges as "strict" or "lenient"; Hogarth, 1971, who measured Canadian magistrates for cognitive complexity as well as attitudes toward punishment). Most of these studies have shown a substantial impact of judge variables. A few have shown no judge effect (e.g., Rhodes, 1977). One reason for the lack of judge effects in some studies of sentence outcomes is that such studies include case characteristics that may anticipate or reflect judicial reaction. Bail status, for example, was a predictor of sentence in Rhodes's study. Yet, as Rhodes mentions, the bail decision may reflect an earlier judicial decision on probable sentence. In this event the role of judge effects in both sentence outcomes *and* bail decisions must be investigated together.

A more general problem with using statistical controls to create comparable subgroups of cases is that, whenever the models fail to measure some variables adequately or omit them altogether, the ability of these models to assess the effects of judicial variables will be impaired. In general, the statistical controls cannot be assumed to have adequately controlled for case differences in evaluations of the separate impact of judicial identity.

To avoid the problems of lack of comparability, a number of researchers have submitted identical cases to several judges, asking each judge to indicate a recommended sentence for the case. The "cases" have varied in detail from a list of eight case characteristics—offense, age, record, defendant's role in the offense, plea, injury to victim, weapon, dollar amount—(Forst and Wellford, 1981) through presentence reports (Partridge and Eldridge, 1974) to excerpts from trial record, testimony, and a detailed description of the offender (Hood, 1972; Kapardis and Farrington, 1982). In each study, the results have shown substantial differences in the sentencing recommendations of different judges. Forst and Wellford (1981) found that for 9 of their 16 scenarios, some judges recommended sentences of at least 20 years, while other judges recommended against imprisonment; for 2 of the cases half of the judges recommended prison and half did not. The judges in this study were all federal court judges and came from different districts. The results are similar, however, in studies comparing judges in a single district. In a study of the federal Second Circuit (Partridge and Eldridge, 1974), judges in one district disagreed on whether to incarcerate in 13 of 20 cases; in another district they disagreed in 15 of 20 cases.

While the sentencing experiments described here are able to have multiple judges "sentence" identical cases, it is possible that the "sentences" in the experiment would not reflect sentences given when the decision had real consequences for a flesh-and-blood offender. While the effect of personal interaction between judge and offender is probably very limited (the defendant usually pleads guilty, and the judge learns about the defendant through the presentence report and from statements by opposing counsel), the absence of real consequences in experiments and the use of often limited case information that leaves considerable room for judicial interpretation or imputation of relevant but missing information are potentially more troublesome.

One study that reduced these problems took advantage of a naturally occurring collegial sentencing structure—the sentencing council (Diamond and Zeisel, 1975). Federal judges in several courts meet regularly to discuss their sentencing decisions. Before each meeting every council member receives presentence reports on the offenders to be discussed at the meeting. Before the council convenes, each judge privately records a favored sentence for each case. These recommendations are discussed at the council meeting and are expected to influence the decision of the sentencing judge, who retains full power to determine the actual sentence. Thus, unlike a decision in sentencing experiments, a sentencing council recommendation has real consequences for the offender through its potential influence on the sentencing judge. The information supplied to the council judges also closely approximates the information available to the sentencing judge. The results of this study indicate substantial disparity in sentence recommendations: in 30 percent of the cases, a random sample of three judges disagreed about whether to incarcerate the offender. The figure is almost identical for sentencing councils in Chicago and in New York.

The sentencing council study generally controls for case attributes and defendant vulnerability. Hence, the only remaining problem is the extent to which the measure of disparity is influenced by interpersonal processes of the council itself, so that the recommended sentences do not completely reflect the sentences of individual judges sitting alone. Judicial disparity may be somewhat understated in council cases if the prospect of formal review of individual judicial decisions in council deliberations leads judges to be more circumspect in their sentence recommendations. It is also possible that the prospect of a moderating effect of council deliberations may lead individual judges to initially recommend sentences that are more extreme than they would actually desire as a result. This situation would exaggerate or overstate the extent of judicial disparity.

In considering potential sources of systematic judicial variation, it is generally acknowledged that pursuing different goals in sentencing can often result in very different sentences in the same case. For example, general deterrence may suggest a prison sentence for the first-offender tax evader, while the goals of specific deterrence and rehabilitation would argue for a fine or probation. To the extent that different judges emphasize different goals, as found in Forst and Wellford (1981), for example, one would expect their sentences to differ.

Aside from general judicial predilections, the particular goals of sentencing deemed appropriate in any case may be influenced by a variety of cues reflecting the degree of offender culpability (or responsibility for the offense) and the stability or enduring quality of offending behavior for the defendant. The extent of blameworthiness of the offender affects judgments of the punishment deserved, and increases in blameworthiness may well evoke sentences based on goals of retribution. To the extent that an offender is judged to be fully responsible for his or her actions and the offending is viewed as a stable attribute of the offender, the likelihood of incapacitative sentences increases. Sentences for the purposes of rehabilitation or deterrence are more likely when offending is perceived to be a temporary attribute of the offender. This perception increases the potential that a sentence can actually affect future offending behavior, both for the sanctioned offender and for others who witness the sanction.

Various elements have been suggested as influencing attributions of offender culpability and stability. The level of responsibility for an offense varies with the offender's motivation and ability to commit the offense. Motivational factors like victim provocation (Harvey and Engle, 1978) and the extent of planning or forethought involved (Harvey and Engle, 1978; Joseph et al., 1976) have been found to affect attributions of culpability, as have ability factors like level of mental or psychological functioning (Monahan and Hood, 1976) and abuses of authority or position (Diamond and Herhold, 1981; Thomas, 1979). Another factor in culpability is the level of harm done (Hood, 1972; Kapardis and Farrington, 1982; Walster, 1966; Wheeler et al., 1981). There is little empirical work on cues affecting judgments of stability; some potentially important factors might include remorse, cooperation with authorities, and indicators of more general social stability, like family support and employment opportunities.

Few of these variables—effort, planning, level of psychological functioning, provocation, harm, and stability cues—have been directly measured in studies of judicial sentencing. To the extent that they influence judges differently in different cases, they might well account for inter-judge and intrajudge disparity.

It is also possible that the origins of judicial disparity may have little to do with judges. Several studies have identified the importance of the recommendations by the prosecutor or probation officers in determining sentence outcomes (Carter and Wilkins, 1967; Hagan, 1975, 1977; Hagan et al., 1979; Myers, 1979; Unnever et al., 1980). Variations in sentences among judges and even for the same judge thus may arise from variations in the individual prosecutor or probation officer making sentence recommendations in different cases.

The evidence for sentence disparity is extensive, but data on the sources of that disparity are scarce. One plausible direction for research is to examine the sentencing goals of different judges, how the goals are formed, and where they lead. If sentences are in part a product of the goals they are meant to achieve, the absence of consensus on appropriate sentencing goals may be a major factor contributing to inter-judge disparity.

The extent to which disparity is unwarranted remains an important policy question whose resolution depends on the weight given to competing values. On the one hand, there is concern that sentences result from the evenhanded application of general sentencing principles. On the other hand, there is a recognition that there are often legitimate social, cultural, and philosophical differences over what those principles should be, as reflected, for example, in conflicting interpretations of the goals of sentencing. Resolution of this policy issue would benefit from continued efforts to clarify and articulate the principles that currently do and those that ought to underlie sentence decisions. Such work would help to illuminate the dimensions of the choices that must be made.

CONCLUSION

Evidence on the determinants of sentences is beginning to emerge from several research approaches. The available research provides some general information on which factors may be important and which may not. Estimates of the magnitude of these effects are considerably less precise.

One limitation of existing research is inadequate controls for potentially important determinants of sentences arising from omitted or poorly measured variables. This limitation contributes to statistical biases of often unknown direction and magnitude in the estimated effects.

Sentence decisions are also typically analyzed using simple linear models involving weighted sums of individual variables to characterize the relationship between determinants and sentence outcomes. These analyses often fail to address even simple forms of interactions among explanatory variables. Instead, all variables are considered simultaneously and always enter the decision with the same impact. However, sentence decisions may be more complex and may require richer characterizations of the decision process. For example, it may be that sentencing decisions are a multistage process that first involves an attempt by the decision maker to allocate the case to one of a small number of case patterns, where each case pattern is subject to a different sentencing rule. One pattern of cases, for example, may be viewed as particularly well suited to rehabilitation, and the sentences imposed would be intended to enhance rehabilitation opportunities. Another pattern of cases may elicit an incapacitative response, while still another pattern may be distinguished for its potential general deterrent effects and be sentenced accordingly.

The sentencing rules characterizing sentence decisions within each case pattern may vary in terms of the variables included and the weights given these variables and may invoke interactions among variables and hierarchical treatments of the variables. In a hierarchical sentencing rule, the sentence decision follows a branching process in which the weight given some factors depends on the presence or absence of other factors. For example, in a particularly heinous crime, the viciousness of the crime alone may be sufficient to lead to incarceration. In less heinous crimes, a variety of factors, like the defendant's prior criminal record and general community ties, may enter the decision to imprison or not.

There may also be some cases that do not fit any of the identified case patterns. Such cases may be sentenced on the basis of the particularly unique features of the case and so be difficult to characterize by a general rule.

This characterization of sentencing decisions is quite different from existing analyses in which the same simple linear model is applied uniformly to all cases. The alternate formulation involves first a process of pattern recognition and then the application of potentially complex decision rules. Specifying the actual forms of alternate models of sentencing decisions to be tried will probably benefit from the insights derived from interviews of participants and extensive observations of the process.

It is also important to remember that sentencing decisions are not made in isolation; they occur in the context of a variety of earlier decisions that potentially influence sentence outcomes. As a result, when attempting to sort out the determinants of sentences, one cannot focus only on the outcomes of the convicted cases that appear before a judge for sentencing. Sentencing decisions must be viewed more broadly to reflect the impact of earlier decisions that result in convictions in some cases, thus making offenders vulnerable to sentencing. This larger system approach to the process will also help to address the methodological problems arising from selection, as well as an indirect basis for resolving the measurement problems in key concepts like seriousness, prior record, and case quality.[24]

[24] See Garber et al. (Volume II), Klepper et al. (Volume II), and Berk and Ray (1982) for a more detailed treatment of the ways in which explicit consideration of the broader case-processing system can help to alleviate the biases arising from measurement error and sample selection.

3

Structuring
Sentencing Decisions

American sentencing laws and practices underwent more extensive changes in the 1976–1980 period than in any other 5-year period in American history. In this chapter we review the range of sentencing innovations adopted since 1960, examine the uses of research in the development of sentencing standards, and consider problems related to the implementation and enforcement of sentencing policy innovations.

THE VARIETY OF INNOVATIONS

THE RETREAT FROM INDETERMINACY

Twentieth-century American sentencing systems before 1976 are commonly referred to as "indeterminate." Under indeterminate sentencing judges and parole boards have wide discretion in setting prison terms within broad statutory ranges for sentence length. Usually the actual length of a prison term remains unknown to a prisoner until the parole board authorizes release. This broad discretion and uncertainty was intended to facilitate individualized treatment for purposes of rehabilitation.

In the state of Washington during much of this century, for example, judges only decided who received prison sentences: they were required by law to impose the statutory maximum sentence on all offenders to be imprisoned, and the parole board decided how long any prisoner actually remained in prison. Under the indeterminate sentencing laws

126

of other states, judges have more influence. In Pennsylvania, for example, judges set both the maximum and the minimum sentence; the minimum cannot exceed half the maximum, and the parole board's authority is confined within the range set by the judge. Although the division of authority between judges and parole boards varies from state to state, the systems are indeterminate: discretion is broad and the duration of imprisonment remains unknown until the parole authorities actually release the prisoner.

What most of the sentencing changes of recent years have in common is their rejection of this pattern in which judges and parole boards make ad hoc decisions, subject to few meaningful constraints, and are effectively immune from review. The narrowing of discretion and the introduction of greater certainty into sentencing have taken many different forms. Some jurisdictions abolished parole release entirely: California established detailed statutory standards for prison sentences, Minnesota established a detailed system of presumptive sentencing guidelines, and Maine established no standards at all. Other jurisdictions made other changes: Pennsylvania adopted both mandatory minimum sentences and sentencing guidelines while retaining parole release; and in Washington the parole board established parole guidelines, the judiciary established sentencing guidelines, and the legislature later created a commission charged to develop sentencing guidelines to take effect in 1984.

CLASSIFICATION OF OFFENSES

The federal criminal laws and those of most states developed adventitiously. New offenses were created and existing sentencing laws were amended in response to particular notorious events or social changes. Sentences authorized for particular offenses varied widely, reflecting the emotions, personalities, attitudes, and political imperatives of particular times (see National Commission on Reform of Federal Criminal Laws, 1970:1246–49). As a result, anomalies characterize the sentencing laws of many jurisdictions. Offenses of comparable seriousness are often subject to substantially different penalties: federal law, for example, recently specified a maximum 20-year prison sentence for robbery of a federally insured bank and a 10-year maximum for robbery of a post office (see Senate Report 96-553:5, 1980), and offenses of different seriousness are often subject to the same maximum penalties.

Consistent and evenhanded application of sentences is unlikely to be achieved in a system in which offenses and authorized sanctions are internally inconsistent and reflect no discernible logic. To introduce greater consistency to criminal law, the Model Penal Code developed by the American Law Institute (1962) classified all felonies into three classes, each bearing a specific maximum sentence of fine, probation, or imprisonment. More than 30 states have enacted new criminal codes in recent years, and these have followed the Model Penal Code's lead in classifying felonies into a small number of categories, usually three or five. Every proposed federal criminal code, from *Study Draft of a New Federal Criminal Code* (National Commission on Reform of Federal Criminal Laws, 1970) to S. 1630, which was approved by the Senate judiciary committee on November 18, 1981, has provided for classification of felonies.

REASONS REQUIREMENTS AND PRESUMPTIONS

Accountability is enhanced if decision makers must justify their decisions. In most contexts judges must give reasons for their decisions: this allows affected parties to understand the rationale for the decision and facilitates appellate review by providing appellate judges with a basis for knowing whether the trial judge applied the appropriate rule to the case under consideration and for evaluating the persuasiveness of the reasons for the decision.

Until recently, sentencing decisions were anomalous. Judges were seldom required to give reasons for the sentences they imposed, and sentence appeals were not usually available in most jurisdictions. There were for all practical purposes no bases or procedures for holding judges accountable for sentencing. Now, however, reasons requirements have been proposed and enacted in a number of forms.

Criminal codes sometimes provide that judges may not impose particular sentences unless they give reasons for doing so. The study draft of the National Commission on Reform of Federal Criminal Laws (1970) provides that judges may impose minimum sentences (Sec. 3201) or maximum sentences beyond specified lengths (Sec. 3202) only if the court "shall set forth in detail" the reasons for its decision. In a variation, the study draft established presumptions in favor of nonincarcerative sentences and parole release at first eligibility (Secs. 3101, 3402) along with criteria for determining when the presumptions are overcome. These provisions do not expressly require that reasons be given for decisions, but the effect is the same. A defendant who contests a sentence to incarceration or retention in prison would assert that the presumption has not been overcome; the sufficiency of the decision-maker's contrary judgment and the reasons for it would be the issues under consideration on appeal.

Most major sentencing innovations and proposals that provide criteria for decisions contain reasons requirements. The California Uniform Determinate Sentencing Law, for example, requires judges to give reasons for imposing a sentence not specified by the applicable statutory sections. Both sentencing guidelines systems and parole guidelines systems typically require that decision makers provide reasons for decisions that do not adhere to the apparently applicable guidelines.

While the commonsense case for reasons requirements in sentencing is straightforward and seldom contested, implementing these requirements raises some practical questions. For example, requiring that judges give reasons for their sentencing decisions in every case may result in the trivialization of reasons; those given may become routine and mechanical. Consequently, most reasons requirements obligate judges to give reasons only for exceptional decisions. A related practical question concerns the form for providing reasons—whether decision makers should be provided checklists that contain possible reasons for decisions or whether they be required to write out reasons of their own devising. (See Zeisel and Diamond [1977] for discussion of some of the difficulties involved in making reasons requirements meaningful.)

SENTENCING INSTITUTES

American trial judges work alone. Under indeterminate sentencing laws they have broad statutory flexibility, and they are typically not required to account for their decisions. Partly to facilitate communication among judges, the U.S. Congress in 1958 authorized sentencing institutes for the federal judiciary, and similar sentencing institutes have been held by many states. At these institutes judges discuss sentencing developments and often engage in simulated sentencing exercises; they then discuss their respective reactions to the simulated cases and the sentences they would have imposed. The premises of sentencing institutes are that they familiarize judges with the views of their colleagues, thus allowing them to learn whether their own attitudes and opinions are consistent with general patterns; that newly appointed judges benefit from the accumulated experience and "going rates" of their colleagues; and that all participating judges become more self-conscious in sentencing. Every major criminal law reform body in recent decades has declared its support for sentencing institutes. Widespread participation by judges in institutes over the last two decades may have increased their awareness of the dilemmas sentencing poses and their receptivity to proposals for reform.

SENTENCING COUNCILS

Sentencing councils are groups of judges who meet on a regular basis to discuss sentences for pending cases. Established in several federal district courts beginning in 1960, they were the first modern institutional innovation expressly aimed at reducing sentencing disparity. Each participating judge reviews presentence reports and prepares sentencing recommendations before attending the council meeting at which the recommendations are discussed. The recommendations are advisory, and the responsible judge in a case may disregard the recommendations.

One of the rationales for sentencing councils is that the exchanges of views would sometimes cause judges to reconsider their initial sentencing recommendations because of incongruity with the recommendations of their colleagues. Several accounts indicate that the initial recommendations of judges *do* differ from their ultimate sentences in one-third or more of the cases that come before the councils (Levin, 1966:511; Phillips, 1980:36). However, several major evaluations of sentencing councils find evidence that sentencing councils do not eliminate substantial sentence disparity (Diamond and Zeisel, 1975; Phillips, 1980). Like sentencing institutes, sentencing councils have been endorsed by every major criminal law reform body of recent years.

ABOLITION OR REGULATION OF PLEA NEGOTIATION

The legitimacy of the American dependence on plea negotiation as a primary method of case disposition has long been questioned. The President's Crime Commission (1967) and the American Bar Association Task Force on Sentencing Alternatives and Procedures (1980) both reviewed objections to plea bargaining and proposed methods to bring it into the open and to subject it to regulation. The National Advisory Commission on Criminal Justice Standards and Goals (1973:46) recommended abolition of plea bargaining.

At least nine major objections to plea bargaining have been asserted. First, until the 1970s, most plea negotiation was hypocritical: a majority of convictions resulted from guilty pleas, but defendants were required to deny in court that they had been offered inducements to plead guilty (President's Crime Commission, 1967:9). Second, serious principled objections can be made to the propriety of offering defendants inducements to waive their constitutional right to trial: in effect, prosecutors threaten to punish the assertion of trial rights by withholding from defendants benefits they would receive if they pleaded guilty. Third, there is always a risk that an innocent defendant will plead guilty from fear of being sentenced more harshly if convicted after trial: this risk is especially great when the defendant is offered a probationary sentence for pleading guilty and is threatened with going to prison if convicted. Fourth, plea-bargaining conflicts with the public interest in soundly administered justice: presentence reports and other investigations of the defendant are generally only available after conviction and are not available at the plea-bargaining stage. Thus the judge must often approve or disapprove a proposed bargain without adequate information about the defendant. Fifth, plea bargaining can result in excessive leniency for professional criminals who are familiar with the courts' operations and are represented by courtroom regulars: unsophisticated minor offenders who are unaware of the manipulative benefits of plea bargaining may simply plead guilty to the original charges and be treated relatively harshly. Sixth, institutionalized plea bargaining undermines the substantive criminal law: defendants plead guilty not to the offense they committed but to some lesser offense that has been negotiated. One often cannot know from the offense of conviction what offense was actually committed. Seventh, plea bargaining effectively shifts power to set sentences from judges to prosecutors. Eighth, plea bargaining reduces judges' awareness of investigations and arrests and thereby lessens their knowledge of police practices and their influence on them. Ninth, by merging the conviction and sanctioning decisions, plea bargaining increases the risk that each decision will not receive the separate attention that it should.

Although the moral and practical case against plea bargaining is quite strong, several arguments have been made in its defense. First, it is sometimes said that the criminal courts would be grossly overburdened if plea bargains did not induce most defendants to plead guilty.[1] Supreme Court Chief Justice Warren Burger has observed (*Santobello* v. *New York* 404 U.S. 257, 260 [1971]):

[Plea bargaining] is an essential component of the administration of justice. Properly administered, it is to be encouraged. If every criminal charge were subjected to a full-scale trial, the States and the Federal Government would need to multiply by many times the number of judges and court facilities.

Second, plea bargaining relieves defendants and prosecutors of the uncertainties of trial. Third, it can be used to mitigate the harshness of mandatory sentencing laws that prescribe punishments more severe than

---

[1] For the contrary argument and supporting evidence that the majority of defendants would continue to plead guilty without plea bargains, see Feeley (1979:Ch. 8), Heumann (1978), and Rubinstein et al. (1980).

a prosecutor believes are warranted. Fourth, plea bargaining in which leniency is exchanged for information, assistance, and testimony in other prosecutions can serve important law enforcement interests. Fifth, plea bargaining can be viewed as a form of dispute resolution in which the parties compromise their differences and thereby achieve a more mutually satisfactory resolution than if the parties were unfailingly adversarial. Sixth, plea bargaining permits prosecutors to achieve convictions in cases in which evidentiary or procedural problems might otherwise result in acquittals.

Efforts have been made to "abolish" plea bargaining in full, or in part, in several jurisdictions. In Wayne County, Michigan, for example, the prosecutor forbade plea bargaining by his assistants in cases in which a firearm was used in the course of a felony (see Heumann and Loftin, 1979). The most dramatic plea-bargaining ban occurred in Alaska. Effective August 15, 1975, the attorney general banned plea bargaining in all its forms (Rubinstein et al., 1980).[2]

For much the same reasons that some prosecutors have attempted to ban plea bargaining, others have attempted to regulate it by establishing internal office policies governing charge and sentence bargains and sentence recommendations (e.g., Kuh, 1975a,b). Plea bargaining has also been regulated as part of more general efforts to establish and enforce office policies and systems of managerial controls (see Eisenstein and Jacob, 1977; Jacoby, 1980). Efforts have been made in a number of jurisdictions to institutionalize plea bargaining. In one series of projects supported by the National Institute of Justice, scheduled plea conferences included the judge, the lawyers, and—if they wished to participate—the defendant, the victim, and the involved police officer. (See Kerstetter and Heinz [1979] for a report on the Dade County, Florida, experience.)

MANDATORY MINIMUM SENTENCES

Between 1977 and 1980, mandatory minimum sentencing laws were adopted in 27 states and were under consideration in at least 14 others (U.S. Department of Justice, 1980a). Mandatory minimum sentencing laws take several forms but have as their common characteristic the statutory directive that convicted defendants whose offenses and prior

---

[2] Because public prosecution is generally organized at local levels, most state attorneys general lack authority to promulgate such a ban and the means to enforce it. In Alaska, however, public prosecution is organized on a statewide basis.

record fall within specified categories be sentenced to a prison term of not less than a specified period of years. Under some mandatory sentencing laws, judges retain the option to impose a nonincarcerative sentence but must impose a sentence of at least the mandatory minimum term on those whom they send to prison. Other laws expressly preclude nonincarcerative sentencing options and direct that all persons convicted of the designated offense receive a term of imprisonment of not less than the mandatory minimum term. Massachusetts's Bartley-Fox law, for example, provides that all persons convicted of unlawfully carrying a firearm be imprisoned for a term not less than 1 year. Other variants are more complicated. A Michigan law enacted in 1977 requires that persons convicted of the use of a firearm in a felony receive a prison sentence of not less than 1 year; both the firearms charge and the underlying felony charge have to be either pled or proved, and the minimum sentence law does not apply if either charge is not proved.

STATUTORY DETERMINATE SENTENCING LAWS (ABOLITION OF PAROLE)

Determinate sentencing laws take two forms. In the first, discussed in this section, a legislature specifies the presumptive sentences or sentence ranges. In the second, discussed in the next section, a legislature sets the general outlines of the sentencing system and the standards for sentences but delegates the responsibility for developing guidelines to a sentencing commission.

Determinate sentencing exists in those jurisdictions in which the lengths of prison sentences can be determined, assuming the prisoner's good conduct in prison,[3] at the time the judge announces the sentence; the release date is not determined later, by a parole-type agency.[4] By that criterion, at least nine states have enacted determinate sentencing laws:

[3] Most state prisons operate good-time systems under which the length of any prison sentence can be reduced as a reward for good behavior while in prison. Throughout this report, discussion of the lengths of prison sentences should include the qualification "assuming good behavior in prison and that good-time credits are not administratively reduced or increased."

[4] A somewhat different concept of determinacy includes parole systems under which release dates are set in the early months of confinement but excludes those jurisdictions that have not established relatively detailed standards for sentencing and parole decisions. (See von Hirsch and Hanrahan [1979:25–35] on the desirability and practicality of parole systems that set release dates early; on definitions of determinacy, see von Hirsch and Hanrahan [1981:294–296].)

Alaska, California, Colorado, Indiana, Illinois, Maine, Minnesota, New Mexico, and North Carolina. The statutory determinate sentencing systems in those states vary widely.

At one extreme, Maine abolished its parole board in 1975 when it enacted a comprehensive criminal code based on the Model Penal Code. Except for the maximum sanctions specified for each class of felonies, no criteria were provided to guide judicial sentencing decisions. Thus Maine judges retain the substantial unregulated discretion that judges typically have had under indeterminate sentencing systems. Because of the abolition of parole, however, prisoners can predict at sentencing when they will be released (see Zarr, 1976). California's Uniform Determinate Sentencing Law, at the other extreme, abolished parole release for most prisoners and enacted detailed statutory sentencing standards. That law provides that, when sentencing offenders to prison, judges choose one of three specified sentences as the "base term" for persons convicted of a particular offense (for example, 2, 3, or 5 years for robbery). The middle term is to be imposed in an ordinary case. The higher or lower term may be imposed in cases with aggravating or mitigating circumstances. In addition, the California law provides for a variety of increments (called "enhancements") that can be added to the base term if various prior-record factors (primarily prior incarcerations) or aggravating offense circumstances are alleged and proved. Among the specified aggravating circumstances are use of a firearm or other dangerous weapon, serious bodily injury, and major property loss or damage.

The other existing determinate sentencing laws range between those of Maine and California. They provide more guidance to judges than the former but less than the latter.

Several criticisms of such laws have been offered. Zimring (1976) notes that sentencing is especially vulnerable to being politicized when detailed sentence criteria are placed before a legislature: introduction of amendments to increase sentences is politically effective evidence of a legislator's devotion to law and order. However carefully developed proposed statutory sentencing criteria may be, they can be altered simply by changing a number in a committee room or even on the floor of the legislature. The many bills introduced in the California legislature to increase sentence severity since adoption of the original determinate sentencing law provide some support for Zimring's observation.

A related objection is that legislatures are not institutionally suited to the development and review of detailed sentencing policy. Sentencing is but one among many subjects competing for legislators' time and attention, and they lack special expertise in the subject. The legislative floor is a poor place for consideration of any subject that requires detailed, sustained attention. While legislatures are well suited to the adoption and enunciation of broad normative choices, they are institutionally less capable of the detailed policy making and gradual refinement of policy over time. For these reasons, legislatures have frequently delegated rule-making authority over technical subjects, such as regulation of securities and public utilities and, recently, sentencing, to administrative agencies.

A third objection is that statutory sentence criteria tend to shift discretion from judges to prosecutors. When, as under California law, the offense of conviction and any pled and proved enhancements determine the applicable sentence, some sentencing power may be shifted from judges and placed in the hands of the lawyers participating in the plea-bargaining process.

PRESUMPTIVE/PRESCRIPTIVE SENTENCING GUIDELINES AND SENTENCING COMMISSIONS

Existing sentencing guideline systems differ on two important dimensions: their legal authority and the influence and role of empirical information on past sentencing practices in generating the guideline sentences. Guidelines are presumptive or voluntary, depending on their legal force. Guidelines are also labeled "descriptive" or "prescriptive," depending on whether they are designed largely to articulate and codify past sentencing practices (descriptive) or are focused primarily on developing new sentencing policies (prescriptive). Although there are four possible combinations of these dimensions, two principal combinations are actually found: presumptive/prescriptive guidelines, illustrated by those in Minnesota, Pennsylvania, and Washington; and voluntary/descriptive guidelines, illustrated by those in Denver and Massachusetts.[5]

In three jurisdictions, Minnesota, Pennsylvania, and Washington, the legislatures have delegated authority for developing detailed sentencing criteria to sentencing commissions. The sentencing commissions are charged to develop presumptive sentencing guidelines. Judges are expected to impose sentences recommended by the guidelines in ordinary

---

[5] Depending on the dimension of particular interest in each context, we may refer to sentencing guidelines simply as presumptive or voluntary or as "descriptive" or "prescriptive." Also, "descriptive" and "prescriptive" are in quotation marks because these terms are widely used but not literally accurate: regardless of their origins, all guidelines are statements prescribing policy and most have used data describing past practice in some way in their development.

cases and to provide reasons for sentences that do not follow the guidelines. Minnesota's is a determinate sentencing system. Parole release has been abolished, and the sentencing guidelines specify "real-time" sentences. Pennsylvania's guidelines are indeterminate and affect only the minimum sentence to be served before parole eligibility: the parole board continues to decide when prisoners are released. The Washington guidelines will establish determinate sentences for offenders convicted after July 1, 1984, while the parole board will establish release dates for offenders convicted prior to that date until it ceases to exist on July 1, 1988.

These presumptive guidelines have substantial legal authority, deriving from the sentencing commission's legislative mandate. The guideline sentence must be imposed or an explanation provided as to why some other sentence was imposed. Both defendants and prosecutors have the right to have the sufficiency of that explanation reviewed by an appellate court. (By contrast, voluntary sentencing guidelines are hortatory and create no defendants' rights; noncompliance by judges does not give rise to a right of appeal. Voluntary guidelines have thus far been initiated by judges and not legislatures.)

The operation of a presumptive guidelines system can be illustrated by the Minnesota guidelines. Table 3–1 shows the sentencing grid of the Minnesota Sentencing Guidelines Commission. The left-hand column lists the 10 categories of criminal offenses, and the top row lists the 7 categories of criminal offenders. The offense categories include all commonly occurring criminal offenses, ranked in order of their seriousness. The offender categories are based on a defendant's "criminal history" (prior record), using a weighted scoring system developed by the commission.

The sentence for any defendant is found by first determining the offense severity and criminal history ranking and then consulting the cell of the sentencing grid in the applicable row and column. The cells above the bold block line call for sentences other than state imprisonment: the numbers in these cells represent the prescribed lengths of stayed (i.e., unexecuted) sentences.[6] Each cell below the bold line con-

---

[6] In general, a stayed sentence is one that is not carried out. Two types of stayed sentences are permitted under Minnesota law: a stay of imposition and a stay of execution. A stay of imposition means the defendant is convicted of a felony, is given a probationary sentence (that may include up to 12 months in jail), and upon completion of the sentence the felony conviction is reduced to a misdemeanor on the record. If the offender violates probation, a felony prison term may be imposed. A stay of execution means that the defendant is convicted, a felony conviction is placed on the offender's record, the offender is placed on probation, and the felony prison term that is pronounced but not carried out may be executed if probation is violated.

TABLE 3–1 Minnesota Sentencing Grid: Sentencing by Severity of Offense and Criminal History

SEVERITY LEVELS OF CONVICTION OFFENSE		CRIMINAL HISTORY SCORE						
		0	1	2	3	4	5	6 or more
Unauthorized Use of Motor Vehicle Possession of Marijuana	I	12*	12*	12*	15	18	21	24
Theft-related Crimes ($150-$2500) Sale of Marijuana	II	12*	12*	14	17	20	23	27 25–29
Theft Crimes ($150-$2500)	III	12*	13	16	19	22 21–23	27 25–29	32 30–34
Burglary—Felony Intent Receiving Stolen Goods ($150-$2500)	IV	12*	15	18	21	25 24–26	32 30–34	41 37–45
Simple Robbery	V	18	23	27	30 29–31	38 36–40	46 43–49	54 50–58
Assault, 2nd Degree	VI	21	26	30	34 33–35	44 42–46	54 50–58	65 60–70
Aggravated Robbery	VII	24 23–25	32 30–34	41 38–44	49 45–53	65 60–70	81 75–87	98 90–104
Assault, 1st Degree Criminal Sexual Conduct, 1st Degree	VIII	43 41–45	54 50–58	65 60–70	76 71–81	95 89–101	113 106–120	132 124–140
Murder, 3rd Degree	IX	97 94–100	119 116–122	127 124–130	149 143–155	176 168–184	205 195–215	230 218–242
Murder, 2nd Degree	X	116 111–121	140 133–147	162 153–171	203 192–214	243 231–255	284 270–298	324 309–339

NOTE: 1st Degree Murder is excluded from the guidelines by law and continues to have a mandatory life sentence.

*one year and one day

SOURCE: Minnesota Sentencing Guidelines Commission (1981:23).

tains a single number—the guideline sentence expressed in months— and a range of months that varies by plus or minus 5–8 percent from the guideline sentence. The judge may impose any sentence within this narrow range, without providing reasons for doing so, in recognition of the fact that there are legitimate differences among cases to justify slight deviations from the guideline sentence. According to commission rules, judges may "depart" from the guidelines and impose sentences not contained in the applicable cell only if "the individual case involves substantial and compelling circumstances." Commission rules contain nonexclusive lists of possible aggravating and mitigating circumstances that might justify departures, and they expressly forbid consideration of some social status factors. The sufficiency of the reasons for departures is subject to review by the Minnesota supreme court (see Minnesota Sentencing Guidelines Commission, 1980).

The guidelines of the Pennsylvania Commission on Sentencing are similar in concept but provide much broader ranges. The Washington state sentencing commission statute was passed in April 1981; the commission is in the preliminary stages of developing its guidelines.

VOLUNTARY/DESCRIPTIVE SENTENCING GUIDELINES

The first sentencing guidelines system was established in Denver in 1976 (see Wilkins et al., 1978). The Denver guidelines resulted from an effort to apply to sentencing the research experience and technology developed in establishing the U.S. Parole Commission's parole guidelines (see the next section). The premises of the Denver guidelines feasibility project stated that "the gradual build-up of case-by-case decisions results in the incremental development of a sentencing policy" and that an empirically based guidelines system "takes advantage of, and incorporates, the collective wisdom of experienced and capable sentencing judges by developing representations of underlying court policies" (Wilkins et al., 1978:xiii, 10). The researchers attempted to develop a mathematical model of the determinants of sentence outcomes in Denver (and also in Vermont, where the effort was abandoned before guidelines were implemented) as the basis for guideline formulation. Various models of sentences in Denver were developed based on the results of multiple regression analyses applied to data on already sentenced cases. The models were then tested on a validation sample, and voluntary/descriptive sentencing guidelines were developed that ostensibly embodied the existing latent sentencing policies of the court (see Wilkins et al., 1978).

The initial Denver guidelines were expressed as a matrix. Separate matrices were developed for three felony classes and for each misdemeanor class. The offense severity score resulted from efforts to scale the severity of offenses within each statutory offense class, and the offender scores were based on offender variables found to explain significant amounts of variation in sentences. Judicial compliance with the guidelines was voluntary, and noncompliance did not give rise to rights of appeal by either defendants or prosecutors.

The Law Enforcement Assistance Administration, which had provided support for the Denver feasibility study, supported the development of a second generation of judicial sentencing guidelines in Cook County (Chicago), Illinois; Essex County (Newark), New Jersey; and Maricopa County (Phoenix), Arizona (see Kress, 1980). Similar guidelines were developed with local funds in Philadelphia.

A third generation of federally funded "descriptive" sentencing guidelines has been developed in demographically diverse counties of Maryland and Florida in order to assess the impact of uniform guidelines in different regions of a single state. The National Institute of Justice has supported an ongoing evaluation (by Abt Associates) of the construction and impact of those guidelines.

Voluntary guidelines need not necessarily be based on statistical efforts to model past sentencing practices. Judges in a particular court could agree to certain normative propositions about the purposes of sentencing and adopt voluntary/"prescriptive" guidelines reflecting that agreement. To date, however, most sentencing guidelines projects have followed the general pattern of the Denver guidelines: collect data on a sample of disposed cases; perform multivariate analyses to develop a model of the independent variables, with their respective weights, that influence sentences; and design a guideline format by which sentences in pending cases can be calculated on the basis of the model. Such processes to generate voluntary/"descriptive" sentencing guidelines have been undertaken by the judiciary at the state level in Michigan, Massachusetts, and New Jersey. State-level sentencing guidelines for selected offenses have been established in several states, including Alaska and Washington. Voluntary/"descriptive" sentencing guidelines projects at the local level have been initiated in at least 11 states (see Criminal Courts Technical Assistance Project, 1980).

PAROLE GUIDELINES

Parole guidelines have been adopted by the U.S. Parole Commission and by the parole boards of several states, including Florida, Georgia, Maryland, Minnesota, New York, Oklahoma, Oregon, and Washington.

The first parole guidelines system was initiated by the (then) U.S. Board of Parole in October 1972 as part of a pilot project to test the feasibility of regionalization of the board's work. The matrix-type parole guidelines developed for use in the northeast region were subsequently modified and in March 1976 were mandated by the Parole Commission and Reorganization Act for use throughout the federal system. Most of the state parole guidelines systems are patterned after the federal guidelines.

The U.S. parole guidelines emanated from the Parole Decision-Making Project of the National Council on Crime and Delinquency Research Center, in collaboration with the U.S. Board of Parole. One phase of that project was an attempt to identify the weights given by decision makers to various criteria in the parole decision. Research showed that decision makers' primary concerns were the severity of the offense, the prisoner's parole prognosis, and the prisoner's institutional behavior and "that a parole board's decisions could be predicted fairly accurately by knowledge of its ratings on these three factors" (Gottfredson et al., 1978).

There have been spirited political conflicts in various jurisdictions between proponents of parole guidelines and proponents of parole abolition. At the federal level, for example, bills to abolish parole and establish a sentencing commission and presumptive sentencing guidelines have twice been approved by the Senate judiciary committee. The bills developed by the House judiciary committee, in contrast, have consistently contained provisions calling for the retention of the Parole Commission and parole guidelines. Minnesota operated a parole guidelines system for almost 5 years, only to abolish it when the state's sentencing guidelines system took effect on May 1, 1980. Washington first established parole guidelines in 1976, but, as we noted above, recent legislation created a sentencing commission charged to develop presumptive sentencing guidelines and provides for abolition of parole.

Supporters of parole guidelines assert that well-organized, well-managed parole boards can achieve greater policy consistency than judges because parole boards are small, continuing collegial bodies; that parole boards applying consistent policies can reduce sentencing disparity by compensating for the disparate prison sentences imposed by dozens of judges throughout a jurisdiction, thereby in effect performing an appellate sentence review function; that parole boards can act as prison population control mechanisms by speeding releases when necessary to relieve population pressures; that parole boards, by being less visible, are less subject to public pressures and are freer to take risks in releasing inmates; and that parole guidelines are likelier to be followed than criteria for judicial sentencing because the status of hearing examiners as institutional employees makes them more amenable to discipline and managerial controls and their decisions more easily subject to review than are those of judges.

Critics of parole guidelines note that they cannot supplant promulgation of standards for judicial decisions because they have no relevance to the "in/out" decisions (whether or not to imprison); that they perpetuate a "Rube Goldberg" system of sentencing in which parole boards reduce the lengths of sentences that judges have increased in expectation that parole boards will reduce them; that sentencing is a decision of immense symbolic importance and is more appropriately a judicial than an administrative decision; and that because defendants are entitled to greater procedural protections in court than at parole hearings, the factual quality of the evidence considered in making the sentencing decision is likely to be of higher quality.

APPELLATE SENTENCE REVIEW

In virtually all common law jurisdictions except the United States, appellate review of sentences has been the principal method used to develop principles for and achieve consistency in sentencing. Approximately 40 percent of all criminal appeals heard by the English Court of Appeal between 1956 and 1976 resulted in affirmance of the defendant's conviction but variation in the sentence imposed (Advisory Council on the Penal System, 1978, App. H:202; also see Cross, 1975; Thomas, 1979). Appellate review of sentences is also extensively used in the Scandinavian countries (Andenaes, 1983) and West Germany (Weigend, 1983). In all of these countries the standards for sentencing that are the bases for review derive from the accumulation over time of a body of case law from which a national sentencing tariff has been extracted and gradually refined.

Numerous U.S. law reform bodies have proposed the adoption and invigoration of sentence appeal in this country.[7] A sizable minority of American states have long had systems of appellate sentence review, established by statute, by constitutional provisions, or by judicial interpretation of state law, but in most cases they appear to be ineffectual. The report of the Criminal Justice Standards Project of the American Bar Association (1980:18.193–18.197) notes:

A number of careful studies have examined the operation of state appellate review systems under which an offender can appeal a sentence as excessively severe. . . . Without serious exception, these studies found that appellate review had little more than a negligible impact, generally providing a remedy only in egregious cases but not capable of developing clearly articulated criteria or standards by which to guide future sentencing decisions.

Several organizational factors appear to contribute to the limited importance of appellate sentence review in the United States. In Massachusetts and Connecticut, the review divisions are composed of trial court judges sitting 20–25 days per year. Their infrequent sittings and limited organizational resources do not facilitate the development of policy. Moreover, since the division members are trial court judges, it is not clear that their colleagues would expect them to develop policies.

---

[7] A partial list includes the American Bar Association's Criminal Justice Standards Project (1980), the National Advisory Commission on Criminal Justice Standards and Goals (1973:116–118), the National Commission on Reform of Federal Criminal Laws (1970, Sec. 1291), and the President's Commission on Law Enforcement and the Administration of Justice (1967:145–146).

Even if the review divisions constructed sentencing standards, it is unclear how they would be communicated to other judges. In Massachusetts the review division gives no reasons for its decisions, and its decisions are communicated only to the trial court judge who sentenced the offender. In Connecticut reasons are supplied by the division and may be published, but in practice the reasons are very general and rarely appear in print.

This ineffectiveness should not be surprising. Under the indeterminate sentencing systems that characterized U.S. state systems for most of this century, the prison sentences that judges imposed were often nominal: the parole boards had primary responsibility for deciding how long people remained in prison. There was little reason for appellate judges to interfere with sentences that would be adjusted by a parole board in any event, especially when the effect of doing so would be to increase the appellate work load without benefit of correspondingly increased resources or personnel. Plea bargaining may also have impeded the development of appellate sentence review. In sentence bargains, the defendant expressly agrees to the sentence received and is not well placed to later object to that sentence. Judges may believe that defendants who have had charge bargains, similarly, are not entitled to object to any sentence that can be imposed for the offense to which the defendant pled guilty. Finally, sentencing was not subject to established criteria, except for the maximum sentences authorized by statute (or in some cases the common law), and there were, accordingly, no standards that an appellate judge could invoke to determine whether a particular sentence was excessive in length or otherwise inappropriate.

The prospects for meaningful appellate sentence review may be greater under some determinate sentencing systems than they were under indeterminate sentencing. Determinate systems have as one of their aims increased accountability for the sentences judges impose. Appellate review may be facilitated by the combination of published detailed standards for sentences and the requirements that judges give written reasons for imposing sentences that deviate from the apparently applicable standards. Together these new rules may provide substantial bases for assessing the appropriateness of appealed sentences. Under the Minnesota guidelines system, for example, judges are authorized to depart from the guidelines only when "substantial and compelling circumstances" are present and must provide a written statement of the reasons for doing so. Minnesota law (1978 Laws, Ch. 723, Sec. 11) enjoins the Minnesota supreme court to

. . . review the sentence imposed or stayed to determine whether the sentence is inconsistent with statutory requirements, unreasonable, inappropriate, excessive, unjustifiably disparate, or not warranted by the findings of fact issued by the district court.

There are a number of controversial questions associated with appellate sentence review. Should both prosecutors and defendants be entitled to appeal, or only defendants? Should sentence appeals be available in cases in which a sentence was explicitly or implicitly negotiated? Should an appellate court's power be limited to granting or denying the relief sought by the appealing party or should the court be able to increase the sentences of defendants who appeal (or decrease sentences appealed by the prosecutor)? Should appeals be heard by regular appellate courts, by specially constituted sentence appeals courts, or by panels of trial judges (as is now done in Massachusetts and Maryland)?

In summary, the changes in sentencing described in this section vary substantially in form and ambition. Some, like sentencing councils and institutes, seem primarily aimed at making decision making more self-conscious. Others, like classification of offenses, reasons requirements, presumptions, and voluntary/"descriptive" sentencing guidelines, are modest efforts to encourage greater consistency. Still others—bans on plea bargaining and abolition of parole—are radical breaks with tradition that signal a fundamental reappraisal of the criminal justice process. The other changes—statutory determinate sentencing, presumptive/ "prescriptive" sentencing guidelines, parole guidelines, mandatory minimum sentences, and appellate sentence review—can be seen as efforts to establish general sentencing criteria and to work toward sentencing that is evenhanded, accountable, and reasonably consistent.

Despite apparent agreement on the need to increase consistency and accountability in sentencing, however, the contemporary sentencing reform movement, in contrast to earlier movements in U.S. history, is characterized by sharp disagreements over the normative goals of sentencing (or the justifying aims of sanctions) and the amount of punishment appropriate for various situations (see Rothman, 1981). In addition, there are tensions between attainment of the normative goals of a reform and the interests and functional goals of people and organizations that constitute the criminal justice system. These conflicts and tensions have shaped contemporary reform efforts.

DEVELOPING GUIDELINES: MODELING AND DATA ISSUES

Social science research methods have been extensively used in the development of sentencing and parole guidelines. The three principal bodies of research concern: modeling past practices to guide or inform formulation of future standards; developing devices to predict recidivism; and projecting the impact of proposed changes. In principle, the methods involved are equally pertinent to legislative consideration of statutory presumptive sentencing laws, prosecutorial consideration of charging and plea-bargaining policies, and judicial sentencing commission and parole board consideration of guidelines. In practice, however, the methods have been most commonly used in parole and sentencing guidelines projects. The rest of this chapter reviews a series of research and policy issues that must be addressed when empirical analyses of past practices are used in establishing standards. Sentencing guidelines are treated as the archetypal case for illustrative purposes, but the discussion is generally applicable to other forms of sentencing standards.

MODELING PAST PRACTICE

The first empirically based sentencing standards were the U.S. parole guidelines. Although social scientists have long been developing "experience tables" that set out base-expectancy recidivism rates, the novel aspect of the Parole Decision-Making Project was that it used estimates of recidivism risk from experience tables as one of the factors in making parole release decisions (Gottfredson et al., 1975; see also Hoffman, 1975; Hoffman and Gottfredson, 1973).

Building on that parole guidelines experience, a sentencing guidelines project was established in Denver (Wilkins et al., 1978) to test the feasibility of developing similar, empirically based guidelines for sentencing. The researchers recognized that sentencing is a more complex process than parole decision making: parole boards decide whether to release prisoners, while judges decide both whom to imprison and for what maximum period. Nonetheless, the researchers (Wilkins et al., 1978:7)

[were] confident that there did exist an implicit policy formulation which acted as an underpinning for judicial decision-making in the sentencing area. Through careful analysis of present practice, [they] believed it possible to discover that implicit policy and make it explicit.

It was expected that this process would inform judges of the elements of that "implicit policy" so that some of those elements could be incorporated into sentencing guidelines.

The notion of descriptive guidelines implies an intent to do little more than create a statistical restatement of what a court has been doing. For this reason, judges have been expected to be less likely to resist guidelines than other sentencing reform innovations (Wilkins et al., 1978:30–31):

When comparing sentencing guidelines to legislatively mandated sentencing proposals, the most striking positive practical aspect of the guideline system is that it is judicially implemented and judicially controlled. . . . The use of sentencing guidelines should lead to less circumvention because it is the existing policies of the court itself that are initially being made explicit. . . . Guideline use . . . will significantly reduce unjustified variation from the established norm by making the established policy of the court explicit.

The first generation of sentencing guidelines led to several challenges to "descriptive" guidelines: first, whether such a thing as an "implicit policy" of a court exists; second, the degree to which the statistical models intended to capture the "implicit policy" reflected actual sentencing practice and, more generally, whether any simple linear model can adequately reflect the complex considerations that influence sentencing decisions (and thereby serve as the basis for establishing a sentence for any particular case); and third, whether the availability of models of past practice obviates the need to make normative choices when developing guidelines.

There remains considerable disagreement over whether any implicit policy exists in any court. Some argue that different judges invoke different considerations in any given case—some will focus on retributive principles while others are primarily concerned with incapacitation—and that shared considerations are weighed differently by different judges, so that talk of a common implicit policy can be misleading. Any model of past practice based on pooling cases of different judges may lead not to the discovery of a single implicit policy but to an average of several different implicit policies. This is most clearly illustrated when views on sentencing within a court are polarized and the averaged implicit policy constitutes a position that no individual judge would endorse.

Others hold that there are observable consistencies in the sentencing practices of different judges in a court. Judges all take offense seriousness into account, whether because a more serious offense deserves a more severe punishment or because a person who committed a more severe offense may be perceived as a greater threat to society if set free. Thus, analysis of past decisions of a court allows one to describe the practice of that court in terms of the case attributes that are taken into account, the weights associated with each attribute, and the particular mathematical form in which those weighted attributes can be combined to predict the expected sentence that would be handed down by a judge of that court in any particular case.

The degree to which any model represents actual court practices depends on the skills of the modeler in incorporating the complexity of the considerations that enter sentencing decisions. If a model represents a court's practices poorly, or if it incorporates discriminatory practices of a court, then its use would be undesirable and could be misleading as a guide to future decisions.

A model that is generally representative of a court's decisions on sentence outcome can have several policy uses. First, the articulation of past sentencing practices can serve as a standard for judges in their individual sentencing decisions, and also as a basis for possible reconsideration of prevailing practices in an iterative process of description, evaluation, and modification of sentencing policies. Second, information about past practices can provide a basis for assessing how much proposed standards diverge from traditional patterns. Because radical changes may engender resistance by those officials whose decisions are at issue, identification of sharp divergences may help policy makers anticipate likely sources of resistance. Third, knowledge of past practices can provide benchmark information that educates policy makers to the actual rather than the presumed operation of the criminal justice system. For example, legislators generally consider prison sentences in terms of statutory maximums while judges deal with maximum sentences to be served; knowledge of the much shorter prison terms actually served may facilitate informed consideration of realistic policy choices. Fourth, reliable data on past practices can be used to project the impact of alternative proposed policies and thereby enable decision makers to assess the costs and feasibility of various policy options.

A statistical model of past practice should not be used merely as a "sentencing machine" or as the sole or primary basis for formulating sentencing policy. Sentencing policy and practice are both dynamic; blindly incorporating past practice into "descriptive" sentencing guidelines may institutionalize a behavior that no longer reflects current practice or policy (if it ever did). Furthermore, the mathematical form of the model of past practice that has generally been used has been a simple linear model, but actual decision behavior almost inevitably uses much more complex logic; that logic should be explored in discussions with court personnel and should inform modeling efforts.

And even if a model can be formulated that is a credible statistical characterization of past practice, such a model cannot be transformed into "descriptive" sentencing guidelines without making ethical judgments. The Denver report (Wilkins et al., 1978:31–32) notes that

the research which undergirds the guidelines development, and the guidelines themselves, are essentially descriptive, not prescriptive. . . . They do not tell what the sentences or the criteria *ought* to be.

However, some ethical judgments are inevitably required.

In the case of the simplest hypothetical descriptive sentencing guidelines (in which no ethically objectionable variables, such as race, directly influence sentences), if there is unacceptably large variation in average judicial behavior, there must be a decision on how great a divergence from the mean will be accepted. The range of accepted variation will depend on the extent to which one wishes to reduce disparity, and it thus requires a judgment about the optimum amount of variation to be encouraged or permitted.

Even in this simple case, however, omitted or mismeasured variables can introduce errors in the estimates of effects and result in misleading guidelines, particularly if the omitted variables are correlated with included variables. If the omitted variables are not correlated with any of the included ones, the estimates of the parameters of the model will not be biased, but they will be inefficient. This could lead to errors in assessing the statistical significance of individual variables.

The problem becomes particularly important when an omitted variable is ethically objectionable. Suppose, for example, that the race variable is omitted from the model—presumably to avoid perpetuating any racial discrimination in sentences in the resulting guidelines—and that race is correlated with one of the included variables, such as prior record. Then, if race had actually mattered in the past, the estimation of the equation without the race variable will lead to an erroneously estimated equation and to guidelines that *build in* the ethically unacceptable effect of race by giving an excessive weight to prior record, which incorporates the role of race as well as that of prior record. Under such guidelines defendants who have poor prior records would receive severe sentences not simply because of the effect of prior record on judicial decisions but also because in the past those with poor prior records tended to be black and blacks were sentenced more severely. Past racism would thereby be incorporated in the guidelines through the prior-record variable.

Although one cannot eliminate the effect of ethically objectionable variables by eliminating them from the equation being estimated, it is possible to purge the models of past decisions of the contaminating effect of objectionable variables and use the purged equations in guidelines construction. However, this task also necessarily involves an ethical choice. The model must be formulated initially with the race variable (for example) included, and then any estimation of discrimination-free sentencing would use that model with the race variable suppressed. But in using the model with the purged estimates to inform future decisions, one must decide how *all* offenders should be treated: one can decide they should be treated as whites have previously been treated, as blacks have been treated, as the average of the prior treatment of blacks and whites, or as some other combination. (For a more technical discussion of this and related issues, see Fisher and Kadane [Volume II].)

Thus, "descriptive" guidelines do not provide a way to achieve a value-free depiction of past sentencing practices. Efforts to model past practices are useful tools in the development of sentencing guidelines, but the guidelines developers must inevitably make normative choices.

USING EMPIRICAL DATA

All sentencing guidelines are prescriptive in the sense that they involve normative choices and are hortatory in recommending future sentences; they vary with respect to the role of empirical data in their formulation. At one extreme are empirically derived guidelines purported to be based only on statistical description; these we regard as inappropriate and illusory. Efforts to develop such guidelines place researchers in the position of making policy choices, sometimes by default (see Coffee, 1978). At the other extreme are guidelines uninformed by considerations of empirical data on past practices or the likely impact of policy choices. While feasible, we view this approach (most closely approximated in past experiences of legislatures in adopting mandatory minimum sentencing laws) as undesirable. In the middle is a policy-development process in which empirical data on past practices and projections of future impact are considered and inform policy choices. Such a middle ground appears to have characterized the development of the U.S. Parole Board's guidelines and the Minnesota and Pennsylvania sentencing guidelines.

There have been many efforts to develop empirically informed sentencing guidelines. In each case, data have been collected on a sample of previously sentenced cases, generally from official court records. The efforts to model past practices have typically involved multivariate analyses aimed at identifying the combination of variables that explains the greatest proportion of variation in sentence outcomes.

The resulting multivariate models have several important limitations. First, they can only describe what judges have done on the average: individual deviations are lost, and polar opposites are represented only poorly by their midpoint. The variables reflected in the model may not be the ones that influenced the judge's decision (the judge may not have seen them or may have ignored them), and the data contained in court records, presentence reports, and similar official and agency records are often unreliable. Also, the records may fail to include influential variables (e.g., the defendant's demeanor). These factors contribute to the error in any model that is estimated. Furthermore, even if the models reflect the variables and their weights, they may not adequately reflect the logic with which the variables are combined. As a result, sentencing models seldom explain more than a third of the variance in sentences, often less, and consequently provide at best a blurred picture of past patterns.

These limitations require that modeling and data collection efforts be undertaken together. Both must start with careful observation of all the relevant participants, and especially prosecutors, probation officers, and judges. Representatives of each of these groups must be interviewed in systematic ways to elicit the considerations that they believe enter their own decisions and recommendations. This will give rise to the formulation of models that are potentially richer than those based solely on a simple linear enumeration of the variables available from court records. In developing data collection forms, researchers must be sensitive to the variables identified in interviews. If those variables are not available in the records, they may have to be collected independently or prospectively as part of the research.

Despite their flaws, multivariate analyses can be useful. They can provide crude but otherwise unavailable information on the relative weight apparently given by judges to important variables like offense seriousness and prior record. Multivariate analyses can be used to test for interactions among variables, e.g., the influence of offense seriousness on sentence type and the influence on that relationship of a third factor, such as race. They can suggest how the various relevant variables have been treated in the past; they can warn of the potential role of inappropriate variables; they can permit comparison of the treatment of typical cases in the past with normative judgments as to how they should be treated. They should not, however, be viewed as dictating sentencing standards. Rather they should represent a starting point for the application of judgment and expertise. In many jurisdictions, these models, however crude, would represent the first attempt at articulating existing sentencing practices, and, if used with discretion, such efforts are likely to lead to more rational policy discussion and development.

Many of the methodological and modeling issues raised by multivariate analyses in guidelines development are not generically different from those raised by sentencing research generally. The problems of omitted variables, variable measurement and scaling, measurement error biases, and selection error biases discussed in Chapter 2 are equally troubling in this applied context. Sparks (Volume II) reviews the efforts of a number of sentencing guidelines projects to gather data, model past practices, and translate the findings into empirically informed guidelines, and he discusses specific difficulties of those endeavors.

Assuming that guidelines development will continue to include efforts to model past practices, three aspects of data analysis warrant consideration: data definition, data collection, and sample design.

DATA DEFINITION

There is no simple answer to the question of what data on past practices should be collected. At one extreme, the New Jersey guidelines project codebook contained 847 variables because the project staff "decided that every bit of data could possibly affect sentences, and that therefore no assumptions should be made at the onset to dismiss any data" (McCarthy, 1978:10). At the other extreme, information might be collected only on variables that are both theoretically reasonable and believed to be correlated with sentencing practices—namely the variables that will be used in later analyses and in the formulation of guidelines.

Neither polar strategy is satisfactory. Collection of data on all conceivable variables is likely to prove unwieldy and to be highly vulnerable to problems of missing items and data unreliability. Data even on such relatively concrete offender variables as prior record are often incomplete and inaccurate. Data on offender variables like past employment, education, and social stability are less reliable and are more often missing. Data on variables such as offenders' parents, income, employment, and place of birth are often unavailable in the records of operating criminal justice agencies and are likely to be of exceedingly low reliability. In the New Jersey effort, for example, data on "education of offender's parent/guardian" were recorded in only 7 percent of the cases, and the reliability of these data is unknown (McCarthy, 1978:16, fn12; Sparks and Stecher, 1979). Perhaps the best prescription is that data should be collected on all variables that are reliably available and that can reasonably be believed to be associated with outcomes in a nontrivial number of cases. It would also be important to attempt to determine the kinds of information that are available to judges at the time sentences are imposed.

Data Collection

All of the empirically informed sentencing guidelines projects to date have collected data retrospectively, usually from court records and probation office presentence reports. Several serious problems arise with such data: some official data may not have been available to the judge at sentencing; the judge may not have used some of the information that was available; and environmental and subjective factors (e.g., defendant demeanor) that may have been influential in the decision are not contained in readily available court records. Models based on data not available to or used by a judge and missing data on the factors that actually influenced a sentencing decision will be subject to potentially large errors in estimation. One alternative strategy that has been suggested (Sparks, 1981) is prospective data collection, i.e., obtaining data on cases sentenced after beginning the research, using observation and interviews as well as official records. This would usually require a longer period for guidelines development to ensure a rich sample of sentenced cases.

Sample Design

Sample design choices depend on the intended uses of the data. For example, quite large samples may be required if separate models are to be developed for subcategories of defendants. At least several hundred cases would be required for each subset if separate models were to be developed for (1) different offense classes, (2) guilty-plea and trial dispositions, (3) male and female defendants, (4) white, black, hispanic, native-American, and other racial or ethnic groups, or (5) for separate judicial districts, counties, or urban-suburban-rural areas. In addition, concern for missing data and for variables that have skewed distributions would argue for large or stratified samples. On the other hand, all these models need not be formulated on independent samples, and more efficient sampling designs are possible. However, the sample must be large enough to validate the statistical model of sentencing on a sample of cases that were not used in model construction. To control for problems of changing case mix or of changing judicial practice, the validation sample ideally should be contemporaneous with the construction sample.

Whatever the method used to develop the data base, the resulting data and estimated models are but raw material for informing the development of sentencing standards. Guidelines developers must still confront a large number of policy and technical choices.

DEVELOPING GUIDELINES: POLICY AND TECHNICAL CHOICES

Reformers seeking to change official behavior and generate some desired distribution of sentences are subject to a recurring tension between the normative and policy goals they wish to achieve and the need to obtain cooperation from decision makers. They must figure out how to make officials do what they want them to do. The tensions between reformers' desires to specify criteria that exactly express their normative goals and the need to promulgate standards in forms that will gain compliance from decision makers are present in a number of critical policy and technical choices. Some of these choices can be illustrated by reviewing options examined and selected by the Minnesota Sentencing Guidelines Commission.

UNAVOIDABLE POLICY CHOICES

The Guidelines Offense

Guilty plea rates vary, but typically between 75 and 95 percent of convictions in a jurisdiction result from guilty pleas (*Sourcebook*, 1980:Table 5.19), many of which follow plea negotiations. Where charge bargaining is prevalent, the conviction offense is the offense to which the defendant pled guilty, not necessarily the offense that was originally charged. Policy makers must decide whether sentencing standards should be applied to the conviction offense, which may be an artifact of plea bargaining, or to some other offense measure. No solution is ideal. Using conviction offenses rewards defendants who have the most effective lawyers and punishes those who, for whatever reason (sometimes naivete or contrition), decide to plead guilty to the offense originally charged. Other options are available. For example, a critical provision of the Model Sentencing and Corrections Act (National Conference of Commissioners on Uniform State Laws, 1979) prescribes: "In determining the appropriate guideline to follow the court shall consider the nature and characteristics of the criminal conduct involved *without regard* to the offense charged" [emphasis added]. Such provisions are common in parole guideline systems. Basing guidelines on defendant's "actual offense behavior" arguably deprives defendants of the benefits of the bargains in return for which they waived their trial rights and can result in the punishment of defendants for alleged but unproven behavior. The choice is between a principled approach that may be impractical and a realistic choice that is unprincipled. The Minnesota Sentencing Guidelines Commission opted for principle and elected to base guidelines on conviction offenses because "serious legal and ethical questions would be raised if punishment were to be determined on the basis of alleged, but unproven, behavior" (Minnesota Sentencing Guidelines Commission, 1981:2).

Guilty-Plea Discounts

"Plea or trial" is a commonly used variable in sentencing research. Substantial evidence suggests that defendants who plead guilty receive sentencing leniency or a discount in exchange for a guilty plea (see Chapter 2). If such discounts are common, and if counsel and judges believe they are necessary to induce the majority of defendants to plead guilty, sentencing policy makers are presented with a dilemma. If they provide discounts for guilty pleas, as suggested by Schulhofer (1979, 1980), they can be accused of encouraging an unattractive aspect of the criminal justice process and of placing unwarranted pressure on defendants to plead guilty—especially when the guilty plea means the difference between probation and prison. If they do not provide discounts, they can be accused of inviting future circumvention of guidelines because they have deliberately defied courtroom conventions in which defendants, lawyers, and judges have an interest.

The Minnesota commission "determined that the severity of offenders' sanctions should not vary depending on whether or not they exercise constitutional rights during the adjudication process" (Minnesota Sentencing Guidelines Commission, 1981:13). In other words, willingness or refusal to plead guilty and waive one's constitutional right to a trial and related rights may not be used to justify departures from applicable guidelines based on conviction offenses. But the informal practice of discounting through a charge-bargaining arrangement in which the defendant agrees to plead guilty to a lesser charge has not been regulated by the Minnesota guidelines.

Social Variables

Most empirical analyses of sentencing practices and outcomes have concluded that the seriousness of the offense and the offender's prior record (e.g., prior convictions or incarcerations, custody status at the time of the offense) are the best predictors of sentences. Various status variables (e.g., education, employment, marital status, and residential stability) are also commonly thought to be germane to sentencing outcomes. But such variables are significantly correlated with race, class, income level, and sex. While direct use of race as a sentencing criterion would be unconstitutional, the use of other criteria correlated with race is unlikely to be declared unconstitutional (see Coffee, 1976), and the use of variables that are correlated with class or sex is even less likely to present constitutional problems.

The Minnesota commission identified status variables "as factors that should not be used as reasons for departure from the presumptive sentence because these factors are highly correlated with sex, race, or income levels" (Minnesota Sentencing Guidelines Commission, 1981:13). The other option, of course, is to use such variables, especially when they have been shown to be significantly predictive of sentence outcomes. Early versions of the U.S. Parole Commission's guidelines used employment, educational, and residential pattern variables in a "salient factor score" used to place prisoners in parole prognosis categories. Over the years, however, for policy reasons the Parole Commission has eliminated those variables. The version that became effective September 1, 1981, contained none of them.

Urban/Rural Differences

Much anecdotal and some empirical evidence (see Martin, Volume II) suggests that, in many states, there are significant local and regional differences in sentencing severity. In Pennsylvania, for example, offenses against the person are punished substantially more severely in suburban and rural counties than in Philadelphia. The Minnesota Sentencing Guidelines Commission also found evidence of some regional differences in sentencing, especially for offenses against the person. There is a tension between the generally perceived need to establish uniform sentencing criteria throughout the jurisdiction contributing to the state prison population (it is in prison that disparities become most apparent, when prisoners compare their sentences) and the competing consideration of deference to local experiences, culture, and attitudes. It is difficult in principle to justify sentencing variations that are attributable solely to local experiences and attitudes, but as a practical matter, uniform state standards that depart substantially from local practices are especially likely to be resisted.

In Minnesota the guidelines commission's decision to promulgate standards that do not authorize local differences does not appear to have been especially controversial. While no jurisdiction with statewide guidelines has explicitly taken account of local differences or authorized their invocation as the justification for departures from otherwise applicable standards, in some states this issue has been sidestepped by adopting guidelines with wide ranges that implicitly allow regional differences in sentencing to continue. In Pennsylvania the initially proposed guidelines would have resulted in substantial increases in sentence severity in Philadelphia and Pittsburgh and decreases of severity in suburban and rural areas. This aroused strong opposition to "uniformity," which contributed to the rejection of the guidelines and their subsequent revision to permit broad judicial discretion, indirectly allowing for local variation.

Comment

The preceding list of unavoidable policy choices does not exhaust the variety of major issues that must be resolved in formulating sentencing standards. Some others include: whether prior arrests not resulting in conviction may be considered in sentencing standards; whether juvenile court records may be considered, and to what extent; and whether some sort of "decay" device should be developed so that prior criminality ceases to be considered or is given less significance after some period of time at liberty without offending.

The policy questions discussed in this section are subject to a common tension: they are often perceived and discussed in terms of principle, yet practical concerns urge pragmatic compromises. To the extent that policy makers resolve issues in terms of principle, they risk irrelevance: implementation of policy requires the cooperation of the practitioners who operate the process. The more that sentencing standards are viewed as unrealistic and unresponsive to real needs, the less likely is compliance with them. Minnesota's decision not to acknowledge a guilty-plea discount in its sentencing guidelines, for example, presents prosecutors and defense lawyers with a choice: either to stop negotiating pleas and sentencing concessions or to devise ways to reward guilty pleas (by charge reductions) even though the guidelines would appear to ban that practice. Of course responses by practitioners need not be uniform. Prosecutors could manipulate guidelines for some kinds of defendants but not others. For example, persons charged with less serious offenses could be offered charge concessions that would make a prison sentence unlikely, while serious offenders might not be offered any concessions. Preliminary analysis of changing practices in Minnesota suggests that this is what is happening in aggravated robbery cases (Minnesota Sentencing Guidelines Commission, 1982).

PRACTICAL ISSUES IN STRUCTURING SENTENCING DISCRETION

In establishing criteria for sentencing that will be followed, the developers of guidelines face a number of practical questions with respect to approach, specificity, and methods for scaling offense and offender variables. Mechanisms to structure sentencing vary in the range of the factors to be considered and in the specificity of the criteria to be used for decision making. At one extreme are traditional indeterminate sentencing systems, in which statutes specify only maximum (and occasionally minimum) lawful sentences for each offense. At the other extreme, one could design a detailed sentencing schedule that specifies precisely the in/out and sentence-length decisions for each offense type. Most recently adopted statutory presumptive sentencing and guidelines systems fall between these extremes.

Approaches for Formatting and Presenting Sentencing Standards

Sentencing reform initiatives have taken various approaches in formatting and presenting sentencing criteria. Some are quite complex and involve many variables; others are simple. Theoretically the differences among them are purely formal, since each approach could be designed to use the same information in making sentencing decisions. As is indicated below, however, the differences may have important effects in practice.

Statutory Formulation of Standards   Statutory presumptive sentence laws are one form of sentencing standard. Typically they specify presumptive sentences or ranges. (See Lagoy et al. [1978] for descriptions of determinate sentence laws in California, Illinois, Indiana, and Maine.) Most such statutes limit their specifications to the dimension of offense severity; other salient sentencing information is left for consideration by judges as aggravating or mitigating circumstances. In contrast, California's Uniform Determinate Sentencing Law provides for sentence "enhancements" based on various prior-record and offense circumstances. Although the California law is expressed in conventional statutory prose form, in substance California's sentencing criteria could be expressed as a matrix. For robbery, the matrix would look like Table 3-2. The rows divide robberies into three categories (ordinary, aggravated, and mitigated) in order to specify base terms. The columns show the incre-

TABLE 3–2   California Robbery Matrix

Offense	Years				
	Base Term	Enhanced Term			
		1	2	3	4 . . .
Aggravated robbery	5	6	7	8	9
Ordinary robbery	3	4	5	6	7
Mitigated robbery	2	3	4	5	6

mental consequences of having various prior incarcerations and offense circumstances (weapon use, serious injury, large property loss or damage) pled and proved.

Although no other state has adopted statutory sentencing criteria that are as detailed as California's, a number of bills prescribing detailed statutory sentence criteria were introduced in the U.S. Congress in the mid-1970s. The proposed Fair and Certain Punishment Act (S. 3752, 1976), for example, subdivided offense definitions on the basis of the offender's intent and the resulting harm and specified a presumptive sentence for each subcategory that could be increased or decreased by no more than 40 percent for aggravating or mitigating circumstances.

Matrix Format   The original U.S. Parole Commission guidelines were expressed as a matrix. The earliest state parole guidelines (in Minnesota, Oregon, and Washington), and the initial "descriptive" sentencing guidelines (in Denver, Chicago, and Philadelphia) also used a matrix format, as do most of the parole and sentencing guidelines systems now in effect.

The widespread adoption of the matrix approach results largely from its practicality. It is compact and efficient and can convey information much more efficiently than can statutory prose. This makes it easy to understand and apply and thereby fosters consistency. Offense severity is ordinally scaled, and offender scores are scaled and uniformly applied. Some variables are explicitly included, and this implicitly diminishes the significance of others that might otherwise be used. Some variables are explicitly excluded. Consequently, there is less likelihood of arbitrary choices or policy inconsistencies that arise from oversight.

Sequential Guidelines   Another approach, illustrated by the Washington State parole guidelines, involves a sequential series of calculations. There are guidelines for eight different offense categories (e.g., robbery, property offenses, assault, drugs). For each offense category the guidelines specify variables that, if present, prescribe addition of a specified increment (or range) of months of imprisonment. For each offender a term of months is calculated for the present offense. A similar prior-record guideline sets out prior conviction variables, each specifying increments in months. The sum of these increments is then added to the offender's base sentence. Finally, a "public safety" guideline containing variables characterizing criminal history, social stability, and institutional behavior is used to predict recidivism probabilities and on the basis of that calculation to reduce the prison term by a specified percentage. The guideline release date is determined by combining the results of the present offense, prior-record, and "public safety" calculations. The range and complexity of detail that can be considered in sentencing using sequential guidelines is greater than that available through matrices but less than with computerized guidelines.

Formula Guidelines   In this approach, exemplified by the Massachusetts sentencing guidelines, the applicable guideline sentence is determined by use of a weighted formula. Values are assigned to the seriousness of the offense (A), to weapons use (B), to injury inflicted (C), and to prior convictions (D), in the formula $X = 2.1A + 9B + 9C + 1.6D$. The weights derive in part from regression coefficients obtained during efforts to develop a statistical characterization of sentencing practices in Massachusetts. The guideline sentence range in months is given by X plus or minus 50 percent of X.

Manuals   Several jurisdictions have developed highly particularized guidelines manuals that provide detailed offense and offender criteria for every offense type. New Jersey's statewide guidelines may be the extreme case (see Sparks and Stecher, 1979). Because the manuals contain a mass of detailed information, considerable internal cross-referencing is required in order to use them.

The primary advantage of such manuals is that their specificity provides highly detailed offense-specific information. This may be particularly appropriate under a guidelines system like New Jersey's in which the manual contains the raw aggregate data derived from a guideline construction research effort and in effect provides a judge with information on past practice but then leaves to the judge the decision of how to use that information. The basic disadvantage of such a complex approach is that it may be especially vulnerable to calculation errors.

Computer-Assisted Guidelines   One obvious solution to the complexity of a manual lies in coding its rules into a computer. The Institute for Law and Social Research, Inc., and Yankelovich, Skelly and White, Inc. (1981:xviii, hereafter cited as INSLAW) recently proposed development of computer-calculated guidelines:

As the offense and offender descriptions grow rich in detail. . . the mechanics of translating all that detail into specific sentences will grow increasingly complex. In an era of sophisticated information processing capabilities this problem is clearly one that is not especially difficult.

In principle, there need be no difference between computerized guidelines and guidelines that take other forms. The sentencing equations in any sentencing system are intended to transform the attributes of a case and an offender into a guidelines sentence. This can be done with the aid of a printed form that leads a court staff person through a series of calculations, including reference to some guideline matrix, or by a computer, probably more easily and with less chance of mechanical error.

However, the INSLAW report (1981:VI-3) concludes that "computer assistance in sentencing may be an idea whose time has not yet come." Sentencing is highly symbolic, expressing as it does community denunciation of an offender and often an effort by the judge to impose a sentence that is commensurate with the offender's blameworthiness. As a matter of fundamental justice, individuals are entitled to a punishment process in which the circumstances of their offenses, and any aggravating or mitigating circumstances, are taken into account. Thus, any use of computer assistance in generating guideline sentences must take considerable care to avoid being seen as a mysterious and mechanical "dehumanization" of this process.

A related proposal involves computer-assisted sentencing in which the judge (or the probation officer) can retrieve statistical information on selected aspects of past practices on a case-by-case basis (see Rhodes and Conly, 1981:Ch. 16). If a decision maker wants to know whether the educational attainment of robbery defendants has been associated with sentence severity in the past, that information can be obtained using a computer. This scenario is not peculiar to guidelines systems; in substance it involves no more than a standard computerized information retrieval system, different only in its efficiency from conventional statistical records systems.

General Observations Simple approaches, like prose guidelines and matrices, are easy to understand and so intuitively clear. Such approaches, therefore, may enhance the credibility of the sentencing standards that they express and thereby be more likely to elicit cooperation. This may be particularly desirable when decision makers are not legally obliged to comply with the standards. Conversely, when policy makers want to prescribe detailed, weighted, criteria involving complex combinations of variables for sentencing, using a computer is much less cumbersome than using many cross-referenced matrices. When decision makers' compliance can be controlled, the nonintuitive character of more complex approaches may be less important. Whether such approaches result in diminished credibility of the guidelines in the eyes of decision makers, and accordingly in lower rates of compliance with them, is a subject on which interviews or experimental research might provide insights.

Organizing Principles of Guidelines Matrices

Existing guidelines systems range from those like Minnesota's and Pennsylvania's, in which all sentences are included in one general matrix, to those like New Jersey's, which effectively establishes a separate matrix for each offense type. In between are a number of guidelines systems that use different organizing principles.[8]

Type of Offender   The U.S. Parole Commission's guidelines (September 1, 1981) consist of two matrices, one applicable to "youthful offenders" and persons imprisoned under the Narcotics Addict Rehabilitation Act (NARA) and the other applicable to all other adult, federal prisoners. Each matrix encompasses all federal offenses and uses a common method of grouping offenders on the basis of predicted group recidivism rates. Recommended prison terms in the youthful offender/NARA matrix are shorter than those for the other matrix.

Statutory Offense Classification   Several guidelines systems have developed separate matrices for each statutory offense class. Thus the Denver guidelines (as set forth in Kress, 1980: Appendix A) contain separate matrices for three felony classes and three misdemeanor classes. The principal argument for this organizing principle is that it defers to legislative assessments of the relative seriousness of the various statutory classes. For similar reasons, the Michigan guidelines provide matrices that distinguish among offenses on the basis of the statutory maximum sentences. In several jurisdictions, guidelines developers have concluded that individual statutory classifications can cover an extremely wide range of offense behavior under a single offense type, thereby inadequately distinguishing among offenses, and that such classifications emphasize the worst case in setting a maximum rather than reflecting punishment for the usual case. Hence, developers have created their own scales of offense severity; the Pennsylvania sentencing guidelines and the U.S. Parole Commission's guidelines are examples.

---

[8] Guidelines and related materials are developed and used by operating agencies and tend to be unavailable in published form. Kress (1980) discusses at length the Denver, Newark, Cook County, Philadelphia, Phoenix, and Washington guidelines and in appendixes reprints the guidelines and informational booklets for Denver, Philadelphia, Phoenix, and the state of Washington.

Generic Offense Groupings   Several of the early "descriptive" guidelines systems grouped offenses in broad general categories. For example, the Essex County (Newark) sentencing guidelines contained four grids (violent, drug, property, and miscellaneous crimes), and the Philadelphia sentencing guidelines contained two grids (offenses against the person and all other offenses). The Washington parole guidelines contain eight generic groupings (murder II, manslaughter, sex offenses, robbery, assault, property offenses, drugs, and escape). One advantage of the generic approach is that it permits greater specificity of criteria than statutory offense classes.

Linking Offender Score to Current Offense

Guidelines may be designed to link an offender's prior-record score to the class and seriousness of the current offense in various ways. The Washington parole guidelines, for example, accord different weights to various kinds of prior felony convictions, depending on the present offense. Thus, a prior assault conviction adds 48 months to a base sentence when the current offense is murder; 24 months for assault; 12 months for robbery; and 6 months for drugs. By contrast, although statutory offense classes are typically heterogeneous, guidelines like the original ones in Denver use the same criminal history criteria for all persons sentenced under a single matrix and cannot weight prior-record items differently in accordance with their relevance to the nature of the current offense.

The same sentencing criteria can be expressed under various grouping systems. Even a single comprehensive matrix system like Minnesota's could be particularized by adopting different criminal history scoring systems for each offense type: the consequences of having a particular prior-record score could be uniform even though the factors contributing to the scores might vary among offense types. For example, separate scoring systems could be devised for each offense so that a single variable (e.g., a prior rape conviction) might represent three points in connection with a current rape conviction, two points for a current assault conviction, one for theft, and zero for tax evasion.

Specificity of Sentencing Standards

An important goal of sentencing policy changes is achieving substantial consistency in sentencing patterns while permitting special treatment for special cases. For example, under the presumptive Minnesota sentencing guidelines, the judge is directed to impose sentences from within narrow ranges (plus or minus 5–8 percent from the midpoint) "unless the case involves substantial and compelling circumstances." When the sentence departs from the guidelines the judge must provide a written explanation as to why the sentence imposed is more appropriate than that provided in the guidelines. The adequacy of this explanation is subject to review by the state supreme court.

The aim of "descriptive" sentencing guidelines was similar. The developers sought to establish guideline ranges that covered 80–85 percent of the sentences imposed in the construction and validation samples. Some of the remaining "outliers," the other 15–20 percent, may have been extraordinary cases, but others may have been ordinary cases that received aberrant sentences. The developers of those guidelines expected that extraordinary cases would continue to receive extraordinary treatment (see, e.g., Wilkins, 1981). The ordinary outliers were a primary target of descriptive sentencing guidelines: the judge, considering imposing a 5-year sentence in a case for which, according to the guidelines, 85 percent of convicted persons receive a sentence of 1–1½ years, may reconsider and impose a sentence from within the guideline range.

To achieve greater consistency in sentencing and at the same time allow sufficient flexibility to accommodate cases presenting special circumstances, guidelines developers have had to address various other technical issues.

Points and Ranges Developers of sentencing guidelines distinguish between points and ranges. A point guideline specifies a single punishment for a particular combination of offense and offender circumstances: for example, persons convicted of burglary who have two previous felony convictions shall be imprisoned for 17 months. A range guideline specifies outer limits on permissible sentences: for example, persons convicted of burglary who have two previous felony convictions shall be imprisoned for a specified term from within the range of 14 to 20 months. Point guidelines have been discussed in the literature (e.g., Sparks et al., 1982) but have not been adopted in any jurisdiction.

The practical distinction is between ranges and point/range combinations. The U.S. Parole Commission's guidelines provide a range in months from which examiners are to set the release date in ordinary cases. Most statutory determinate sentence laws (see, e.g., Lagoy et al., 1978:Table 5) and various sentencing guideline systems (e.g., those in Massachusetts and Michigan) also establish range guidelines.

A few jurisdictions, including Minnesota (see Table 3–1), have adopted point/range sentencing criteria that designate a single term of months for ordinary cases and also a range within which a sentence can vary to reflect aggravating and mitigating circumstances that warrant some modification but do not justify a major deviation from the ordinary sentence. As noted above, California established three prison terms for every felony (for robbery, the terms are 2, 3, and 5 years). Section 1170(b) of the California Penal Code provides "the court shall order imposition of the middle term unless there are circumstances in aggravation or mitigation of the crime." Thus for robbery, 3 years is the point and 2–5 years is the range. The enhancements have the effect of raising the upper limit of the range.

No research findings have been published comparing the effects of range and point/range guidelines on compliance rates. Proponents of the Minnesota guidelines suggest that point/range guidelines are optimally structured to foster compliance and allow flexibility. By setting a point, they provide a benchmark. By setting a narrow range within which judges may set sentences in ordinary cases to reflect special circumstances, they encourage judges to adjust sentence lengths within the range rather than to depart from it. And by permitting departures from the range when there are substantial and compelling circumstances, subject to a reasons requirement and review, they also accommodate highly unusual cases without sacrificing the integrity of the guidelines.

The Widths of Ranges   Guidelines systems and statutory presumptive sentence laws differ substantially in the widths of the sentence ranges from which decision makers may choose. At one extreme, the Massachusetts guideline range (for date of first parole eligibility) is the number of months calculated from the Massachusetts guideline formula, plus or minus 50 percent. Thus, if the formula yielded 60 months, the guideline range would be 30 to 90 months. At the other extreme, the Minnesota sentencing guidelines range is the point guideline term plus or minus only 5–8 percent, and the Washington parole guideline range is the term of months determined in accordance with the state's sequential calculation plus or minus 12.5 percent. Table 3–3 sets out sample ranges for the Massachusetts, Minnesota, and Washington guidelines.

The Minnesota and Washington guideline ranges are narrow. The Massachusetts ranges are wide. If Minnesota judges and Washington parole hearing examiners comply with their guidelines in a substantial majority of cases, one would expect those jurisdictions to achieve substantial consistency in the lengths of prison sentences served. However, because the ranges are narrow, one might expect that decision makers will depart from the narrow guidelines more often than under broad ranges. Conversely, one might predict relatively high apparent compliance rates with the Massachusetts sentencing guidelines, especially for longer sentences, although critics of sentencing disparities might not be

TABLE 3–3   Ranges of Presumptive Sentences Under
Massachusetts, Minnesota, and Washington Guidelines

State	Presumptive Sentence			
	10^a	20^a	30^a	60^a
Massachusetts[b]	5–15	10–30	15–45	30–90
Minnesota[c]	9–11	19–21	28–32	57–63
Washington[d]	9–11	18–22	26–34	53–67

[a] Midpoint of interval (in months).
[b] Actual Massachusetts range.
[c] Ranges derived from Minnesota sentencing guidelines grid.
[d] Estimated and rounded.

impressed by a claim of 85 percent compliance rates with guidelines that specify such broad ranges for permissible sentences.

Questions about ranges cannot be answered without discussion of normative premises and without reference to the context in which the guidelines will be implemented. An adherent of the goal of just deserts, who places high value on equality in sentencing and the reduction of disparities, would favor narrow ranges. One with utilitarian goals, in contrast, might urge broad ranges that permit lengthy incarceration when incapacitative, deterrent, or rehabilitative considerations appear germane and relatively short incarceration in other cases.

One's view of the width of ranges may also depend on predictions about official reactions to guidelines. If one predicts that decision makers will reject the precise guidance of narrow guidelines, a plausible reform tactic would involve setting ranges wider than would ideally be preferred. If narrow guidelines were often rejected, there would be no residual guidance, and the result might be wide disparities in sentences. Broader guidelines might channel more decisions into the guideline range and thereby achieve less overall disparity in sentences. In a context in which administrative or other controls, such as credible appellate review systems, can be brought to bear on decision makers, the prospects for compliance with narrow ranges may be greater than when such controls are absent. Thus narrow guidelines may be more practicable in Washington, where parole examiners are subject to administrative controls, and in Minnesota, where appellate courts review sentences and a sentencing commission monitors sentences, than in Massachusetts, where judicial compliance with the guidelines is voluntary and judges can simply ignore the guidelines if they find them too confining.

In/Out Guidelines   Systems of sentencing criteria, including those that have adopted sophisticated graduated standards for determining sentence lengths for persons to be imprisoned, face a more difficult dilemma in finding a satisfactory approach for deciding who should be imprisoned. Even California's detailed statutory standards do not tell judges whom to imprison. Most convicted California felons are eligible for probation or suspended sentences, and the law is silent on that choice (except for a few offenses that are not "probationable").

The Minnesota sentencing guidelines embody a clear policy on the question, but they can also result in outcomes that may be viewed as unfair. Under the Minnesota sentencing matrix, cells below the "in/out line" (see Table 3–1) specify a state prison sentence; those above that line specify a sentence other than state prison. The magnitude of the difference in sentences is highlighted by the cells adjoining the in/out line. A prior felony conviction adds one point to a defendant's criminal history score. Thus the difference between two persons convicted of second-degree assault but whose sentences are governed by adjacent cells could be one felony conviction. Yet one defendant (Row VI, Column 3) should receive a nonimprisonment sentence and the other (Row VI, Column 2) should receive a 34-month prison sentence—a dramatic difference. It is possible, and ironic, that the Minnesota guidelines, generally designed to reduce disparities and treat similar cases similarly, may result in increasing the differences in sentences received by similarly situated offenders whose cases fall close to the in/out line, particularly in light of the continuation of charge negotiation that may affect the offender's location in the guideline grid.

The Minnesota commission carefully considered the philosophical and policy implications of the placement of the line on the grid. Yet any rigid single line (or mandatory decision rule) treats adjacent cells on different sides of the line differently. And in Minnesota the impact of that line on sentences is very substantial, although the difference between cases just above and below it is not necessarily greater than the difference found between cases in adjacent cells on the same side of the line. Thus both the policy embodied in the line and its impact in cases is likely to be particularly troubling to judges and others concerned about the fairness and appropriateness of the punishment in cases involving close calls. While someone who supports retributive goals may be comfortable with the placement of the line on the Minnesota grid and the commission's effort to treat similarly situated offenders the same and to eliminate certain factors defined as illegal from decision making in individual cases, a utilitarian who is more concerned with individualized justice may be more troubled by a clear policy that is rigidly or arbitrarily applied or overlooks subtle distinctions in individual cases.

The same dilemma also arises in "descriptive" sentencing guidelines. Suppose statistical efforts to characterize past practices indicate that persons falling within a particular cell have been imprisoned in 55 percent of cases. The choices presented to the guidelines developers are to make that 55/45 cell an "in" cell, which would change sentencing practice if followed and probably undermine the guidelines in the eyes of judges who know that this is an ambiguous category of cases, or to adopt guidelines that have probation as one end of the guideline range. This latter option acknowledges the ambiguity of cases in that cell but provides no guidance to judges.

The alternatives—a clear but possibly arbitrary policy or no policy guidance—pose a difficult dilemma because in many jurisdictions a substantial proportion of cases in which imprisonment is a realistic possibility fall in cells abutting the in/out line. In developing its guidelines, the Minnesota Sentencing Guidelines Commission conducted a study of case dispositions for a weighted sample (weighted N = 4,369) of cases decided in fiscal 1978.[9] After designing the grid, the commission examined what percentage of persons would have been imprisoned, by guideline cell, had the guidelines been in effect (Knapp, 1982; Minnesota Sentencing Guidelines Commission, 1980, 1982). Table 3–4 shows that 575 of the preguideline cases analyzed in the study would have fallen within sentencing guideline cells that specify imprisonment. Slightly more than half of those defendants (302) would have fallen within cells abutting the in/out line. Another 542 defendants would have fallen within nonimprisonment cells immediately above the in/out line. Thus only 273 persons would have fallen clearly within the imprisonment cells, and 844 would have fallen in the cells adjacent to the in/out line. In other words, 83 percent of the convicted offenders for whom prison was a realistic option fell in guideline cells abutting the in/out line.

We do not pretend to have an answer to this problem. It may lie in having more refined and detailed criteria for categories of cases that abut an in/out line than are required for those cells that pertain to low-probability or high-probability imprisonment cases.

---

[9] The Minnesota Sentencing Guidelines Commission's dispositional study consisted of data on 2,332 cases sentenced before guidelines: a 42 percent random sample of male offenders convicted and receiving a felony or gross misdemeanor sentence in fiscal 1978 and all females similarly convicted in that year. Counties with large Indian populations were oversampled. The cases were then weighted to reflect the distribution of all felony convictions.

TABLE 3–4 Hypothetical Application of Minnesota Guidelines to Preguideline Cases Sentenced in Fiscal 1978, Classified by Guideline Categories

Offense Severity	History/Risk Score							TOTALS
	0	1	2	3	4	5	6+	
I	4 (474)	13 (126)	44 (69)	59 (32)	56 (23)	26 (8)	74 (16)	15 [a] (748)
II	6 (477)	24 (90)	27 (82)	56 (24)	85 (14)	53 (18)	100 (11)	16 (716)
III	6 (534)	16 (171)	40 (100)	57 (79)	79 (35)	72 (16)	58 (21)	20 (956)
IV	6 (563)	19 (185)	42 (139)	44 (34)	86 (30)	62 (23)	77 (11)	19 (986)
V	17 (119)	37 (34)	78 (14)	83 (13)	80 (10)	100 (2)	50 (4)	33 (197)
VI[b]	12 (231)	22 (78)	45 (58)	86 (15)	66 (13)	61 (14)	100 (2)	25 (412)
VII	39 (97)	68 (57)	86 (28)	85 (15)	100 (11)	100 (4)	100 (7)	62 (219)
VIII	42 (46)	38 (26)	87 (16)	100 (6)	100 (10)	100 (2)	— (0)	58 (106)
IX	35 (6)	— (0)	— (0)	100 (4)	100 (2)	— (0)	— (0)	68 (13)
X	100 (13)	100 (5)	100 (4)	— (0)	— (0)	— (0)	— (0)	100 (17)
TOTALS	9 (2571)	24 (774)	45 (511)	63 (222)	80 (149)	62 (88)	77 (72)	23 (4387)

NOTE: The numbers of cases shown in the figure are estimates of the cases represented by the sample, i.e., 4,369 cases estimated from the 2,332 cases in sample. The weighting procedure used to estimate the cases contains a rounding procedure that will occasionally cause the product of the percent and number of cases to yield fractions.

[a] In/out line: the presumptive guideline sentence below the line is state prison; the presumptive sentence above the line is something other than state prison.

[b] The significant number of cases at level VI are presumptive imprisonment cases because of the application of mandatory minimum laws.

SOURCE: Minnesota Sentencing Guidelines Commission (1982:18, Fig. 3).

Scaling Offenses and Offenders   The scaling problems that confound sentencing research also arise in guidelines development. For guidelines developers there are at least two principal problems: first, how to scale offenses in terms of their seriousness; and second, how to weight individual attributes in offense and prior-record scoring systems.

The offense scaling problem is generally posed as a choice between adoption of statutory offense classifications (either directly in terms of formal offense classes or indirectly in terms of statutory maximum sentences), and independent development of an offense severity scale. As a practical matter, statutory sentence criteria are necessarily governed by statutory classes, but most administrative or judicial guidelines projects have developed their own severity rankings. Thus the U.S. Parole Commission (see Gottfredson et al., 1978) and the Minnesota and Pennsylvania sentencing commissions developed their own offense severity rankings (see Martin, Volume II). Those jurisdictions that base their guidelines on statutory categories have typically developed intraclass variables for scaling offenses (see Kress, 1980:Appendix, for examples).

The weighting question reduces to whether scoring systems require simple addition of zero or one point for each attribute or call for the calculation of scores using a differentially weighted sum of those attributes to express offense and offender scores. Most guidelines systems have used simple, zero/one scoring systems for attributes (e.g., one point for each prior conviction, one point if on parole at the time of the offense, etc.). Although in theory the use of different weights for the variables in scoring systems (like Massachusetts's) could make more subtle distinctions between cases, as a practical matter there are several arguments against using a differentially weighted scoring system. First, since even sophisticated statistical analyses seldom explain more than one-third of the variation in sentences, the weights derived in such analyses may fail to accurately reflect the relative importance of variables in empirically derived guidelines. Second, the need for the potential precision of a differentially weighted system is greatly diminished in developing empirically informed guidelines. Third, simple zero/one scoring systems have been found to perform about as well as more statistically sophisticated procedures in tests of the predictive powers of various scoring systems (see, e.g., Gottfredson and Gottfredson, 1979).

How Many Models?   Researchers attempting to characterize past sentencing practices frequently find that the variables that explain the in/out decision are different from those that explain the sentence-length decision. In developing "descriptive" sentencing guidelines, the most accurate model is a bifurcated one in which one set of variables guides the incarceration decision, and another set of variables (or the same variables with different weights) guides the sentence-length decision, and possibly yet another set of variables guides the choice among non-incarcerative sentence options. So far as the panel is aware, no such multistage sentencing guidelines models have been developed, although some bifurcated models of past sentence outcomes have been estimated (see, for example, Rhodes, 1981).[10]

Philosophical Implications

The growing interest in the philosophy of punishment in the 1970s has influenced sentencing policy. For example, several recent innovations have expressly embodied retributive premises and rejected the legitimacy of rehabilitative goals of punishment (see Chapter 1). The panel takes no position in the philosophical debates on punishment but seeks to call attention to the fact that adoption of particular premises has important implications for the development of sentencing guidelines.

In the interest of clarity the issues discussed in this section are assessed from the perspective of stereotyped punishment models: "thoroughgoing retribution" and "modern orthodoxy" (see White, 1978:7). A retributivist believes that the moral quality of offenders' acts defines the amount of punishment they deserve, and the achievement of equality and proportionality in the distribution of punishment are given high priority. In Hart's (1968:231) words, a retributive theory asserts:

first, that a person may be punished if, and only if, he has voluntarily done something morally wrong; secondly, that his punishment must in some way match, or be the equivalent of, the wickedness of his offense; and, thirdly, that the justification of punishing men under such conditions is that the return of suffering for moral evil voluntarily done, is itself just or morally good.

A modernist "allows some place, though a subordinate one, to ideas of equality and proportion in the gradation of the severity of punishment" (Hart, 1968:233), while placing greater emphasis on the utilitarian goals of deterrence, rehabilitation, and incapacitation.

Scaling of Offenses Retributivists are especially concerned with the coherence of offense severity scales. A theory of equality necessarily entails a theory of significant differences. Criminal codes often do not

---

[10] Kress (1980:132) reports that, in developing the early "descriptive" guidelines systems, bifurcated guideline models were considered but rejected in several cities.

provide bases for drawing sufficiently detailed distinctions between offenses of different moral consequence. In the federal system, for example, offenses are not classified, and the maximum sentences authorized for various offenses are arbitrary (see Low, 1970a,b). In states having offense classification systems, each of the three or four felony classes encompasses acts of diverse characters. Consequently, most guidelines projects have developed their own systems of offense classification based on the decision makers' determination of the relative seriousness of various offenses. A related problem is that criminal code sections are often drawn in general terms that do not make distinctions that sentencing policy makers consider relevant. From a single statutory definition of extortion (18 Pa. C.S. 3923), Pennsylvania's sentencing commission crafted five different extortion offenses (on the basis of the amount of money involved and the circumstances) and gave each of them a different severity ranking (*Pennsylvania Bulletin* 12:431, 1982).

When policy makers adopt retributive premises, offense scaling will be a matter of substantial importance, and efforts like those in Pennsylvania will likely be required. To a modernist, scaling is less important (though not irrelevant) because retributive concerns are but one among many sets of punishment goals that should influence sentencing decisions.

The Range of Discretion   We noted earlier that ranges for sentences vary substantially in the amount of discretion that they allow decision makers, from Minnesota's plus or minus 5–8 percent to Massachusetts's plus or minus 50 percent. Retributivists, given the high value they attach to the achievement of equality and proportionality, would insist on narrow sentencing ranges. The enabling statute in Minnesota, for example, permitted the commission to establish ranges of plus or minus 15 percent, but the commission chose the narrower 5–8 percent range because "the Commission felt that broad ranges would increase the disparate treatment of similar cases and, in a sense, would allow disparity to continue in practice while defining it away in theory" (Minnesota Sentencing Guidelines Commission, 1980:12). A modernist, by contrast, would prefer broader ranges because they permit a decision maker to give substantial weight to such considerations as deterrent and incapacitive effects when they appear appropriate. Thus, Morris (1974:75) argues that equality of suffering should not be a primary goal of sentencing:

To say that a punishment is deserved . . . is not to say that it ought to be imposed. The concept of desert . . . is one of a retributive maximum; a license to punish the criminal up to that point but by no means an obligation to do so.

Considerations other than retribution determine how much punishment should be imposed short of that maximum.

The Punitive Content of Guidelines   All sentencing and parole guidelines systems include some measure of the seriousness of the present offense and some measure of the offender's prior record. Philosophical premises affect the relative significance accorded the present offense and the past record. This can be illustrated by reference to the U.S. Parole Commission's adult parole guideline matrix, which is set out in Table 3–5.

A retributivist, who believes in looking only at the severity of the current offense, would find much to fault in the sentences specified in this matrix. If an offender's punishment should exactly "match the wickedness of his offense," the past criminality or risk of recidivism of the offender is irrelevant, and all persons convicted of a particular offense should receive the same punishment (but see von Hirsch [1981] for an argument that retributive sentencing schemes can appropriately take prior record into account). The U.S. parole guidelines take a dramatically different position. A comparison of the first and last numbers in the three middle offense severity rows indicates that an offender's criminal history can increase the severity of the prescribed sentence by a factor of three (10–32, 14–44, 24–72). A "very good" offender convicted of a "high" severity offense (14–20 months) could serve the same sentence as a "poor" offender convicted of a "low" severity offense (12–16 months). In the U.S. Parole Commission's guidelines, the "of-

TABLE 3–5   U.S. Parole Guidelines: Recommended Months of Incarceration Before Release on Parole for Adults

	Offender Characteristics			
Offense Severity	Very Good	Good	Fair	Poor
Low	0–6	6–9	9–12	12–16
Low moderate	0–8	8–12	12–16	16–22
Moderate	10–14	14–18	18–24	24–32
High	14–20	20–26	26–34	34–44
Very high	24–36	36–48	48–60	60–72
Greatest I	40–52	52–64	64–78	78–100
Greatest II	52+	64+	78+	100+

SOURCE: U.S. Parole Commission Rules Sec. 2–20 (effective September 1, 1981); 28 Code of Federal Regulations 2–20.

fender characteristics" score is based on a recidivism prediction table, and they effectively embody an incapacitative premise.

The Minnesota Sentencing Guidelines Commission selected its final guidelines grid from among several that were variously characterized as "just deserts," "modified just deserts," "incapacitation," and "modified incapacitation" (see Knapp, 1980). Figure 3–1 sets out the four sample grids. The commission discussed the philosophical implications of the sentence patterns in each grid and ultimately settled on a slightly revised version of the "modified just deserts" grid (see Table 3–1).

The Minnesota commission's choice is slightly ironic. In selecting the "modified just deserts" model, the commission devoted most of its attention to the location of the in/out line. In the guidelines that were promulgated, the left-to-right differentials are more pronounced than in the U.S. parole guidelines. In one row (Row VI, Table 3–1), the most severe sentence (104 months) is more than four times more severe than the least severe (23 months). Thus the guidelines adopted by the Minnesota commission do not fully reflect the just deserts premises embraced by the commission.

In summary, to a retributivist, an offender's prior record should play little if any role in determining the nature of the punishment and so sentencing guidelines should be weighted to give little significance to prior criminal history. To a modernist, conviction makes an offender subject to a wide range of possible sanctions, and incapacitative, deterrent, and rehabilitative considerations then enter in setting sentences.

Philosophical premises not limited to the retributivist/modernist contrast can also influence decisions about the legitimacy of various sentencing variables. General moral considerations may lead decision makers to eliminate certain possible sentencing criteria like race, sex, and class that are overtly invidious and such social variables as employment history, education, and residential stability that are neutral on their face but correlated with invidious variables. General moral or ideological views may also lead to rejection of sentencing concessions to reward guilty pleas. The Minnesota commission, for example, decided that none of these criteria should be given weight in sentencing.

Questions of the practical ramifications of philosophical views of punishment are not new, but such questions have become more widely debated in recent years. When parole and sentencing decisions were mostly invisible and unreviewable, as they were under indeterminate sentencing systems, there was little need to ponder such matters as the systematic role of prior record or social variables in sentencing. With the development and promulgation of detailed sentencing and parole

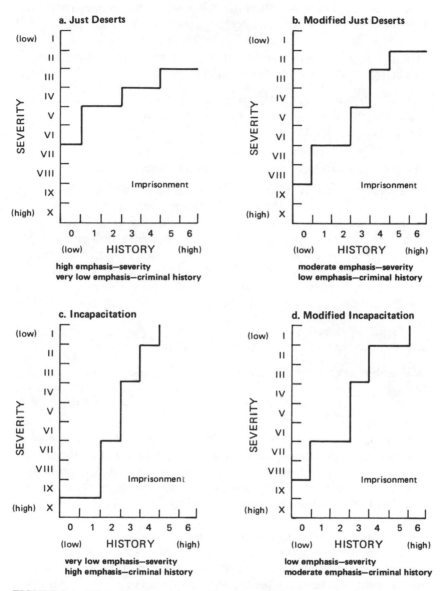

FIGURE 3–1 Dispositional models considered by the Minnesota Sentencing Guidelines Commission. SOURCE: Knapp (1980:13).

criteria, many of these questions have become salient and are receiving more attention from policy makers.

THE PROCESSES OF DEVELOPING, IMPLEMENTING, AND ENFORCING NEW SENTENCING STANDARDS

This section is concerned with political choices and planning questions that confront policy makers as they develop, implement, and enforce new sentencing standards and try to maximize compliance with them.

DEVELOPMENT PROCESSES AND IMPLEMENTATION

Sentencing is a complex process involving discretionary decisions by many people. Attempts to promulgate new sentencing standards that result in institutional changes have varied markedly in the processes by which reforms have been designed and the consideration given to political repercussions of policy choices. Those jurisdictions that have made extensive efforts to obtain the understanding and support of all affected interest groups appear to have been more successful in gaining legislative approval when needed and fuller compliance when implemented than those that have not made such efforts.

Martin's (Volume II) case study of the politics of sentencing reform in Minnesota and Pennsylvania indicates that:

the complexities of developing sentencing guidelines involve not only the technical issues related to the development of statistical models of past sentencing practices and projections of future prison populations, but also the political aspects of the policy-making process.

In both states the legislature created a sentencing guidelines commission to promulgate guidelines that would go into effect unless rejected by the legislature. The differences in mandates, development processes, products, and outcomes illustrate the political problems of attempting to redistribute discretionary authority and change local sentencing practices.

In Minnesota the legislature determined that disparities in the punishment of offenders convicted of felonies should be reduced through presumptive sentencing guidelines and the abolition of the parole board's discretionary releasing authority. The commission defined its task primarily as the development of public policy rather than as a technical activity. To gain support for its guidelines, the commission conducted a broad campaign to influence individuals and interest groups that would be affected by the guidelines and to involve them in the development process. The commission held a series of public meetings to publicize its activities and solicit policy recommendations; cultivated close relations with the media; had its members establish and maintain good relations with their respective constituencies; and held open meetings and arranged final hearings on the draft guidelines at meetings of associations of trial judges, county prosecutors, and public defenders prior to submission to the legislature. The final guidelines embodied compromises negotiated within the commission to reflect the views of interest groups and the extensive public debate the commission's work fostered. Consequently, all of the concerned groups perceived themselves as having a stake in the guidelines and viewed the resulting standards as preferable to the status quo; hearing no criticism, the legislature allowed the guidelines to go into effect without change.

In Pennsylvania the commission was created to design guidelines for both felony and misdemeanor offenses (a broader mandate than in Minnesota) and without clear guidance concerning the prison population ramifications of its possible decisions. When the commission designed guidelines similar to those in Minnesota, they met with criticism from virtually every interest group. This resulted in part from the commission's limited effort to build a constituency and from the likely effect of the proposed guidelines. To reduce disparity in a state characterized by wide variation in local sentencing patterns, the commission proposed to average sentences statewide and restrict judicial discretion. Judges were angered at this limitation of their authority, and suburban and rural judges, prosecutors, and legislators opposed the reduction of sentence severity in their jurisdictions. These groups joined forces to press for legislative adoption of a resolution directing the commission to revise its guidelines to widen ranges and increase sentence severity. The revised guidelines now in effect aroused little opposition because they maintain symbolic acceptance of statewide standards but are broad enough to accommodate traditional local sentencing practices.

The voluntary sentencing guidelines that have been adopted in several jurisdictions had neither legislative authorization nor broad support from or involvement of the local judiciary. Nor were defense bars and prosecutors' offices involved in the development process or, in several instances, even informed about the guidelines after they had been promulgated. In Denver, Rich et al. (1981:165) note:

the criminal division decided *en banc* that the probation department . . . should distribute the guideline work sheets to the judges but not to the attorneys. . . . Sentencing guidelines . . . were to be downplayed as much as possible.

In Chicago (Rich et al., 1981:180):

with a few exceptions, Chicago prosecutors and defense attorneys were unaware of the existence of sentencing guidelines.

Given these limited efforts to obtain cooperation and support from lawyers, who jointly with judges influence the sentences that convicted persons receive, it should come as no surprise that Rich et al. (1981) found little evidence of commitment to or impact of voluntary sentencing guidelines in the cities they studied. Sparks et al. (1982) point to the likely importance of efforts to inform affected interested groups of the nature and intent of sentencing guidelines. In contrast to the Minnesota commission's efforts to build bridges to affected interests during the development process, in Massachusetts only minimal information about the guidelines was disseminated before the guidelines were introduced.

Equally important as political bridge-building during the development stage is attention to the mechanical operation of a new sentencing system to facilitate compliance. Proposed sentencing and parole guidelines or determinate sentencing schemes are often complex. Applicable sentences can be identified only after numerical and statistical calculations have been made, based on the availability of necessary information. All such systems, but especially the more complex ones, are vulnerable to missing data and administrative errors, which can be reduced by careful planning, attention to detail, and the development of quality control procedures to verify adherence to the new policies. Officials cannot be expected to comply with a complex system without adequate familiarity with their responsibilities, information about its operation, and a disincentive for continuing "business as usual." Furthermore, efforts must be made to ensure that all the information necessary for calculating guideline sentences is routinely available.

The effect of careful attention to implementation issues, including training the people who must implement new sentencing standards, developing mechanisms that facilitate implementation, and creating procedures for monitoring compliance, is illustrated by the contrast in approach and results in Minnesota and several jurisdictions with voluntary sentencing guidelines. To facilitate successful implementation of its guidelines, the Minnesota Sentencing Guidelines Commission undertook the following activities (among others):

• Prepared commentary, which was included in training materials on the guidelines, to clarify the commission's intent, the relevant statutory provisions, and the applicable rules of criminal procedure to aid court personnel.

• Worked with the corrections department to supplement the statewide criminal records information system to ensure the availability of necessary data.

• In conjunction with the Minnesota Corrections Association, devised a new presentence investigation form that includes information necessary for the calculation of guideline sentences.

• Recommended several legislative changes necessary to facilitate transition to the new system.

• Conducted extensive training sessions for all judges, prosecutors, probation personnel, and defense attorneys to familiarize them with the guidelines.

In addition, smooth implementation in Minnesota was facilitated by the following activities by affected participants:

1. Establishment of procedures for sentencing hearings by an ad hoc judicial committee.[11]

2. Development of rules and standards for appellate review of sentences under the guidelines by the state supreme court.

3. Revision of prerelease and furlough policies consistent with the guidelines policy by the Department of Corrections.

In contrast to Minnesota's approach, in Chicago and Newark training was limited and implementation mechanisms were largely ignored. The results were chronic problems with missing data and errors in computing guideline sentences, disputes about the accuracy of the facts on which computations were made, and disagreements over definitions of guideline variables, e.g., what constitutes a weapon or injury (Rich et al., 1981). And Sparks et al. (1982) observe that the Massachusetts guidelines were not effectively presented even to the Massachusetts judiciary. Their presentation was very brief (2 hours), written materials were limited to the guidelines themselves, and the description of the guidelines by one of the judges on the committee that produced them was inadequate.

ENFORCEMENT

The legal authority of sentencing standards and the existence, nature, and credibility of enforcement mechanisms also appear to affect the likelihood that the standards will be followed. Because there is little

---

[11] Judge Douglas Amdahl, a member of the Minnesota Sentencing Guidelines Commission and chief judge of the Hennepin County (Minneapolis) District Court (and, subsequently, chief justice of the Minnesota supreme court), took the initiative by establishing an ad hoc committee of judges and lawyers to propose procedures for sentence hearings. The committee's proposed rules were presented to a statewide meeting of trial court judges, modified in light of comments received at the meeting, and submitted to the chief judges in each judicial district for voluntary administrative adoption. The rules have been adopted in most judicial districts.

research on these issues, this section simply suggests several distinctions that may usefully inform efforts to implement sentencing innovations.

Legal Authority

Rules are characterized by various degrees of legal authority, and decision makers can be expected to give greater weight to rules of greater authority. Three levels of legal authority can be distinguished in the sentencing initiatives implemented to date, and a fourth level may soon exist.

Voluntary   Voluntary standards such as voluntary sentencing guidelines typically possess only collegial authority, so their surface credibility may be critical. Part of the rationale of the early "descriptive" guidelines was that, by articulating the prevailing norms and embodying the implicit policies of a court, voluntary compliance would be achieved. One might hypothesize, however, that compliance with voluntary sentencing standards will be low: (1) when the development process is not understood and respected by the judges who must use or ignore them; (2) when the standards take a form that is alien to judges, such as Massachusetts's weighted formula guidelines; and (3) when the ranges for sentencing are narrow and deviate from prevailing practices in a large percentage of cases.[12] Since these guidelines by definition are voluntary, a primary aim of developers must be to persuade judges that compliance with the guidelines is a good idea and that compliance will achieve important public aims.[13]

Presumptive   Presumptive sentencing and parole guidelines and statutory sentencing standards have presumptive authority; they are to be observed in the ordinary case and are to be disregarded only under

---

[12] The original Denver guidelines were intended to encompass 80–85 percent of the sentencing decisions in the construction and validation samples (Wilkins et al., 1978). Consequently, assuming that individual judges did not drastically change their respective sentencing standards, one would expect 80–85 percent of the sentences to be consistent with the guidelines. Such *consistency* with guidelines, however, does not mean that judges were *compliant*; judges could sentence consistently with the guidelines even if unaware of them.

[13] The developers of the original guidelines recognized the importance of judicial support. They made strenuous efforts to induce the judges to perceive guidelines development as a collaborative process in which the judges make the critical policy decisions (Wilkins, 1981).

special circumstances. Decision makers are generally required to give reasons for their decisions when they depart from the presumptive sentence. Thus under the federal parole guidelines, the Minnesota sentencing guidelines, and California's Uniform Determinate Sentencing Law, decision makers are required to provide written reasons for decisions contrary to the applicable presumptive standards. However, merely establishing presumptive standards does not necessarily lead to high compliance rates. Without effective appellate or other review, the reasons requirement may be meaningless. Or if the range of discretion permitted by the presumptive standards is large, substantial disparity may exist even though most sentences are in formal compliance with the applicable standards.[14]

Mandatory Mandatory sentencing laws formally require that decision makers make particular dispositions. The mandatory sentence generally establishes a fixed minimum penalty for a broad class of cases that may vary widely in their individual circumstances. Such laws are vulnerable to circumvention because they are inflexible and require imposition of penalties that judges and prosecutors may believe to be inappropriate in individual cases. Their rigid and often severe penalties provide a powerful plea-bargaining weapon to a prosecutor who can promise to dismiss the crucial charge if a defendant pleads guilty to other charges. Their inflexibility can thus alter the balance of power relations in plea bargaining.

Judicial Rules Judicial rules for sentencing, which do not yet exist in any jurisdiction, are an intermediate case. In several jurisdictions, notably Massachusetts and Michigan, statewide sentencing guideline projects may eventually result in promulgation of court rules that give guidelines presumptive force. Trial judges are subject to numerous court rules on case processing and procedure; they are accustomed to adhering to such rules. Other things being equal, one might expect that sentencing guidelines that are promulgated as court rules are likely to possess greater authority than are voluntary guidelines and would be likely to result in greater levels of judicial compliance.

---

[14] Under the original Illinois and Indiana presumptive sentencing laws, the statutory ranges applicable to persons convicted of forcible rape and to those who had two prior nonviolent felony convictions were 6–50 and 6–60 years, respectively (Lagoy et al., 1978:399). Under such presumptive standards, 100 percent compliance rates could easily exist along with gross unwarranted disparity.

Review Mechanisms

Legal authority by itself affords little basis for predictions about substantive compliance with sentencing standards. Judges, parole examiners, and lawyers can ignore or willfully circumvent even presumptive and mandatory sentencing standards. Legal authority becomes meaningful in the presence of credible review mechanisms that pose a realistic threat that failure to comply will lead to appeal to and overrule by a higher authority.

Appellate Sentence Review   Obtaining judicial compliance with sentencing standards may present some difficulties. Appellate sentence review appears to provide reasonably searching scrutiny of sentencing decisions in other countries. In the United States, however, there is no tradition of rigorous appellate review of sentences. Indeterminate sentencing laws gave immense discretion to sentencing judges, and there were no obvious criteria that appellate judges could invoke in order to assess the appropriateness of particular sentences.

Recent presumptive sentencing guidelines and statutes may provide meaningful standards for appellate review in the United States. The Minnesota supreme court, for example, is carefully reviewing appeals arising from departures from the Minnesota guidelines. As a result, case law is now developing in that state articulating certain basic principles governing the choice of appropriate sentences. Two principles in particular have been affirmed in various Minnesota supreme court rulings: (1) that the sentence be based on the conviction offense and not on alleged but unproved offenses and (2) that the severity of the sentence should be proportional to the seriousness of the offense when compared with other offenses (see Minnesota Sentencing Guidelines Commision, 1982).

One should not, however, be sanguine about the prospects of appellate sentence review as a policing mechanism. Its greatest drawback is that it is dependent on appeals by the parties. If no one appeals, appellate courts will have no opportunity to review sentences, and quite substantial departures from guidelines or from statutory presumptive or mandatory sentencing laws will be beyond the ken of the courts. Most convictions result from guilty pleas, often pursuant to plea negotiations, and neither party has an interest in appealing such negotiated sentences. If a prosecutor has agreed to accept a plea conditioned on the defendant's receiving a below-guideline sentence, later appeal of the defendant's sentence is unlikely. Thus the only cases in which appeals are likely are those in which there was no agreement about a sentence and in which the judge failed to impose a sentence within the prescribed range, or there was an agreement the judge did not honor.

Even if the number of appeals is small, however, appellate sentence review may have a powerful indirect effect on the application of presumptive sentencing standards by providing an evolving frame of reference within which plea bargaining occurs. Both prosecutors and defense counsel must negotiate in the shadow of the threat that if they are uncompromising, the case may be appealed. A possible result, therefore, is the gradual development of "going rates" for negotiated sentences, shaped and limited by the formal sentencing standards.

Administrative Review   The U.S. Parole Commission is in effect a sentence review agency for the federal district courts. Its parole guidelines are based on offense seriousness rankings and a parole prognosis (the "salient factor" score). The judge's sentence is not taken into account except when a minimum sentence is longer than the maximum guideline sentence or when a maximum sentence is shorter than the minimum guideline sentence: in these relatively rare cases (10 to 20 percent) the sentence prevails and the guidelines are overridden. Thus the Parole Commission in effect applies its own sentencing standards post hoc in reviewing sentence lengths to set release dates.

Administrative sentence review of this sort has some advantages over appellate sentence review. Because parole review is not dependent on initiation by a party, it is less subject to collusive evasion of applicable sentencing standards. (However, it is not immune from collusive manipulation: sentence bargaining with judicial acquiescence can ensure a sentence shorter than the earliest applicable parole guideline release date.) To avoid the effects of charge bargaining, the Parole Commission applies its guidelines on the basis of actual offense behavior, not the conviction offense, thereby adjusting for the effects of varying charging and bargaining patterns in different parts of the country. Moreover, because the Parole Commission has its own internal system of administrative review, the quality of the reviewing decision can be assessed and revised when appropriate.

Review mechanisms also are more likely to affect behavior in administrative sentencing systems like parole than in judicially dominated systems. Administrative review procedures that have both formal and informal authority can be established. The formal authority resides in the review body's capacity to decide that the reasons provided for a noncompliant decision are unconvincing and to unilaterally change that decision. The informal authority results from the bureaucratic nature of parole organizations: as civil servants, examiners have career advancement concerns that encourage compliance with agency policy.

There has been some discussion in Congress of various ways to enhance the Parole Commission's sentence review function. For example, it has been proposed that, in connection with a presumptive sentencing guideline system resembling Minnesota's, parole release be available only in those cases in which a judge has imposed a sentence longer than is provided in the applicable guideline.

No comprehensive system of administrative review of sentences has, to the panel's knowledge, been established. California has established a partial administrative review system, but it does not yet appear to have had significant effect. California Penal Code Section 1170(f) initially directed the Board of Prison Terms:

not later than one year after the commencement of the term of imprisonment [to] review the sentence [in all cases] and . . . by motion recommend that the court recall the sentence and commitment previously ordered and resentence the defendant in the same manner as if he had not previously been sentenced *if the board determines that the sentence is disparate* [emphasis added].

Whether this injunction will be effective in the future remains to be seen.

Informal Review Mechanisms   Several informal processes can be used for review of compliance with sentencing standards. Efforts can be made to attract media attention to sentencing. On numerous occasions citizens groups have organized court observation systems in order to monitor judicial sentencing behavior. The Minnesota commission has established an internal monitoring system. Sentencing information forms must be completed by the trial court for every case and must include reasons for departures in cases where the sentence departs from the guidelines. One copy of the sentencing report form is sent by the court to the commission for review. The commission has established a review and follow-up procedure by its staff that involves initially calling the probation officer to obtain missing information or correct errors in sentence calculation prior to sentencing; contacting the judge if written reasons for a departure are missing following sentencing; and, if these are not forthcoming, contacting the chief judge in the judicial district. This monitoring system provides the sentencing commission with records on compliance and departures and serves as a constant reminder to judges that sentences are reviewed by the commission in every case, which may encourage judges to follow the guidelines.

Such monitoring devices, if well designed, may also be essential in the process of amending sentencing standards. They can provide feedback on the effects of the new standards on the system as a whole and on the congruence between actual and desired sentencing practices. This information can serve as the basis for modifying guidelines to overcome unanticipated problems and to accommodate changes in community standards and values affecting sentencing.

4

Sentencing Reforms and Their Effects

Recent changes in sentencing laws and practices have variously affected judges, prosecutors, parole boards, and other officials in the criminal justice system. Many sentencing reforms have been directed only at one set of officials and have not addressed or attempted to anticipate shifts of discretion to other officials. For example, the California legislature eliminated parole release for most prisoners and established detailed statutory criteria for prison sentences but did nothing to control the discretion of prosecutors—whose influence on sentencing through charging and plea negotiation increased. Because the punishment process is complex, it is important—if the effects of changes are to be recognized and understood—to look not only at processes that are formally and immediately affected by a change but also at earlier and later processes. Thus, an adequate assessment of the impact of sentence reforms requires that consideration be given to its implications for court procedures and plea-bargaining practices as well as to its apparent impact on sentences received by offenders.

This chapter summarizes the findings of the literature on evaluations of the impact of sentencing reforms. A detailed review of that literature is contained in Cohen and Tonry (Volume II). We are primarily concerned with the effectiveness of sentencing reforms as a means of reducing disparities, altering sentence severity, and making decision making systematic. Consequently, we focus on how innovations affect what happens to defendants and how participants in the system have altered their behaviors in reaction to innovations. The innovations we considered were directed at the actions and decisions of prosecutors, judges, and parole authorities. More specifically, we review evaluations of efforts to abolish plea bargaining in three jurisdictions; mandatory minimum sentencing laws in Michigan, Massachusetts, and New York; California's Uniform Determinate Sentencing Law; presumptive and voluntary sentencing guidelines; and parole guidelines in four jurisdictions.

This chapter is divided into four sections. The first section summarizes research findings on the extent of formal compliance with several sentencing innovations. The second section examines evidence of efforts by lawyers and judges to dispose of cases in ways inconsistent with apparently applicable rules and laws. The third section reviews evidence concerning the impact of sentencing innovations on sentence outcomes. Section four describes the major methodological shortcomings that characterize the evaluations. (The organization of this chapter requires that we discuss particular studies and innovations in more than one section. In order to minimize repetition, studies are described relatively fully when first mentioned and are thereafter described by cross-reference.)

The corpus of sentencing reform impact evaluations is small, and most published reports suffer from serious methodological shortcomings. There has not yet been a sufficient number of well-executed evaluations to permit the panel to offer detailed conclusions about the effects of diverse sentencing innovations. However, the following four broad generalizations emerged from many of the evaluations considered:

1. Formal compliance with the requirements of innovations has been widespread: assistant prosecutors have adhered to plea-bargaining bans and restrictions; parole board examiners have tended to set release dates that are consistent with applicable parole guidelines provisions; judges have tended to adhere to statutory sentencing standards, especially mandatory minimum sentence laws. Outside the parole context, however, compliance has often been formal rather than substantive.

2. Judges and lawyers have often substantially modified case-processing procedures in order to achieve dispositions of cases that were different from those specified in applicable rules or laws. Partial plea-bargaining bans and mandatory minimum sentencing laws appear especially vulnerable to circumvention.

3. Parole and sentencing guidelines systems that have legal or administrative force and are subject to credible enforcement mechanisms have operated to reduce the extent of sentencing disparities.

4. Plea-bargaining bans and mandatory and determinate sentencing laws have produced modest changes in sentencing outcomes, particularly some increases in prison use. Typically, increases in severity have been

experienced by marginal offenders, who previously might or might not have received prison sentences.

COMPLIANCE WITH SENTENCING REFORMS

Whether officials comply with the formal requirements of sentencing innovations appears to depend on the legal authority of an innovation and whether it is subject to credible enforcement mechanisms. Plea-bargaining bans, mandatory minimum sentencing laws, Minnesota's presumptive sentencing guidelines, California's determinate sentencing law, and parole guidelines commonly result in substantial formal compliance. Voluntary sentencing guidelines have not been shown to achieve high rates of formal compliance.

ABOLITION OF PLEA BARGAINING

There have been several efforts to "abolish" plea bargaining in full or in part. Some of these efforts have been evaluated: the Alaskan attorney general's 1975 ban on plea bargaining in that state (Rubinstein et al., 1980); the actions of a county prosecutor in Michigan to abolish charge bargaining in drug trafficking cases (Church, 1976); the Wayne County (Detroit) prosecutor's prohibition of bargaining in firearms cases subject to a mandatory 2-year sentence (Heumann and Loftin, 1979); and the restrictions placed on charge reductions in New York's mandatory sentencing laws for drug offenses (Joint Committee on New York Drug Law Evaluation, 1978).

These evaluations found that plea bargaining can be substantially controlled when the chief prosecutor wishes to do so, establishes internal review and management systems that effectively monitor assistant prosecutors' behavior, and wins the support of assistant prosecutors. When the ban is only partial (only charge bargaining is banned or only sentencing bargaining), judges and lawyers tend to shift to alternative bargaining systems.

Alaska is the only jurisdiction to attempt the statewide elimination of plea bargaining in all its variant forms. On July 3, 1975, effective August 15, 1975, the attorney general of Alaska ordered state prosecutors to desist from plea bargaining and sentence recommendations. Charge dismissals or reductions as inducements to guilty pleas were later forbidden, but unilateral charge dismissals for good-faith professional reasons were permitted. The Alaska Judicial Council evaluated the impact of the abolition in Anchorage, Fairbanks, and Juneau (Rubinstein et al., 1980). Case record data were collected on case dispositions in the 12-month periods before and after the ban, and interviews were conducted covering more extended periods. The credibility of the study's statistical analyses is doubtful, as are the conclusions deriving from the statistical data, but the rich interview data provide a firmer basis for most of the study's major conclusions. The study concluded that "plea bargaining *as an institution* was clearly curtailed" (Rubinstein et al., 1980:31). Sentence bargaining and prosecutorial sentence recommendations declined abruptly from 43.5 to 13.1 percent of all cases in the three jurisdictions. The interview data from judges, prosecutors, and defense attorneys supported the statistical indications that sentence bargaining had essentially ceased. The study concluded that charge bargaining also had substantially disappeared.

An effort to eliminate prevailing charge-bargaining practices was initiated by the newly elected prosecutor in "Hampton" County, Michigan,[1] in January 1973. He instituted a strict policy forbidding bargained charge reductions in drug sale cases and, at the same time, substantially tightened the standards under which drug prosecutions were authorized. Church (1976) collected information on drug sale warrants and dispositions for the 12-month periods before and after January 1, 1973. These data were supplemented by data from interviews with judges, defense counsel, prosecutors, and the court administrator. Church concluded that guilty pleas to reduced charges fell from 81 percent of cases before the ban to 7.1 percent afterward but that charge bargaining was quickly replaced by sentence bargaining involving judges and defense lawyers.

The Michigan Felony Firearms Statute created a new offense of possessing a firearm while engaging in a felony and mandated a 2-year prison sentence, which could not be suspended or shortened by release on parole, to be served consecutively to the sentence imposed for the predicate (underlying) felony. Since the gun possession charge had to be separately charged, its applicability depended on the decisions of Michigan prosecutors. The law took effect on January 1, 1977, and was supplemented by the Wayne County prosecutor's ban on charge dismissals of firearms charges pursuant to plea bargains. Since the charge determined the mandatory incremental sentence, prohibition of charge bargaining also accomplished a prohibition on sentence bargaining. Heumann and Loftin collected data from court records on cases disposed in the 6-month periods before and after the ban took effect and conducted interviews with lawyers and judges. They found that the prosecutor was

---

[1] "Hampton" County is a pseudonym used by the researcher to conceal the identity of the research site.

generally successful in obtaining formal compliance with the ban (Heumann and Loftin, 1979:402).

MANDATORY SENTENCING LAWS

Numerous mandatory sentencing laws have been passed in recent years. Evaluations of three of the laws have been published (Beha, 1977; Heumann and Loftin, 1979; and Joint Committee on New York Drug Law Evaluation, 1978). All three evaluations were largely concerned with the deterrent effects of the laws studied: case processing and dispositions received subsidiary attention, and, accordingly, the data are sometimes unsatisfying and must be interpreted cautiously.

There appear to have been few blatant refusals to impose the prescribed sentences on defendants convicted under the mandatory minimum sentencing laws. However, in each jurisdiction studied the percentage of prosecutions resulting in convictions declined, which suggests that officials attempted to shelter some defendants from the law's effects. In the case of the Michigan felony gun law, for example, the proportion of offenders incarcerated after conviction in "other assault" cases (a category of assault cases of moderate severity) rose from 57 percent to 83 percent; however, the conviction rate declined by 20 percent (Heuman and Loftin, 1979:Table 3).

Under New York's "Rockefeller" drug laws, which went into effect on September 1, 1973, severe mandatory prison sentences were prescribed for narcotics offenses at all levels, and selective statutory limits were placed on plea bargaining. The Joint Committee on New York Drug Law Evaluation (1978) found that the risk of incarceration after conviction increased substantially, from 34 percent in 1972 to 55 percent in 1976. However, the likelihood that a person arrested for a drug offense would be incarcerated remained the same because indictment and conviction rates declined. Sentence lengths did increase substantially: the percentage of sentenced drug felons receiving minimum prison terms longer than 3 years increased from 3 to 22 percent.

In Massachusetts the Bartley-Fox Amendment, effective April 1, 1975, required imposition of a 1-year mandatory minimum prison sentence, without suspension, furlough, or parole, for anyone convicted of carrying an unlicensed firearm. Beha (1977) collected data on all prosecutions for firearms crimes in the 6 months after the law took effect and for the corresponding 6 months of the preceding year. Only indirect evidence is available regarding compliance by lower court judges in imposing the 1-year minimum prison term for carrying a gun. The percentage of cases proceeding to superior court either on an appeal, as a trial de novo, or bound over directly from the lower court, increased from less than one-fifth of cases to more than one-half after implementation of the new law, suggesting that lower court judges imposed more severe sentences in compliance with the law. However, these increases in severity were offset by sharp reductions in the number of cases available for sentencing because dismissals and acquittals increased.

DETERMINATE SENTENCING IN CALIFORNIA

The original California Determinate Sentencing Law (DSL) took effect July 1, 1977, and was amended twice in 1978 to increase the severity of penalties for some offenses.[2] The DSL prescribes three base terms for each crime (e.g., for robbery the terms are 2, 3, or 5 years). The middle term is the presumptive term to be imposed except in cases in which the judge concludes that mitigating or aggravating circumstances warrant the use of the lower or upper base terms.

Seven major research projects have examined the postimplementation impact of determinate sentencing in California. As summarized in Table 4–1, these studies vary considerably in questions addressed, in the jurisdiction levels and stages in case processing studied, and in the relative strengths or weaknesses of their evaluation designs. Together they provide a comprehensive picture of the impact of determinate sentencing in California.

The available evidence indicates a high degree of formal compliance with the requirements of DSL in California. Available evidence for fiscal 1977–1978 and for 1979 indicates that most offenders sentenced to prison in those years received the presumptive middle base term (61 percent in 1977–1978 and 54 percent in 1979). The use of the lower and upper base terms for mitigating and aggravating circumstances varied among offenses. Upper base terms were more likely to be imposed than lower base terms for crimes against persons, and lower base terms were more common than upper base terms for property and drug offenses. In more recent years there has been a marked increase in the proportion of convicted persons who receive the lower base term; possible explanations for this trend are discussed in Cohen and Tonry (Volume II).

The law also prescribes additions to prison sentences ("enhancements") when particular aggravating circumstances, including weapon

[2] The crime types directly affected by the amendments were first-degree burglary, robbery, voluntary manslaughter, rape, crimes against children, and oral copulation. Both the middle and upper terms were increased for all these offenses except robbery, where only the upper term was increased.

TABLE 4-1 Variations in Impact Evaluation Design: California Determinate Sentencing Law

Characteristics of Evaluations	Sparks (1981)	Hubay[a] (1979)	Brewer et al. (1980)	Lipsom and Peterson (1980)	Ku (1980)	Casper et al. (1982)	Utz (1981)
Jurisdiction studied	Statewide	County	Statewide	Statewide	Statewide	Counties	Counties
States of case processing studied		N.A.					
charging						yes	yes
plea bargaining				yes		yes	yes
sentence outcomes in Superior Court	yes		yes	yes	yes	yes	yes
Controls for variation in case seriousness		N.A.					
limited to control for crime types (legal categories)	yes		yes	yes	yes	yes	
consideration of wide variety of factors, in addition to crime type, contributing to case seriousness							yes
Time frame studied		N.A.					
simple two-point pre/post design			yes	yes	yes	yes	yes
multiple observations in pre/post design	yes				yes	yes	

[a] Because the final report was not available at the time of writing, many of the details of the study design were not available.

use, great bodily injury to the victim, large property loss, or prior prison terms, are charged and proved. Statewide, among persons committed to the Department of Corrections, the use of enhancements tends to be limited to weapon or firearm use, especially in robbery cases, for which the enhancement was charged in 90 percent of eligible cases and proved in 74 percent of charged cases. This contrasts sharply with enhancements for victim injury and prior prison, which were charged and proved in less than 25 percent of eligible cases among persons admitted to prison. The statutes impose no obligation on prosecutors to charge or prove facts that would support an enhancement. Charging patterns vary from county to county in California, and thus the imposition of enhancements also varies (see Casper et al., 1982; Utz, 1981).

Contrary to the wide discretion exhibited by prosecutors in charging and proving enhancements, once enhancements were proved judges routinely added the prescribed additional years to the base sentence. Thus, with respect to the enhancements, there was considerable compliance by judges with the formal requirements of DSL (see Cohen and Tonry, Volume II:Table 7-17).

SENTENCING GUIDELINES

As we discussed in Chapter 3, sentencing guidelines have taken many forms and approaches. A distinction is sometimes drawn between "descriptive" guidelines, which are based on statistical characterizations of past practice, and "prescriptive" guidelines, which are in the first instance the result of policy decisions about appropriate punishments. They are also distinguished by their respective legal authority. "Voluntary" guidelines do not have legal authority: judges are not required or authoritatively encouraged to comply with voluntary guidelines, and defendants have no recourse against judges who fail to do so. "Presumptive" sentencing guidelines, like Minnesota's, do have legal authority: judges are directed to impose sentences prescribed by the guidelines unless "substantial and compelling" circumstances are present that justify departure from them, and defendants and prosecutors may seek review of the appropriateness of a departure.

Several examinations of the construction and effects of voluntary/ descriptive guidelines have been conducted: Rich et al. (1981) assessed the construction and subsequent impact of judicially adopted guidelines in Denver and Philadelphia; Sparks et al. (1982) reviewed the construction of the Massachusetts guidelines in depth and those of other jurisdictions in less detail; Cohen and Helland (1982) examined guidelines in Newark.

Formal compliance with voluntary/descriptive guidelines has apparently been limited in the jurisdictions studied. It is important to note that in this context we distinguish between "compliance" and "consistency." A sentence is compliant with guidelines when a judge has consciously considered the sentences indicated by the applicable guidelines and elected to impose a sentence from within the guideline range. A sentence may be consistent with guidelines even if a judge was unaware of their existence. Thus sentencing in a court could be consistent with guidelines but not compliant. Indeed, the original Denver guidelines were drafted with the intent that 80–85 percent of the cases in the construction sample would fall within ("be consistent with") the guidelines.

Rich et al. (1981) found that in Denver judicial decisions to incarcerate were consistent with guidelines in about 70 percent of cases, both before and after guideline implementation. Postimplementation consistency in terms of sentence length was lower, about 40 percent of those sentenced to prison. In Philadelphia and Denver, there was consistency on both the in/out and length decisions in only about one-half of all cases. Similar results were found in Newark (Cohen and Helland, 1982). Lawyers and judges interviewed in Philadelphia and Denver indicated that few judges made significant efforts to comply with the guidelines. Thus there was little evidence of formal compliance and evidence of even *less* consistency than had been expected given the avowedly descriptive basis of the guidelines.

As of early 1982, Minnesota was the only jurisdiction that had implemented sentencing guidelines that are both presumptive and prescriptive. The early indication from internal evaluations by the guidelines

TABLE 4–2 Percentage of Cases Sentenced
Consistently With Minnesota Sentencing Guidelines

	Presumptive "Outs" Who Were Sentenced "Out"	Presumptive "Ins" Who Were Sentenced "In"
1978 baseline cases	86	44
1980–1981 sentences imposed	96	77

NOTE: The figures in this table were estimated from data provided by Knapp (1982). They are not precise because some cases that appear among the presumptive "outs" are actually treated as presumptive "ins" under separate statutory provisions for mandatory sentencing.

TABLE 4–3   Percentage of Cases Sentenced Consistently With
Presumptive Sentences Within Selected Cells of Minnesota
Sentencing Guidelines

	Percentage Actually Sentenced "Out"	
Presumptive "Out" Cells	1978 Baseline Cases	1980–1981 Sentences Imposed
Offense 5, history 1	60.7	95.0
Offense 5, history 2	21.8	74.2
Offense 3, history 3	45.4	80.3
	Percentage Actually Sentenced "In"	
Presumptive "In" Cells	1978 Baseline Cases	1980–1981 Sentences Imposed
Offense 7, history 0	39.1	71.8
Offense 8, history 0	41.9	85.4
Offense 8, history 1	29.1	75.0

SOURCE: Knapp (1982).

commission is that there is substantial formal compliance by judges in
both decisions to incarcerate and decisions about sentence length. As
shown in Table 3–1, the Minnesota guidelines are expressed in a grid
format; cases falling in cells above the in/out line should receive "out"
sentences (i.e., stayed state prison terms), and cases falling in cells below
the line should receive state prison sentences.

Table 4–2 shows the percentages of cases in the commission's 1978
baseline sample that would have been sentenced consistently with the
presumptive "in" and "out" sentences had the guidelines been in effect
in 1978 and the percentages of cases sentenced consistently with the
presumptive sentences under the guidelines in 1980–1981. For both "in"
and "out" decisions there were marked shifts in sentences consistent
with the guidelines. As Table 4–3 reveals, these shifts in sentencing are
often larger when individual cells in the guideline grid are examined
than is apparent overall.

The relatively low preguideline consistency with the guidelines illus-
trates the extent to which the guidelines departed from previous sentencing practices in Minnesota. Since this is one of the few sentencing
reforms that has resulted in substantial changes in the behavior of a
state court system and its participants—at least in the preliminary findings—the panel encourages a longer-term and more extensive examination of the nature and extent of compliance with the Minnesota sentencing guidelines.

PAROLE REFORMS

Parole Abolition

On May 1, 1976, Maine became the first state in modern times to abolish parole release and establish a determinate sentencing system in which the duration of prison terms could be calculated at the time of sentencing. Maine is not an ideal jurisdiction in which to assess the impact of parole abolition. The small numbers of criminal prosecutions and convictions in that state make meaningful statistical analyses of changes in sentences by offense type virtually impossible. However, two evaluations of Maine's innovations have been completed. Kramer et al. (1978) assessed the impact of the change during its first 12 months; Anspach's (1981) report provides a content analysis of changes in Maine's substantive criminal law without data on the impact of the parole abolition.

Both of the evaluations are fundamentally flawed, and neither provides credible findings on the impact of Maine's abolition of parole. Plausible arguments have been made that parole release operates in important respects as a monitoring system for sentencing—evening out disparities in the lengths of prison terms and providing a device to relieve prison crowding; the Maine evaluations have not provided insights into these or other questions. It is to be hoped that other evaluations will be undertaken that are designed to test hypotheses about the comparative advantages of judicial and parole systems for determining the lengths of prison sentences.

Parole Guidelines

There have been three major evaluations of the operations of parole guidelines systems. Arthur D. Little, Inc., and Goldfarb, Singer, and Austern (1981, hereafter cited as ADL, 1981) examined the U.S. Parole Commission's parole guidelines system and state systems in Washington, Oregon, and Minnesota. Mueller and Sparks (1982) studied the operation of the Oregon parole guidelines. In 1982 the General Accounting Office released a study on the operation of the federal parole guidelines system. Four primary questions have been studied: the extent to which parole guidelines are correctly applied in prison release decisions; the extent to which parole release decisions are consistent with apparently applicable guidelines; the extent to which parole guidelines serve to reduce disparities in punishment compared with parole release without guidelines and compared with the distribution of sentences imposed by judges; and the effect of parole guidelines on the overall severity of prison sentences. Findings on the first two questions are reviewed here. Findings on the third and fourth questions are reviewed later in this chapter.

Using parole guidelines, the Arthur D. Little and the General Accounting Office studies investigated consistency of decisions in two senses. The first, which we refer to here as error proneness, concerns the consistency with which different decision makers apply the guidelines to individual cases. This was tested by having researchers or, in the General Accounting Office study, parole hearings examiners, calculate guidelines sentences for cases already decided and comparing those sentences to the ones actually imposed.

Both the General Accounting Office and the Arthur D. Little studies of the U.S. Parole Commission's guidelines found serious error-proneness problems. Arthur D. Little researchers—using a method in which two individuals separately evaluated each file, reconciled their decisions, and compared them with the actual case decisions—were in agreement with the actual Parole Commission offense seriousness and salient factor score calculations in 61 percent of the cases studied (ADL, 1981b:49). The General Accounting Office (1982:15–22) study found greater inconsistency, even when it had experienced parole examiners calculate guidelines sentences for 30 prisoners previously released.

In the three states studied, Arthur D. Little researchers found wide variation in rates of error proneness. In Minnesota, from a sample of prisoners released in 1979, the researchers concluded that the parole board "applies parole decision guidelines in a highly consistent manner" (ADL, 1981d:97). In Oregon, calculations were completely consistent with parole board calculations in 67 percent of the cases studied (ADL, 1981a:8). In stark contrast, the complete agreement rate in Washington was only 13 percent (ADL, 1981c:2). The evaluators point out that their analyses may, for several reasons, overstate discordance. Nonetheless, for all but Minnesota's "simple and explicit" system, all of the guidelines systems appear highly subject to calculation errors, owing to various combinations of inherent complexity, poor quality-control procedures, insufficiently specific policy rules, and problems of missing and unreliable data.

Consistency in its second sense concerns the extent to which release dates are consistent with the apparently applicable guidelines (that is, the guideline term as determined by the examiner, which, as noted above, may be inaccurate). An important caveat must be noted: all parole guidelines systems authorize examiners to depart from the guidelines in exceptional cases. Thus a release date not authorized by the guidelines does not necessarily mean that it is not in compliance with the guidelines system. The discretionary "departure rates" under the U.S. parole guidelines have varied between 10 percent and 20 percent. Under the Minnesota guidelines, the overall discretionary departure rate in 1977–1979 was less than 10 percent (ADL, 1981d:40). Compliance with Washington's first set of guidelines occurred in only about 30 percent of the cases, but those guidelines were later repealed and replaced with guidelines expressed in a different format; release dates were set within the new guidelines in 74 percent of cases (ADL, 1981c:14).

ADAPTIVE RESPONSES TO SENTENCING REFORMS

Most sentencing innovations are designed to alter existing processes, procedures, or outcomes, and they generally originate outside the organizational contexts in which decisions are made in individual cases. Legislatures, parole commissions, sentencing commissions, or chief prosecutors prescribe the new systems, but judges, assistant prosecutors, and parole hearing examiners must carry them out. There are numerous ways that officials can alter their behaviors to adapt to new procedures or rules that they believe to be inconvenient, impractical, or unwise. Most impact evaluations of sentencing innovations have identified ways in which the officials who make decisions have altered their operations in order to nullify new policies in some respects.

ADAPTATIONS TO PLEA-BARGAINING BANS

Courtroom personnel have personal and bureaucratic interests in the expeditious disposition of cases that they often believe are satisfied by plea bargaining. One might expect plea-bargaining bans to disrupt case processing by reducing guilty-plea rates and by increasing trial rates, case backlogs, and case-processing time. Or one might expect widespread efforts to circumvent such bans, particularly through adoption of forms of plea bargaining or consensual case disposition that have not been banned.

The evidence is mixed. The evaluators of the Alaska plea-bargaining ban concluded that overt plea bargaining ceased to be an important factor in case processing in the jurisdictions studied and that implicit plea bargaining (in which a defendant is assured that guilty pleas will be rewarded by sentencing concessions) replaced overt bargaining only for some offenses. In Wayne County, "Hampton" County, and Blackhawk County, plea-bargaining bans produced shifts to forms of consensual case disposition that were not banned (Church, 1976; Heumann and Loftin, 1979; *Iowa Law Review*, 1975).

Alaska

Sentence bargaining was the predominant form of bargaining prior to the plea-bargaining ban. For a brief period after the ban, charge bargaining increased in Fairbanks, but it ceased when it was prohibited by the state prosecutor there. Overall the ban appears to have been effective (Rubinstein et al., 1980). Case processing changed little: there was a slight tendency toward earlier dismissal of cases, but overall dismissal rates and guilty-plea rates were substantially unchanged. Trial rates increased, but the absolute numbers remained small. Court-processing times decreased.

There was some evidence of changes in the handling of cases. Case screening tightened: the percentage of cases screened out increased from 10.0 to 12.9 percent in the year after the ban. Screening rejections of drug and morals felonies increased substantially; there may have been a tendency after the ban took effect to prosecute as misdemeanors cases that previously were handled as felonies. There was no increase in outright dismissals: the overall dismissal rate prior to the ban (52.3 percent) was essentially unchanged after the ban (52.7 percent).

Both the interviews and the statistical analyses indicated that sentence bargaining was *not* replaced by charge bargaining or by forms of implicit plea bargaining. And, contrary to expectations, the rate of guilty pleas to offenses originally charged declined only slightly: from 23.6 percent of the cases available after screening before the ban to 22.5 percent of such cases after the ban.

"Hampton" County

In "Hampton" County, where charge bargaining in drug cases was prohibited, the system adapted to the ban in ways that permitted consensual case dispositions to continue. First, sentence bargaining increased: roughly one-half the judges made some form of preplea sentence commitment in applicable cases—a sizable behavioral shift given former practices and strong system norms against judicial participation in plea bargaining (Church, 1976:387). Second, there was a substantial increase in the rate at which cases were dismissed outright. Under the plea-bargaining ban, nolle prosequi rates declined slightly from 15 to 10 percent. Judicial dismissal rates after the ban took effect increased from 19 percent for

1972 warrants to 28 percent after the ban, as did "youthful trainee" convictions (which permit a sentence of probation) from 3 to 17 percent. Thus some drug sale cases that formerly were likely to result in a conviction through a guilty plea to reduced charges before the ban were removed from the system following the ban.

Wayne County, Michigan

Although the county prosecutors filed and pursued gun law charges in conformance with the state law (which required a mandatory prison term), two types of adaptive mechanisms to avoid the law's impact and the simultaneous ban on plea bargaining greatly limited increases in sentence severity. First, especially for assault cases of moderate severity, "waiver trials" were used to avoid the mandatory 2-year sentence: sometimes judges gave explicit prior indications that they would dismiss the gun charge at trial, often with the prosecutor's acquiescence; other times there were no explicit understandings, but judges acknowledged to researchers that they considered every possible defense and sought any available technical loophole. Second, researchers' interviews suggested that judges routinely nullified the 2-year mandatory sentence increment for a firearms offense by reducing the sentence otherwise imposed on the primary convicted felony offense by an offsetting 2 years (Heumann and Loftin, 1979).

MANDATORY SENTENCING LAWS

One conventional hypothesis concerning mandatory sentencing laws is that lawyers and judges will dismiss charges, acquit defendants, and otherwise alter their practices in order to avoid imposing sentences they believe to be unduly harsh or otherwise inappropriate. Although the number of evaluations of the impact of mandatory sentencing laws is too small and their quality too uneven to permit confident generalizations, the avoidance hypothesis appears to be confirmed by the few published evaluations.

In Wayne County, Michigan, there is evidence from interviews and also from statistical analyses that efforts were made to prevent sympathetic defendants from being subject to mandatory imprisonment under the firearms law. Although there was little change in the disposition patterns for the most serious offense studied (armed robbery offenders continued to be imprisoned at high rates) or the least serious (few offenders were imprisoned for felonious assault, which often involved acquaintances), marked changes characterized the more ambiguous category, "other assault." Early dismissal rates doubled, and there was an offsetting decline in the percentage of convictions (Heumann and Loftin, 1979).

Beha's (1977) evaluation of Massachusetts's Bartley-Fox law revealed few signs of widespread efforts to avoid compliance with the mandatory sentence provision in the lower courts. The only significant sign was a substantial increase—from 16 to 36 percent of dispositions—in the acquittal rate for defendants charged *only* with illegal carrying of a firearm. Beha only studied case dispositions in lower trial courts, from which convicted offenders could appeal to a trial de novo in the superior courts; he does not indicate whether circumvention of the mandatory sentence law occurred in the higher court.

In the evaluation of the mandatory sentencing provisions of the Rockcfeller drug laws in New York (Joint Committee on New York Drug Law Evaluation, 1978), there are also indications that cases were screened more carefully at early stages of the process after the law took effect. The numbers of arrests for drug felonies in New York State declined substantially, as did indictment rates given arrest and conviction rates given indictment.

Most of the mandatory sentencing law evaluations have been primarily concerned with the deterrent effects of the new laws, and the effects on case processing have received less attention. Neither Beha nor the Joint Committee conducted extensive interviews or used participant observation methods. Cautiously phrased, our conclusion is that the evidence is not inconsistent with the avoidance hypothesis, especially when defendants have been charged with relatively less serious offenses. However, it is important to note that there were high rates of formal compliance for cases that were not screened out.

CALIFORNIA'S DETERMINATE SENTENCING LAW

Case processing in California changed little after implementation of DSL. The law left substantial discretion in charging and dismissing cases in the hands of prosecutors, whose processing and plea-bargaining activities apparently continued much as before. However, as in other jurisdictions in which sentencing standards made sentences more predictable, there was a tendency toward disposition of cases earlier in the process. Some observers expected a shift of sentencing power to the prosecutor (Alschuler, 1979). However, it appears that the new law did not significantly alter power relations: in jurisdictions in which judges traditionally dominated sentencing, they continued to do so; where prosecutors traditionally dominated, this too continued.

Charging

Prosecutors in the jurisdictions studied typically adhered to an explicit policy of full initial charging (although screening on the merits of the case was permitted) and used various administrative procedures to ensure that assistant prosecutors complied. Both observation and interview data and the statistical analyses found little evidence of any major changes in initial charging for cases finally disposed of in superior court. For example, Utz's (1981) multivariate analysis of changes in initial charging for burglary cases in Alameda and Sacramento counties indicates that, after controlling for other attributes of the case, initial charging was not affected by DSL.

Unfortunately, all analyses of charging are limited to cases finally disposed of in superior courts. It is possible to circumvent the determinate sentence provisions by initially charging cases as misdemeanors rather than felonies, in which instance they do not appear in superior court at all. From existing data it is impossible to determine if such changes have occurred.

Plea Bargaining

Utz (1981) and Casper et al. (1982), who between them studied five California counties, found little change in local plea-bargaining practices as a result of DSL. Jurisdictions that engaged in substantial bargaining before DSL incorporated explicit sentence length agreements into their bargaining practices after DSL; those jurisdictions with limited bargaining before DSL continued to refrain from bargaining after DSL.

Controlling for crime type, there were no marked changes after DSL in the already high proportion of guilty pleas among convictions found in the five counties and for the state as a whole, although *early* guilty-plea rates (e.g., at initial court appearance) increased. As indicated in Figure 4–1, without controlling for any variations in crime-type mix over time, a simple two-point comparison between 1976 before DSL and 1978 after DSL shows sharp increases in the proportion of early pleas entered at initial appearance among all guilty pleas in superior courts. Consideration of a longer time period before DSL implementation, however, reveals a long-term decline in the rate of early pleas from the late 1960s to 1976, making it unclear whether the increases in the early guilty-plea rate after DSL represent a real effect of the law on early guilty pleas or merely a random fluctuation in a cyclic phenomenon.

Despite explicit prosecution policies in all five counties of "full enforcement" of enhancement and probation ineligibility provisions, both

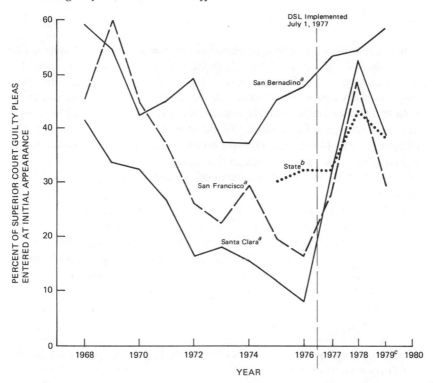

FIGURE 4–1   Trends in the timing of guilty pleas in California: percent of all superior court guilty pleas entered at initial appearance. SOURCES: [a] From Casper et al. (1982:Figure 13); [b] Derived from Lipson and Peterson (1980:Table 3); [c] The rates for 1979 derived from data reported in California Department of Justice (1980).

Casper et al. (1982) and Utz (1981) report that the opportunities for prosecutors to drop such allegations played a significant part in plea negotiations. As expected, the allegations were used by prosecutors as bargaining chips, to be dropped in return for a guilty plea to the basic offense charge or an agreement on a prison sentence.

SENTENCING GUIDELINES

The Rich et al. (1981) evaluation of the initial voluntary sentencing guidelines systems attempted to study the effects of the guidelines on plea negotiations. Interview data from Philadelphia, Chicago, and Denver indicate that lawyers did not consider the guidelines to be important and accordingly did not take them into account when negotiating plea agreements.

Because Minnesota's presumptive sentencing guidelines have legal force and prescribe narrow ranges from which prison sentence lengths must be selected, some guideline critics have suggested that opposing counsel would incorporate the guidelines into their plea negotiations. Since the applicable guideline range is based on conviction offenses, the outcomes of charge bargains would determine the applicable guideline sentence. Preliminary analyses by the Minnesota Sentencing Guidelines Commission found some evidence of changes in charge reduction patterns for cases in which aggravated robbery was the most serious initial charge. As evidenced in Table 4–4, the proportion of charge reductions from aggravated robbery to a lesser charge increased for defendants with low criminal history scores—fewer of these defendants were actually convicted of aggravated robbery. Once again, there were apparently adjustments in case processing to avoid imposing the prescribed prison term when prison was not deemed appropriate by court personnel. For defendants with high criminal history scores, on the other hand, the proportion of charge reductions declined, and more cases resulted in convictions on the original aggravated robbery charge. This pattern suggests that prosecutors and judges were operating to preserve distinctions among cases on the basis of criminal history despite the explicit guidelines policy that prescribed prison terms for aggravated robbery cases.

TABLE 4–4   Changes in Charge Reductions After Implementation of the Minnesota Sentencing Guidelines

| Criminal History Score | Percentage of Cases Convicted of Aggravated Robbery When Aggravated Robbery Was the Most Serious Original Charge | |
	1978 Baseline Cases	Cases Sentenced Under Guidelines, 1980–1981
0	59	49
1	75	60
2	64	66
3	54	70
4	58	70

SOURCE: Knapp (1982).

It was also anticipated by some that the guidelines would result in increases in the rate of cases going to trial. No such increase was observed during the first year after full implementation of the guidelines; the trial rate among felony convictions was 5 percent in 1978 and 4 percent among 5,500 cases disposed under the guidelines (Knapp, 1982). However, in assessing the impact on trial rates it is important to also examine disposition time. If disposition time increased, especially for trial cases, increases in trial rates might not be evident during the early implementation period. This remains an issue for further exploration in the continuing evaluation of the impact of the Minnesota guidelines.

PAROLE GUIDELINES

In most jurisdictions decisions under parole guidelines are not the result of an adversary process. Parole boards may responsively adapt policies to various pressures, but hearing examiners have few opportunities for adaptive responses. Although there has been wide variation in compliance with parole guidelines, this seems to result from ambiguities in the guidelines themselves rather than from systematic attempts to evade the guidelines.

Two other forms of adaptive response to parole guidelines at *sentencing* have been hypothesized: sentence bargains in which the maximum sentence imposed expires *before* the presumptive parole release date, thus avoiding the parole decision entirely; and judicial imposition of minimum sentences that expire *later* than the presumptive release date. There is considerable anecdotal evidence of such bargaining and sentencing by reference to parole guidelines, but no systematic studies are available.

THE USE AND SEVERITY OF SANCTIONS

Most sentencing innovations that affect the behavior of prosecutors and judges operate to make sentencing more predictable. If plea bargaining has been banned or regulated or if a case is subject to a mandatory sentence, statutory determinate sentencing, or presumptive sentencing guidelines, the parties can better predict the likely sentence than under indeterminate sentencing systems. For many defendants the increased predictability may affect plea negotiations, but it is unlikely to affect the nature of the sanction to be imposed. Offenders who have committed venial offenses are often unlikely to receive prison sentences. Offenders who have committed major violent crimes or who have extensive criminal records are likely to receive prison sentences whatever the sentencing system. Generally, the innovations studied have not resulted in dramatic increases in the proportion of cases sentenced to prison for either venial or repetitive serious offenders. However, there have been increases in the lengths of prison terms imposed for an intermediate category of offender who might or might not have been imprisoned before an innovation.

New sentencing standards could also substantially affect the sentences of marginal offenders. By definition these are ambiguous cases. New sentencing standards may resolve the ambiguity of the cases by directing that marginal offenders fitting a particular profile be imprisoned. Yet these are cases in which judges may often be loathe to impose prison sentences. It is hypothesized that at least two arguably undesirable outcomes may result. Judges and lawyers may circumvent applicable new standards when they appear to be too harsh in a particular marginal case, or they may apply them inappropriately, punishing marginal offenders more severely—with prison terms—than they want to. There is evidence to support both hypotheses: the findings on adaptive responses (discussed above) confirm the first hypothesis; other evidence (discussed below) suggests that sentencing outcomes do not appear to have been altered substantially except for marginal offenders, who often seem to receive harsher sentences.

PLEA-BARGAINING BANS

Bans on plea bargaining did not have a substantial overall impact on sentencing outcomes in any of the three jurisdictions in which evaluations are available; they did, however, affect the severity of sentences, especially for marginal offenders. In Alaska, although there were few marked changes in imprisonment rates, Rubinstein et al. (1980) conclude that there were some selected changes in sanction severity. Sentences did not become more severe where the original charge was a violent felony or "high-risk"[3] larceny, but drug cases experienced large increases in sentence severity as did "low-risk" burglary, larceny, and receiving cases.

In Wayne County, Michigan, there was no substantial overall change in sentences for defendants processed by the court (including those dismissed and acquitted). The proportion of all defendants who received incarcerative sentences did not increase. There were, however, some

---

[3] "High-risk" and "low-risk" characterizations were based on indicators of persistent criminality.

increases in the severity of prison terms imposed. The proportion of armed robbery defendants who received sentences of 5 or more years increased from 34 to 41 percent. The proportion of defendants who received sentences of at least the 2-year minimum increased by at least 50 percent, for "other assaults" (from 22 to 33 percent of defendants) and for felonious assaults (from 4 to 13 percent of defendants).

MANDATORY MINIMUM SENTENCING LAWS

In Wayne County, the percentage of convicted defendants who were incarcerated did not change markedly after passage of Michigan's firearms law (Heumann and Loftin, 1979). However, the likelihood of incarceration after conviction did change significantly, from 57 to 82 percent for the marginal "other assault" offenders. Also, after the new law took effect, there was an increase in the length of sentences for imprisoned offenders. Of offenders imprisoned for felonious assault, the proportion sentenced to terms of 2 or more years increased from 30 to 71 percent. For offenders imprisoned for other assaults, the proportion receiving terms of 2 years rose from 59 to 81 percent after the law. There was little increase (from 87 to 93 percent) in use of 2-year terms for armed robbery offenders.[4]

Beha's (1977) data do not permit conclusions regarding changes in sanctions in Massachusetts. The substantial increase in the rate of appeals of lower court convictions suggests that the imposition of prison sentences increased substantially, but whether these sentences survived superior court processing is unknown.

In New York State, the risk of incarceration for the small numbers of defendants who were convicted of drug offenses after passage of the Rockefeller drug laws increased significantly, but the steady decline in the number of drug felony convictions from 1972 to 1976 offset that development to yield a stable probability of incarceration given arrest. Overall and statewide, the proportion of persons arrested for a drug felony who were imprisoned remained essentially the same in 1972 (10.6 percent) and the first half of 1976 (11.6 percent). However, the severity of prison terms imposed on those New York drug offenders who were

---

[4] Loftin and McDowall (1981) report similar effects on a considerably expanded data set. Though they report no effect of the gun law on the expected time served by offenders charged with murder or armed robbery, the expected sentences for felonious assault and other assaults did increase more for cases involving guns. Similar results were found for the probability of prison among charged offenders.

sentenced to prison increased markedly. Under the old law (between 1972 and 1974) only 3 percent of sentenced drug felons received minimum sentences of more than 3 years. Under the new law, the use of long minimum sentences increased to 22 percent. Between September 1973 and June 1976, 1,777 offenders were sentenced to indeterminate lifetime prison terms, a sentence rarely imposed before the new drug law (Joint Committee on New York Drug Law Evaluation, 1978:99–103).

CALIFORNIA'S DETERMINATE SENTENCING LAW

Trends in Prison Use

Prison use definitely increased after DSL, whether measured by the commitment rate to prison (commitments/population) or by the likelihood of a prison sentence after conviction in superior court. The increased use of prison has been accompanied by increased imprisonment of less serious, marginal offenders: persons convicted of less serious offenses constitute a larger proportion of persons sent to prison, and imposition of prison sentences has increased relative to jail sentences. However, these increases continue preexisting trends toward increased prison use in California and may not be an effect of DSL.

Because of the greater certainty about lengths of prison terms, it was generally hypothesized that prison use would increase as a result of DSL. Under indeterminate sentencing laws, judges could not impose short prison sentences because all prison terms were for the statutory maximum sentence subject to earlier release at the parole agency's discretion. It was widely believed that judges were hesitant to imprison persons convicted of less serious crimes for fear that they might be kept in prison unduly long. Under DSL's determinate provisions, a judge could impose a short sentence and know when the defendant would be released. Consistent with this hypothesis, most studies have found a definite increase in prison use, measured by commitment rates based on population and by rates based on superior court convictions.

As indicated in Table 4–5, the commitment rate for all offenses increased between 1976 and 1978 for the state as a whole and for individual jurisdictions within the state. Similar increases were generally found for the proportion of convicted offenders sentenced to prison in superior courts (see Table 4–6), both across jurisdictions and for different kinds of offenses (except in Santa Clara County). When the observation period is extended to include multiple observations, however, several studies conclude that the increase in prison use after DSL is best viewed as a

TABLE 4–5   California Adult Prison Commitment
Rate (Commitments/100,000 Residents)

Jurisdiction	Commitment Rate	
	1976 (Before DSL)	1978 (After DSL)
Males only[a]		
State total	30.0	39.3
Counties		
Southern California	25.1	37.6
Los Angeles	27.9	39.1
9 other counties	22.5	35.9
San Francisco Bay	29.3	39.4
Alameda	25.0	46.0
San Francisco	50.2	83.7
7 others	26.5	37.1
Rest of state	37.8	44.8
10 Sacramento Valley	40.9	43.3
7 San Joaquin Valley	37.5	51.4
22 others	34.3	37.1
All adults[b]		
State total	32.1	41.8

[a] Data from Lipson and Peterson (1980:Table 12). The reported rates represent the number of males committed to state prisons per 100,000 total resident population (males *and* females).
[b] Data from Brewer et al. (1980:Table 5). The rates are total adult commitments (male and female) to state prisons per 100,000 total resident population.

continuation of a preexisting trend toward increased prison use in California (Brewer et al., 1980; Casper et al., 1982; Ku, 1980; Lipson and Peterson, 1980), both for all offenses for the state as a whole (Figure 4–2) and in San Bernardino and San Francisco counties (Casper et al., 1982).

Factors Contributing to Increased Prison Use

Public and judicial attitudes toward criminals may simply have become more punitive in the late 1970s. However, several factors are also potentially important in accounting for the trend toward greater prison use in California.

The Changing Impact of Probation Subsidies on Local Jurisdictions Brewer et al. (1980) note the contributing role of changes in the probation subsidy program to counties. This program, initiated in 1965 to provide economic incentives for local jurisdictions to keep offenders under local supervision within their own communities, achieved this end through 1971. Because of growing dissatisfaction with local programs and escalating costs of these programs, prison commitments began to rise again in the early 1970s. Under the provisions of the act, however, the amount of the probation subsidy was determined by the extent of prison use in a county; any increase in prison use relative to a baseline figure decreased the probation subsidy the county received. Thus, as prison use began to increase, the amount of the probation subsidies received by counties decreased. With this decline in probation subsidies, prison commitments rose even higher, and the use of probation declined further.

TABLE 4–6   Proportion of Convicted Offenders
Sentenced to Prison in California Superior Courts

Jurisdiction and Offense	Percentage to Prison Among Convictions	
	1976 (Before DSL)	1978 (After DSL)
All offenses		
State total[a]	17.8	23.0
Counties		
Alameda[b]	14.2	23.2
Sacramento[b]	25.4	26.9
San Bernadino[c]	29.5	38.5
San Francisco[c]	25.0	31.5
Santa Clara[c]	25.0	16.5
Burglary		
Alameda[d]	17.8	42.5
Sacramento[d]	23.0	21.3
San Bernadino[e]	29.5	38.5
San Francisco[e]	24.5	32.0
Santa Clara[e]	24.5	16.0
Robbery		
San Bernadino[e]	65.0	63.0
San Francisco[e]	44.0	49.5
Santa Clara[e]	59.5	57.0

[a] These data from the California Bureau of Criminal Statistics are reported in Brewer et al. (1980) and Lipson and Peterson (1980).
[b] Derived from data reported in Utz (1981:Appendix F).
[c] Data from Casper et al. (1982:Figure 5).
[d] Data from Utz (1981:Table 39).
[e] Data from Casper et al. (1982:Figures 6 and 7).

FIGURE 4-2 Prison use in California. SOURCES: [a] Data from Brewer et al. (1980:Table 5) and Lipson and Peterson (1980:Figure 2); [b] Data from Brewer et al. (1980:Table 5); [c] Data for 1979 were obtained from the California Department of Justice (1980).

Increased Seriousness Another factor in the increased use of prison is that the seriousness of cases sentenced in superior courts may have increased. This could have resulted from increases in judicial punitiveness, increases in the seriousness of the cases that result in convictions, or changes in the distribution of cases between superior and municipal courts.

Including elaborate controls for the seriousness of burglary cases disposed in superior courts in Alameda and Sacramento counties in 1976 (pre-DSL) and in 1978 (post-DSL), Utz's (1981:22–27) data indicate some increase in case seriousness between 1976 and 1978.

Increases in prison sentences among those convicted in superior courts also may have resulted from changes in the pretrial filtering process that affected the case mix in superior courts. In particular, a shift of less serious cases to municipal courts for final disposition would leave the superior courts with increasing proportions of more serious, prison-eligible cases. If so, the increase in prison sentences for superior court cases would be more apparent than real: the cases sentenced to prison remain essentially unchanged, while more cases of moderate seriousness are eliminated from the available pool of convictions. (However, this would not explain the increases in the prison commitment rate per population.)

Major changes have occurred in the distribution of cases between superior and municipal courts. The proportion of total court dispositions for felony arrests that were handled in superior courts dropped dramatically from 70.7 percent in 1968 to 30.4 percent in 1979. During this same period the proportion of felonies among superior court cases increased from 59.6 percent in 1968 to 89.1 percent in 1979. These changes result in part from statutory changes that permitted prosecutors to handle as misdemeanors or felonies certain offenses previously handled exclusively as felonies (Penal Code 17b(4)). Other changes similarly permitted judges to sentence certain cases as misdemeanors, even if they were filed as felonies (Penal Code 17b(5)).

A variety of system changes could account for the recent concentration of felonies among superior court convictions and for recent increases in the prison sentence rates among these convictions. The increased representation of felonies at superior courts could have resulted from a shift in offending behavior to more serious crimes, resulting in an increase in serious felonies at each stage of the process. Alternatively, there might have been a general shift to greater punitiveness manifested by prosecuting as felonies less serious offense incidents previously prosecuted as misdemeanors.

These possible explanations for observed changes indicate the need to monitor and control for changes in the presentence filtering processes that affect the character of cases available for sentencing. Without such controls, changes in the way cases are filtered (which may be unrelated to a sentencing reform) could be mistakenly interpreted as changes in sentencing policy for "like" cases. Collecting data on control variables that reflect important aspects of the character of cases—i.e., attributes that identify "like" cases for sentencing purposes—increases the likelihood of distinguishing sentence changes due to differences in the character of cases available for sentencing from sentence changes due to real shifts in the sentencing policy for "like" cases.

Demographic Shifts   General demographic shifts, not mentioned in any of the studies, also may have contributed to the recent rise of prison use in California. Both in the United States as a whole and in California, the anomalous pattern of a decrease in prison admission rates through the 1960s, during a period of rapidly rising crime rates, and an increase in prison admission rates in the 1970s, when crime rates increased much less, could be attributed to the changing demographic composition of the population (Blumstein et al., 1980). In the 1960s the post-World War II baby-boom generation was moving into the high-crime ages, but as juveniles or first-offender adults these individuals were not likely to be sent to prison even if convicted. On the other hand, the increase in prison commitments in the 1970s occurred as a sizable portion of the baby-boom offenders became old enough to have developed adult criminal records. Based on population projections, these increases in prison commitments are likely to continue nationally at least until the end of the 1980s. In California the continuing high inmigration of persons ages 18 to 29 is likely to delay any reversal of the upward trend in prison commitments and prison populations in that state.

Increased Punitiveness   If the increases in prison use in California reflect a real shift toward increased punitiveness in the state, this increase should be reflected in increases in the proportion of persons committed to prison for less serious crimes and in increases in time served (controlling for offense seriousness). Data from both Ku (1980) and the California Bureau of Criminal Statistics on prison sentences do indicate a trend toward increased representation among prison commitments of the less serious offense of burglary. This apparent increase in burglars among prison commitments cannot be attributed to a shift in the seriousness mix for burglary offenders sent to prison (Utz, 1981).

Sparks (1981) finds that the greatest increases in prison use after conviction occur for less serious offenders, whether defined by offense type, prior criminal record, or custody status at the time of the offense. These changes served to narrow the differences in the likelihood of prison after conviction for cases of differing seriousness. In all cases, however, the pattern of increasing punitiveness for less serious cases began before DSL.

Other studies find evidence of a slight increase in prison use relative to jail beginning in 1975, predating the implementation of DSL (Brewer, 1980; Casper et al., 1982). This is consistent with a continuing increase in punitiveness as increasing portions of marginal cases are shifted from jail to prison.

The weight of the evidence indicates no perceptible change in prison use *as a result* of DSL. The increases in prison use for superior court cases and associated shifts away from probation and jail sentences evident after DSL implementation appear to be continuations of preexisting trends. These trends toward increased prison use are consistent with, and probably reflect the effects of some combination of increased punitiveness, general increases in the seriousness of cases handled at all levels of the criminal justice system, shifts of less serious cases from superior to municipal courts, and changes in the age structure of the population.

Impact on Length and Disparity of Prison Terms

Two issues are of central concern in considering the impact of DSL on prison terms: changes in the average severity of prison terms reflected in either increases or decreases in mean or median time served and changes in the variability or disparity in time served for similar cases.

All the evidence points to a *decrease* in sentence lengths after DSL, but the post-DSL changes are part of a continuing trend that began *before* the law was implemented. There was also a tendency toward greater uniformity in sentences under DSL as sentence variation declined and the difference in sentences of men and women was essentially eliminated. Nevertheless, the range of sentences imposed for individual convicted offenses remained surprisingly broad.

The impact of DSL on average prison terms was difficult to anticipate prior to implementation. The original base terms were selected to reflect recent time actually served under releasing policies of the California Adult Authority (the state parole board for adults). The good-time provisions under DSL, which allowed for a maximum of one-third off a sentence, the application of separate enhancements, and subsequent enactment of increased base terms all contributed to uncertainty in predictions about changes in average time served under DSL.

A decrease in the variation or spread of prison terms was anticipated since an important goal of DSL was introduction of greater uniformity in sentences for offenders convicted of the same offense (Casper et al., 1982; Lipson and Peterson, 1980).

Length of Prison Terms   Studies comparing the average length of terms under the old and new laws use both actual sentences imposed under DSL and adjusted DSL terms reflecting credits for jail time already served and/or good time off the sentence.[5] These comparisons generally find *decreases* in mean or median time served under the new law, es-

---

[5] Since most of the studies were undertaken in the first few years after DSL implementation, the number of individuals sentenced *and* subsequently released under DSL is

pecially when allowing for jail and maximum good time-discounts from the term imposed at sentencing. Brewer et al. (1980), for example, report that the mean time served for all offenses increased very slightly from the old to the new law (from 40.0 to 41.4 months) using the *actual* sentence imposed under DSL; but allowing for maximum good-time credits, the *adjusted* DSL mean time served is only 28.7 months. Similarly, for robbery, the mean time served from actual DSL sentences is higher than for actual time served before the law but is lower when adjusted for good time. For burglary, both the mean time served from actual DSL sentences and the mean from adjusted DSL sentences are *lower* after DSL than the mean time served found for prisoners released under indeterminate sentencing laws.

Different post-DSL changes in time served for men and women were observed as the substantial gap between men's and women's terms was closed under DSL (Brewer et al., 1980); see Table 4–7. Greater uniformity in time served by sex has been accomplished by DSL through increasing the terms of women imprisoned for offenses against persons, keeping women's terms for property offenses about the same, and reducing men's prison terms for all types of offenses.

When the observation period is increased, the general decline in time served evident after DSL appears to be a continuation of a trend toward shorter terms that began several years *before* DSL implementation. Median prison terms between 1968 and 1975 for all offenses were consistently longer (about 36 months) than those in the preceding 23 years (about 26 months). From 1975 through 1978, however, the length of terms declined, falling to pre-1968 levels in 1978. The shorter DSL terms after discounting for jail and maximum good-time credits are fully consistent with this recent decline in time served.

Variability in Prison Terms   The statutory declaration that punishment is the primary purpose of imprisonment under DSL suggests that sentences for similar convicted offenses should receive similar sentences. In meeting this objective, reductions in the level of variation in prison terms for "like" offenses would be expected. Several of the studies explicitly addressing this issue report reductions in the variation or spread of prison terms after DSL when controlling for the offense of conviction,

---

quite small. Information from the Department of Corrections indicates that, so far, with the admittedly limited experience with implementation of the early-release, good-time provisions, most prisoners have been released with maximum good time off their sentences (Brewer et al., 1980:14–15; Lipson and Peterson, 1980:25; Utz, 1981:150).

TABLE 4–7   Changes in Length of Prison Terms by Sex Based on Statewide Data

| Offense | Mean Prison Terms, in Months | | Time Served by Women as a Percent of Time Served by Men |
	Men	Women	
All offenses			
Pre-DSL: 1972–1976	40.0	23.7	59
DSL adjusted:[a] 1977–1978	28.7	24.8	86
2nd degree burglary			
Pre-DSL: 1972–1976	30.0	19.5	65
DSL adjusted:[a] 1977–1978	18.4	16.0	87
Robbery			
Pre-DSL: 1972–1976	44.8	26.7	60
DSL adjusted:[a] 1977–1978	35.7	29.6	83
Assault with deadly weapon			
Pre-DSL: 1972–1976	40.9	22.3	55
DSL adjusted:[a] 1977–1978	32.9	34.7	105

[a] Adjusted to reflect maximum allowable good-time credits.

SOURCE: Derived from data in Brewer et al. (1980:Tables 7 and 8).

particularly when discounted DSL terms are used. For men, for example, the comparisons of DSL terms actually imposed with time served before DSL in Brewer et al. (1980:Table 7) indicate that the standard deviation decreased from 20 to 50 percent for five of the seven crime types with increases in means (Brewer et al., 1980). However, Casper et al. (1982:Table 17) note that the range of DSL sentences actually imposed in robbery and burglary cases is quite broad, due principally to the use of enhancements and consecutive terms on multiple charges in sentences for offenders convicted of the same crime type.

In sum, despite the magnitude of the change in sentencing procedures under DSL, there is no compelling evidence of substantial changes in sentence outcomes attributable to DSL. While prison use increased and time served decreased after the new sentencing law, both changes represented continuations of trends that began several years before determinate sentencing was implemented.

SENTENCING GUIDELINES

When the impact of various voluntary sentencing guidelines has been examined, there is little or no evidence of changes in sentencing practices. In particular, the relative use of different sanctions and the length of prison terms imposed have remained unchanged, and there has been little effect on the extent of variation in sentences imposed on like cases, as classified by the guidelines. This absence of substantial differences in sentences can be attributed largely to the nature of the guidelines themselves.

In addition to being voluntary in their implementation, the guidelines were largely "descriptive," articulating past sentencing practices without intending to substantially alter them. As a result, very little change from past practices was expected from even strict compliance with the guidelines. Instead, the guidelines were intended to provide judges with a description of prevailing practices in their jurisdiction, to be used as a standard in their own sentencing decisions and to serve as a basis for possible reconsideration of those practices in an iterative process of description, evaluation, and modification of the guidelines.

The Minnesota guidelines represent a complete departure from this model of voluntary/descriptive guidelines. The Minnesota guidelines are presumptive, having the force of a legislative requirement, and the prescribed sentences represent a deliberate departure from past sentencing practices. On the basis of early in-house data, Minnesota's presumptive guidelines appear to have significantly altered sentencing patterns in that state.

The Minnesota guidelines included an explicit policy choice to increase the use of prison for serious offenses against persons by offenders with limited criminal histories while decreasing the use of prison for property offenders, regardless of their prior criminal history. Consistent with the guidelines, the proportion of total commitments to state prisons represented by individuals convicted of person offenses increased from 32 to 46 percent. There was no increase in the proportion of convictions for person offenses; cases with presumptive prison sentences represented about 13 percent of convictions before (1978) and after (1980–1981) guidelines implementation. Table 4–8 provides further evidence of the effectiveness of the guidelines in shifting prison sentences from property to person offenses. The proportion of low-history offenders convicted of serious offenses who were sentenced to prison increased sharply, from 45 to 77 percent after implementation of the guidelines, while the proportion of high-history offenders convicted of the least serious felonies who were sentenced to prison decreased from 53 to 16 percent (Knapp, 1982; Minnesota Sentencing Guidelines Commission, 1982).

Another explicit choice articulated in the Minnesota guidelines was in the direction of uniform sentences, in particular that sentences should be neutral with respect to the race, sex, and socioeconomic status of the defendant. One indicator of the success of the guidelines in achieving more uniform sentencing is the rate of departure of sentences from the guidelines for different demographic groups. The data in Table 4–9 indicate that variations in sentences remained after implementation of the guidelines. The total in/out departure rate was reduced from 19.4 to 6.2 percent after guidelines were implemented, and similar reductions in departures were found for all demographic groups. Nevertheless, minority, male, and unemployed offenders continued to experience higher rates of departures from the presumptive sentences, and these departures tended to be in the direction of more severe sentences: presumptive "outs" who were in fact sentenced to the state prison.

The mix of cases differed sharply among different demographic groups: cases of convicted whites, females, and employed offenders were more likely to involve low-seriousness offenses and low criminal history scores. Departure rates were also generally lower for these less serious cases; the typical reasons for departures related to the extent of injury to victims—conditions that do not apply in low-seriousness property offenses. These differences in the distribution of cases could affect comparisons of departure rates across demographic groups. As a minimum control for the potential influence of differences in the distribution of cases, departure rates were estimated separately among presumptive "ins" and presumptive "outs." As indicated in Table 4–10, the differences across race and sex remain after minimally controlling for case distribution and the differences between employed and unemployed offenders are increased.

TABLE 4–8   Shift in Prison Sentences From Property to Persons Offenses Under Minnesota Sentencing Guidelines

Offense Severity Level	Criminal History Score	Percent of Cases Sentenced to State Prisons	
		1978 Baseline Cases	Cases Sentenced Under Guidelines, 1980–1981
VII, VIII, IX (high)	0,1 (low)	45	77
I, II (low)	3, 4, 5 (high)	53	16

SOURCE: Data from Minnesota Sentencing Guidelines Commission (1982). Also available from Knapp (1982).

TABLE 4–9   In/Out Departure Rates for Cases Sentenced Under Minnesota Sentencing Guidelines in 1980–1981

Demographic Group	Percentage of Departures, All Cases	Percentage of Severe Departures Among Total (Presumptive "Outs" Who Were Sentenced "In")	Percentage of Lenient Departures Among Total (Presumptive "Ins" Who Were Sentenced "Out")
Total	6.2	3.1	3.1
Race			
Whites	5.2	2.6	2.7
Blacks	9.6	4.9	4.7
Native Americans	12.4	7.5	4.9
Sex			
Males	6.5	Not reported	Not reported
Females	3.1	Not reported	Not reported
Employment			
Employed	3.4	0.2	3.2
Unemployed	8.9	5.0	3.9

SOURCE: Data from Minnesota Sentencing Guidelines Commission (1982).

The actual departure rates were compared with an independent assessment of justified departures by the guidelines commission, and similar differences by race and sex were found. Based on this analysis, it appears that differences in case seriousness account for a large part of the differences found in departure rates by sex and race.[6] The rate of severe departures for blacks relative to whites is, however, somewhat higher than expected and remains a matter of concern.

PAROLE GUIDELINES

Departure Rates

As we noted earlier, evaluations of parole guidelines have noted departure rates that have varied from under 10 percent (Minnesota in 1979) to 68 percent (Washington in 1976) (ADL, 1981c,d). Unfortunately, departure rates alone are not informative—their salience depends on several factors, including the specificity of policy guidance, the width of guidelines ranges, whether the applicable guideline has

[6] No independent assessment is available for the unemployment variable.

TABLE 4–10   Departure Rates Among Presumptive "Ins" and Presumptive "Outs" (Under Minnesota Sentencing Guidelines)

Demographic Group	Percentage Sentenced "In" Among Presumptive "Outs"[a]	Percentage Sentenced "Out" Among Presumptive "Ins"
Race		
Whites	3.1	15.4
Blacks	6.8	10.7
Native Americans	9.5	17.2
Sex		
Male	4.0	14.2
Female	1.6	25.9
Employment[b]		
Employed	0.2	46.4
Unemployed	6.3	18.8

[a] Severity level VI offenses are excluded from the presumptive "outs" because some of these offenses are in fact presumptive "ins" under the terms of separate mandatory sentencing laws.

[b] The departure rates by employment status are estimated from data on departure rates and the distribution of cases for different categories of offenders available from the Minnesota Sentencing Guidelines Commission. The figures estimated here are approximations based on estimates of both the number of departures and the total number of cases in each category. They include severity level VI offenses among presumptive "outs."

SOURCE: Data from Minnesota Sentencing Guidelines Commission (1982).

been correctly identified, and clarity about the character of a departure. To elaborate this last point, we repeat our earlier distinction between consistency and compliance: a decision may be inconsistent with guidelines but compliant if the case is one which the developers intended the offender to receive an aggravated or mitigated sentence outside a normal range; conversely, a decision may be consistent but noncompliant if the case is one that *should* have been handled by a departure but was not. Consequently, data on departure rates are necessarily ambiguous unless full and detailed contextual information is available.

Changes in Disparity and Severity

All of the studies we reviewed that assessed the impact of parole guidelines on disparity found evidence that the guidelines reduced sentencing disparities. For Oregon, Mueller and Sparks (1982:20–21, 36) concluded that, controlling for offense seriousness and using the parole board's offender scoring system, the variability of prison terms in that state was less in 1976 and 1978, under guidelines, than it had been in 1974, before guidelines were implemented. The Arthur D. Little study of the impact of the U.S. parole guidelines on disparity compared actual times served by prisoners convicted of robbery and selected property offenses who were released in 1970 (preguidelines) and 1979 (postguidelines) and found "measurably less dispersion in the distribution of actual time served" for the 1979 releases that could not be explained by reduced variability in sentences imposed by judges (ADL, 1981e:3). Finally, for Minnesota, Arthur D. Little found that for persons convicted of aggravated robbery, "offenders released in 1979 under the guidelines system tended to serve more nearly the same amount of time . . . when stratified into subgroups based upon prior history" than did aggravated robbery prisoners who were released in 1974, before guidelines (ADL, 1981d:63). Thus it appears that well-managed parole guidelines systems can operate to reduce sentence disparity among persons imprisoned.

Only one study has addressed the question of whether the overall severity of prison sentences served increased with the implementation of parole guidelines. Mueller and Sparks (1982:20) concluded that in Oregon between 1974, before guidelines were implemented, and 1978, when guidelines had been in effect for several years, there was "an overall increase in severity of terms." They cautioned, however, as we do in regard to the California evaluations, that one cannot conclude that "the guidelines *caused* the observed changes" (Mueller and Sparks, 1982:1).

CONCLUSIONS

SUBSTANTIVE FINDINGS

Most of the studies we reviewed reported that formal compliance with the procedural requirements of reforms has been achieved. Prosecutors have refrained from bargaining, judges have imposed the mandated sentences on convicted offenders, and parole boards have released prisoners according to guideline requirements. But this behavioral change often represented compliance more in form than substance. When participants considered the new rules inappropriate, they routinely attempted to circumvent the procedural changes by filtering out those cases they believed should not be subject to those rules. With respect to sentence outcomes, the impact of the sentencing reforms has been modest. There has been some increase in prison use, some increase in sentence severity for marginal cases, and some decrease in disparity. These changes have varied by type of reform and jurisdiction.

Formal Compliance

The mechanisms for achieving compliance with new sentencing rules differ. Plea-bargaining and parole reforms have been successfully implemented through administrative orders. The three evaluations of plea-bargaining bans indicate that when prosecutors sought to abolish plea bargaining in general or in a particular form and were serious about it they were able to do so. Similarly, the evaluations of parole guidelines indicate that parole examiners attempt to follow the guidelines of parole boards.

High compliance of prosecutors and parole boards with sentencing reforms, when it occurs, is likely to be the result of both administrative controls within the relevant agencies and favorable responses to the sentencing innovations by participants. Prosecutors working in systems that have prohibited plea bargaining tend to prefer the new regime (although defense lawyers dislike it). For prosecutors, the shift from haggling over sentences and charges to expending greater effort to develop cases for trial enhances their self-image and demands more "professional" behavior. The support for parole guidelines sometimes expressed by hearing examiners and parole board members, too, was not surprising, since the guidelines represent the policy of the board that initiated their development, can be changed by the board when guidelines and practice tend to diverge, and relieve individual members of some of the difficulties of decision making.

Judges, who traditionally operate as independent agents relatively free of administratively imposed changes and organizational controls, have complied with new sentencing provisions only when changes have been mandated by statute, as in the instances of mandatory and determinate sentencing laws and statutory sentencing guidelines. In the jurisdictions studied, voluntary sentencing guidelines have produced no measurable judicial compliance.

Adaptive Responses

There is much evidence of adaptive responses by officials who alter case-processing methods in order to circumvent new rules and procedures for some categories of offenders. Increased case screening or other early disposition of cases effectively avoids application of sentencing laws. Voluntary sentencing guidelines have had no discernible impact on judicial behavior or court processing; they have simply been ignored.

Sentencing Outcomes, Disparity, and Marginal Cases

Modest changes in sentencing outcomes, particularly in the use of prison sentences, followed implementation of sentencing innovations. Increases in sentence severity were most typically found in those marginal cases for which imprisonment had been most uncertain prior to the innovations. Both high-seriousness cases, for which imprisonment had been and continued to be likely, and low-seriousness cases, which were unlikely to be given a prison term, experienced little change.

Concerns that defendants with minor records or those accused of minor offenses would become enmeshed in the rigidity of the new scheme were expressed by critics of plea-bargaining bans and mandatory sentencing laws. The evidence from virtually every study indicates that these apprehensions were well founded: marginal offenders who did not benefit from early filtering decisions have been subject to harsher sentences.

Ironically, while the severity of those sanctions that were imposed for certain offense types sometimes increased, the rate of persons imprisoned and the likelihood of imprisonment declined. In New York, for example, about 11 percent of those arrested on drug charges were imprisoned in both 1972 and the first half of 1976, but the number of drug arrests was much smaller in 1976 so that there were fewer prison sentences imposed overall.

One of the goals of the sentencing reforms was the reduction of disparity in time served by like offenders with like cases. Several studies present some evidence suggesting that reduction in sentence variation did result from DSL in California, Minnesota's sentencing guidelines, and parole guidelines in several jurisdictions. However, this does not address variations in case processing before the sentencing stage and their effects. For example, two cases in which the underlying offense behavior is the same might still result in different charges at conviction and thus still be sentenced differently as a result.

METHODOLOGICAL CONCERNS

Our review of impact evaluations suggests the need to address a number of key methodological issues in subsequent evaluations of criminal justice reforms generally and of sentence reforms particularly.

The Need for Extended Observation Periods

Several of the evaluations reviewed here involved simple two-point, prereform and postreform designs that are inadequate for a number of reasons. First, such designs do not permit distinguishing discrete changes or effects associated with a reform from the continuation of preexisting trends. Multiple observations of outcomes before implementation of a change are highly desirable, as indicated by several studies of DSL in California; those extended observations were crucial to the conclusion that introduction of determinate sentencing in California resulted in no substantial changes in sentencing outcomes in that state.

Ideally, the postreform observation period should also extend for multiple observations after the reform, because case processing often takes months or even years. Thus a sentencing reform that is to apply to all cases involving offenses committed after January 1 of a year may not be applied to any substantial number of cases until well into the second year after the reform is implemented. If the reform increases case-processing time, there will be further delay before full impact. To the extent that cases disposed early differ significantly from cases that take longer to resolve, early evaluations of effects are likely to be biased and may indicate opposite effects from later evaluations.

The possibility of delayed impact was strongly suggested both by the dramatic increase in early guilty-plea rates in California and under the New York drug laws, where median disposition times increased and conviction and imprisonment rates for drug felonies fell immediately after the law went into effect. A gradual increase of sanction rates in New York by 1976 and a drop in early guilty pleas in the second year under DSL in California suggest the need for more data points.

To avoid possible spurious findings of effects arising from delays, evaluations should routinely include measures of case-processing times and changes in work loads and backlogs. These variables are important not only as direct indicators of impact, but also for identifying necessary follow-up periods after a reform.

The Need for Outcome Measures at All Levels of Case Processing

Evaluations are often limited to aspects of the process directly affected by a reform and fail to address processing at earlier or later stages in the criminal justice system. This narrowness of focus fails to acknowledge the complexity of criminal case processing and the many opportunities for the exercise of discretion that it affords. While in a literal sense criminal sentences are limited to the sanctions imposed by the court on convicted offenders, the character of these sentence outcomes is substantially influenced by factors determining which cases are actually available for sentencing.

If those cases least likely to end in a prison sentence if convicted are weeded out by changes in screening, charging, case dismissal, or shifting final disposition from higher to lower courts, the cases that reach the higher courts will be increasingly restricted to the more likely prison cases. An observed increase in prison use among higher court convictions then might be more apparent than real, because it derives at least in part from a change in the mix of cases at the higher court rather than from a real change in policy to extend prison use to cases previously sentenced to nonprison outcomes.

The importance of changes in the filtering process is clearest in the evaluations of the New York drug laws (Joint Committee on New York Drug Law Evaluation, 1978) and the mandatory sentencing law for firearms violations in Detroit, Michigan (Heumann and Loftin, 1979). In both jurisdictions prison use for convicted offenders increased dramatically after the reform, but conviction rates fell and fewer cases entered the system; consequently, there was virtually no change in the proportion of all cases entering the system that resulted in imprisonment.

The considerable opportunities for filtering cases before they reach the sentencing stage cannot be ignored. The need to adequately address the effects of changes in filtering is a central lesson from our review.

The Need for Adequate Controls for Changes in Case Attributes

General changes in the character of cases—particularly changes in the seriousness of cases—are related to but certainly not limited to the filtering process. Case attributes relevant to sentencing outcomes might also be affected by general changes in offending patterns and demographic changes in the offender population. Failure to control for any resulting changes in case attributes before and after a reform can seriously jeopardize the validity of conclusions about the impact of that reform on case outcomes at various stages, particularly sentencing outcomes.

The Need for Qualitative Analysis of System Functioning

Many evaluations are limited entirely to statistical analysis of abstracted case-processing data, often available from centralized automated data systems. While such analyses can provide aggregate average characterizations of case processing for large numbers of cases, they seldom provide adequate data to understand the ways courtroom participants alter their behavior to cope with the changes. The complexity of the sentencing process strongly indicates that statistical research based on official records cannot adequately address the system impact of legal changes. Although statistical analyses are an important component of evaluation research, they must be augmented by extensive use of participant observation, systematic interviewing, and other qualitative methods.

5

Sentencing Policies and Their Impact on Prison Populations

One of the important consequences of changes in sentencing policies is their impact on prison populations. This issue is especially important at a time when prisons are increasingly crowded. However, both short-term and longer-term perspectives on prison populations must be considered in policy making, since population projections suggest a decrease in the number of prisoners by the end of the 1980s in a number of states.

The size of the prison population is shaped by the number of offenders committed, the length of their sentences, and the time they actually serve. These, in turn, may be affected by demographic changes in the population, changes in demographic-specific crime rates, legislatively established sentencing policies, police and prosecutorial policies, judicial decision-making practices, the exercise of authority by prison officials in awarding and revoking good time, and parole boards' release and revocation policies.

The panel examined the relationship between sentencing policies and prison populations because anticipation of the impact on prison of existing and alternative sentencing policies makes explicit the choices among levels of punitiveness and their costs and is an important aid to responsible policy making.

In this chapter we examine recent changes in prison populations and the implications of these changes for the health and safety of inmates and correctional staff; the methods, uses, and limitations of projections of future prison populations for policy making; and alternative strategies for coping with prison populations that have grown beyond the capacities of existing prison facilities.

CHANGES IN PRISON POPULATIONS AND THEIR IMPLICATIONS

INCREASES IN PRISON POPULATIONS

Except during World War II, American prison populations increased at about the same rate as the civilian population from 1930 until the early 1970s, when a dramatic increase began in the number of prisoners incarcerated in federal and state prisons (see Figure 5–1). The rate of incarceration in state and federal prisons rose 62 percent between 1972 and 1981: from 95 per 100,000 population to 154 per 100,000 population.[1] Between the end of 1972 and the end of 1978, the federal and state prisoner population sentenced for more than 1 year increased by about 50 percent, from 196,183 to 294,580 (U.S. Department of Justice, 1975, 1976, 1977, 1978b, 1979). Since then, sentenced state and federal prisoner populations have continued to rise to 352,476 at the end of 1981, another 19 percent in 3 years (U.S. Department of Justice, 1982a).

The sharpest inmate increases occurred in state prisons, which hold about 60 percent of all offenders. Between 1972 and 1981, net state prison populations increased by 89 percent, from 174,470 to 330,307 inmates. Between 1939 and 1970 the median state prison incarceration rate was 98.8 per 100,000 civilian population; in 1972 this rate had fallen to 84, but by 1978 it had risen to 124, an increase of 48 percent in 6 years; by December 31, 1981, it had climbed to 144, a further increase of 16 percent in 3 years (U.S. Department of Justice, 1982a).

Increases in state prison population were most pronounced in the South. For decades the rate of incarceration in the South was higher than in other regions, and the gap grew during the 1970s. Between 1970 and 1978 state prison populations grew by 84.1 percent in the South, while they increased by 41 and 44 percent, respectively, in the North and North Central states, and by only 8.6 percent in the West (see Table 5–1). In 1970, the South accounted for 39 percent of all state prisoners; by 1978, that number was 48 percent. The greater increases in the South far outpaced population increases there: the incarceration rate increased 63 percent in the South and only 43 percent for the nation as a whole.

Though federal prisoners make up only 6 percent of the national prisoner total, recent changes in federal prison populations illustrate the

---

[1] Rates of incarceration are computed as the ratio of inmates in a jurisdiction for every 100,000 civilian population in that jurisdiction as estimated by the Bureau of the Census. State rates vary due both to different policies regarding incarceration and differences in accounting practices; for details, see Mullen and Smith (1980:11).

TABLE 5–1 State Prison Population Change by Region Between 1970 and 1978

Region	1970 Prison Population	1978 Prison Population	1978 Percentage Change in Population	1970 Rate per 100,000 Civilian Population	1978 Rate per 100,000 Civilian Population	1978 Percentage Change in Rate per 100,000 Civilian Population
Northeast[a]	28,595	40,425	+41.4	59	83	+41
North Central[b]	41,941	60,246	+43.6	74	104	+41
South[c]	69,590	128,108	+84.1	112	183	+63
West[d]	36,277	39,410	+8.6	106	99	−7
Total State prison population	176,403	268,189	+52.0	87	124	+43

[a] Connecticut, Maine, Massachusetts, New Hampshire, New Jersey, New York, Pennsylvania, Rhode Island, and Vermont.

[b] Illinois, Indiana, Iowa, Kansas, Michigan, Minnesota, Missouri, Nebraska, North Dakota, Ohio, South Dakota, and Wisconsin.

[c] Alabama, Arkansas, Delaware, District of Columbia, Florida, Georgia, Kentucky, Louisiana, Maryland, Mississippi, North Carolina, Oklahoma, South Carolina, Tennessee, Texas, Virginia, and West Virginia.

[d] Alaska, Arizona, California, Colorado, Hawaii, Idaho, Montana, Nevada, New Mexico, Oregon, Utah, Washington, and Wyoming.

SOURCE: Adapted from Carlson et al. (1980:20).

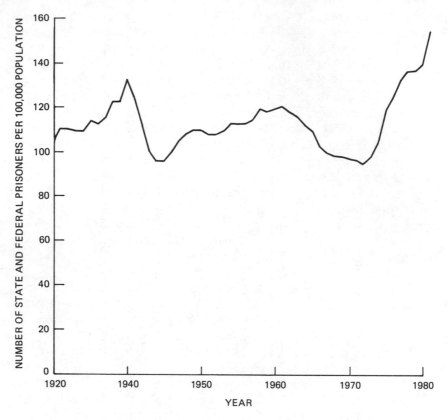

FIGURE 5–1   Annual imprisonment rate in the United States: 1930–1981. SOURCES: Adapted from Blumstein and Cohen (1973:203), Carlson et al. (1980:114), and U.S. Department of Justice 2(1982a).

impact of changes in prosecutorial policy on prison populations. Between 1977 and 1980, federal prison populations dropped, principally due to a change in emphasis in the Justice Department that sharply reduced prosecution of auto theft and bank robbery cases and increased resources for prosecution of white-collar crime, major narcotics violations, organized crime, and political corruption cases, all of which take longer to convict and result in shorter sentences.

PRISON CAPACITY AND CONDITIONS OF CONFINEMENT

The dramatic increases in prison population have not been accompanied by corresponding increases in prison capacity, resulting in overcrowding and a decline in living standards in prisons. The decline in prison populations through most of the 1960s led to selective closing of facilities and a virtual halt in the construction of new prison facilities. When the downward trend was reversed and prison populations increased by more than one-third between 1972 and 1976, crowding became common, and the conditions in many older facilities became a cause for many legal actions. The greater activism of courts in addressing conditions of confinement in prison as a constitutional issue and emerging professional standards and accreditation procedures[2] have limited legally acceptable options in dealing with population pressures and created a critical problem in many corrections systems. By March 1982, prison authorities in 28 states and the District of Columbia were operating under court orders arising from violations of the constitutional rights of prisoners related to the conditions of confinement or overcrowding, including sweeping orders covering entire correctional systems in 10 states. In addition, according to the American Civil Liberties Union Foundation, legal challenges to major prisons were pending in 9 other states (*Criminal Justice Newsletter*, 1982).

A congressionally mandated national study of prison inmates and facilities found that 61 percent of federal prisoners, 65 percent of state prisoners, and 68 percent of prisoners in local jails had less than 60 square feet of floor space, the minimum standard promulgated by the Commission on Accreditation for Corrections (Mullen et al., 1980:61, 75). Because definitions of capacity vary widely, there is no single or clear estimate of the number of inmates that can be held in existing state and federal prisons, and the study used three different measures of capacity. Using the reported capacity measure, the study found that state and federal prisons had slightly more than sufficient capacity to hold all inmates confined in 1978 in state and federal prisons together (i.e., 96 percent of all space was used). By the measured capacity standard—one inmate per cell of any size or, for dormitories, the smaller of (1) the number of square feet of floor space/60 or (2) the jurisdictionally reported capacity—state and federal prisons were operating at 115 percent of capacity. By the most stringent physical capacity standard, de-

---

[2] In 1974 the American Correctional Association established the Commission on Accreditation for Corrections to develop a set of uniform standards that would provide measurable criteria for assessing the safety and well-being of correctional system inmates and staff. It has published 10 volumes of standards, including *Adult Correctional Institutions* and *Adult Local Detention Facilities* (Commission on Accreditation for Corrections, 1977a,b). Other standard-setting efforts include the American Bar Association's *Tentative Draft of Standards Relating to the Legal Status of Prisoners* (1977) and the *Federal Standards for Corrections* drafted by the U.S. Department of Justice (1978a).

fined as a minimum of 60 square feet of floor space per inmate, prisons were operating at 171 percent of capacity (Mullen et al., 1980:65). An additional indicator of crowded conditions in state prison facilities is the extent to which state prisoners are housed in local facilities. According to the Bureau of Justice Statistics, 6,497 inmates (2.1 percent of the total) were housed in local jails at the end of 1979, including 39.4 percent of Mississippi's state prisoners and 24.6 percent of Alabama's (U.S. Department of Justice, 1981c:15).

Relief from population pressures through expansion of prison and jail facilities is not anticipated. In its survey of facility construction, renovation, acquisition, and closing plans between March 31, 1978, and December 31, 1982, an Abt survey found jurisdictions planning a total increase of 52,843 beds or an overall increase of about 24 percent in net additional capacity (Mullen and Smith, 1980:80). But these increases are in rated capacity, not in the measured capacity standard of 60 square feet (suggesting the possibility of capacity increases achieved by changing definitions, greater use of double-celling, and a decline in living standards). They also include intended expansions for which appropriations had not yet been authorized by state legislatures and so they may be inflated.[3] The increase of 48,651 state and federal prisoners between year-end 1977 and mid-year 1981 (U.S. Department of Justice, 1981b) and the time lag between planning, appropriation, and construction of a facility suggest that facility expansion is not keeping pace with expanding populations, that prison crowding is increasing, and that short-term approaches to correctional population pressures are badly needed now.

The dramatic increases in prison populations, as well as changes in sentencing policies, raise two major questions for institutional management: What is the general effect of crowded prison conditions on inmate health and behavior and on institutional management? What is the effect of determinate sentences on institutional programs, offender misconduct, and disciplinary procedures?

Inmate Health and Behavior

It is widely believed among prison administrators and researchers that crowding has adverse affects on inmate health and behavior and, by

---

[3] Another survey of prison construction plans completed in May 1981 (National Moratorium on Prison Construction, 1981) found that, although states "planned" to expand by a total of 102,350 beds, if "planned construction" is defined as a facility that has been approved by a legislative body or been included in a governor's budget, only 25,316 additional beds were authorized or under construction.

increasing tension and aggression, may contribute to inmate violence and prison riots. But systematic research on these subjects is recent and limited. Cumulation of knowledge has been hindered by variation in the definitions and measures of crowding and density and their behavioral, physical, and attitudinal outcomes, resulting in noncomparable findings.

The initial research on crowding involved studies that documented its deleterious effects on animal health and behavior.[4] Studies of the relationship between population density and human behavior have yielded more ambiguous results than the animal research. Correlational studies of the incidence of social pathology in communities and households differing in population density have been a primary source of empirical conclusions about the effects of crowding (see Bordua, 1958; Galle et al., 1972; Schmid, 1960; Schmitt, 1957; Shaw and McKay, 1942). But these ecological approaches must be viewed with great caution because of the danger of making inferences about individuals from aggregate data, particularly where findings may be confounded by high correlations of deleterious factors like economic and educational deprivation with density.

Observational studies of hospital patients and of children in groups of varying size have yielded inconsistent results (see Hutt and Vaizey, 1966; Ittelson et al., 1972; Loo, 1972; McGrew, 1970). Individuals consistently interacted less in larger groups, but Loo reported less aggression in the denser situation, while Hutt and Vaizey found more.

Sample surveys have found positive correlations between persons per room or perceptions of the household as crowded and disrupted interpersonal relationships within the home (Baldassare, 1978; Mitchell, 1971), stress diseases (Booth and Cowell, 1976), and poor mental health (Gove et al., 1979). Again the correlation of density with other potentially deleterious factors may confound the findings.

In addition to these general studies of crowding, several studies have examined the effects of crowding and high density in prisons. (Although the terms "density" and "crowding" sometimes are used interchangeably, "density" refers to a physical condition and "crowding" to a subjective reaction to that condition. Further, there is a distinction between social density, the number of occupants per living unit, and physical

---

[4] Conditions of high density were found to impair fertility and reproduction in mice (Christian, 1960); to disrupt maternal ties, lead to homosexuality, and produce social withdrawal in rats (Calhoun, 1966a,b); and to cause increased aggression and emotionality, prostration, convulsions, and death in several mammalian species (Ader et al., 1963; Barnett et al., 1960; Bullough, 1952; Calhoun, 1956, 1962; Christian, 1960; Keeley, 1962; Rosen, 1961; Turner, 1961).

density, the number of square feet per individual.) Studies of the effects of social density have found that inmates living in open dormitories feel more crowded, rate their environments more negatively, have higher rates of illness complaints, and feel greater psychological stress than inmates living in single or double occupant rooms (Cox et al., 1979, 1980; Paulus et al., 1975). Some of the negative effects were reduced through use of dividers in dormitories, permitting an increase in privacy without an increase in space (McCain et al., 1980). McCain et al. (1976) also found that increased physical density led to progressive and measurable increases in negative effects on inmates, including higher rates of illness complaints, perceived crowding, mood states, rating of the environment, perception of choice and control, and nonaggressive disciplinary infractions. Increased social density was a more important contributor to the physical and psychological effects than increased physical density. The disciplinary data were obtained in only one institution, however, and only nonaggressive infractions were considered.

Some studies of the effects of crowding-related stress in prison, as measured by blood pressure, find that inmates in open dormitories have higher blood pressure than those in single cells, that increased social density in dormitories increases blood pressure (D'Atri, 1975; Paulus et al., 1978; Ray, 1978), and that transfers from single occupancy cells to multiple occupancy dormitories cause increases in blood pressure (D'Atri et al., 1981). However, McCain et al. (1980) found no density-related blood pressure effects.

Nacci et al. (1977) report that the federal correctional institutions that were most overcrowded relative to rated capacity, particularly those that had a large number of young offenders, had the highest disciplinary infraction rates. Similar results are reported by Megargee (1977) where the amount of living space available and the density were significantly associated with both the number and rate of disciplinary violations. However, Megargee found that the rate at which disciplinary reports (not distinguished by level of seriousness) were given over a 36-month period was not significantly related to the overall population in the institution, but he looked only at medium-sized institutions that varied within a narrow range (450–550 inmates). A third study (McCain et al., 1980) found both sheer population size and increased density in prisons associated with negative effects, including disproportionate increases in rates of disciplinary infractions, violent death, suicide, and death of inmates more than 50 years old.

In sum, research is just beginning to sort out the complex and often overlapping effects of social and physical density, crowding, and institutional size on inmate perceptions, morale, health, and behavior. A variety of negative effects have been hypothesized to result from sustained high-density living conditions, particularly in large institutions. The evidence, however, is still fragmentary due to methodological shortcomings, divergent measures, and correlations that may result from uncontrolled confounding variables like prison age and condition, security level of the institution, and the amount of time prisoners are confined to cells. It is very difficult to separate the individual physical, psychological, and behavioral effects of crowding from the effects of the many other undesirable aspects and deprivations of a prison environment.

In order to provide a comprehensive interpretation of the variety of crowding effects on inmates, future research on crowding effects should look across institutions; introduce richer controls for other attributes of these institutions; examine variations in the effects of crowding over time, including long-term effects (more than 3 years); compare housing types explore individual and group differences in reaction to high-density living arrangements; and develop a wider variety of measures of behavioral effects to supplement attitudinal measures.

Determinate Sentencing and Institutional Programs

Under indeterminate sentencing policies, corrections institutions developed a broad range of rehabilitation programs, including vocational, educational, and social skills development; individual and group therapy; and partial physical custody (i.e., work release and placement in halfway houses). Some expected that the shift to determinate sentencing policies would result in a reallocation of institutional resources from rehabilitation programs to custodial uses, a drop in program participation as inmates no longer felt coerced in such programs, and greater motivation from those inmates who continued to participate voluntarily.

To date, only two preliminary studies have been completed on the effects of determinate sentencing on institutional programs in three jurisdictions; both studies have serious limitations. Brady (1981) examined the impact of determinate sentencing in Oregon and California on prison programs and inmate attitudes toward them. His interviews with administrators, custodial and program staff, and inmates indicated that participation in programs in both states continued at about the same level as before determinate sentencing, but that many staff members sensed some change in inmate behavior and attitudes toward participation: many inmates were more negative; a few were more motivated. The contribution of California's Uniform Determinate Sentencing Law (DSL) to these attitudinal changes is unclear; what is clear to prison staff is that "rehabilitation and programs have less general appeal [to inmates] than perhaps five years ago" (Brady, 1981:9). California's institutional programs have continued, but a clear shift in goals and policies has occurred due to both disciplinary problems in institutions and DSL. Prisoners are being reclassified according to their background and "prior incarceration behavior" rather than their amenability to rehabilitation. While the programs themselves have not been altered, internal security dominates the prison atmosphere and staff view prisoners as less cooperative than they were prior to implementation of DSL.

Brady's findings must be viewed as preliminary. There are no comparative data on pre-DSL and post-DSL levels of participation, and other changes occurred simultaneously with implementation of the new law, including more crowding and an increasingly youthful and violent inmate population.

Stone-Meierhoefer and Hoffman (1980) examined the effects on program participation of setting presumptive parole release dates within 120 days of admission to prison. Comparing program participation by an experimental group (randomly assigned prisoners given presumptive parole release dates) and a control group (prisoners considered for parole after serving one-third of their sentence), they found that experimental group members enrolled in somewhat fewer programs, particularly education programs, than control group members and appeared to drop out of a slightly higher percentage of the programs in which they enrolled. No significant difference was found between the groups in the number of persons enrolling in at least one type of educational or work program, but experimental group members joined significantly fewer programs than did those in the control group. The authors attribute this difference to the fixed parole date that obviates the need for program participation in order to impress the parole board.

The generalizability of these findings is limited. Staff and prisoners were aware that the experiment was part of a pilot study of the U.S. Parole Commission's new parole guidelines. The guidelines had already been implemented, so all inmates already could predict their parole dates, thereby reducing parole-related incentives for program participation for both experimental and control groups.

Inmate Misconduct, Disciplinary Procedures, and Determinate Sentencing

Determinate sentencing was also expected to affect disciplinary problems and procedures in prisons (Goodstein, 1980; Morris, 1974; von Hirsch, 1976). Supporters of determinacy reasoned that uncertainty about the length of time to be served caused anxieties, tensions, and frustrations among inmates that contributed to more institutional misbehavior and interpersonal violence (Bennett, 1976; Park, 1976). Conversely, critics of this viewpoint suggested that determinacy would increase disciplinary problems by removing the threat of longer imprisonment.

Three studies have produced data on the effects of determinacy on prison discipline (Forst, 1981; Goodstein, 1981; Stone-Meierhoefer and Hoffman, 1980). Their methodologies, research questions, and findings vary and provide at best preliminary and suggestive obervations rather than reliable conclusions.

Stone-Meierhoefer and Hoffman (1980) found that granting presumptive parole dates did not appear to adversely affect discipline within federal prisons. Comparisons of experimental and control groups (as described above) indicated no significant differences in the proportion of inmates committing disciplinary infractions, the total number of infractions, or the number of inmates committing major infractions (after controlling for months of exposure). However, because federal prisoners differ in both offense type and background from state prisoners and the sample pool underrepresented long-term prisoners—arguably those with little incentive to conform—the disciplinary impact of a fixed parole date may have been underestimated.

Goodstein (1981) used a quasi-experimental design to compare prisoners with determinate and indeterminate sentences in three South Carolina prisons on a number of attitudinal and behavioral measures.[5] Controlling for differences in sentence length (because those with indeterminate sentences had committed different offenses and had longer terms), Goodstein found no difference between the prisoner groups with respect to rate of institutional misconduct. She did find, however, that inmates with determinate sentences reported experiencing significantly less stress than did those with indeterminate terms.

Forst (1981) examined the impact of determinate sentencing on inmate misconduct and institutional discipline in Oregon and California. His interview and observational data indicate that determinacy has not been the answer to prison unrest that its supporters had hoped, nor has knowledge of a fixed release date led directly to increases in misconduct

---

[5] In South Carolina, judges have the discretion of sentencing offenders to terms with fixed release dates (via a "split sentence" requiring that an offender serve a specified portion of the total sentence in prison) or to long maximum terms with the expectation of earlier parole release. Since the criminal code makes all inmates eligible for parole after serving one-third of their maximum sentences, it is possible for an offender with a split sentence to be released from prison at a fixed date prior to his parole eligibility date.

as others had feared. Indeed, it now appears that "prison violence. . . is little affected by the type of sentencing structure" (Forst, 1981:88).

In California, the change from indeterminate to determinate sentencing both eliminated the parole board that previously set parole release dates and reinstituted the use of good time. The law left untouched the authority of corrections officials to refer serious misconduct to the district attorney for prosecution as a new offense and their ability to alter the *quality* of time served by means of a variety of sanctions, including isolation and segregation.[6]

Between 1970 and 1979, serious disciplinary infractions of all types rose steadily in California prisons.[7] Since implementation of DSL in July 1977, however, forfeiture of good time as a disciplinary mechanism has been used modestly, but it is gradually increasing. Between July 1, and September 30, 1977, 1.7 percent of prisoners found guilty of serious disciplinary infractions (but not necessarily "good-time offenses") lost some good time; for the same quarter of 1979, good-time forfeitures had increased tenfold, to 17.2 percent of such prisoners. The median number of days of good time lost in 1978 was 10 (Forst, 1981:97–8).[8] Felony referrals to district attorneys have also increased steadily, from 931 in 1975 to 1,744 in 1978, but prison officials attribute this principally to the increase in the number of serious felonies committed in prison, rather than to a change in policy associated with DSL (Forst, 1981:58–59).

In Oregon, increased use of parole release after 1972 and subsequent adoption of the parole guidelines in 1977 diminished the role of good-time forfeiture as a sanction by corrections authorities. To regain some leverage over time served as a means of controlling inmates, corrections officials in 1978 obtained parole board approval of a system for changing inmates' parole release dates under certain circumstances on prison

---

[6] Segregation is a classification decision in California: while technically a change in an offender's placement to a more secure housing unit is not a punishment, reclassification of custody status actually functions as a qualitative sanction as well as a mechanism for protecting inmates who request it.

[7] During that 9-year period, the rate of incidents per 100 average institutional population increased almost 10-fold, from 1.36 to 10.07 (Management Information Section, Policy and Planning Division, California Department of Corrections, February 26, 1979, cited in Forst, 1981:77). Another indicator of the increase in serious misconduct is the increase in assaults on staff, which rose from 94 in 1976 to 182 in 1978 (Forst, 1981:80).

[8] Some of the prisoners found guilty of an infraction were "lifers" not subject to good-time loss. Some of the forfeiture was loss of participation credits. In 1978 a department policy directed all inmates to be assigned to a program; as jinmates failed to participate, more participation credits were forfeited.

authorities' initiative, thereby reintroducing an element of indetermi-nacy.[9] Actual use of changed release dates for handling discipline prob-lems varies among institutions and seems to be (inversely) related to crowding rather than to the rate of misconduct.[10]

Data on changes in inmate misconduct as a result of the introduction of determinacy in Oregon, however, are incomplete because of a court order to expunge all records of disciplinary matters between December 6, 1977, and October 22, 1979. Nevertheless, from the data that were available Forst (1981:85) observed: "We cannot distinguish any rela-tionship between inmate misconduct (as measured by disciplinary re-ports) and the change from an indeterminate to a determinate sentencing system."

An apparent trend in both states is reliance on disciplinary devices that affect the quality rather than the amount of time in prison, prin-cipally through reclassification of inmates and the resulting transfers among housing units that vary in degree of security. This is viewed as having two advantages for prison administrators: it does not increase the prison population, and it has a more direct and immediate effect on the inmate, which is viewed as a more effective deterrent to misconduct.

Forst also found that corrections administrators in both Oregon and California report decreased tension and anxiety over uncertainty of re-lease date but no concomitant reduction in misconduct. Though no statistical data were available to support their view, they suggest that determinacy has *indirectly* increased misconduct in two ways: first, it contributes to prison overcrowding, which results in heightened tension and disciplinary infractions; second, it leads to feelings of hopelessness

---

[9] There now are four categories of prison misconduct that can result in a change in release date. The range of possible extensions to a term varies with the seriousness of the misconduct. Misconduct that is hazardous to human life can result in a change of from 50 to 100 percent of an inmate's term with a maximum extension of 5 years. Misconduct that is a hazard to security can increase a term from 25 to 50 percent to a maximum 2-year extension. Hazard to property can increase a term from 10 to 20 percent to a maximum 1-year extension, and the third in a series of rule violations within a 3-month period can increase a prison term from 5 to 10 percent to a maximum 6-month extension.

[10] At Oregon State Prison, which was very crowded at the end of 1979, only two or three term changes were made of 4,120 disciplinary reports filed (Forst, 1981:98), as prison authorities relied on segregation (which does not increase time and thereby prison population) in preference to changes in parole release dates. At Oregon State Correctional Institution, where crowding was less critical and most inmates live in dormitories, changes in release dates were more frequent, although only 2.8 percent of all disciplinary actions filed in that institution in 1979 led to recommendations for changed release dates (Forst, 1981:98).

and frustration among prisoners who have long sentences that may be extended but which they can do nothing to shorten. This view is ironic in light of the rejection of indeterminacy by some because it was believed to lead to frustration and hopelessness.

Prison officials are reported to favorably regard changes in disciplinary procedures stemming from the determinate sentencing laws in Oregon, since the parole board has agreed to a procedure for changing parole release dâtes that increases the officials' influence. In California some administrators prefer the current system that specifies acceptable behavior, while others feel they have diminished control over inmates.

In sum, all three studies of determinacy and offender misconduct, though preliminary, suggest that both critics and supporters of determinacy exaggerated the effect of the change. Determinate sentencing may have limited impact on prisoners' misconduct because, in relation to peer pressures and other concerns, it has little influence on the daily environment of a prison inmate.

PROJECTION OF PRISON POPULATIONS: NEED, TECHNOLOGY, AND USES

NEED FOR PROJECTIONS OF PRISON POPULATIONS

The need to develop improved methods for estimating the impact of changes in sentencing policies on prison populations has become especially important in the face of capacity constraints and increased crowding in U.S. prisons. Without consideration of the impact of policy changes on prison populations, two undesirable consequences are likely to occur: prosecutors and judges will adhere to new policies, and prisons will become severely overcrowded; prosecutors and judges will informally seek to limit prison populations through accommodations that modify mandated policies.

The effects of a sentencing policy on the corrections system are generally ignored by judges and often are not considered by legislatures. Some have asserted that such effects *should* be ignored when considering broad principles of justice or weighing individual cases. Such a perspective, however, may be impractical during the 1980s when prisons are at or near capacity and substantial additional prison space is unlikely to be available soon. Consequently, consideration of policy changes likely to significantly increase prison population should weigh the desirability of the change in light of available prison capacity and the costs of increasing that capacity.

Adopting a policy without providing the resources needed to implement it tends to undermine respect for the law by participants in the system and to encourage violation through a variety of ad hoc adaptations. Furthermore, many jurisdictions are likely to experience increases in prison populations, even without explicit changes in sentencing policy, and these jurisdictions will need more capacity just to maintain current practices. Thus, whether considering policy changes or assessing current policies, projection of the impact on future prison populations of existing and alternative practices is a necessary component of sound public policy formulation.

In making prison population projections, three factors must be kept in mind: the amount of time necessary for the full effect to be felt, the amount of compliance, and the nature and composition of the prison population. The time dimension is important in distinguishing short-term and long-term effects. A policy of incarcerating a higher proportion of a certain type of offender (e.g., a mandatory minimum sentence of 5 years for all robbers) would increase prison populations more rapidly than an increase in the average length of sentence of those categories of offenders who are already being imprisoned (e.g., an increase in the average sentence of incarcerated robbers from 4 to 7 years). The latter change will lead to a gradual population buildup over several years. The former will have an immediate, dramatic short-term effect, through increases in commitments, as well as long-term consequences.

Prison population projections must also consider likely rates of compliance with new policies. The simplest assumptions, no compliance (i.e., a continuation of existing policy) and complete compliance, are likely to be inaccurate; actual compliance will probably lie between these extremes. Therefore, several estimates that assume different levels of compliance by justice system personnel are desirable.

Policy changes may alter the composition of prison populations and the length of the inmates' sentences. These effects, in turn, may have repercussions for programs and levels of control in institutions. For example, an increase in the number of violent youthful offenders serving long terms may suggest a need for increased custodial staffs, since such offenders have lower rates of participation in institutional programs and worse disciplinary records than other offenders.

PROJECTION METHODS: THEIR USES AND SHORTCOMINGS

Naive Projections Using the Existing Situation as a Baseline

The simplest projection method rests on the assumption that next year's prison population—in the absence of a policy change—will be the same as the current population. (For a more detailed discussion of projection methods, see Blumstein [Volume II].) This method, while offering the considerable advantage of simplicity, assumes stability of prison populations over time, absent any policy changes, despite evidence of changes in crime rates, sentencing practices, and the demographic characteristics of offenders. The further one projects into the future, the less accurate the baseline data are likely to be as projections.

Extrapolations of Time-Series Data

Simple linear extrapolations of future prison population based on recent trends have often been used by researchers and corrections planners. Over the last decade, however, forecasting procedures have become more sophisticated than trend analyses (see Box and Jenkins, 1976; Granger and Newbold, 1977; Nerlove et al., 1979). To the degree that the future is like the past, it is possible to accurately forecast the future of a wide variety of historical patterns using techniques that include linear trends, shifts in level, shifts in slope, seasonal cycles, and other temporal regularities. Once these historical patterns are captured in a small set of parameters whose values are estimated from the observed time series, optimal forecasts are available (i.e., with minimum mean square forecasting errors).

These forecasts do not invoke any causal structure, which is both a strength and a weakness of the technique. The strength is that they do not rely on current social science theory, which may not be able to explain incarceration rates. There is no need to collect data on causal variables and forecast *their* values (which would be required for forecasts of the outcome variable of interest): pure induction from the outcome variable alone will suffice. The weakness is that, if the underlying causal relationships produce *new* temporal patterns, time-series forecasts will be inaccurate. Thus, such forecasts tend to be more useful in making short-term projections than long-term ones. Furthermore, because extrapolations from time-series data only consider the time variable and assume a constant rate of change in other factors that influence prison populations, they are of limited utility to a legislature considering the effect of a policy change.

There is still lively debate about the accuracy of time-series extrapolations compared to alternate approaches. A great deal depends on specific applications, and experience with forecasts of prison populations is limited. Nevertheless, time-series forecasts are valuable procedures when (1) there is no reason to believe that structural changes will occur; (2) the time-series model easily survives statistical tests of its validity; (3) the time series includes many observations (e.g., more than 100); and (4) the time horizon of the forecasts is short.

Use of Predictor Variables

Prison populations can also be projected by relying on a variety of other variables, which are believed to be causally related to prison population, as predictor variables in an estimated regression equation. Some of the predictor variables that have been included in a prison population forecast model are the consumer price index (Fox, 1978), unemployment (Robinson et al., 1977), the demographic mix in the population (Crago and Hromas, 1976), and prison capacity (Abt, 1980).

There are three problems with using predictor variables. First, in projecting future prison populations, they often include variables in the model that are more difficult to project than prison population itself. Use of the unemployment rate, for example, in the absence of accurate projections of that rate, adds little to one's ability to project prison populations. Demographic variables are more easily projected because data on individuals in a demographic group, such as males aged 20–29, are available and fairly easy to project. Second, these forecast models usually do not include changes in intervening sentencing policy variables, such as the probability of imprisonment and the length of prison sentences. Even if sentencing policy variables are included directly as predictors in models, the changes in these policy variables must then be projected. Finally, these models are at present relatively simple. They fail to consider the many interrelated political, socioeconomic, and demographic variables that appear to influence sentencing. But adding more variables to the model is often not feasible given the difficulty in making future projections of many of them.

Projections Based on Demographic-Specific Incarceration Rates

A variation of projections using general predictor variables uses demographic-specific incarceration rates as the predictor variable. These projections rely on marked differences in involvement with the criminal justice system among different age, race, and sex groups. In 1979, for example, the incarceration rate of males was 25 times that of females; the incarceration rate of black males was 6.7 times that of white males; and the incarceration rate of white males aged 23 (the peak age of incarceration) was 8.8 times that of white males aged 40 and older (see Blumstein, Volume II).

Projections of prison populations for demographic-specific subgroups are particularly attractive when one has fairly reliable projections of demographic changes in the general population and when incarceration rates, especially for the high-rate groups (e.g., males aged 20–29), are fairly constant over time. Examination of incarceration rates within demographic groups, however, indicates the possibility of substantial changes in these demographic-specific rates over time (see Blumstein, Volume II; U.S. Department of Justice, 1981b). In addition, this approach does not include in the projection model sentencing policy variables, such as an increase in the proportion of burglars incarcerated as a result of new legislation or an administrative decision. While the absence of sentencing policy variables could theoretically be remedied by generating demographic-specific conviction rates by offense type and then applying sentencing variables to them, data systems found in most jurisdictions do not provide sufficient information to permit estimation of conviction rates that are demographic- and offense-specific.

Disaggregated Flow Models

Disaggregated flow models permit detailed disaggregated examination of future prison populations. They require a data base that contains records on individual cases as they proceed through the criminal justice system. Development of such models, therefore, is feasible principally in jurisdictions with operational offender-based transaction statistics (OBTS) systems.[11] The OBTS system includes attributes of the offender and the offense and describes the experiences of individuals as they are processed through the criminal justice system. An individual case record is created for each arrest or court filing; additional information is added to the record as the case moves through the successive stages of processing in the criminal justice system. Analyses of the records of indi-

---

[11] The OBTS system was initiated in 1969 with funding from the Law Enforcement Assistance Administration (LEAA) to Project SEARCH in an effort to computerize reports from existing criminal justice statistical series. When the SEARCH task force found that such series did not yet exist, they turned their attention to the design of statewide statistical systems and concluded that such systems should be based on data on offenders as they passed through the system. A model system, proposed for adoption by states, emphasized selection of certain common data elements and use of a common unit of analysis (i.e., the defendant who is charged with a felony and fingerprinted). In 1973 LEAA awarded two separate grants to Project SEARCH: one to design an offender-based state corrections information system, the other to design a state judicial information system. Several states were selected to participate in the development and testing of these systems, which were intended to collect management information for daily operation, and at the same time meet the OBTS data requirements and transfer appropriate data into master OBTS files in each state. Since then a number of states have developed OBTS systems that include common court and correctional system data on individual offenders.

vidual cases completed during a given period (e.g., a year) permits disaggregated estimates of the nature of case processing at various decision points in the criminal justice system.

In these flow models the state or local criminal justice system is represented as a series of stages processing defendants, or "units of flow." The flow through each stage of the system can be represented by a matrix of branching ratios or transition probabilities representing the percentage of cases at any stage that proceed to the next stage. These transition probabilities can be disaggregated by crime type (or any other relevant characteristic of the units of flow) to allow for differences in the way different cases flow through the system. Sentencing policy variables are explicitly included in this detailed characterization of case processing. This kind of model can then be applied to disaggregated projections of system inputs (e.g., crimes, arrests, or convictions) to generate projections of prison population.

A disaggregated flow model permits a fuller characterization of case processing than is available from incarceration rates alone. The model's flow parameters are, nevertheless, generally treated as fixed quantities because of inadequate knowledge about likely system responses to changing flow levels through the system. This is not an inherent limitation, however; to the extent that plausible assumptions about changes in case processing at various points can be made, the model's flow parameters can be manipulated to reflect anticipated processing or policy changes.

One example of this approach is found in Blumstein et al. (1980). Demographic- and offense-specific arrest rates are used in combination with population projections to estimate future arrests. Then, similarly— estimates of the disaggregated probability of imprisonment and time served are applied to the arrests to yield projections of the size and composition of future prison populations. Using data for Pennsylvania from 1970 through 1975 and projections of demographic changes in the state's population, the model estimated future arrests and prison commitments for Pennsylvania to the year 2000. The projections to the year 2000, reflecting the strong effect of the postwar baby boom on the criminal justice system, suggest that arrest rates in Pennsylvania will peak about 1980, prison commitments will peak in 1985, and prison population will peak in 1990, then gradually decline. Because the projections ignore possible policy changes and the likely adaptive responses in the criminal justice system to increasing population pressures on the prison system, they are likely to be increasingly inaccurate the farther they extend in time. The model is useful, nevertheless, in suggesting the likely point at which additional capacity or policy alternatives will be needed to accommodate mounting population pressures, thereby helping decision makers select among alternatives.

Microsimulation Models

Disaggregated flow models examine the distribution of average flow rates through the criminal justice system. Microsimulation models permit estimation of total distributions of flow parameters by simulating the flow of *individual* offenders through the system, then combining their individual experiences into aggregate statistics.

A microsimulation can use a group of actual case records. Such an approach was used by the projection estimates developed by the Minnesota Sentencing Guidelines Commission (MSGC), which permitted estimation of the effect on prison populations over a 5-year period of any guidelines sentencing schedule or policy option considered by the commission. In the MSGC model, the primary determinants of future prison populations are current prison population, future commitments to the prison population for 5 years, and the length of current and future prisoners' sentences. In the simulation, the movement of individual cases through the criminal justice system is governed by flow probabilities and by the length of time spent at each processing point, both of which are adjustable parameters in the model.

The MSGC model was designed to permit flexibility in testing alternative sentencing policies. When sentencing decision rules are proposed, the new sentences imposed on each of the simulated cases and the aggregate consequences for prison populations of the particular policy can be examined for a multiyear period (see Knapp, 1980; Knapp et al., 1979). In using the microsimulation to project long-term future population, it is important that the microsimulation be augmented by projections reflecting anticipated changes in the size and composition of the cases that serve as input to the simulation.

ESTIMATING THE EFFECTS OF SENTENCING POLICY CHANGES ON PRISON POPULATIONS

Since sentencing policies are shaped and implemented in states (or in some instances at a local level), jurisdiction-specific projections that estimate the consequences of changes in sentencing policy for prison populations are needed in advance of a policy change. To be useful as a policy-impact estimating technique, a projection model must contain estimates of sentencing variables, including commitment rates and sentence lengths by offense type; disaggregated flow and microsimulation models are best suited for this purpose. Development of impact assessments involves four steps, each subject to data and methodological difficulties.

The first step is identifying the subset of cases to which the policy change would apply. A mandatory sentence for use of a gun, for example, would apply to cases involving guns. Unfortunately, most data sets do not contain adequate individual or aggregate data on details of the offense and relevant attributes of the offender to permit accurate determination of which or how many cases would be affected by such a proposed policy. Approximations of missing data are thus often necessary, adding uncertainty to the projection.

The second step is establishing the future values of policy variables. With adequate data, a proposed sentencing policy can be characterized by specifying corresponding sentencing variables for each affected offense/offender subset. For example, in the case of a mandatory minimum sentencing law, it is necessary to determine which offenders previously not incarcerated for a particular offense type would be subject to incarceration under the new law and to specify the sentence lengths both for those newly incarcerated and for those who were previously incarcerated for less than the proposed mandatory minimum sentence. (Those already receiving sentences above the mandatory minimum and those committing offenses not addressed by the mandatory law would not be affected by the law.)

The third step is estimating behavioral responses to a new policy. Policies are often not implemented as planned. Actors in the criminal justice system follow a variety of adaptive strategies that may affect the number of commitments and time served under a new policy. Responses by judges to a mandatory minimum sentence law might include, for example: literal interpretations, with prison sentences, for all who satisfy the conditions of the law, for the specified mandatory minimum sentence; increased sentences of up to the new required minimum for all who formerly went to prison but continued sentences of probation for those previously sentenced to probation (perhaps through agreement to a plea to a lesser charge); or probation sentences for some of those formerly sent to prison for terms shorter than the new minimum (perhaps through conviction on a lesser charge or invoking a mitigating circumstances provision) in order to avoid the longer sentences. An assumption of literal compliance is likely to overestimate the impact of a policy; it is preferable to test several possible response patterns to establish a likely range of outcomes.

The final step is calculating the effects of a change in sentencing policies on prison populations. This step involves comparing prison populations expected under the old and new policies using various behavioral assumptions. The difference in projected populations reflects the effect of a new policy.

Both projections of prison populations that do not include consideration of policy changes and those designed specifically to examine the effects of particular policy choices permit fuller appreciation of the factors that affect prison populations, provide estimates of the ranges for those populations, and encourage the development of an ongoing monitoring system that includes data on the behavior of participants and the flow of offenders through the criminal justice system. In addition, estimates of the impact of changes on prisons represent an important methodological device for forcing consideration of policy issues.

In jurisdictions where proposed sentencing policies increase punitiveness and further exacerbate pressures on already crowded prisons, policy makers face a dilemma: Should they increase prison capacity, which is costly and may not be needed soon after construction is completed, or look for alternative punishment strategies? Impact estimates can aid in responsible decision making by focusing attention on the explicit value trade-offs associated with a desired level of punitiveness and its costs. A note of caution is necessary in considering prison population projections, however, to avoid overconfidence in projected figures and the possibility that reactions to projections will lead to self-fulfilling prophecies. It must be remembered that all projections are vulnerable to errors arising from data inadequacies and the uncertainty of system responses to new policies.

ALTERNATIVE STRATEGIES FOR HANDLING INCREASING PRISON POPULATIONS

Three general strategies are available to achieve a balance between prison capacity and prison population: expansion of capacity through changes in existing facilities and new construction; limitation on admissions through use of alternatives to imprisonment; and direct regulation of prison population through controls on intake and release. Most states now appear to be using at least one of these approaches to some extent. While selection among these options is primarily a policy question, policy choices can be informed by consideration of the relative short-term and long-term effects of each strategy.

INCREASING PRISON CAPACITY: THE POPULATION-CONSTRUCTION NEXUS

There are no simple explanations of why some states build new prisons and others do not. The decision to construct new prison facilities appears to be influenced by a variety of demographic, social, economic, and political considerations often in combinations unique to each state.

Some of the factors that tend to accelerate the decision to build are the apparent failure of alternatives to incarceration, leading to a renewed reliance on imprisonment; the need for specialized new facilities; court orders; prison disturbances or riots; state population growth; and the availability of federal funds or facilities. Prison riots and disturbances, for example, seem to contribute to construction both by the focusing of public attention on the need for more or better facilities and through the destruction of existing housing that necessitates replacement construction. States that are growing in overall population appear to be expanding prison capacity faster than states with stable or declining populations and also building at a higher rate than the rate of increase in the number of prisoners. The availability of existing federal facilities that require only modest renovation and involve moderate operating costs has contributed to the expansion of state prison capacities (Benton and Silberstein, 1983).

Other factors tend to retard capacity expansion. These include the existence of excess capacity in some state prison facilities; redefinition of rated "capacity" to meet population increases;[12] political circumstances that prevent development of a consensus on the need to build or block implementation of a decision to do so; budgetary constraints and competition for funds; site-related opposition; regulatory limitations on location and construction; and effective prison management.

Increasing prison populations are costly in terms of both capital outlays to expand capacity and increases in direct operating expenditures (cash outlays for purchase of noncapital goods and services). Such expenditures for adult correctional institutions—both jails and prisons—for all levels of government in fiscal 1977 were about $2.46 billion. The average annual per-inmate cost for all adult inmates of state prisons was $5,461, with a range of costs across states from $2,241 to $14,946 (Mullen and Smith, 1980:115–117). Direct current expenditures of federal, state,

---

[12] The Supreme Court decision in *Rhodes* v. *Chapman* (452 U.S. 337 [1981]), permitting two prisoners in a single cell under certain circumstances, may have discouraged construction by enabling many states to legally increase prison density.

and local governments steadily increased between 1971 and 1977; the $2.46 billion spent in 1977 represented an increase of 45 percent over the 1971 figure after adjustment for inflation. It has been estimated that these expenditures would increase an additional 10–17 percent by 1982 (Mullen and Smith, 1980:134).

Capital outlays for correctional institutions (including juvenile detention facilities for state and local governments) in 1977 amounted to $415 million (only a small fraction of which was spent on equipment). Estimating future prison construction costs is difficult, however, due to wide variations in estimated costs depending on institutional size, region, and security level (see Singer and Wright, 1976). The National Council on Crime and Delinquency (1977:7) estimated that construction costs per new bed range from $25,000 to $50,000; according to the Federal Bureau of Prisons, a new 500-bed facility would cost about $35,000 per new bed (U.S. General Accounting Office, 1978:13).

Financial costs are only one consideration in the complex decision regarding construction of new prison facilities, but the millions of dollars for each new prison that might be spent on other government services and facilities, particularly in a time of fiscal austerity, appear to have been a major inhibitor of prison capacity expansion. In the past few years, voters in several states, including New York and Michigan, have rejected bond issues to finance prison construction.

Several studies have attempted to develop and test general hypotheses about why particular states build new prisons. Given the range of factors that might affect the construction decision, these analyses have been rather simplistic, and, thus far, the models have not fit the evidence very well. Nonetheless, a consideration of their shortcomings may be instructive.

One approach, termed the "population model," suggests that the supply of prison housing is expanded in direct response to increased demand in the form of prison population increases. However, neither recent national prisoner statistics nor a preliminary test of the correlation between measures of prison population growth between 1975 and 1981 and estimates of planned net capacity increase from 1978 through 1982 for the 50 states (Benton and Silberstein, 1983) support this model without the addition of other factors that mediate the population-construction relationship.

An alternative "capacity model," suggested by William Nagel (1973), postulates that prison construction is itself a stimulus to prison population expansion. In this model, expanded prison capacity affects sentencing decisions, resulting in more prisoners to fill that capacity, renewed population pressures, and further construction.

Carlson et al. (1980) sought to test both the capacity and population models and to clarify the relationship between capacity and population. They found no relationship between current capacity and present population, i.e., construction does not appear to be significantly stimulated by existing or past prison population pressure. However, they report a significant and substantial relationship between past capacity change and future populations with a 2-year lag and concluded that (Carlson et al., 1980:56):

On the average . . . additions are filled to rated capacity by the second year after opening additional space; within five years the occupancy of the new space averages 130 percent of rated capacity.

Because the finding that prison capacity generates the population to fill it has been widely cited by the press and accorded importance by policy makers, the panel believed it important to assess the validity of the finding.[13] The independent review of the data indicates that the empirical evidence cited in the Carlson et al. study provides no valid support for the capacity model (Blumstein et al., 1983). Errors in the study include an excessively simplistic formulation of the problem and associated statistical model; failure to test the sensitivity of the computed results to undue influence by several extreme data points; a serious computational error in calculating the univariate estimates of the coefficients; a highly questionable assumption that there were no changes in prison capacity in years when no new facilities were opened; inadequate correction for errors associated with serial correlation in a model including lagged dependent variables; and failure to analyze the aggregate data at a state level to discern whether the conclusions were reflected in individual states.

While the results of the reanalysis do *not* demonstrate that there is no causal relationship between prison capacity and prison population—indeed, anecdotal evidence supports such a relationship—it is clear that the relationship is complex, that the construction decision rests on a number of factors that stimulate or discourage building, that conditions vary greatly from state to state, and that further research is needed to explain the prison construction-prison population relationship. If prison

[13] The replication was made possible by Carlson, who generously made the data tape available to the panel. It was initiated by Alfred Blumstein and carried out at Carnegie-Mellon University, and the findings are available in Blumstein et al. (1983). The data tape contained reported prison population and reported increases in prison capacity for each of the 50 states and the District of Columbia for each year from 1955 to 1976 (1,122 cases) plus one observation from 1954 and four from 1977, for a total of 1,127 cases.

population forecasts are correct, populations in a number of states should decline in the 1990s without policy changes. This likely situation provides an opportunity to test the capacity model directly to determine whether and under what circumstances the availability of "spare" capacity affects the threshhold for selecting offenders to be incarcerated in order to fill the space.

ALTERNATIVES TO INCARCERATION

The effort to develop alternatives to incarceration and community-based corrections programs was stimulated by the President's Commission on Law Enforcement and the Administration of Justice (1967), which called for the integration of offenders into the community rather than their removal from it. In the early 1970s, when prisons in most states were not under population pressure, a variety of alternative programs were initiated to alter traditional case processing by prosecutors, provide alternative sanctions to prison and jail confinement, reduce the use of secure confinement facilities, and provide alternatives to continual confinement in state prisons. The initiatives included pretrial diversion, restitution and community service programs at all stages of the criminal justice process, increased use of probation and intensive community supervision, development of halfway houses, early release programs, and statewide community corrections legislation.

As prison populations mushroomed between 1972 and 1978 and persistent evidence indicated the unproductive effect of rehabilitation programs in prisons, many groups pressed for greater use of community-based sanctions instead of incarceration for nondangerous offenders. While some advocated these programs as a way of reducing prison populations, others regarded alternative sanctions as more punitive alternatives to simple probation and fines and as a way of providing supervision and control of those offenders who were released into the community.

From the perspective of the pressure of growing prison populations, our concern is the extent to which the proliferation of alternative sanctions actually displaced or reduced incarceration. Little of the existing research has been designed to answer this question. What limited evidence there is, however, suggests that alternative sanctions have more frequently increased the level of nonincarcerative punishment for those offenders who otherwise would not have been incarcerated than they have served as an alternative sanction for those who otherwise would have been incarcerated. Rather than reducing the use of incarceration for certain types of offenders, alternative programs have extended the

level and scope of formal mechanisms of social control exercised b̶
criminal justice system (Austin and Krisberg, 1982). For example, m̶
persons who previously would have had their cases dismissed or bee̶
given a nominal sanction are now subject to greater supervision by the
state through use of pretrial diversion programs. And restitution and
community service sentences often have been added to probation or
incarcerative sentences, compounding the amount and duration of punishment received by minor offenders. Indeed, it appears that most restitution and community service programs were established to serve as
supplements to probation and parole supervision or fines imposed on
minor offenders (Austin and Krisberg, 1982). Those programs deliberately designed to reduce incarceration do not appear to have been
effective in doing so (Flowers, 1977; Schneider and Schneider, 1979;
Pease et al., 1977).

Postincarcerative release options such as work release, work furlough,
halfway houses, and prerelease facilities have been designed to permit
incarcerated offenders to move to lower-security facilities or to community supervision several months prior to parole or conditional release.
One study that examined the impact of community-based correctional
programs on prison populations (Hylton, 1980) found that prison populations increased significantly between 1962 and 1979 in Saskatchewan,
Canada, despite the introduction of community corrections programs.
Hylton's failure to control for or examine increases in crime and police
arrests and their potential effect on prison populations weakens confidence in his conclusion that community corrections programs had little
effect. Bass's (1975) study of California's work furlough program reported that it experienced high rates of violations and technical escapes
and, consequently, resulted in increasing the rate and length of incarceration for many violators. Although postrelease alternatives have removed incarcerated offenders from prisons earlier than they might otherwise have been released, the empty beds have been filled quickly by
new admissions from the ample pool of convicted offenders eligible for
incarceration.

Four states (California, Colorado, Minnesota, and Oregon) have
adopted community corrections acts intended to encourage communities
to treat offenders locally rather than send them to state prisons by
providing financial subsidies for local programs. Because the Colorado
and Oregon laws are relatively recent (1976 and 1978, respectively),
impact data are limited. Studies of the California probation subsidy
program initiated in 1965 suggest that, although it succeeded in shifting
responsibility for offenders formerly destined for state facilities to local
jurisdictions, it increased the rate of incarceration at the local level and

rsons under some type of criminal justice system and Dill, 1978; Lerman, 1975; Miller, 1980). A Minnesota's Community Corrections Act (CCA))81) suggests that CCA-supported programs were :nt local sentencing options, previously limited to ut were having negligible impact on state prison inately, the CCA evaluation was oriented toward with little attention to illuminating the processes underlying them. Neither the question of why the financial incentive to handle offenders locally (on which the act was premised) was less effective than had been expected nor the impact of other changes in sentencing policy that occurred at the same time (including the adoption of parole guidelines) was addressed in the report.

The finding that alternative sanctions have not served as alternatives to incarceration is disappointing to those who sought to reduce imprisonment rates, but it is hardly surprising. Austin and Krisberg (1982) suggest that programs designed as alternatives to incarceration, like many other "reforms," have failed due to a combination of circumstances. These include the interests, values, and power of key decision makers and criminal justice system agencies that oppose reductions in incarceration (including police, prosecutors, judges, and corrections administrators); the limited economic and political clout of probation and parole agencies and private reform organizations that support wider use of alternatives to incarceration; the effectiveness of powerful agencies in reshaping innovations to serve their own interests, particularly through redefinition of the client population; public concern with "lenient" (i.e., nonincarcerative) sentences given to serious offenders; and the diverse and often conflicting objectives of supporters of alternative programs.

MECHANISMS TO CONTROL INFLOW AND RELEASE OF PRISONERS

A third approach to maintaining an equilibrium between the population and capacity of prisons and jails is to directly regulate the inflow and release of prisoners. Some state judges have taken prison crowding into consideration by refusing to send offenders to overcrowded institutions or sending them to jail to serve prison terms.[14] Others concerned with crowding (Blumstein and Kadane, forthcoming; Manson, 1981) have

---

[14] For example, the chief justice of the Massachusetts Superior Court would not sentence offenders to the Massachusetts Correctional Institution at Concord due to overcrowding (WCVB-TV Editorial, March 14, 1975, cited in Mullen et al. [1980:143]).

suggested more formal inflow control mechanisms such as allocating existing prison space to sentencing judges.

The only state to have adopted an explicit limit on the inflow of offenders to state prisons (but not to jails) is Minnesota. The legislation creating the Sentencing Guidelines Commission required the commission to "take into substantial consideration . . . correctional resources including but not limited to the capacities of local and state correctional facilities." The commission interpreted the law as a directive that the guidelines not generate prison populations that exceed the capacities of state institutions. The commission's prison population projection model permitted it to test various sentencing options, consider only those that did not increase populations beyond existing capacity, and finally adopt an imprisonment policy and sanction levels that would maintain prison populations at about 95 percent of existing capacity, assuming no change in crime rates or sentencing laws, for 5 years. The guidelines have been in effect since May 1980. Thus far, destabilizing policy changes have been limited: in 1980 the legislature increased the mandatory minimum sentence for possession and use of a firearm but has defeated several more drastic bills, and the commission has withstood pressures to increase sentence severity. As a result, Minnesota was one of the few states to reduce prison population in 1980 and in the first half of 1981 (U.S. Department of Justice, 1981b).

Inflow mechanisms may be effective planning tools for allocating existing space in prisons, but they cannot provide immediate relief when prison overcrowding occurs. To handle such situations, a variety of discretionary release controls are currently in use as population safety valves, the most important of which is parole. In many jurisdictions the sentencing judge maintains parole release authority over offenders sent to the local jail; when population pressures become severe, early release for jailed offenders is authorized. State parole boards have sometimes acted to control prison populations by adopting accelerated parole release policies when crowding or administrative concerns require it; many continue to do so.

For example, in 1961 the California legislature approved a program based on screening of inmates by base expectancy (parole prediction) scores combined with programs for more intensive parole supervision. By 1963 the Department of Corrections' research division had screened the entire prisoner population, a number of prisoners were referred for parole consideration earlier than originally scheduled, and some of these were released on parole by the Adult Authority. The Department of Corrections estimated that the program had reduced the prison population by more than 840 offenders and had saved at least $840,000. In the early and mid-1970s the California Adult Authority again lowered prison populations dramatically by informally changing its parole release strategy. Recently, the Mississippi legislature, in response to a court order, authorized "early parole" and "supervised earned release" (Mullen and Smith, 1980:123). Under a similar court order, Maryland's parole board authorized extended preparole furloughs of 60–90 days for nonviolent offenders (Ney, 1980:8). In Oregon in May 1980 the parole board, working closely with the Department of Corrections, modified the history risk component of the guidelines to make the earlier release of some inmates possible in December 1980 to comply with a court order directing the Department of Corrections to reduce prison crowding (Arthur D. Little, 1981).

Whatever the other shortcomings of parole boards, their ability to manage prison population size is a valuable feature at a time when the number of inmates exceeds prison capacity. A parole board's insulation from political pressure enables it to make necessary but unpopular early release decisions more quickly and unobtrusively than can a governor or legislature.

As part of the movement to determinate sentencing, several states have abolished their parole authorities and have adopted fixed sentences; others have proposed such changes. Whatever the merits of these changes, they have curtailed the ability of a centralized release authority to use early release as a population management tool. Several states that had substantial recent increases in prison populations have found it necessary to adopt alternative means of early release, including emergency release powers acts, executive clemency, and increases in the rate at which good time is awarded.

Michigan's Prison Overcrowding Emergency Powers Act of 1980 (Public Act 519) provides that, if the state's prison system is overcrowded for 30 consecutive days, the governor shall declare a prison overcrowding state of emergency. This declaration will reduce by 90 days the minimum sentences of all prisoners who have minimum terms. The result is an enlargement of the pool of prisoners eligible for parole by making inmates eligible for parole release earlier than they otherwise would have been. The parole board then makes case-by-case release decisions. If the 90-day sentence reduction does not result in reduction of prison population to 95 percent of rated capacity within 90 days of the declaration of the state of emergency, minimum sentences will be reduced by another 90 days, increasing further the pool of prisoners eligible for parole. The governor must rescind the state of emergency once the population is reduced to 95 percent of rated capacity. The act was first invoked in the summer of 1981, permitting a reduction in prison population.

Various forms of executive clemency date back to colonial times in the United States, but information on their historical or contemporary uses is limited.[15] Until the end of the nineteenth century, executive clemency was the only way to obtain early release from prison. With the adoption of indeterminate sentences, parole boards were created to regularize release procedures; nevertheless, states retained the executive clemency authority, as a safety valve for providing mercy and dealing with extraordinary circumstances and organizational problems (Berecochea, 1982).

Existing state clemency structures, eligibility criteria, and decision-making procedures vary widely. In 31 states the governor has sole authority to grant clemency; in 10 states authority rests entirely in the hands of a special board; and in 9 states the governor's authority is limited to granting clemency to applicants receiving affirmative recommendations from a special board or advisory body (Stafford, 1977).

A recent study of the uses of sentence commutation—the form of clemency that reduces a sentence and is most frequently used to grant early release for a prisoner—found that regular commutations are granted very sparingly (Martin, 1982b). For example, in Illinois between 1977 and 1981, there were an average of 160 applications per year for commutation, with only an average of 9 granted per year. In Texas, which has very narrow grounds for commuting a sentence, there were an average of 20 applications and 15 commutations annually during those years. And in New York, with a prison population of more than 25,000 inmates in 1981, a total of 102 sentences were commuted between 1977 and 1981; 50 of those were granted under a special commutation procedure adopted to reduce sentences of offenders given mandatory minimum sentences of more than 15 years under the Rockefeller drug laws after those laws were revised in 1979.

Special commutations have been used by 5 states—Georgia, Maryland, Oklahoma, Utah, and Wyoming—to reduce prison populations by releasing large numbers of inmates, generally those imprisoned for

---

[15] There are several types of clemency: pardons, which usually involve a recognition of guilt but the need to mitigate the penalty (or remove a civil disability); commutations, which substitute a less severe punishment for that originally imposed (often reducing a minimum sentence, thereby making the offender eligible for earlier supervised parole release); and reprieves, which postpone the execution of a sentence, particularly in capital cases.

nonviolent offenses who are within 6 months of parole release. (Most other recipients of commutations have life or very long sentences.) In Utah between November 1981 and March 31, 1982, in response to a declaration of crowding by the director of the Division of Corrections, the Board of Pardons advanced the release dates of 93 inmates within 90 days of parole release. Maryland granted 543 "seasonal" commutations in 1978 and 297 in 1979 to inmates who had served at least one-half their sentences for nonviolent offenses and who were nearing parole eligibility. And in Georgia between July 1, 1980, and June 30, 1981, the parole board first released 2,436 inmates on special paroles and reprieves with conditional commutations and then released 2,001 more inmates up to 6 months early on special commutations without parole supervision (Martin, 1982b).

A third, also limited, population control mechanism is use of good time. Prison authorities may affect the time served on a sentence by the grant, forfeiture, and restoration of statutory and meritorious good time. If today's nominal sentences were served without good-time reductions, prisons would be far more crowded than they are. But statutory good time is of limited value as a population control mechanism in many jurisdictions because it is automatically credited to prisoners at the beginning of their sentence and thereafter may only be taken away for a disciplinary infraction. Furthermore, its use as a mechanism for disciplining inmates by adding time to be served back onto their sentences conflicts with the goal of reducing prison populations. For that reason, several state agencies, including the Illinois Department of Corrections, have taken steps to limit forfeiture of good time (Jacobs, 1982) and have given prison officials more flexibility in awarding meritorious good time. In Illinois, for example, the Director of Corrections has wide power to reward a prisoner who performs meritorious service by granting up to 90 days additional good time. Although the effect of good-time provisions may not be realized immediately, and good time poses a greater risk of arbitrary application than uniformly applied emergency-power release provisions, it can reduce prison populations.

Offender classification provides a fourth tool for addressing some of the problems of overcrowding. Increases in crowding have tended to undermine existing classification procedures by increasing the frequency of assignment on the basis of available space. This situation has resulted in a vicious circle of misclassification, which can retard offenders' progress through the prison system, thereby leading to longer terms, continued crowding problems, and classification errors. In Alabama, for example, the team involved in court-ordered classification of the entire prison system found that at least one-half of the inmates could be classified for minimum or community custody although only 10 percent were so classified (Clements, 1982:75). Solomon (1980) reports that two-thirds of prisoners classified as needing medium security in Tennessee required only minimum security. Crowding is worst in maximum security prisons. Here, due to overcrowding, jobs and other opportunities are reduced, offenders have less chance to demonstrate "progress" or adjustment, and when they do not meet the criteria of demonstrating "improvement" their movement out of the system is slowed.

Comprehensive classification criteria for management purposes, following the principle of using the least restrictive alternative possible, should help break this vicious circle. Consistent application of such criteria should relieve crowding, particularly in maximum security institutions and, by increasing opportunities for program participation and "normalization," should lead to swifter movement of inmates through the prison system.

IMPACT OF ALTERNATIVE STRATEGIES

In the face of crowded prisons, rising prison populations, court orders to reduce crowding and improve prison conditions, and determinate sentencing laws that limit system flexibility, policy makers in every state must develop their own strategies to maintain a balance between population and capacity through a combination of construction to expand capacity, increased use of alternatives to incarceration, and systematic use of inflow and release control mechanisms. Research can facilitate decision making by systematically examining the implementation and effects of policies and programs in various jurisdictions and by projecting the effects of policy options under a variety of conditions.

Every option has both short-term and long-term advantages and costs. Construction may be necessary to replace obsolete facilities or expand capacity in systems that have long-term expected increases in inmate populations. But prison construction is very costly, and these costs are compounded by steady increases in operating costs. Alternative policies may be more cost-effective ways of preventing crowding and avoiding the costs of new construction in jurisdictions with short-term population pressures but long-term expectations of decreased inmate populations. Because it takes about 5 years to complete construction of a new prison facility, expansion of capacity by new construction will not solve the immediate capacity needs of many jurisdictions and may have the long-term effect of increasing what is viewed as the "normal" size of the prison population.

Nonincarcerative programs often are advertised as less costly and more humane than incarceration (see National Council on Crime and Delinquency, 1980; Thalheimer, 1978), but others (e.g., Greenberg, 1975; Strathman et al., 1981) have expressed doubt that alternative programs result in actual savings, more humane sanctions, and reduced recidivism, or even that they are functioning as alternatives to incarceration. Although alternative programs promise some relief for prison crowding and may be appropriate and less costly ways of dealing with some nonviolent offenders, institutional pressures for "success" and public resistance to community facilities suggest their continued use predominantly for offenders who are unlikely to be imprisoned, thus limiting their short-term ability to provide substantial relief for prison crowding.

Prison population control mechanisms appear to offer the greatest opportunities for short-term relief from crowding. Explicit control of prisoner intake, while desirable, requires a high degree of political consensus, shared social attitudes toward crime control, and agreement on a decision rule or formula for determining who should be incarcerated; such consensus is not likely to prevail or be easily developed in many jurisdictions. Early release of large numbers of prisoners—through expanded use of early parole release, executive clemency, or emergency powers acts—can be implemented quickly, is less costly than construction or alternative programs (in the short run), is preferable to reliance on less visible ad hoc adaptive mechanisms that are likely to prevail otherwise, and is more flexible in emergency situations than intake controls. In a situation of sudden and severe overcrowding or an emergency such as a natural disaster, a prison release mechanism permits reduction of all terms or only those of certain types of offenders by a fixed amount of time to provide immediate relief to the corrections system, while intake controls cannot deal with prison populations after inmates are committed. Furthermore, if social attitudes or sentencing policies change, leading to different sentences for offenders whose offenses are similar but who are convicted several years apart, these differences can be addressed by a parole board or some other early release mechanism.

In sum, the current state of knowledge is uncertain regarding the effects and effectiveness of various alternatives for dealing with expanding prison populations. What is clear, however, is that the link between sentencing policy and prison populations should be considered when developing new sentencing policies. To ensure such consideration, some formal means should be developed in each state to provide regular projections of prison populations and assessments of the likely impact of proposed policy changes.

6

Research Agenda
for the Study of
Sentencing

GENERAL RESEARCH STRATEGY

The rapid pace of changes in sentencing policies and practices has stimulated research designed to assess those changes and to aid future reforms. If it is to be useful to policy makers, future research on sentencing must balance short-term and long-term perspectives and research goals, capitalize on the natural experiments associated with changes in sentencing, improve the quality and availability of data, and use a variety of methodological approaches.

A Balanced Program

A balance between quick-response, highly targeted research projects and longer-term, more basic efforts is needed. Changes in sentencing policy must be viewed from a longer-term and broader perspective so that results of policy shifts can be assessed in the context of larger social processes and changes. For example, crime rates rose sharply in the 1960s and early 1970s and leveled off in the late 1970s. Meanwhile, during the 1970s deterrence became an increasingly important goal of the criminal justice system. Some have argued that the leveling off of crime rates in the late 1970s was attributable to the deterrent effects of sanctions. However, the changes in the crime rate could also have been related to demographic shifts associated with the postwar baby boom and a variety of other social changes. Understanding the changes in

259

crime rates requires partitioning these, and other, possible causes, which in turn necessitates long-range as well as short-range studies. Historical and theoretical analyses of long-range changes, in addition to their intrinsic value, are necessary to provide a context for interpreting the results of specific, short-range policy evaluations.

CAPITALIZING ON NATURAL EXPERIMENTS: THE IMPORTANCE OF TIMING

Because of the limited opportunities for planned or designed interventions, evaluations of the impact of policy changes must rely heavily on natural experiments. Natural experiments arise, for example, when a prosecutor decides to test a new case-screening policy or a legislature enacts a new sentencing statute. In supporting studies and evaluations of natural experiments, funding agencies are caught in a dilemma. To provide useful and timely information to the criminal justice community, programs and policy changes must be evaluated promptly. Because of the variety of potential changes that might be evaluated, the need to collect baseline data on operations *before* a change is put into effect, and the amount of time required to develop and publish requests for proposals, select a contractor, and implement a research project, funding agencies must anticipate changes and support short-term evaluations. But in so doing they risk jumping the gun, selecting the wrong program to evaluate, and supporting evaluations and studies that are completed before the changes being studied have been fully implemented and operations have become normal.

One promising strategy for capitalizing on natural experiments, evaluating them promptly, and minimizing the costs of false starts would be the creation of an ongoing center with operational and technical expertise to identify opportunities for experiments and to advise on the formulation and execution of study designs. The National Institute of Justice should create such a center. The center could have discretionary funds to award selected applicants up to $10,000 to conduct early feasibility studies to determine the existence and viability of research opportunities arising from policy changes. Applicants for feasibility grants could submit informal proposals providing adequate evidence that (1) relevant data are available and accessible, (2) qualified research staff are available to pursue the opportunity, and (3) the opportunity is worth pursuing as a longer-term study. Feasibility studies could establish the key variables, examine the availability of baseline data, and develop a detailed design of the research project that would then be submitted as a proposal to the National Institute of Justice for longer-term funding.

A small center staff, augmented by consultants, could screen opportunities as they arise by reviewing submissions on a continuous basis (providing approval or rejection to applicants within a few weeks) and providing technical assistance to grantees in the development and execution of their research designs. Such quick reaction and initial assessments of feasibility would permit timely screening of opportunities to prevent premature funding of extensive and costly evaluations prior to adequate exploration of their potential and problems.

DATA NEEDS

Modest improvements in the data available in the existing data series and statistical systems maintained by various jurisdictions and the Bureau of Justice Statistics (BJS) could significantly enhance the opportunity for answering questions related to sentencing policy. An important limitation of the FBI's *Uniform Crime Reports (UCR)*, for example, is the absence of a full characterization of the demographic attributes of arrestees, particularly by age, race, and sex, simultaneously partitioned for each offense type. Such a full partition would permit comparison of the consistency of the attributes of arrestees with those of prisoners. The development of such characterization should be considered in the impending reassessment of the *UCR* being undertaken by the Bureau of Justice Statistics and the FBI.

Easily accessible data on prosecutorial and court processing are rarely compiled, thereby making it difficult for researchers to follow cases systematically through the criminal justice process. In view of the varying quality and sophistication of prosecutorial and court data systems, the most fruitful strategy for developing indicators of court-processing characteristics would be to support further development of more uniform and consistent data and management information systems in those jurisdictions already collecting such data rather than by attempting a uniform nationwide collection system.

On corrections, the *Prisoners in State and Federal Institutions* series provides annual data on gross prison populations by state but does not include a detailed breakdown of the composition of the prison population in each state. The *Profiles of State Prison Inmates* provides valuable detailed individual data on a national sample of prisoners in correctional institutions, but these data are available only for 1974 and 1979, and they cannot be disaggregated by state; hence, they cannot be used by individual states for their planning purposes. State-level disaggregation, at least for the larger states, should be included in subsequent national surveys. Furthermore, these two sources (the annual counts and the detailed profiles of inmates) cannot be combined to study offenders in the various state prison systems by crime type, sentence length, and demographic characteristics. For example, one cannot determine from existing national data the changes over time or variations across jurisdictions in the demographic characteristics, prior conviction records, offense types, and sentence characteristics of prisoners.

In order for legislatures to consider the impact of sentencing policy on prisons, it is necessary to estimate the consequences of a particular policy, for example: imposing a particular determinate sentence for specified groups of offenses or imposing a particular mandatory minimum sentence for offenses involving weapons or for second-time felons. While each state can be expected to formulate its own estimation models and to collect its own data for this purpose, a national project should be organized to foster such developments, including surveying the provisions being considered in various sentencing legislation and designing for common use a standard sampling and data collection protocol that could be easily adapted by any state considering changes in sentencing policy.

Census data on jail inmates are far cruder than those for prison inmates, both because of the rapid turnover of the jailed population and because of the large number and variety of jail facilities across the nation. Attention should be given to a periodic sample of jail populations to learn more about their composition and how it changes over time. This kind of data would be especially important when significant changes in sentencing legislation are being considered. Such changes are likely to affect the plea-bargaining process and, as a result, the jail populations in pretrial detention. For example, stiffer sentences such as those called for by a mandatory minimum sentencing law may encourage more of the people vulnerable to the terms of the law to demand a trial, and this might slow processing through the courts and so increase the pretrial detention population. Detailed surveys of jail populations should be taken before a major sentencing change and at several points following its implementation. Aside from assessments of the direct impact of legislative changes on jail populations, analyses of such survey data could shed some light on the plea-bargaining process.

In most jurisdictions, only highly aggregated data are collected on the number of cases disposed of by the courts, on flows into probation or prison, and on releases on parole. Even a partition by offense type is often not available. These crude data cannot provide useful information on the effects of alternate sentences or sentencing policies to the key participants in the sentencing process. These objectives are best pursued with individually based data that record attributes of defendants, their offenses, and their prior records, and follow the movement of their cases through the criminal justice system. Offender-based transaction statistics (OBTS) systems found in a number of jurisdictions are intended to collect such data, but very few jurisdictions maintain such data completely and reliably. Recognizing the political, logistical, and fiscal constraints on widespread development and improvement of such data systems, it is important, at a minimum, to focus attention on the most serious offenders—e.g., those indicted for serious offenses—and to develop an individually based statistics system for them.

At a time of severe budget cuts, the identification of a minimum uniform core of standard data items on case processing through the court and corrections systems for collection across jurisdictions becomes particularly important. Standard items would include the basic demographic attributes of an offender; a characterization of the key elements in prior record; the current arrest charges, including certain key attributes of the offense (e.g., weapon use); whether there was a charge reduction associated with a guilty plea; and final disposition data, including conviction charges, sentences, and data on the execution of the sentence, such as date received and released by supervising agencies.

Improved and expanded common data bases containing two important classes of information at the state level are needed to advance knowledge about sentencing: cross-sectional aggregate information on numbers of crimes and on the processing of suspects, defendants, and offenders by the criminal justice system; and disaggregated longitudinal information on the processing of individual cases from arrest through the courts and into the corrections system. Most jurisdictions collect the former but each in its own idiosyncratic way; only a few collect the latter. Such disaggregated data are essential for understanding the outcomes of the criminal justice process and for developing projections of the impact on prison populations of various policy options. A number of states have pursued this objective through OBTS systems. Development and support for improved uniform systems should be continued and other states encouraged to set up such systems.

In addition, it would be useful to invest some research effort in studies of the quality of these sorts of administrative data. If official data are to figure significantly in future research, their strengths and weaknesses should be better documented. Much has been learned, for example, from comparisons between the National Crime Survey (an annual survey of criminal victimization) and the *Uniform Crime Reports* data, and these kinds of projects should be continued. In addition, similar comparisons are needed for court and prison statistics.

DIVERSIFYING RESEARCH APPROACHES

Research based on observation and interview techniques is an essential aspect of a broad research strategy designed to illuminate the sentencing process. Quantitative methods alone cannot adequately capture or control for many features of social interaction, the importance of the subjective dimension of behavior, the need to tap the meaning of a situation in shaping decisions made by actors in the criminal justice system, and the effects of subtle behavioral cues. Qualitative techniques are particularly valuable in generating hypotheses about how and why actors behave as they do, in interpreting the meanings individuals give to their decisions, in clarifying relationships and patterns of interaction among actors in various criminal justice agencies, and in describing the informal decision rules by which agencies and their officials create a gap between the law on the books and the law in action. Qualitative approaches to learning about prosecutorial decisions—which are fundamental to sentencing and very poorly understood—are especially important.

Since a choice of research method must be related to the research question, no single approach can be given highest priority in all situations. However, we believe there has been too much reliance on simple statistical analyses of cross-sectional data, and we urge vigorous efforts to broaden the range of methods used in the study of sentencing. These should include qualitative studies that provide new insights and hypotheses for further testing and, when appropriate, greater use of experimental and quasi-experimental designs that will permit causal inferences associated with specific operational changes.

DETERMINANTS OF SENTENCES

DISCRIMINATION

It is not likely that research will provide a definitive estimate of the influence of racial discrimination on sentence outcomes in general. A more useful alternative to a global approach is to focus on the effect of race in particular jurisdictions, time periods, and sets of circumstances. Furthermore, the methodological problems that impede knowledge about the effect of race also characterize efforts to assess the impact of sex, age, and socioeconomic status on sentence as well as the effect of case-processing variables such as attorney type and type of plea.

We have defined sentencing broadly to include a series of decisions affecting cases as they pass through the criminal justice system. In addressing the issue of discrimination in sentencing, several problems must be addressed. Detecting the presence of discrimination based on race, socioeconomic status, sex, or some other case attribute is difficult because the effect of discrimination is often small in comparison with the effects of current offense and prior record. Hence, sensitive measurements of these latter variables are required to discover small effects. This problem is further complicated by aggregation effects, which may mask individual instances of discrimination for certain crime types, in certain jurisdictions or courts, or on the part of individual decision makers.

These different settings and circumstances should be explicitly examined in future research through use of sufficiently disaggregated data. This research should also explore the role of situational variables in different jurisdictions in making inappropriate factors more or less salient in the sentencing decision.

To reduce the risk of selection bias, which can be a problem when one examines only sentence outcomes, research on discrimination should examine the handling of cases as early as possible in the criminal justice system. Studies of discrimination should emphasize the treatment of less serious offenses, which offer greater room for discretion and greater opportunity for discrimination, and should examine in detail the various stages between arrest and imprisonment to discern the degree to which discrimination exists at any of these intermediate stages.

Research on discrimination requires a variety of complementary methodological approaches—including structural modeling, longitudinal studies, statistical analyses of aggregate court-processing data, observation and interview techniques, and experimental and quasi-experimental designs—to supplement the cross-sectional studies of discrimination that currently predominate.

The social importance of discrimination suggests the need for continued research on this topic, but this research should not simply continue existing approaches to this topic. New studies should be designed to answer questions like the following: In what ways are particular groups of offenders benefited or disadvantaged by differential treatment? Is discrimination related to crime type or offense seriousness? Is discrimination related to victim-offender relationships or case-processing variables? In which jurisdictions or types of jurisdictions is discrimination found?

CASE-PROCESSING VARIABLES

The role of case-processing variables in sentencing is also a fertile area for further research. The belief that a guilty-plea discount exists and is necessary for court functioning is an important source of support for plea bargaining. However, the extent of such a discount remains unknown.

One useful approach to the discount question is an examination of the defendant's decision to plead guilty or go to trial, a topic on which only limited research is currently available. It is assumed that the differential between sentences in pled and tried cases accounts for the decision to plead guilty, but many other factors (e.g., the expense of a trial attorney, loss of time from work while in court, and the cost of time spent in jail prior to a trial) may also contribute to the decision. Further research examining why defendants plead guilty is desirable. This research should look across jurisdictions and courtroom cultures and should separate case-processing from other variables.

Heumann's (1978) suggestion that there are subtleties in sentence discount policies needs further investigation. In particular, research should explore the extent to which court personnel in various settings distinguish between "dead bang" cases, in which conviction is a virtual certainty and for which the defendant may be "punished" for going to trial, and cases in which there is a real factual dispute and the legal ambiguities are felt to justify the additional expense of a trial.

An additional question for research is whether the elimination of plea bargaining leads to an increase in trials. Rubinstein et al. (1980) report that the ban on plea bargaining in Alaska resulted in only a slight increase in the number of trials with no backlog of such cases. However, a differential between sentences for those convicted at trial and those who pled guilty may have discouraged trials and may actually have resulted in a shift from overt to covert bargaining.

Another approach that might be considered for studying the plea/trial sentence differential involves gathering data on the final sentence offers of the prosecution in a set of cases. Among those that go to trial, the sentence imposed after trial can be compared with the sentence that would have been imposed had the defendant agreed to plead guilty. Such a research strategy has a set of natural controls for case attributes since it involves the same cases.

Two difficulties arise in this type of research. First, since most cases involve guilty pleas, such a research strategy requires prospectively gathering data on a large number of cases in order to obtain enough trial cases for analysis. (A retrospective approach is unlikely to work because offers are not recorded and participants' recall is not sufficiently good.) Second, interpretation of a sentence differential—if it emerges—is not simple. A harsher sentence after trial *may* indicate punishing defendants for failing to plead guilty, but other explanations may also account for the finding: the trial may bring out details about the crime (particularly aspects indicating a heinous nature) or more extensive prior-record information; when defendants take the stand and deny their guilt, judges or juries may be punishing them for two crimes, the one for which they have been convicted and the crime of perjury; or defendants' failure to take the first step toward rehabilitation that admission of guilt is sometimes said to imply may be the basis for harsher sentences after trial. Interviews with judges after they sentence trial cases might illuminate the extent to which a differential is produced by the mode of disposition itself as opposed to the other factors. It would also be useful in sorting out Heumann's assertion that frivolous trial cases are punished while "real" triable cases are not.

DISPARITY

There are two principal unanswered questions in studies of disparity: How much unexplained variation is due to systematic differences among decision makers rather than to planned or to apparent disparity? What are the nature, magnitude, and sources of the differences that are found? Providing answers to these questions will help to clarify the sources of disparity, thus focusing debate on whether the identified differences are warranted or not, which is a value question.

Research on disparity, however, faces problems of measurement error arising from inadequately measured variables, omitted variables, and sample selection biases. In addition, there is the problem of classifying "like cases" and the identifying criteria to be used in grouping cases as similar or different. Cases that appear alike initially may, on closer scrutiny, differ in subtle ways (e.g., one defendant may be emotionally disturbed) or in not-so-subtle ways (e.g., two cases in which the conviction offenses are the same as a result of plea negotiations may differ substantially in the actual underlying offense behavior). Conversely, two cases that differ with respect to the conviction offenses may involve essentially similar offense behavior. Consequently, research to improve the estimates of the determinants of sentences will also contribute to the identification of disparity.

Often what appears to be disparity in sentences may actually result from inadequate models of the sentencing decision. The extent of this seeming disparity can only be reduced with improved models of sentencing, but existing models will not be improved simply by adding more variables. Instead, observation, interview, and experimental studies are needed to create models that better reflect the processes by which interactions among court personnel affect decision making and improve the measurement of key variables such as offender culpability and offense seriousness.

To shed further light on interjurisdictional variation in sentencing and the influence of community attitudes as environmental constraints on judicial behavior, further studies might follow up on Gibson's (1978a) study of judges who "ride circuit." Controlling for defendant and case attributes and for judge attributes and role conceptions, the decisions of judges who serve in several diverse communities can be examined to assess their responsiveness to local norms and to explore the sources of public influence on judicial decisions.

An additional source of disparity associated with environmental constraints on judicial decisions, which may limit judges' willingness to sentence convicted offenders to confinement, is the physical conditions in local jail facilities and the availability of alternative sanctions (as well as judges' knowledge of each). Many judges may be reluctant to send minor offenders to crowded and dangerous jails for even brief periods; new or uncrowded facilities, conversely, may encourage greater use of incarceration. Tests of the impact of conditions of incarceration on sentencing outcomes might be carried out through an interrupted time-series analysis of the sentences of individual judges prior to and following the opening of new jail facilities.

PUBLIC OPINION

Better understanding of public perceptions of crime seriousness and the severity of penalties and how these affect judicial behavior is also desirable. Blumstein and Cohen (1980) found that, although there is strong consistency in the *relative* ranking of sentence severity across crime types, there are important differences among social and demographic groups about the *absolute* magnitude of sentences to be imposed. Similarly, the public's chosen sentences correspond to the actual sentences and time served in relative terms across crime types, but they differ considerably in absolute magnitudes.

In opinion polls, respondents' recommended sentences generally reflect their responses to only brief abstract offense descriptions. A respondent is told little about the circumstances of the offense and less about the offender. One might come closer to actual sentences with studies that measure opinions in response to more fully elaborated descriptions that reflect the typical offense-offender scenario. Overall, there is a need for further study of the public's judgment about appropriate sentences, the information bases on which people make those judgments, and further exploration of the role of public opinion in shaping sentencing policy.

RESEARCH APPROACHES

A mixed research strategy is needed to increase understanding of the determinants of sentences. Progress in modeling sentencing decisions requires fuller knowledge of the decision-making process. Methodological advances are needed to address problems of sample selection and measurement error and to develop better measures of the key variables. These, in turn, require qualitative and experimental research.

Qualitative studies can be especially fruitful in identifying variables that motivate decisions but do not appear in official data and in illuminating how the interactions among criminal justice system actors affect decision making. Research on the flow of information and influence among criminal justice system personnel and the impact of this information on decision making, for example, can contribute to an understanding of the ways in which these decision makers view case seriousness. Studies detailing the interactions between judges and prosecutors, between prosecutors and defense attorneys, and between judges and probation officers should illuminate the kinds of issues these actors raise in discussions of cases, the questions they ask, and the manner in which they talk about offender culpability, offense seriousness, and prior record. In considering prior record, for example, it may be that some individuals or work groups emphasize the length of an offender's arrest record while others focus on previous imprisonment.

Efforts to explore the determinants of sentence outcomes often are hampered by reliance on the available data, which tend to be retrospective and reflect only official sources. Instead, researchers might attempt prospective data collection, interviewing and observing the actors whose behavior will subsequently be modeled and collecting detailed data on the variables that appear to be important but are often neglected. This preliminary exploration of the decision-making process could be especially fruitful in identifying variables that motivate decisions but do not appear in official records. In particular, data related to variables that affect the assessment of offender culpability are often not recorded in court archives or, when available, are often ignored by researchers because they are not easily quantified or coded. For example, a presentence report may describe how circumstances like the loss of a job, a death in the family, or an older brother's influence contributed to a defendant's behavior. These factors, along with variables like motive, level of planning, vulnerability of the victim, and foreknowledge of the likely level of harm, may strongly affect judicial and prosecutorial assessments of culpability, predictions about future criminal activity and dangerousness, and, ultimately, the sentence.

One way to illuminate the subtle factors influencing sentencing decisions is to trace a set of sentences as they are formulated. In conducting such prospective research on sentence development, a researcher can independently measure variables like level of planning and can tap decision makers' assessments of these variables by interviewing them prior to and following the decision. For example, judges might be interviewed immediately after a sentencing hearing or after reviewing case records in chambers; probation officers might be interviewed after completing a presentence report that includes sentencing recommendations; and prosecutors and defense lawyers might be interviewed immediately after pretrial negotiation conferences. Such data could be used to generate hypotheses about the nature of the decision-making process and models of sentencing decisions. These models can also be used to explore whether variations among decision makers are associated with consideration of different case characteristics, different assessments of culpability and prognosis, or different weights given to the variables in the formulation of sentences.

The results of such *process* explorations can then be directly tested in experimental studies and structural modeling efforts. One such experimental technique for manipulating variables like level of planning, type of motive, and victim provocation that are difficult to measure is "the vignette procedure" (e.g., Rossi and Nock, 1982). Briefly, one designs a set of "stories" or "cases" in which the parts can be randomly interchanged. For example, in one story or case the offender is black and the victim is white, in another the offender is white and the victim black. One might also use such a set of vignettes to explore assessments of the strength of evidence with a sample of attorneys and judges who would be asked to rate the stories on such dimensions as likelihood of indictment, of a substantial charge reduction through negotiation, and of a verdict of guilty if the case were tried. By regressing the ratings of such vignettes on the vignette characteristics, one might estimate the relative importance of factors determining the strength of evidence in a case.

Experimental simulations of sentencing by judges or others in a laboratory or other experimental setting also provide useful data, particularly when used in conjunction with nonexperimental data to validate results obtained by the latter or to provide alternative estimates that are subject to different sorts of biases. A number of studies have used simulations and experiments to analyze the details of judges' decision processes, including the variables they used in making decisions and the order in which those variables were considered. Such studies of decision making should be performed with participants throughout the criminal justice system, including probation officers and prosecutors. The results might provide information on the relative importance of otherwise unobserved factors in the selection process, thereby helping researchers to identify additional variables that are important to measure. If conducted in a variety of jurisdictions, they could indicate the consistency or variability of the effect of these factors.

Experimental simulations can also be used to address some questions that cannot be answered by observational data. For example, judges might be asked to choose for hypothetical cases both a determinate sentence and a minimum and maximum sentence. Their answers could be used to evaluate the implications of laws on determinate sentencing.

Experimental work with judges and prosecutors, guided by the results of the kind of field studies outlined above, would permit a direct test of the impact of individual case characteristics on sentence outcomes. Such experimental research would also make it possible to evaluate the impact of case characteristics that occur infrequently but exert a major influence when they do appear.

Modeling is the most frequently used approach to the study of the determinants of sentences. Among the modeling problems that need to be addressed by future research on sentencing are those of omitted and inadequately measured variables and sample selection biases. Many potentially relevant variables are omitted from models of sentencing outcomes, particularly those investigating discrimination in sentencing. These omissions can lead to biases in the estimated effects of the included variables when the included variables are correlated with the omitted or inadequately measured variables. Similar problems can occur when such variables are poorly measured. An obvious remedy, simple to prescribe but often difficult to accomplish when research is conducted with inadequate data sets, is the inclusion of a richer set of adequately measured independent variables. New research projects should make every effort to include information on a wide variety of individual case and offender attributes and to explore the relative usefulness of alternative measures of included variables.

One approach to addressing the problem of inadequate measures of various determinants of sentences is to use a model that explicitly links multiple observed indicator variables with the unobserved determinants of case disposition (Garber et al., Volume II). Such models, often called structural models involving latent variables, estimate the effects of unobserved variables from observations of the outcomes on other variables whose values are postulated to be determined as functions of the unobserved variables. In studying sentencing using such structural models, the primary determinants of case disposition (seriousness, quality of evidence, and prior record) are treated as unobserved or latent variables. The model consists of a series of structural equations representing principal indicators for which data are available (e.g., charge, pretrial release, bail amount, type of legal representation, conviction at trial, and severity of punishment). Using data on available observed determinants, it is then possible to estimate the *effects* of unobserved variables on case outcomes without directly measuring these unobserved variables. For the study of racial discrimination, this approach may make it possible to disentangle the various sources of race-outcome correlations that are likely to reflect both discriminatory and nondiscriminatory factors at distinct stages of criminal justice processing without requiring improved measures of the unobserved variables.

Structural equation models must be based on a comprehensive theory of the operation of the criminal justice system and the motivations of its principal actors and on a theory of measurement error. Such theories do not yet exist, so that any model will rest on a variety of questionable assumptions. Nevertheless, structural modeling presents an alternative approach to cross-sectional studies that rely on largely inadequate measures of the primary determinants of sentencing to understand sentencing outcomes; structural models of the case disposition process sharpen researchers' focus on areas of ignorance and suggest new hypotheses for further testing. Wide agreement on any particular formulation of an identified structural model is unlikely, but consistent findings obtained under a variety of different model formulations can increase confidence in the validity of the findings.

The handling of sample selection biases depends fundamentally on the source of the correlation between the unmeasured and measured determinants of sentences in the selected sample. If the correlation arises from unmeasured factors common to selection and sentencing that are *independent* of included variables in the full population, there are a number of available adjustments that rely on explicit estimates of the selection process to generate unbiased estimates of the determinants of sentences (e.g., Berk and Ray, 1982). The key is obtaining data for the full population before selection occurs. For example, the data set might include cases as they enter the criminal justice system, and it must include measures on the kinds of factors that determine how deeply a case is likely to penetrate into the system in addition to measures of the determinants of sentences.

These estimation techniques are not appropriate when there is also a correlation between the unmeasured and measured factors in the full population. Use of these techniques requires having adequate measures of any correlated but unmeasured determinants of selection and sentences. An alternative to improved measurement is to develop models of both the selection and sentencing processes, including in the models, when appropriate, the unmeasured determinants of these processes. Having specified a system of structural equations for the various processes that includes common latent (i.e., unmeasured) variables in several of the equations, the effects of the latent variables can be estimated from common movements observed in multiple outcome variables. Once again, estimating this combined system of selection and sentencing requires data for a sample of cases before selection occurs (see, e.g., Garber et al., Volume II; Klepper et al., Volume II).

Further research addressing the problems of measurement error and sample selection biases should include basic methodological work that formally compares the alternative correction techniques and documents the relative effectiveness of each and the trade-offs among them. Research is also needed to assess the robustness of proposed alternative methods to correct for sample selection biases. In particular, future research should explore the sensitivity of the estimated effects of various determinants of sentences to measurement error and sample selection biases. This analysis would include use of a variety of alternative measures of offense seriousness and prior record, both in replications with the same data sets and with independent data sets, to assess the sensitivity of the results to the particular measures used. Alternative models of the selection and sentencing processes should also be explored within any single data set to test the sensitivity of the results to the particular sets of assumptions in any model. To the extent that consistent results are found under a variety of alternative measures and model formulations, it will increase confidence in the available estimates for the determinants of sentences. On the other hand, substantial variations in the results would signal that biases arising from measurement error and sample selection are likely to be serious problems in any estimates of the determinants of sentences.

Important progress in modeling sentencing outcomes is likely to result from more adequate treatments of the complexity of the dependent variable, sentence outcome. Instead of using a single scale to represent sentence severity, with all the arbitrariness such a scale represents, there should first be a qualitative dependent variable representing the choice among the various kinds of sentence options being considered. Then the second part of the model would address the magnitude of each selected sentence type.

An adequate model of the determinants of such a multivariate sentence outcome variable is likely to be a complicated function of many input variables, some related to the crime, some to the criminal, some to the decision maker, and some to the context in which the decision is made. These variables may interact in important ways that need to be explored in future research. Once such a model has been specified and validated, e.g., by comparing its predictions with new sentence outcomes, it is possible that simplifying approximations can be found that would isolate those essential variables relating to the crime, those relating to the criminal, etc. If an approximation adequately reflecting sentence outcomes can be found, one might then consider using this approximation as a basis for developing single-scale variables that combine the many individual measures of independent variables into a single variable, reflecting offense seriousness, for example. Given the generally limited state of knowledge in modeling the determinants of sentences at this time, however, resources should be devoted primarily to model development and data collection, with secondary emphasis on developing scales of the determinants of sentences. Efforts to scale certain key variables like offense seriousness and prior record, however, may usefully contribute to the model development effort proposed by providing useful insights into cognitive issues involved in individual decision making.

STRUCTURING SENTENCING DECISIONS

PREDICTION RESEARCH AND SELECTIVE INCAPACITATION

The sentencing guidelines developed to date have emphasized current offense seriousness and prior criminal record. This is in sharp contrast to the original guidelines of the U.S. Parole Commission, which explicitly considered factors related to predictions of future recidivism in making release decisions. It has been suggested that sentencing guidelines might be similarly designed to emphasize selective incapacitation. This would require research to identify those factor(s) that best predict subsequent rates of offending and weighting them in the guidelines to ensure long sentences for the relatively small number of high-rate violent offenders. Greenwood and Abrahamse (1982) suggest that it may be fruitful in terms of reductions in both crime and prison population to identify high-rate violent offenders (measured by the number of serious crimes per year of liberty) from the larger number of low-rate offenders on the basis of background and other characteristics.

Such an effort may be viewed from several perspectives. Supporters suggest that it can be viewed as a way of reallocating scarce prison cells so that they will confine that group of offenders likely to commit the most crimes and as a means of decreasing the sentence lengths of the large number of offenders with low offense rates without substantially increasing crime. Critics point to the injustice of basing any individual's punishment in any respect on behavior that has not happened and may not happen.

The principle of selective incapacitation and research on it thus involves value and legal questions about which there is disagreement. For some, the value choice would be influenced by the question of how good a prediction of individual criminality can be made. If the prediction is good and if it would not result in imprisonment of individuals who would not otherwise be in prison but would result in a reallocation of time in prison, they would consider such an approach to be permissible. For others, any use of selective incapacitation raises insurmountable ethical and legal problems. Their view is that specific individuals ought not be punished on the basis of some prediction about their future criminality and that the criminal justice system must scrupulously avoid taking such actions. There is also fundamental concern about the variables that would be used in any such prediction. The use of an individual's social or economic characteristics for such a purpose presents the greatest hazard, and there are important legal questions that challenge the use of juvenile record information and records of official contacts that do not result in convictions. Furthermore, since many variables that predict recidivism may be correlated with race or minority status, their use could have disturbing discriminatory consequences.

An additional concern arises from the problem of errors inherent in all predictions of future behavior. If an explicit selective incapacitation policy were implemented, the false negatives (i.e., those released who commit new crimes) would be easily identified, but the false positives (i.e., those imprisoned because they were predicted to commit crimes but who would not have done so) could not be identified—they could not demonstrate that they would not have committed new crimes if released. Thus only one of the two types of error that might occur can be observed, the erroneous release, and there is some danger that the pressure to avoid such errors would lead to increasingly tight standards for release. While the increased use of such prediction methods for parole decision making in recent years does not appear to have resulted in tightened release standards, the relatively hidden nature of the parole process, compared with the much more visible sentencing decisions, may make the experience with parole not applicable to sentencing.

Even those who are prepared to consider such approaches remain skeptical that good prediction models invoking only legally valid variables can be devised and validated and result in decisions that are appreciably better than those of good practitioners. Most prediction research has been based on retrospective data and is always subject to "shrinkage" in predictive validity when applied in new settings. Furthermore, even when the internal predictions are good, the predictive quality diminishes appreciably when the variables that may be used in the prediction are restricted to official records of convictions (see, for example, Chaiken and Chaiken, 1982).

Interviews with judges reveal that most do take into account their own assessment of an individual's subsequent criminality and that they do so using whatever variables they have at hand, including many of questionable quality or predictive validity in presentence investigation reports. Thus careful and validated prediction research may identify particular patterns of variables that offer valuable new insights to judges and prosecutors and thereby enable them to improve their sentencing practice.

The problems of predicting offender criminality involve all the issues previously discussed regarding efforts to model sentencing outcomes: measurement, scaling, model misspecification, and selection bias. Any selective incapacitation scheme should have valid and reliable answers to the following questions: What are the magnitudes of the anticipated prediction errors? How many and which groups of offenders are likely to suffer from such a policy, and which ones are likely to benefit? How much do different variables contribute to predictions? How many of what types of crimes would be averted under the scheme? What crimes might increase as a result? How would the crime and imprisonment consequences differ from current practice? Addressing these questions can facilitate a more informed assessment of the value choices. Ultimately, policy makers considering a sentencing policy based on individual prediction must weigh the benefits of crimes averted against the costs and dangers of incorporating in policy the biases and errors that are inherent in any model. Even with an adequate model, it is extremely important that the agencies that support such research subject any findings to validity testing and also consider carefully the possibility of misuse and the potentially inappropriate consequences of the introduction of selective incapacitation policies.

APPELLATE REVIEW

Appellate review of sentences has had little influence in the United States, but it is institutionalized and widely believed to be quite influential in England. Since there are no systematic data on its effects, further study of the operation and impact of the English system might be useful to guide American reformers, who have urged its widespread adoption. One might examine the impact of major appellate decisions in England by analyzing the impact of several widely cited cases on subsequent lower court decisions to determine the process and pattern by which lower courts adapt. It would also be desirable to examine how appellate sentence review is working in those few jurisdictions in the United States that have established presumptive sentencing standards with appellate review (e.g., Minnesota and Pennsylvania). Such studies should look at the numbers of appeals, the issues raised, and the impact of the decisions on departures from standards over time. Interviews with judges could indicate knowledge of and adherence to appellate decisions.

IMPLEMENTATION OF NEW POLICIES

The adoption of sentencing reform—whether through criminal code revision, statutory determinate sentencing laws, or parole or sentencing guidelines—is a complex political process. In their efforts to understand the relation of legal change and social reform, political scientists and legal scholars have frequently studied the politics of passage and implementation of substantive legal changes, but they have less often focused on the politics attendant on procedural changes in the law and in the judicial process. Comparative case studies of sentencing reform efforts in various jurisdictions would be a first step toward the construction of a theory of change in sentencing institutions. Any such theory would have to incorporate the role of the latent and symbolic functions of policy innovation and should also reflect the sources and limits of change.

The process of implementing a new sentencing policy is too often overlooked by reformers, and research should illuminate that process. A policy change is not self-executing, and preliminary data suggest that the effects of some mandatory minimum sentencing statutes, bans on plea bargaining, and sentencing guidelines vary considerably, depending on the manner in which they were implemented. Qualitative examinations of the implementation process should be a part of impact evaluations, since they may provide the key to understanding the nature and scope of any effects that are observed. Such examinations might include study of the knowledge of a new policy and attitudes toward it both before and after training or distribution of materials among judges, lawyers, and other court personnel.

Sentencing guidelines shift discretion to prosecutors but limit their ability to threaten an extreme penalty. Without such a threat, defendants may be less easily induced to plead guilty and that result might in turn require a larger guilty-plea discount to keep the trial rate at a manageable level. Thus guidelines could bring about a shift in the dynamics of the plea-negotiation process and thereby provide a natural experiment on which research should capitalize. Such studies could examine courtroom work group norms and plea-negotiation practices before and after implementation of guidelines.

EFFECTS OF SENTENCING REFORMS

Evaluations of the impact of sentencing reforms thus far have been preliminary; there is a need for better research designs in any future evaluations. The development of such designs could be fostered by a center to support feasibility studies for impact evaluations (discussed above); more generally, there should be a systematic effort to design a broad evaluation research strategy). Such a strategy should be geared to establishing evaluations that meet both the short-term need for timely management feedback on an innovation and the long-term need for more rigorous evaluations that provide more definitive findings.

A mix of methodological approaches should be used in impact studies. Statistical analyses of case-processing data available from centralized data systems can tell only part of the story of efforts to change complex court and corrections processes. Systematic interview and participant observation need to accompany quantitative evaluations as an essential part of the effort to understand sentencing behavior in a social and institutional context.

Future evaluation studies should have more extended observation periods; time-series analyses should have several observation points rather than simple two-point, preinnovation and postinnovation, research designs. Extended time-series analyses are needed to distinguish effects associated with reforms from continuation of trends. Multiple post-reform observations are desirable to ensure that a reform has actually been implemented and that its effects have reached a stable point. Such an approach also avoids the selection bias associated with cases that are resolved early, which may differ in important ways from those that take a longer time to move through the system. Multiple observations over a longer follow-up period ensure a more representative case mix.

Furthermore, outcome measures must address all stages of case processing, not only those directly affected by a reform. The variety of opportunities for the shift of discretion and the associated potential for nullifying the effects of a reform require observations at both earlier and later stages. Evaluations of mandatory minimum laws and plea-bargaining bans, for example, should include data on pretrial dismissals and charging patterns as well as on sanctions imposed on convicted offenders. Impact studies should examine not only changes in the severity of sentences for those convicted but also changes in the mix of cases that appear for sentencing to identify any associated changes in the pattern of case screening. It is particularly desirable to examine adaptations by actors in the criminal justice system, such as alterations in charging and plea-bargaining practices, to determine how they affect implementation of a reform and may undermine its desired effect. Similarly, exogenous changes in case attributes, such as changes in patterns of offending, perhaps resulting from demographic shifts in the population, may occur; these changes will affect sanction outcomes independently of any reform and must be accounted for.

Statewide statutory sentencing guidelines, which represent an important reform, should be evaluated. Evaluation efforts should examine the extent to which the changes in offender populations projected under the guidelines are realized. They should also test the correspondence between anticipated and actual changes in intrastate disparity.

Studies of individual judicial compliance with guidelines are needed. Compliance is not merely behaving in ways consistent with the guideline rules; rather, it means conscious prescription of a sentence in accordance with the guidelines. In order to determine compliance, one must have at a minimum data on sentences by individual judges before and after introduction of the guidelines so that changes in sentencing patterns can be identified. Cases outside the guidelines may not indicate noncompliance if there are aggravating or mitigating circumstances that justify departures; sentences within the guidelines may ignore such circumstances and thus also represent noncompliance, although those cases would be harder to identify. Pursuing this issue further may require learning how judges actually make decisions and determining why they sentence as they do. Research on compliance should analyze a sample of cases, including those that depart from the guidelines and some of those that ostensibly comply with them. Those analyses must be augmented by interview and observation studies to provide information on the role of plea bargaining in generating outcomes and on the justifications considered in choosing a sentence within or outside the guidelines.

In selecting which policy innovations to evaluate, it is necessary to consider whether a change is really intended and is likely to be effective in changing practices. When the goal of a change appears to be primarily symbolic, an evaluation is not warranted. While there is no simple way to distinguish a real from a symbolic change, certain situational factors may strongly point toward a gesture that is largely symbolic. For example, if a mandatory minimum sentencing law is adopted when prisons are already filled to capacity, and if no provision is made to deal with the expected increase in the number of prisoners if there is compliance with the law, there is likely to be little actual change. While studies documenting a null effect may be valuable, their value lies primarily in the understanding they can provide of the adaptation process itself. Absent such a focus, such studies should be given lower priority for funding than a change that is likely to have real effects and to become a candidate for replication elsewhere.

SENTENCING POLICY AND PRISONS

Sentencing policy should include consideration of the impact of changes on prison populations; hence, there should be support for improving techniques for estimating prison populations. Because such estimates are likely to be used by future sentencing commissions in many jurisdictions, an investment by the National Institute of Justice in development of existing models and technology transfer is likely to be cost-effective. Projection models such as the flow model developed by the Minnesota Sentencing Guidelines Commission could be generalized so that they could be made available to other jurisdictions.

There is a widely held belief that prison crowding has harmful effects on inmate health and behavior. However, few studies adequately document the effects of various conditions of confinement on the prison population. Given the willingness of the Supreme Court (in *Rhodes* v. *Chapman* 452 U.S. 337 [1981]) to consider such studies in setting standards and the paucity of reliable data on which to base such standards, research is needed to sort out the complex and overlapping effects on inmate morale, health, and behavior of a variety of factors: physical and social density; institutional size; control and disciplinary style; inmate composition (especially as it affects inmates' victimization risk); amount of time mandatorily spent in living quarters; and prison term.

Research on the effects of crowding and other prison conditions should look across institutions, controlling for institutional populations and physical attributes. But because those individuals who are viewed by corrections authorities as the most troublesome are often assigned to the institutions with the worst physical conditions, separating the effects of the environment from selection effects arising from the assignment process represents a difficult research problem. Ideally, such research would use an experimental design that randomly assigns prisoners to various conditions. To the extent that it proves impossible to design experimental studies, research could involve quasi-experiments that control for selection processes or natural experiments that take advantage, for example, of the reassignment of prisoners that accompanies the opening or closing of a prison facility or of a unit within an institution.

Only rudimentary data are available on the effects of changes in the goals of sentencing and the shift to determinacy on prisoners—their behavior and program participation—or on management—program availability and disciplinary practices. Further studies of the impact of determinacy on prison management practices and on prisoners would be desirable.

The problem of growing prison populations and their relationship to changes in prison capacity has been the subject of recent debate that is important because of its wide publicity and the difficult policy choices regarding prison expansion now being confronted by many states. Our review of existing evidence indicates that neither capacity nor population alone can account for much variation in the other. There is a need to reconsider the question of the growth of prison populations; to develop models of prison capacity change that include exogenous demographic, social, political, legal, and economic factors that appear to determine variations across states and time periods; and to test the models in different states to provide more complex explanations for the variation found in the population-capacity relationship. For example, one might have expected that the current pressure of crowded prisons would be reflected in a mixture of building to increase capacity and reducing the severity of sanctions imposed on convicted offenders. Generally, however, only a limited amount of building has occurred, and the severity of sanctions imposed appears to have increased. Development of such models should be associated with efforts to explore adaptive responses by various jurisdictions as sentencing policy changes or as new prison capacity becomes available. It has been hypothesized that there will be an excess of prison capacity after 1990 in certain states as the baby boom generation passes through the ages of highest likelihood of imprisonment. This possibility offers an additional opportunity for testing the degree to which sanctions increase in response to the increased availability of prison capacity.

Evaluations of programs intended as alternatives to incarceration have generally failed to provide reliable answers to two related questions: how frequently alternative programs are actually used as alternatives to incarceration and the programs' impact on prison population. To obtain those answers it is necessary to measure the displacement effects of the programs, i.e., the extent to which offenders sent to a particular alternative program would, in its absence, have gone to prison and, conversely, how often the programs are used instead as supplementary sanctions for offenders who would not have been incarcerated. Measurement of the displacement effects, however, requires an adequate model of the in/out decision. Jurisdictions with explicit sentencing policies, such as Minnesota, provide the opportunity to distinguish among offenders on the basis of clearly articulated sentencing policies, thereby allowing a more adequate test of the effects of alternative programs.

In summary, there are a wide variety of important research questions regarding sentencing principles, policies, and practices. Studies are needed to overcome the methodological difficulties and address the substantive issues related to the determinants of sentences; the practical and theoretical implications of various approaches to structuring sentencing decisions; and the effects of changes in sentencing policies on criminal justice system practices, sentence outcomes, and prison populations. These issues pose a difficult but important challenge for the next generation of research on sentencing.

References

Abt Associates, Inc.
 1980   *American Prisons and Jails*. 5 volumes. Washington, D.C.: U.S. Department
        of Justice.
 1981   Chronology of Sentencing Guideline Activity. Prepared for Project to Evaluate
        Multijurisdictional Sentencing Guidelines Field Test. Abt Associates, Inc.,
        Cambridge, Mass.
Ader, R., A. Kreutnew, Jr., and H.L. Jacobs
 1963   Social environment, emotionality, and alloxan diabetes in the rat. *Psychoso-
        matic Medicine* 25(1):60 68.
Advisory Council on the Penal System
 1978   *Sentences of Imprisonment—A Review of Maximum Penalties*. London: Her
        Majesty's Stationery Office.
Aigner, S.J.
 1974   MSE dominance of least squares with errors-of-observation. *Journal of Econ-
        ometrics* 2:365–372.
Alfini, James J.
 1981   *Misdemeanor Courts*. Washington, D.C.: U.S. Department of Justice.
Allen, Francis
 1959   Criminal justice, legal values and the rehabilitative ideal. *Journal of Criminol-
        ogy, Criminal Law and Police Science* 50:226–232.
Alschuler, Albert W.
 1968   The prosecutor's role in plea-bargaining. *University of Chicago Law Review*
        36:50–112.
 1975   The defense attorney's role in plea-bargaining. *Yale Law Journal* 84:1179–1314.
 1976   The trial judge's role in plea-bargaining. Part I. *Columbia Law Review* 76:1059–
        1154.
 1979   Plea bargaining and its history. *Law & Society Review* 13(2):211–246.

American Bar Association
  1977   *Tentative Draft of Standards Relating to the Legal Status of Prisoners*. Chicago, Ill.: American Bar Association.
  1980   *American Bar Association Standards for Criminal Justice*. 2d ed. 4 volumes. Boston, Mass.: Little, Brown.
American Friends Service Committee
  1971   *Struggle for Justice: A Report on Crime and Punishment in America*. New York: Hill and Wang.
American Law Institute
  1962   Model Penal Code. Proposed Official Draft. American Law Institute, Philadelphia, Pa.
Andenaes, Johannes
  1983   The choice of sanction: a Scandinavian perspective. Ch. 1 in M. Tonry and F. Zimring, eds., *Reform and Punish*. Chicago, Ill.: University of Chicago Press.
Anspach, Donald F.
  1981   Crossroads of Justice: Problems with Determinate Sentencing in Maine. University of Southern Maine (Portland).
Arkin, Steven D.
  1980   Discrimination and arbitrariness in capital punishment. *Stanford Law Review* 33:75–101.
Arthur D. Little, Inc., and Goldfarb, Singer and Austern (ADL)
  1981   An Evaluation of Parole Guidelines in Four Jurisdictions. Unpublished report prepared for the National Institute of Corrections. Arthur D. Little, Inc., Washington, D.C.
  1981a Consistency: an analysis of the parole decision guidelines of the Oregon Board of Parole. In ADL, 1981.
  1981b Consistency: an analysis of the parole decision guidelines of the U.S. Parole Commission. In ADL, 1981.
  1981c Consistency: an analysis of the parole decision guidelines of the Washington State Board of Prison Terms and Parole. In ADL, 1981.
  1981d The parole guidelines of the Minnesota Corrections Board. In ADL, 1981.
  1981e The parole guidelines of the U.S. Parole Commission: an analysis of disparity. In ADL, 1981.
Atkinson, David N., and Dale A. Newman
  1970   Judicial attitudes and defendant attributes: some consequences for municipal court decision-making. *Journal of Public Law* 19:68–87.
Austin, James, and Barry Krisberg
  1982   The unmet promise of alternatives. *Crime & Delinquency* 28(July):374–409.
Baab, G.A., and W.R. Furgeson, Jr.
  1968   Texas sentencing practices: a statistical study. *Texas Law Review* 45:471–503.
Baldassare, M.
  1978   *Residential Crowding in Urban America*. Berkeley, Calif.: University of California Press.
Baldwin, John, and Michael McConville
  1977   *Negotiated Justice*. London: Martin Robertson & Co.
Banks, E.
  1964   Reconviction of young offenders. *Current Legal Problems* 17:74.
Barnes, Harry E., and Negley K. Teeters
  1959   *New Horizons in Criminology*. Englewood Cliffs, N.J.: Prentice-Hall.

Barnett, S.A., J.C. Eaton, and H.M. McCallum
  1960   Physiological effects of "social stress" in wild rats—II. Liver glycogen and blood glucose. *Journal of Psychosomatic Research* 4(July):251–260.

Bass, R.A.
  1975   An Analysis of the California Department of Corrections Work Furlough Program in Fiscal Year 1969–70. Research Unit, California Department of Corrections, Sacramento, Calif.

Beattie, R.
  1935   The Public Defender and Private Defense Attorneys. Bureau of Public Administration, Berkeley, Calif.

Bedau, Hugo Adam
  1964   Death sentences in New Jersey. *Rutgers Law Review* 19:1–2.
  1965   Capital punishment in Oregon 1903–1964. *Oregon Law Review* 45:1–39.

Beha, James A.
  1977   "And nobody can get you out"—the impact of a mandatory prison sentence for the illegal carrying of a firearm on the use of firearms and on the administration of criminal justice in Boston. *Boston University Law Review* 57:96–146(Part I), 289–333(Part II).

Bennett, L.
  1976   The study of violence in California prisons: a review with policy implications. In A. Cohen et al., eds., *Prison Violence*. Lexington, Mass.: D.C. Heath.

Bensing, Robert C., and Oliver J. Schroeder
  1960   *Homicide in an Urban Community*. Springfield, Ill.: Charles C Thomas.

Benton, F. Warren, and Judith A. Silberstein
  1983   An explanatory model of state prison expansion. *Journal of Criminal Justice*.

Berecochea, John
  1982   Origins and Early Development of Parole in California. Unpublished Ph.D. dissertation. Law and Society Program. University of California, Berkeley.

Berk, Richard A., and Subhash C. Ray
  1982   Selection biases in sociological data. *Social Science Research* 11(4):352–398.

Bernstein, Ilene Nagel, William R. Kelly, and Patricia A. Doyle
  1977   Societal reaction to deviants: the case of criminal defendants. *American Sociological Review* 42:743–755.

Bing, S., and S. Rosenfeld
  1970   *The Quality of Justice in the Lower Criminal Courts of Metropolitan Boston*. Boston, Mass.: Lawyer's Committee for Civil Rights Under Law.

Bittner, Egon
  1970   *The Functions of Police in Modern Society*. National Institute of Mental Health. Washington, D.C.: U.S. Department of Health and Human Services.

Blomqvist, A.G.
  1972   Approximating the least-squares bias in multiple regression with errors in variables. *The Review of Economics and Statistics* 54:202–204.

Blumberg, A.
  1964   *Criminal Justice*. New York: Quadrangle Books.

Blumstein, Alfred
  1982   On the racial disproportionality of U.S. prison populations. *Journal of Criminal Law & Criminology* 73(3):1259–1281.

Blumstein, Alfred, and Jacqueline Cohen
  1973   A theory of the stability of punishment. *The Journal of Criminal Law & Criminology* 64(2):198–206.

1980   Sentencing of convicted offenders: an analysis of the public's view. *Law & Society Review* 14(2):223–261.

Blumstein, Alfred, and Joseph B. Kadane
forth-   An approach to the allocation of scarce imprisonment resources. *Crime & coming Delinquency*.

Blumstein, Alfred, Jacqueline Cohen, and William Gooding
1983   The influence of capacity on prison population: a critical review of some recent evidence. *Crime & Delinquency* 29(1).

Blumstein, Alfred, Jacqueline Cohen, and Harold D. Miller
1980   Demographically disaggregated projections of prison populations. *Journal of Criminal Justice* 8:1–26.

Blumstein, Alfred, Jacqueline Cohen, and Daniel Nagin, eds.
1978   *Deterrence and Incapacitation: Estimating the Effects of Criminal Sanctions on Crime Rates.* Panel on Research on Deterrent and Incapacitative Effects, Committee on Research on Law Enforcement and Criminal Justice, Assembly of Behavioral and Social Sciences, National Research Council. Washington, D.C.: National Academy of Sciences.

Boland, B., and J.Q. Wilson
1978   Age, crime and punishment. *The Public Interest* 51:22–34.

Booth, Alan, and John Cowell
1976   Crowding and health. *Journal of Health and Social Behavior* 17:204–220.

Bordua, David
1958   Juvenile delinquency and "anomie." *Social Problems* 6:230–238.

Bowers, William J.
1974   *Executions in America.* Lexington, Mass.: D.C. Heath.

Bowers, William J., and Glen L. Pierce
1980   Arbitrariness and discrimination under post-Furman capital studies. *Crime & Delinquency* 26:563–635.

Box, George E.P., and Gwilym M. Jenkins
1976   *Time Series Analysis: Forecasting and Control.* 2d ed. San Francisco, Calif.: Holden-Day.

Brady, James
1981   Determinate sentencing and prison rehabilitation programs in California and Oregon. Ch. 22 in S.L. Messinger et al., Report on Strategies for Determinate Sentencing. Unpublished report prepared for the National Institute of Justice, U.S. Department of Justice, Washington, D.C.

Braithwaite, J.
1981   The myth of social class and criminality reconsidered. *American Sociological Review* 46:36–57.

Brereton, David, and Jonathan D. Casper
1982   Does it pay to plead guilty? *Law & Society Review* 16:1645–1670.

Brewer, D., G.E. Beckett, and N. Holt
1980   Determinate Sentencing in California: The First Year's Experience. California Department of Correction, Chino.

Bridge, Franklin M., and Jeanne Mosure
1961   Capital Punishment. Staff Research Report No. 46. Ohio Legislative Service Commission, Columbus.

Brody, S.R.
1976   *The Effectiveness of Sentencing—A Review of the Literature.* London: Her Majesty's Stationery Office.

Bullock, H.A.
1961   Significance of the racial factor in the length of prison sentences. *Journal of Criminal Law, Criminology and Police Science* 52:411–417.

Bullough, W.S.
1952   Stress and epidermal mitotic activity. I. The effects of the adrenal hormones. *Journal of Endocrinology* 8(July):265–274.

Burke, Peter J., and Austin T. Turk
1975   Factors affecting postarrest dispositions: a model for analysis. *Social Problems* 22:313–332.

Calhoun, John B.
1956   A comparative study of the social behavior of two inbred strains of house mice. *Ecological Monographs* 26:81–103.
1962   A behavioral sink. Pp. 295–315 in E.L. Bliss, ed., *Roots of Behavior; Genetics, Instinct, and Socialization in Animal Behavior*. New York: Harper & Row.
1966a   Population density and social pathology. *Scientific American* 206:139–148.
1966b   The role of space in animal sociology. *Journal of Social Issues* 22:46–58.

California Department of Justice
1980   *Criminal Justice Profile—1979: Statewide*. Division of Law Enforcement, Bureau of Criminal Statistics and Special Services. Sacramento, Calif.: California Department of Justice.

Cameron, M.O.
1964   *The Booster and the Snitch*. New York: Free Press.

Cargan, Leonard, and Mary A. Coates
1974   Indeterminate sentence and judicial bias. *Crime & Delinquency* 20:144–156.

Carlson, Kenneth, Patricia Evans, and John Flanagan
1980   Population trends and projections. Volume II of *American Prisons and Jails*. Washington, D.C.: U.S. Department of Justice.

Carter, Robert M., and Leslie T. Wilkins
1967   Some factors in sentencing policy. *Journal of Criminal Law, Criminology and Police Science* 58(4):503–514.

Casper, Jonathan D.
1972   *American Criminal Justice: The Defendant's Perspective*. Englewood Cliffs, N.J.: Prentice-Hall.

Casper, Jonathan D., David Brereton, and D. Neal
1982   *The Implementation of the California Determinate Sentencing Law*. Washington, D.C.: U.S. Department of Justice.

Chaiken, Jan, and Marcia Chaiken
1982   *Varieties of Criminal Behavior*. Santa Monica, Calif.: Rand Corporation.

Chambers, M.
1981   How the police target young offenders. *New York Times Magazine* (September 20):116–124.

Chiricos, Theodore G., and Gordon P. Waldo
1975   Socioeconomic status and criminal sentencing: an empirical assessment of a conflict proposition. *American Sociological Review* 40:753–772.

Chiricos, Theodore G., Phillip D. Jackson, and Gordon P. Waldo
1972   Inequality in the imposition of a criminal label. *Social Problems* 19:553–572.

Chow, G.C.
1957   *Demand for Automobiles in the United States*. Amsterdam, The Netherland North-Holland.

Christian, J.J.
1960   Endocrine adaptive mechanisms and the physiologic regulations of population growth. Pp. 51–150 in *Lecture and Review Series* No. 60–62. Bethesda, Md.: Naval Medical Research Institute.

Church, Thomas, Jr.
1976   Plea bargains, concessions, and the courts: analysis of a quasi-experiment. *Law & Society Review* 10:377–401.

Clarke, Stevens H., and Gary G. Koch
1976   The influence of income and other factors on whether criminal defendants go to prison. *Law & Society Review* 11:57–92.
1977   Alaska Felony Sentencing Patterns: A Multivariate Statistical Analysis. Alaska Judicial Council, Anchorage.

Clements, Carl B.
1982   The relationship of offender classification to the problems of prison overcrowding. *Crime & Delinquency* 28:72–81.

Coffee, John C., Jr.
1975   The future of sentencing reform: emerging legal issues in the individualization of justice. *Michigan Law Review* 73:1361–1462.
1978   The repressed issues of sentencing: accountability, predictability, and equity. *The Georgetown Law Journal* 66(4):975–1107.

Cohen, Jacqueline, and Joan Helland
1982   Methodology for Evaluating the Impact of Sentencing Guidelines. Urban Systems Institute, School of Urban and Public Affairs, Carnegie-Mellon University.

Commission on Accreditation for Corrections
1977a   A Manual of Standards for Adult Correctional Institutions. Commission on Accreditation for Corrections, Rockville, Md.
1977b   A Manual of Standards for Adult Local Detention Facilities. Commission on Accreditation for Corrections, Rockville, Md.

Conklin, John E.
1972   *Robbery and the Criminal Justice System.* Philadelphia, Pa.: Lippincott.

Cox, Verne C., Paul B. Paulus, Garvin McCain, and J.K. Schkade
1979   Field research on the effects of crowding in prisons and on offshore drilling platforms. In J.R. Aiello and A. Baum, eds., *Residential Crowding and Design.* New York: Plenum.

Crago, T., and Hromas, G.
1976   Beyond a straight line fit—probation [sic] projection techniques which use readily available data. In *Proceedings of the 106th Annual Congress of Corrections.* College Park, Md.: American Corrections Association.

Criminal Courts Technical Assistance Project
1980   Overview of State and Local Sentencing Guidelines and Sentencing Research Activity. Criminal Courts Technical Assistance Project, The American University.

Criminal Justice Newsletter
1982   *Criminal Justice Newsletter* 3(5):2–5.

Criminal Justice Research Center
1980   *Sourcebook of Criminal Justice Statistics—1979.* T.J. Flanagan, M.J. Hindelang, and M.R. Gottfredson, eds. Washington, D.C.: U.S. Department of Justice.

Cross, R.
1975   *The English Sentencing System.* 2d ed. London: Butterworths.

D'Atri, David A.
1975   Psychophysiological responses to crowding. *Environmental Behavior* 7(2):237–252.
D'Atri, David A., Edward F. Fitzgerald, Stanislav V. Kasl, and Adrian M. Ostfeld
1981   Crowding in prison: the relationship between changes in housing mode and blood pressure. *Psychosomatic Medicine* 43(2):95–105.
Davis, Kenneth C.
1969   *Discretionary Justice: A Preliminary Inquiry.* Baton Rouge, La.: Louisiana State University Press.
1976   *Discretionary Justice in Europe and America.* Urbana, Ill.: University of Illinois Press.
De Jong, William
1980   Supplemental report—adult pre-release facilities. Volume V of *American Prisons and Jails.* Washington, D.C.: U.S. Department of Justice.
Diamond, Shari Seidman, and C.J. Herhold
1981   Understanding criminal sentencing: views from law and social psychology. Pp. 67–102 in G. Stephenson and J.H. Davis, eds., *Progress in Applied Social Psychology.* New York: John Wiley.
Diamond, Shari Seidman, and Hans Zeisel
1975   Sentencing councils: a study of sentence disparity and its reduction. *University of Chicago Law Review* 43:109–149.
Dworkin, Ronald
1977   *Taking Rights Seriously.* Cambridge, Mass.: Harvard University Press.
Eisenstein, James, and Herbert Jacob
1977   *Felony Justice.* Boston, Mass.: Little, Brown.
Elliott, Delbert S., and Suzanne S. Ageton
1980   Reconciling race and class differences in self-reported and official estimates of delinquency. *American Sociological Review* 45:95–110.
Everson
1919   The human element in justice. *Journal of Criminal Law & Criminology.*
Farrell, Ronald A.
1971   Class linkages of legal treatment of homosexuals. *Criminology* 9:49–68.
Farrell, Ronald A., and Victoria Lynn Swigert
1978a   Prior offense as a self-fulfilling prophecy. *Law & Society Review* 12:437–453.
1978b   Legal disposition of inter-group and intra-group homicides. *Sociological Quarterly* 19:565–576.
Federal Bureau of Investigation
1980   *Crime in the U.S.—1979.* Uniform Crime Reports. Washington, D.C.: U.S. Department of Justice.
Feeley, Malcolm M.
1979   *The Process is the Punishment: Handling Cases in a Lower Criminal Court.* New York: Russell Sage Foundation.
Florida Civil Liberties Union
1964   Rape: Selective Electrocution Based on Race. Florida Civil Liberties Union, Miami.
Flowers, G.T.
1977   The Georgia Restitution Shelter Program. Evaluation Report No. 1-150. Georgia Department of Offender Rehabilitation, Atlanta.
Foley, L.A., and C.E. Rasche
1979   The effect of race on sentence, actual time served and final disposition of female

offenders. Pp. 93–106 in J.A. Conley, ed., *Theory and Research in Criminal Justice: Current Perspectives*. Cincinnati, Ohio: Anderson.

Foote, Caleb, J. Markle, and E. Woolley
1954   Compelling appearance in court: administration of bail in Philadelphia. *University of Pennsylvania Law Review* 102:1031–1079.

Forst, Brian, and Charles Wellford
1981   Punishment and sentencing: developing sentencing guidelines empirically from principles of punishment. *Rutgers Law Review* 33:799–837.

Forst, Brian, Judith Lucianovic, and Sarah J. Cox
1977   *What Happens After Arrest? A Court Perspective of Police Operations in the District of Columbia*. Washington, D.C.: Institute for Law and Social Research.

Forst, Martin L.
1981   Effects of determinate sentencing on prison disciplinary procedures and inmate misconduct. Ch. 21 in S.L. Messinger et al., Report on Strategies for Determinate Sentencing. Unpublished report prepared for the National Institute of Justice, U.S. Department of Justice, Washington, D.C.

Foucault, Michel
1978   *Discipline and Punish*. Translated by Alan Sheridan. New York: Pantheon.

Fox, James
1978   *Forecasting Crime Data*. Lexington, Mass.: Lexington Books.

Frankel, Marvin E.
1972   *Criminal Sentences: Law Without Order*. New York: Hill and Wang.

Galle, O.R., Walter R. Gove, and J.M. McPherson
1972   Population density and pathology: what are the relationships for men? *Science* 176:23–30.

Garber, Stephen, and Stephen Klepper
1980   Extending the classical normal errors-in-variables model. *Econometrica* 48:1541–1546.

Garfinkel, Harold
1949   Research note on inter- and intra-racial homicides. *Social Forces* 27:369–381.

Gaudet, F.J., G.S. Harris, and C.W. St. John
1933   Individual differences in the sentencing tendencies of judges. *Journal of Criminal Law & Criminology* 23:811–818.

Gerard, Jules, and T.R. Terry
1970   Discrimination against Negroes in the administration of criminal law in Missouri. *Washington University Law Quarterly* 1970:415–437.

Gewirth, Alan
1978   *Reason and Morality*. Chicago, Ill.: University of Chicago Press.

Gibson, James L.
1978a   Judges' role orientations, attitudes and decisions: an interactive model. *American Political Science Review* 72(September):911–924.
1978b   Race as a determinant of criminal sentences: a methodological critique and a case study. *Law & Society Review* 12:455–478.

Goldberger, A.S.
1981   Linear regression after selection. *Journal of Econometrics* 15:357–366.

Goldkamp, J.
1979   *Two Classes of Accused*. Cambridge, Mass.: Ballinger.

Goldstein, Abraham, and Stephen Marcus
1977   Myths of judicial supervision in three "inquisitorial" systems: France, Italy, and Germany. *Yale Law Journal* 78(December):240–283.

Goodstein, Lynne

1980   Psychological effects of the predictability of prison release: implications for the sentencing debate. *Criminology* 18(3):363–384.

1981   A quasi experimental test of prisoner reactions to determinate and indeterminate sentencing. In N. Parise, ed., *Coping with Crime*. Beverly Hills, Calif.: Sage.

Gordon, Robert A.

1976   Prevalence: the rare datum in delinquency measurement and its implications for the theory of delinquency. Pp. 201–284 in Malcolm W. Klein, ed., *The Juvenile Justice System*. Beverly Hills, Calif.: Sage.

Gottfredson, Don M., and Stephen D. Gottfredson

1979   *Screening for Risk: A Comparison of Methods*. National Institute of Corrections. Washington, D.C.: U.S. Department of Justice.

Gottfredson, Don M., Peter B. Hoffman, Maurice H. Sigler, and Leslie T. Wilkins

1975   Making paroling policy explicit. *Crime & Delinquency* 21(1):34–44.

Gottfredson, Don M., Leslie T. Wilkins, and Peter B. Hoffman

1978   *Guidelines for Parole and Sentencing*. Lexington, Mass.: Lexington Books.

Gove, W.R., M. Hughes, and O.R. Galle

1979   Overcrowding in the home: an empirical investigation of its possible pathological consequences. *American Sociological Review* 44:59–80.

Granger, C.W.J., and Paul Newbold

1977   *Forecasting Economic Time Series*. New York: Academic.

Green, Edward

1961   *Judicial Attitudes in Sentencing: A Study of the Factors Underlying the Sentencing Practices of the Criminal Court of Philadelphia*. Vol. 15 in Cambridge Studies in Criminology. London: Macmillan.

1964   Inter- and intra-racial crime relative to sentencing. *Journal of Criminal Law, Criminology and Police Science* 55:348–358.

Greenberg, David F.

1975   Problems in community corrections. *Issues in Criminology*. 10(Spring):1–33.

Greenwood, Peter W., and Allan Abrahamse

1982   *Selective Incapacitation*. Report R-2815-NIJ. Santa Monica, Calif.: Rand Corporation.

Greenwood, Peter W., Joan Petersilia, and Franklin E. Zimring

1980   *Age, Crime, and Sanctions: The Transition from Juvenile to Adult Court*. Report R-2642-NIJ. Santa Monica, Calif.: Rand Corporation.

Greenwood, Peter W., Sorrel Wildhorn, Eugene C. Poggio, Michael J. Strumwasser, and Peter de Leon

1973   *Prosecution of Adult Felony Defendants in L.A. County*. Santa Monica, Calif.: Rand Corporation.

Hagan, John

1974   Extra-legal attributes and criminal sentencing: an assessment of a sociological viewpoint. *Law & Society Review* 8(Spring):357–383.

1975   Parameters of criminal prosecution: an application of path analysis to a problem of criminal justice. *Journal of Criminal Law, Criminology and Police Science* 65:536–544.

1977   Criminal justice in rural and urban communities: a study of the bureaucratization of justice. *Social Forces* 55(3):597–612.

Hagan, John, and Ilene Bernstein
1979   Conflict in context: the sanctioning of draft resisters, 1963–76. *Social Problems* 27:109–122.
Hagan, John, John Hewitt, and Duane Alwin
1979   Ceremonial justice: crime and punishment in a loosely coupled system. *Social Forces* 58(2):506–527.
Hagan, John, Ilene Nagel, and Celesta Albonetti
1980   The differential sentencing of white collar offenders in ten federal district courts. *American Sociological Review* 45(October):802–820.
Hart, H.L.A.
1968   *Punishment and Responsibility*. Oxford: Oxford University.
Hartung, Frank E.
1952   Trends in the use of capital punishment. *The Annals of the American Academy of Political and Social Science* 284(November):8–19.
Harvey, D., and M.E. Engle
1978   Effects of retaliation, latency and provocation level on judged blameworthiness for retaliatory aggression. *Personality and Social Psychology Bulletin* 4:579–582.
Hausman, J.A., and D.A. Wise
1977   Social experimentation, truncated distributions and efficient estimation. *Econometrica* 45:919–938.
Heckman, James
1976   The common structure of statistical models of truncation, sample selection and limited dependent variables and a simple estimation for such models. *Annuals of Economic and Social Measurement* 5:475–492.
1979   Sample selection bias as a specification error. *Econometrica* 45:153–161.
Heider, F.
1958   *The Psychology of Interpersonal Relations*. New York: Wiley.
Heller, N.B., and J.T. McEwen
1973   Application of crime seriousness information in police departments. *Journal of Criminal Justice* 1:241–253.
Heumann, Milton
1978   *Plea Bargaining*. Chicago, Ill.: University of Chicago Press.
Heumann, Milton, and Colin Loftin
1979   Mandatory sentencing and the abolition of plea bargaining: the Michigan Felony Fire Arm Statute. *Law & Society Review* 13:393–430.
Hindelang, M.
1976   *Criminal Victimization in Eight Cities: A Descriptive Analysis of Common Theft and Assault*. Cambridge, Mass.: Ballinger.
1978   Race and involvement in common law personal crimes. *American Sociological Review* 43:93–109.
Hindelang, M., Chris Dunn, Paul Sutton, and A.L. Aumick
1975   *Sourcebook of Criminal Justice Statistics—1974*. Washington, D.C.: U.S. Department of Justice.
Hindelang, Michael J., Travis Hirschi, and Joseph G. Weis
1979   Correlates of delinquency: the illusion of discrepancy between self reports and official measures. *American Sociological Review* 44:995–1014.
Hoffman, Peter B.
1975   A paroling policy feedback method. In W.E. Amos and C.L. Newman, eds.,

Parole: Legal Issues/Decision-Making Research. New York: Federal-Legal Publications.

Hoffman, Peter B., and Don M. Gottfredson
1973   Paroling Policy Guidelines: A Matter of Equity. Supplemental report 9, Parole Decision Making Project. National Council on Crime and Delinquency, Davis, Calif.

Hoffman, Peter B., Barbara Stone-Meierhoefer, and James L. Beck
1978   Salient factor score and release behavior: three validation samples. *Law and Human Behavior* 1:47–62.

Hogarth, John
1971   *Sentencing as a Human Process.* Toronto: University of Toronto Press.

Hood, Roger
1972   *Sentencing the Motoring Offender.* London: Heinemann.

Howard, Joseph C., Jr.
1967   Rape death penalty study reported in the *New York Times,* September 18, 1967, p. 33.

Hubay, Charles
1979   Study of Robbery Cases in Alameda County. Rand Corporation, Santa Monica, Calif.

Hutt, C., and M.J. Vaizey
1966   Differential effects of group density on social behavior. *Nature* 209:1371–1372.

Hylton, John H.
1980   Community Corrections and Social Control: A Canadian Perspective. Paper presented at 110th Congress of the American Correctional Association, San Diego, Calif., August 1980.

Institute for Law and Social Research and Yankelovich, Skelly and White, Inc. (INSLAW)
1981   *Federal Sentencing: Toward a More Explicit Policy of Criminal Sanctions.* Final report. FJRP-81/003. Washington, D.C.: U.S. Department of Justice.

Iowa Law Review
1975   The elimination of plea bargaining in Black Hawk County: a case study. *Iowa Law Review* 61:1053–1071.

Ittelson, W., H. Proshansky, and L. Rivlin
1972   Bedroom size and social interaction of the psychiatric ward. Pp. 95–104 in J. Wohlwill and D. Carson, eds., *Environment and the Social Sciences: Perspectives and Applications.* Washington, D.C.: American Psychological Association.

Jackson, Richard M.
1972   *The Machinery of Justice in England.* 7th ed. Cambridge: Cambridge University Press.

Jacob, Herbert
1962   Politics and criminal prosecutions in New Orleans. *Tulane Studies in Political Science* 8:77–98.

Jacobs, James B.
1982   Sentencing by prison personnel. *UCLA Law Review* 30(November).

Jacoby, Joan
1980   *The American Prosecutor: A Search for Identity.* Lexington, Mass.: Lexington Books.

Johnson, Elmer H.
1957   Selective forces in capital punishment. *Social Forces* 36:165–69.

Johnson, Guy
1941 The Negro and crime. *The Annals of the American Academy of Political and Social Science* 217:93–104.

Johnson, Oakley C.
1951 Is the punishment of rape equally administered to Negroes and whites in the state of Louisiana? Pp. 216–228 in William L. Patterson, eds., *We Charge Genocide*. New York: International Publishers.

Johnston, J.
1972 *Econometric Methods*. 2d ed. New York: McGraw-Hill.

Joint Committee on New York Drug Law Evaluation
1978 *The Nation's Toughest Drug Law: Evaluating the New York Experience*. A project of the Association of the Bar of the City of New York and the Drug Abuse Council, Inc. Washington, D.C.: U.S. Government Printing Office.

Joseph, J.M., T.R. Kane, G.G. Gaes, and J.T. Tedeschi
1976 Effects of effort on attributed intent and perceived aggressiveness. *Perceptual and Motor Skills* 42:706–711.

Judson, Charles J., James J. Pandell, Jack B. Owens, James L. McIntosh, and Dale L. Matschullat
1969 A study of the California penalty jury in first degree murder cases. *Stanford Law Review* 21:1297–1431.

Kapardis, A., and D.P. Farrington
1982 An experimental study of sentencing by magistrates. *Law and Human Behavior* 5:107–121.

Katz, L., L. Litewin, and R. Banberger
1971 *Justice is the Crime: Pretrial Delay in Felony Cases*. A report to the National Institute of Law Enforcement and Criminal Justice, Law Enforcement Assistance Administration. Washington, D.C.: U.S. Department of Justice.

Keeley, Kim
1962 Prenatal influence on behavior of offspring of crowded mice. *Science* 135:44–45.

Kelly, Henry E.
1976 Comparison of defense strategy and race as influences in differential sentencing. *Criminology* 14:241–249.

Kennedy, Edward M.
1978 Speech to the annual conference of International Association of Chiefs of Police, New York, N.Y., October 15–20, 1978. International Association of Chiefs of Police, Gaithersburg, Md.

Kerstetter, Wayne A., and Ann M. Heinz
1979 *Pretrial Settlement Conference: An Evaluation*. Washington, D.C.: U.S. Department of Justice.

Kleck, G.
1981 Racial discrimination in criminal sentencing: a critical evaluation of the evidence with additional evidence on the death penalty. *American Sociological Review* 46:783–805.

Knapp, Kay A.
1980 Estimating the Impact of Sentencing Policies on Prison Populations. Paper presented at 32nd annual meeting of the American Society of Criminology, San Francisco, Calif., November 5–8, 1980.
1982 Impact of the Minnesota sentencing guidelines on sentencing practices. *Hamline Law Review* 5(June):237–256.

Knapp, Kay, Bob Tift, Frank Popplewell, Brad Richardson, and Jim Broucek

1979   Development of Statewide Sentencing Guidelines in Minnesota: Data Collection Instrument. Minnesota Sentencing Guidelines Commission, St. Paul, Minn.

Kramer, John H., F.A. Hussey, S.P. Lagoy, D. Katkin, and C.V. McLaughlin

1978   Assessing the Impact of Determinate Sentencing and Parole Abolition. Draft report to National Institute of Justice, U.S. Department of Justice, Washington, D.C.

Kress, Jack M.

1980   *Prescription for Justice: The Theory and Practice of Sentencing Guidelines.* Cambridge, Mass.: Ballinger Publishing Co.

Ku, R.

1980   Case studies of new legislation governing sentencing and release. Volume IV of *American Prisons and Jails.* Washington, D.C.: U.S. Department of Justice.

Kuh, Richard

1975a   Plea bargaining: guidelines for the Manhattan district attorney's office. *Criminal Law Bulletin* 11:48–61.

1975b   Sentencing: guidelines for the Manhattan district attorney's office. *Criminal Law Bulletin* 11:62–66.

Kulig, Frank

1975   Plea bargaining, probation, and other aspects of conviction and sentencing. *Creighton Law Review* 8:938–954.

LaFree, Gary D.

1980   The effect of sexual stratification by race on official reactions to rape. *American Sociological Review* 45:842–854.

Lagoy, Stephen P., Frederick A. Hussey, and John H. Kramer

1978   A comparative assessment of determinate sentencing in the four pioneer states. *Crime & Delinquency* (October):385–400.

Landes, William

1974   Legality and reality: some evidence on criminal procedure. *Journal of Legal Studies* 3:287–337.

Lemert, Edward M., and Forrest Dill

1978   *Offenders in the Community.* Lexington, Mass.: Lexington Books.

Lemert, Edwin M., and Judy Rosberg

1948   *The Administration of Justice to Minority Groups in L.A. County.* Berkeley, Calif.: University of California Press.

Lerman, Paul

1975   *Community Treatment and Social Control: A Critical Analysis of Juvenile Correctional Policy.* Chicago, Ill.: University of Chicago Press.

Levi, M.D.

1973   Errors in the variables bias in the presence of correctly measured variables. *Econometrica* 41:985–986.

Levin, Martin A.

1972   Urban politics and judicial behavior. *Journal of Legal Studies* 1:220–221.

Levin, Theodore

1966   Toward a more enlightened sentencing procedure. *Alaska Law Review* 45:499–512.

1977   *Urban Politics and the Criminal Courts.* Chicago, Ill.: University of Chicago Press.

Lipson, A.J., and Mark A. Peterson
  1980   *California Justice Under Determinate Sentencing: A Review and Agenda for Research.* Report R-2497-CRB. Santa Monica, Calif.: Rand Corporation.
Lipton, Douglas, Robert Martinson, and Judith Wilks
  1975   *The Effectiveness of Correctional Treatment: A Survey of Treatment Evaluation Studies.* New York: Praeger.
Lizotte, Alan J.
  1978   Extra-legal factors in Chicago's criminal courts: testing the conflict model of criminal justice. *Social Problems* 25:564–580.
Loftin, Colin, and D. McDowall
  1981   "One with a gun gets you two": mandatory sentencing and firearms violence in Detroit. *The Annals of the Academy of Political and Social Science* 455(May):150–167.
Loo, C.
  1972   Effects of spatial density on social behavior of children. *Journal of Applied Social Psychology* 2:372–381.
Lotz, Roy, and John D. Hewitt
  1977   The influence of legally irrelevant factors on felony sentencing. *Sociological Inquiry* 47:39–48.
Low, Peter
  1970a Comment on the sentencing system: part C. Pp. 1289–1337 in *Working Papers of the National Commission on Reform of the Federal Criminal Laws.* Vol. II. Washington, D.C.: U.S. Government Printing Office.
  1970b Preliminary memorandum on sentencing structure. Pp. 1245–1287 in *Working Papers of the National Commission on Reform of the Federal Criminal Laws.* Vol. II. Washington, D.C.: U.S. Government Printing Office.
Mangum, Charles S., Jr.
  1940   *The Legal Status of the Negro.* Chapel Hill, N.C.: North Carolina Press.
Manning, Peter K.
  1980   *The Narc's Game: Organizational and Informational Limits on Drug Law Enforcement.* Cambridge, Mass.: MIT Press.
Manson, John R.
  1981   The Prison Overcrowding Dilemma: A New Approach. Unpublished manuscript. Connecticut Department of Corrections, Hartford.
Martin, Roscoe
  1934   *The Defendant and Criminal Justice.* Bulletin No. 34-37. Bureau of Research in the Social Sciences, University of Texas.
Martin, Susan E.
  1982a Interests and Politics in Sentencing Reform: A Comparative Case Study of the Development of Sentencing Guidelines in Minnesota and Pennsylvania. Committee on Research on Law Enforcement and the Administration of Justice. National Research Council, Washington, D.C.
  1982b Commutation of Prison Sentences: Practice, Promise, and Limitation. Paper presented at meeting of American Society of Criminology, Toronto, November 4–6, 1982.
Martin, Susan E., Lee B. Sechrest, and Robin Redner, eds.
  1981   *New Directions in the Rehabilitation of Criminal Offenders.* Panel on Research on Rehabilitative Techniques, Committee on Research on Law Enforcement and the Administration of Justice, Assembly of Behavioral and Social Sciences, National Research Council. Washington, D.C.: National Academy Press.

Mather, Lynn M.
1974 Some determinants of the method of case disposition: decision-making by public defenders in Los Angeles. *Law & Society Review* 8:187–216.
McCain, Garvin, Verne C. Cox, and Paul B. Paulus
1976 The relationship between illness complaints and degree of crowding in a prison environment. *Environment and Behavior* 8(2):283–290.
1980 *The Effect of Prison Crowding on Inmate Behavior.* Washington, D.C.: U.S. Department of Justice.
McCallum, B.T.
1972 Relative asymptotic bias from errors of omission and measurement. *Econometrica* 40:757–758.
McCarthy, John P.
1978 Report of the Sentencing Guidelines Project to the Administrative Director of the Courts. State of New Jersey Administrative Office of the Courts, Trenton.
McCarthy, J.P., N. Sheflin, and J.J. Barraco
1979 Report on the Sentencing Guidelines Project to the Administrative Director of the Courts: On the Relationship Between Race and Sentencing. Sentencing Guidelines Project, State of New Jersey Administrative Office of the Courts, Trenton.
McGrew, P.
1970 Social and spatial density effects on spacing behavior in preschool children. *Journal of Child Psychology and Psychiatry* 11:197–204.
McKelvey, Blake
1977 *American Prisons.* Montclair, N.J.: Patterson Smith.
Megargee, Edwin I.
1977 The association of population density, reduced space, and uncomfortable temperatures with misconduct in a prison community. *American Journal of Community Psychology* 5(3):289–298.
Mennel, Robert M.
1973 *Thorns and Thistles: Juvenile Delinquents in the United States: 1825–1940.* Hanover, N.H.: University Press of New England.
Messinger, Sheldon L.
1979 Introduction. Pp. xi–xxx in A. von Hirsch and K. Hanrahan, *The Question of Parole.* Cambridge, Mass.: Ballinger.
Messinger, Sheldon L., Andrew von Hirsch, Kathleen Hanrahan, Richard F. Sparks, Pamela J. Utz, Elliot Studt, Martin Forst, and James Brady
1981 Report on Strategies for Determinate Sentencing. Unpublished report prepared for the National Institute of Justice, U.S. Department of Justice, Washington, D.C.
Mileski, Maureen
1971 Courtroom encounters: an observation of a lower criminal court. *Law & Society Review* 5:473–538.
Miller, D.
1980 Alternatives to Incarceration: From Total Institutions to Total Systems. Ph.D. dissertation, University of California, Berkeley.
Minnesota Sentencing Guidelines Commission
1980 Report to the Legislature. January 1, 1980. Minnesota Sentencing Guidelines Commission, St. Paul, Minn.
1981 Minnesota Sentencing Guidelines and Commentary. Rev. ed. Minnesota Sentencing Guidelines Commission, St. Paul, Minn.

1982   Preliminary Report on the Development and Impact of the Minnesota Sentencing Guidelines. Minnesota Sentencing Guidelines Commission, St. Paul, Minn.

Mitchell, R.
1971   Some social implications of high density housing. *American Sociological Review* 36:18–29.

Moitra, Soumyo D.
1981   Analysis of Sentencing Policies Considering Crime-Switching Patterns and Imprisonment Contraints. Ph.D. dissertation, School of Urban and Public Affairs, Carnegie-Mellon University.

Monahan, John, and Hood, Gloria
1976   Psychologically disordered and criminal offenders. *Criminal Justice and Behavior* 3:123–134.

Morris, Norval
1974   *The Future of Imprisonment.* Chicago, Ill.: University of Chicago Press.
1982   Anisonomy, or treating like cases unlike. Ch. 5 (pp. 179–209) in N. Morris, *Madness and the Criminal Law.* Chicago, Ill: University of Chicago Press.

Morse, W., and R. Beattie
1932   *Survey of the Administration of Criminal Justice in Oregon.* New York: Arno Press.

Mueller, Julia M., and Richard F. Sparks
1982   Strategy for determinate sentencing—some statewide statistical results (Oregon). Chapter in S.L. Messinger et al., Report on Strategies for Determinate Sentencing. Unpublished report prepared for the National Institute of Justice, U.S. Department of Justice, Washington, D.C.

Mullen, Joan, and Bradford Smith
1980   Conditions and costs of confinement. Volume III of *American Prisons and Jails.* Washington, D.C.: U.S. Department of Justice.

Mullen, Joan, Kenneth Carlson, and Bradford Smith
1980   Summary findings and policy implications of a national survey. Volume I of *American Prisons and Jails.* Washington, D.C.: U.S. Department of Justice.

Mulvihill, Donald J., Melvin M. Tumin, and Lynne A. Curtis
1969   *Crimes of Violence.* Vol. 11. Staff report submitted to the National Commission on the Causes and Prevention of Violence. Washington, D.C.: U.S. Government Printing Office.

Myers, Martha A.
1979   Offended parties and official reactions: victims and the sentencing of criminal defendants. *Sociological Quarterly* 20:529–540.

Nacci, Peter L., Hugh E. Teitelbaum, and Jerry Prather
1977   Population density and inmate misconduct rates in the federal prison system. *Federal Probation* 41(June):26–31.

Nagel, Ilene, and John Hagan
1983   Gender and crime: offense patterns and criminal court sanctions. Pp. 91–144 in M. Tonry and N. Morris, eds., *Crime and Justice, An Annual Review of Research.* Vol. 4. Chicago, Ill.: University of Chicago Press.

Nagel, Stuart
1969   *The Legal Process from a Behavioral Perspective.* Homewood, Ill.: Dorsey Press.

Nagel, William G.
  1973   *The New Red Barn: A Critical Look at the Modern American Prison*. New York: Walker and Co.
Nardulli, Peter
  1978   *The Courtroom Elite*. Cambridge, Mass.: Ballinger Publishing Co.
National Advisory Commission on Criminal Justice Standards and Goals
  1973   *Courts*. Washington, D.C.: U.S. Department of Justice.
National Commission on Reform of Federal Criminal Laws
  1970   *Study Draft of a New Federal Criminal Code*. Washington, D.C.: U.S. Government Printing Office.
National Conference of Commissioners on Uniform State Laws
  1979   Model Sentencing and Corrections Act. Approved draft—1979. National Conference of Commissioners on Uniform State Laws, Chicago, Ill.
National Council on Crime and Delinquency
  1977   *Prisons: The Price We Pay*. Hackensack, N.J.: National Council on Crime and Delinquency.
  1980   *The Sourcebook on Alternatives to Prison in California*. Report to Joint Rules Committee of the California legislature. San Francisco, Calif.: National Council on Crime and Delinquency.
National Moratorium on Prison Construction
  1981   United States incarceration and prison growth. *Jericho* (May 9):6–7. (Available from Unitarian Universalist Service Committee National Moratorium on Prison Construction, Washington, D.C.).
Nerlove, Marc, David M. Grether, and Jose L. Carvalho
  1979   *Analysis of Economic Time Series*. New York: Academic Press.
Newman, D.
  1956   Pleading guilty for considerations. *Journal of Criminal Law, Criminology and Police Science* 46:780–790.
Ney, Becki
  1980   Release Mechanisms. American Institute of Criminal Justice, Philadelphia, Pa.
Ney, Becki, William Nagel, Polly Smith, and Judi Zucker
  1980   Release Procedures. The American Foundation, Inc., Philadelphia, Pa.
Nozick, Robert
  1974   *Anarchy, State and Utopia*. New York: Basic Books.
Oaks, D.H., and W. Lehman
  1968   *A Criminal Justice System and the Indigent*. Chicago, Ill.: University of Chicago Press.
Olsen, R.
  1980   A least squares correction for selectivity bias. *Econometrica* 48:1815–1820.
Park, J.
  1976   The organization of prison violence. In A. Cohen et al., eds., *Prison Violence*. Lexington, Mass.: D.C. Heath.
Partington, Donald
  1965   The incidence of the death penalty for rape in Virginia. *Washington and Lee Law Review* 22:43–75.
Partridge, Anthony, and William B. Eldridge
  1974   *Second Circuit Sentencing Study: A Report to the Judges of the Second Circuit*. FJC No. 74–4. Washington, D.C.: The Federal Judicial Center.

Paulus, Paul B., Verne C. Cox, Garvin McCain, and Jane Chandler
   1975   Some effects of crowding in a prison environment. *Journal of Applied Social Psychology* 5:86–91.
Paulus, Paul B., Garvin McCain, and Verne C. Cox
   1978   Death rates, psychiatric commitments, blood pressure, and perceived crowding as a function of institutional crowding. *Environmental Psychology and Nonverbal Behavior* 3:107–116.
Pease, K., S. Billingham, and I. Earnshaw
   1977   *Community Service Assessed in 1976.* Home Office Research Unit Report No. 39. London: Her Majesty's Stationery Office.
Perry, R.W.
   1977   Justice system and sentencing: the importance of race in the military. *Criminology* 15:225–234.
Phillips, Charles D.
   1980   *Sentencing Councils in the Federal Courts.* Lexington, Mass.: Lexington Books.
Platt, Anthony M.
   1977   *The Child Savers.* 2d ed. Chicago, Ill.: University of Chicago Press.
Pope, Carl E.
   1975a   *Sentencing of California Felony Offenders.* National Criminal Justice Information and Statistics Service (now Bureau of Justice Statistics). Washington, D.C.: U.S. Department of Justice.
   1975b   *The Judicial Processing of Assault and Burglary Offenders in Selected California Counties.* National Criminal Justice Information and Statistics Service (now Bureau of Justice Statistics). Washington, D.C.: U.S. Department of Justice.
President's Commission on Law Enforcement and the Administration of Justice (President's Crime Commission)
   1967   *The Challenge of Crime in a Free Society.* Washington, D.C.: U.S. Government Printing Office.
Rankin, A.
   1964   The effect of pretrial detention. *New York University Law Review* 39:641–655.
Rao, C.R.
   1973   *Linear Statistical Inference and Its Applications.* 2d ed. New York: John Wiley.
Rau, Richard M.
   1972   *Sentencing in the Federal District Courts.* Law Enforcement Assistance Administration. Washington, D.C.: U.S. Department of Justice.
Rawls, John
   1971   *A Theory of Justice.* Cambridge, Mass.: Harvard University Press.
Ray, D.W.
   1978   *The Effects of High Density in a Juvenile Correctional Institution.* Ph.D. dissertation, George Peabody College for Teachers.
Reiss, Albert J., and A.L. Rhodes
   1961   The distribution of juvenile delinquency in the social class structure. *American Sociological Review* 26:720–732.
Rhodes, William M.
   1976   The economics of criminal courts: a theoretical and empirical investigation. *Journal of Legal Studies* 5:311–340.
   1977   A study of sentencing in the Hennepin County and Ramsey County district courts. *Journal of Legal Studies* 6:333–354.
   1978   *Plea Bargaining.* Washington, D.C.: Institute for Law and Social Research.
   1981   Comments on the Methodology Used in the Construction of Sentencing Guide-

lines. Paper presented at National Research Council Conference on Sentencing Research, Woods Hole, Mass., July 27–31, 1981.

Rhodes, William M., and Catherine Conly
1981   *Analysis of Federal Sentencing.* Final report. FJRP 81/004. Washington, D.C.: U.S. Department of Justice.

Rich, William D., L. Paul Sutton, Todd D. Clear, and Michael J. Saks
1981   Sentencing Guidelines: Their Operation and Impact on the Courts. Draft. National Center for State Courts, Williamsburg, Va.

Robinson, W.H., P. Smith, and J. Wolf
1977   Prison Populations and Costs—Illustrated Projections to 1980. Congressional Research Service, Library of Congress, Washington, D.C.

Robison, James O., and Gerald Smith
1971   The effectiveness of correctional programs. *Crime & Delinquency* 17:67–80.

Rosen, J.
1961   Dominance behavior of the adult rat as a function of early social experience. *Journal of Genetic Psychology* 99:145–151.

Rossi, Peter H., and Steven L. Nock, eds.
1982   *Measuring Social Judgements: The Factorial Survey Approach.* Beverly Hills, Calif.: Sage.

Rothman, David J.
1971   *The Discovery of the Asylum.* Boston, Mass.: Little, Brown and Co.
1980   *Conscience and Convenience: The Asylum and Its Alternatives in Progressive America.* Boston, Mass.: Little, Brown and Co.
1981   Perspectives on the History of Sentencing. Paper presented at National Research Council Conference on Sentencing Research, Woods Hole, Mass., July 27–31, 1981.

Rothman, Meah Dell
1976   The pardoning power: historical perspective and case study of New York and Connecticut. *Columbia Journal of Law and Social Problems* 12(Winter):149–220.

Rubenstein, Jonathan
1974   *City Police.* New York: Ballantine Books

Rubinstein, Michael L., Stevens H. Clarke, and Teresa J. White
1980   *Alaska Bans Plea Bargaining.* Washington, D.C.: U.S. Department of Justice.

Ryan, John P.
1980/   Adjudication and sentencing in a misdemeanor court: the outcome is the pun-
1981   ishment. *Law & Society Review* 15:79–108.

Samuelson, Paula
1977   Sentence review and sentence disparity: a case study of the Connecticut Sentence Review Division. *Connecticut Law Review* 10:5–89.

Schmid, Calvin Fisher
1960   Urban crime areas. *American Sociological Review* 25(August):527–542, 25 (October):655–678.

Schmitt, R.C.
1957   Density, delinquency and crime in Honolulu. *Sociology and Social Research* 41:274–276.

Schneider, Peter R., and Anne L. Schneider
1979   Implementation and Policy Issues in the National Juvenile Restitution Initiative: A Six-Month Evaluation Report. Institute for Policy Analysis, Eugene, Oreg.

Schulhofer, Stephen J.
1979 Prosecutorial Discretion and Federal Sentencing Reform. Vol. 1 and Vol. 2 (Technical Supplement). Federal Judicial Center, Washington, D.C..
1980 Due process of sentencing. *University of Pennsylvania Law Review* 128:733–828.

Sebba, L.
1980 Is mens rea a component of perceived offense seriousness? *Journal of Criminal Law & Criminology* 71:124–135.

Sechrest, Lee B., Susan O. White, and Elizabeth D. Brown, eds.
1979 *The Rehabilitation of Criminal Offenders: Problems and Prospects.* Panel on Research on Rehabilitative Techniques, Committee on Research on Law Enforcement and Criminal Justice, Assembly of Behavioral and Social Sciences, National Research Council. Washington, D.C.: National Academy of Sciences.

Sellin, Thorsten, and Marvin E. Wolfgang
1964 *The Measurement of Delinquency.* New York: Wiley.

Sentencing Guidelines Project
1981 Advisory board makes first guideline modifications. *SGP News* (August). Administrative Office of the Courts, Annapolis, Md.

Shane-Dubow, Sandra, Walter F. Smith, and Kim B. Haralson
1979 *Felony Sentencing in Wisconsin.* Madison, Wis.: Public Policy Press.

Shaw, C.R., and H.D. McKay
1942 *Juvenile Delinquency and Urban Areas.* Rev. ed. Chicago, Ill.: University of Chicago Press.

Singer, N., and V.B. Wright
1976 *Cost Analysis of Corrections Standards: Institutional-Based Programs and Parole.* National Institute of Law Enforcement and Criminal Justice. Washington, D.C.: U.S. Department of Justice.

Singer, Richard G.
1979 *Just Deserts: Sentencing Based on Equality and Desert.* Cambridge, Mass.: Ballinger.

Smith, G.
1970 A Statistical Analysis of Public Defender Activities. Ohio State University Research Foundation, Columbus.

Solomon, L.
1980 Developing an empirically based model for classification decision-making. *Prison Law Monitor* 217:234–42.

Southern Regional Council
1969 Race Makes the Difference. Southern Regional Council, Atlanta, Ga.

Sparks, Richard F.
1981 The Construction of Sentencing Guidelines: A Methodological Critique. Paper presented at National Research Council Conference on Sentencing Research, Woods Hole, Mass., July 27–31, 1981.

Sparks, Richard F., and Bridget A. Stecher
1979 The New Jersey Sentencing Guidelines: An Unauthorized Analysis. Paper presented at the annual meeting of the American Society of Criminology, Philadelphia, Pa., November 8, 1979.

Sparks, Richard F., Bridget A. Stecher, Jay Albanese, and Peggy L. Shelly
1982 Stumbling Toward Justice: Some Overlooked Research and Policy Questions About Statewide Sentencing Guidelines. Final report of the Evaluation of State-

wide Sentencing Guidelines Project. National Institute of Justice, U.S. Department of Justice, Washington, D.C.

Spohn, C., J. Gruhl, and S. Welch
1982   The effect of race on sentencing: a reexamination of an unsettled question. *Law & Society Review* 16:71–88.

Stafford, Samuel P. II
1977   *Clemency : Legal Authority, Procedure and Structure*. Williamsburg, Va: National Center for State Courts.

Stone-Meierhoefer, Barbara, and Peter B. Hoffman
1980   The Effects of Presumptive Parole Dates on Institutional Behavior: A Preliminary Study. Draft. Report 27. Research Unit, U.S. Parole Commission, U.S. Department of Justice, Washington, D.C.

Strathman, Gerald J., et al.
1981   Minnesota Community Corrections Act Evaluation: General Report. Crime Control Planning Board, Minnesota Department of Corrections, St. Paul.

Sutton, P.
1978   *Variations in Federal Criminal Sentences: A Statistical Assessment at the National Level*. National Criminal Justice Information and Statistics Service (now Bureau of Justice Statistics). Washington, D.C.: U.S. Department of Justice.

Swigert, Victoria Lynn, and Ronald A. Farrell
1977   Normal homicides and the law. *American Sociological Review* 42:16–32.

Taylor, J., T. Stanley, B. DeFlorio, and L. Seekamp
1972   An analysis of defense counsel in the processing of felony defendants in San Diego, California. *Denver Law Journal* 49:233–275.

Terry, R.
1967   Discrimination in the handling of juvenile offenders by social-control agencies. *Journal of Research in Crime and Delinquency* 4:218.

Thalheimer, D.J.
1978   *Cost Analysis of Correctional Standards: Community Supervision, Probation, Restitution, Community Service*. Volume II. Washington, D.C.: U.S. Department of Justice.

Thomas, David A.
1979   *The Principles of Sentencing*. 2d ed. London: Heinemann.

Thomson, Randall J., and Matthew T. Zingraff
1981   Detecting sentence disparity: some problems and evidence. *American Journal of Sociology* 86:869–880.

Thornberry, Terence P.
1973   Race, socioeconomic status and sentencing in the juvenile justice system. *Journal of Criminal Law & Criminology* 64:90–98.

Tiffany, Lawrence P., Yakov Avichai, and Geoffrey W. Peters
1975   A statistical analysis of sentencing in federal courts: defendants convicted after trial, 1967–1968. *The Journal of Legal Studies* 4:369–390.

Tobin, James
1958   Estimation of relationships for limited dependent variables. *Econometrica* 26:24–36.

Townsend, David, John W. Palmer, and Jennifer Newton
1978   Technical Issue Paper on Presentence Investigation Reports. Report No. 3, Critical Issues in Adult Probation. Center for Law Enforcement and Correctional Justice, Westerville, Ohio.

Turner, C.D.
1961   *General Endocrinology*. Philadelphia, Pa.: W.B. Saunders.
The Twentieth Century Fund. Task Force on Criminal Sentencing
1976   *Fair and Certain Punishment*. New York: McGraw-Hill.
Uhlman, Thomas M.
1979   *Racial Justice: Black Judges and Defendants in an Urban Trial Court*. Lexington, Mass.: Lexington Books.
Uhlman, Thomas M., and Darlene N. Walker
1980   "He takes some of my time; I take some of his": an analysis of judicial sentencing patterns in jury cases. *Law & Society Review* 14:323–341.
Uniform Parole Reports
1980   Parole in the United States: 1979. James L. Galvin, Cheryl H. Ruby, John J. Galvin, Ellen L. McNeil. *Uniform Parole Reports* Series 1:80:3. San Francisco, Calif.: National Council on Crime and Delinquency.
Unnever, James D., Charles Frazier, and John C. Henretta
1980   Race differences in criminal sentencing. *Sociological Quarterly* 21:197–207.
U.S. Department of Commerce
1980   *Population Estimates and Projections*. Series P-25, No. 870, Bureau of the Census. Washington, D.C.: U.S. Department of Commerce.
U.S. Department of Justice
1975   *Prisoners in State and Federal Institutions on December 31, 1974*. National Prisoner Statistics Bulletin SD-NPS-PSF-2. Law Enforcement Assistance Administration. Washington, D.C.: U.S. Department of Justice.
1976   *Prisoners in State and Federal Institutions on December 31, 1975*. National Prisoner Statistics Bulletin SD-NPS-PSF-3. Law Enforcement Assistance Administration. Washington, D.C.: U.S. Department of Justice.
1977   *Prisoners in State and Federal Institutions on December 31, 1976*. National Prisoner Statistics Bulletin SD-NPS-PSF-4. Law Enforcement Assistance Administration. Washington, D.C.: U.S. Department of Justice.
1978a   *Federal Standards for Corrections*. Washington, D.C.: U.S. Department of Justice.
1978b   *Prisoners in State and Federal Institutions on December 31, 1977*. National Prisoner Statistics Bulletin SD-NPS-PSF-5. Law Enforcement Assistance Administration. Washington, D.C.: U.S. Department of Justice.
1979   *Prisoners in State and Federal Institutions on December 31, 1978*. National Prisoner Statistics Bulletin SD-NPS-PSF-6. Bureau of Justice Statistics. Washington, D.C.: U.S. Department of Justice.
1980a   *Crime in the U.S.—1979*. Washington, D.C.: U.S. Department of Justice.
1980b   *Criminal Victimization in the United States, 1978*. National Crime Survey Report NCS-N-17. GPO NCJ-66480. Bureau of Justice Statistics. Washington, D.C.: U.S. Department of Justice.
1981a   Prisoners at midyear 1981. *Bureau of Justice Statistics Bulletin* (September). NC-78756. Bureau of Justice Statistics. Washington, D.C.: U.S. Department of Justice.
1981b   *Prisoners in State and Federal Institutions on December 31, 1979*. National Prisoner Statistics Bulletin NPS-PSF-7, NCJ-73719. Bureau of Justice Statistics. Washington, D.C.: U.S. Department of Justice.
1981c   *Criminal Victimization in the United States, 1979*. Washington, D.C.: U.S. Department of Justice.

1982a Prisoners in 1981. *Bureau of Justice Statistics Bulletin* (May). NCJ-82262. Bureau of Justice Statistics. Washington, D.C.: U.S. Department of Justice.

1982b *Prisons and Prisoners*. Bureau of Justice Statistics Bulletin NCJ-80697. Washington, D.C.: U.S. Department of Justice

U.S. Department of Labor
1980 *Handbook of Labor Statistics*. Bulletin 2070. Washington, D.C.: U.S. Department of Labor.

U.S. General Accounting Office
1978 *What Can be Done About Overcrowding in Long-Term Federal Correctional Facilities?* Washington, D.C.: U.S. General Accounting Office.

1982 *Federal Parole Practices: Better Management and Legislative Changes are Needed.* Washington, D.C.: U.S. General Accounting Office.

Utz, Pamela J.
1981 Determinate sentencing in two California courts. Ch. 17 in S. L. Messinger et al., Report on Strategies for Determinate Sentencing. Unpublished report prepared for the National Institute of Justice, U.S. Department of Justice, Washington, D.C.

van den Haag, Ernest
1975 *Punishing Criminals: Concerning a Very Old and Painful Question*. New York: Basic.

Vera Institute of Justice
1977 Felony Arrests: Prosecution and Disposition in New York City's Courts. Vera Institute of Justice, New York.

Vetri, D.
1964 Guilty plea bargaining: compromises by prosecutors to secure guilty pleas. *University of Pennsylvania Law Review* 112:865–908.

von Hirsch, Andrew
1976 *Doing Justice: The Choice of Punishments*. New York: Hill and Wang.

1981 Utilitarian sentencing resuscitated: the American Bar Association's second report on criminal sentencing. *Rutgers Law Review* 33(Spring):772–789.

von Hirsch, Andrew, and Kathleen Hanrahan
1979 *The Question of Parole: Retention, Reform, or Abolition?* Cambridge, Mass.: Ballinger.

1981 Determinate penalty systems in America: an overview. *Crime & Delinquency* 27(July):289–316.

Walker, Samuel
1980 *Popular Justice: A History of American Criminal Justice*. New York: Oxford University Press.

1979 *A History of Criminal Justice in America*. New York: Oxford University Press.

Walster, E.
1966 Assignment of responsibility for an accident. *Journal of Personality and Social Psychology* 3:73–79.

Wechsler, Herbert
1961 Sentencing, correction, and the Model Penal Code. *University of Pennsylvania Law Review* 109:465–493.

Weigend, Thomas
1980 Continental cures for American ailments: European criminal procedure as a model for law reform. Pp. 381–428 in M. Tonry and N. Morris, eds., *Crime and Justice: An Annual Review of Research*. Vol. 2. Chicago, Ill.: University of Chicago Press.

1983 Sentencing in West Germany. In Michael H. Tonry and Franklin E. Zimring, eds., *Reform and Punishment*. Chicago, Ill.: University of Chicago Press.

Weiner, B., ed.
1974 *Achievement Motivation and Attribution Theory*. Morristown, N.J.: General Learning Press.

Weiss, Carol H.
1981 The Influence of Research in Criminal Justice: The Case of Sentencing. Harvard University, Cambridge, Mass.

Wheeler, Stanton, E. Bonachich, M.R. Cramer, and I.K. Zola
1981 Agents of delinquency control: a comparative analysis. In S. Wheeler, ed., *Controlling Delinquents*. New York: Wiley.

White, James B.
1978 Making sense of the criminal law. *University of Colorado Law Review* 50:1–27.

Wickens, M.R.
1972 A note on the use of proxy variables. *Econometrica* 40:759–761.

Wilkins, Leslie T.
1981 *The Principles of Guidelines for Sentencing: Methodological and Philosophical Issues in Their Development*. Washington, D.C.: U.S. Department of Justice.

Wilkins, Leslie T., Jack M. Kress, Don M. Gottfredson, Joseph C. Calpin, and Arthur M. Gelman
1978 *Sentencing Guidelines: Structuring Judicial Discretion—Report on the Feasibility Study*. Washington, D.C.: U.S. Department of Justice.

Williams, Glanville
1961 *Criminal Law*. 2d ed. London: Stevens.

Willick, D.H., G. Gehlker, and A.M. Watts
1975 Social class as a factor affecting judicial disposition. *Criminology* 13:57–77.

Wilson, James Q.
1973 *Varieties of Police Behavior*. New York: Atheneum.
1975 *Thinking About Crime*. New York: Basic.

Wolf, Edwin D.
1964 Abstract of analysis of jury sentencing in capital cases. *Rutgers Law Review* 19:56–64.

Wolfgang, M.
1978 Overview of research into violent behavior. Testimony to the Subcommittee on Domestic and International Scientific Planning, Analysis and Cooperation (DISPAC) of the Committee on Science and Technology. U.S. House of Representatives, Washington, D.C.

Wolfgang, Marvin E., and Franco Ferracutti
1967 *The Subculture of Violence: Toward an Integrated Theory in Criminology*. London: Tavistock.

Wolfgang, Marvin E., and Marc Reidel
1973 Race, judicial discretion, and the death penalty. *The Annals of the American Academy of Political and Social Science* 407:119–133.

Wolfgang, Marvin E., Robert Figlio, and Thorsten Sellin
1972 *Delinquency in a Birth Cohort*. Chicago, Ill.: University of Chicago Press.

Wolfgang, Marvin E., Arlene Kelly, and Hans C. Nolde
1962 Comparison of the executed and commuted among admissions to death row. *Journal of Criminal Law, Criminology and Police Science* 53:301–311.

Yale Law Journal
1956 Comment: the influence of the defendant's plea on the judicial determination

of sentence. *Yale Law Journal* 66:204–222.

Zalman, Marvin, Charles W. Ostrom, Jr., Phillip Guilliams, and Garret Peaslee
1979   Sentencing in Michigan: Report on the Michigan Felony Sentencing Project. Michigan State Court Administrative Office, Lansing.

Zarr, Melvyn
1976   Sentencing. *Maine Law Review* 28(Special Issue):117–148.

Zeisel, Hans, and Diamond, Shari S.
1977   Search for sentencing equity: sentence review in Massachusetts and Connecticut. *American Bar Foundation Research Journal*. 4(Fall):881–940.

Zimring, Franklin E.
1976   A Consumer's Guide to Sentencing Reform. Occasional Paper #16. University of Chicago Law School, Chicago, Ill.
1983   Prisoners, professors and politicians—sentencing reform in the decade of the seventies. In Michael H. Tonry and Franklin E. Zimring, eds., *Reform and Punishment*. Chicago, Ill.: University of Chicago Press.

Zimring, Franklin E., Joel Eigen, and Sheila O'Malley
1976   Punishing homicide in Philadelphia: perspectives on the death penalty. *University of Chicago Law Review* 43:227–252.

Participants, Conference on Sentencing Research

Woods Hole, Massachusetts
July 27–29, 1981

JAMES AUSTIN, National Council on Crime and Delinquency, San Francisco, California

HUGO A. BEDAU, Department of Philosophy, Tufts University

WARREN BENTON, John Jay College of Criminal Justice, City University of New York

*RICHARD A. BERK, Department of Sociology, University of California, Santa Barbara

*†ALFRED BLUMSTEIN, School of Urban and Public Affairs, Carnegie-Mellon University

JOHN S. CARROLL, Department of Psychology, Loyola University of Chicago

*JONATHAN D. CASPER, Department of Political Science, University of Illinois, Urbana

*JOHN C. COFFEE, JR., School of Law, Columbia University

JACQUELINE COHEN, School of Urban and Public Affairs, Carnegie-Mellon University

*SHARI S. DIAMOND, Department of Psychology, University of Illinois, Chicago Circle

*FRANKLIN M. FISHER, Department of Economics, Massachusetts Institute of Technology

LAWRENCE M. FRIEDMAN, School of Law, Stanford University

*Member, Panel on Sentencing Research.
†Member, Committee on Research on Law Enforcement and the Administration of Justice.

309

STEVEN GARBER, School of Urban and Public Affairs, Carnegie-Mellon University

*DON M. GOTTFREDSON, School of Criminal Justice, Rutgers University

JOHN HAGAN, Department of Sociology and Faculty of Law, University of Toronto

JAMES B. JACOBS, School of Law, Cornell University

*†JOSEPH B. KADANE, Department of Statistics, Carnegie-Mellon University

STEVEN KLEPPER, Department of Statistics, Carnegie-Mellon University

KAY A. KNAPP, Minnesota Sentencing Guidelines Commission, Minneapolis

BARRY KRISBERG, National Council on Crime and Delinquency, San Francisco, California

RICHARD LEMPERT, School of Law, Cornell University

CHARLES F. MANSKI, Cambridge Systematics, Inc., Cambridge, Massachusetts

SUSAN E. MARTIN, National Research Council

CHERYL MARTORANA, National Institute of Justice, U.S. Department of Justice

SHELDON L. MESSINGER, Center for the Study of Law and Society, University of California, Berkeley

*†NORVAL MORRIS, School of Law, University of Chicago

DANIEL S. NAGIN, Pennsylvania Department of Revenue, Harrisburg

LLOYD OHLIN, Harvard Law School

WILLIAM RHODES, Institute for the Study of Law and Society, Washington, D.C.

*DAVID ROTHMAN, Department of History, Columbia University

*RUTH RUSHEN, Department of Corrections, Sacramento, California

JUDITH SILBERSTEIN, New York City

BRADFORD SMITH, National Council on Crime and Delinquency

RICHARD F. SPARKS, School of Criminal Justice, Rutgers University

LUKE-JON TIERNEY, Department of Statistics, Carnegie-Mellon University

MICHAEL H. TONRY, School of Law, University of Maryland

*†JAMES Q. WILSON, Department of Political Science, Harvard University

---

*Member, Panel on Sentencing Research.
†Member, Committee on Research on Law Enforcement and the Administration of Justice.

APPENDIX **B**

Biographical Sketches,
Panel Members and Staff

ALFRED BLUMSTEIN is J. Erik Jonsson professor of urban systems and operations research and director of the Urban Systems Institute in the School of Urban and Public Affairs, Carnegie-Mellon University. He is chair of the Pennsylvania Commission on Crime and Delinquency, and he previously served as director of the Task Force on Science and Technology for the President's Commission on Law Enforcement and Administration of Justice. He is chair of the National Research Council's Committee on Research on Law Enforcement and the Administration of Justice and was chair of that committee's Panel on Research on Deterrent and Incapacitative Effects. He is a fellow of the American Association for the Advancement of Science; a member of the Law & Society Association, the American Society of Criminology, and the International Society of Criminology; past president of the Operations Research Society of America; and associate editor of several journals. He received a bachelor of engineering physics degree and a PhD degree in operations research from Cornell University.

SYLVIA BACON is associate judge of the District of Columbia Superior Court. Previously she was an assistant U.S. attorney for the District of Columbia and assistant director of the District of Columbia Crime Commission, and she was the U.S. delegate to the Fifth United Nations Congress on Prevention of Crime. She is the author of *Report of the President's Commission on Crime in District of Columbia* (1967). She is chair of the Criminal Justice Section of the American Bar Association

311

and a past member of the Association's Commission on Corrections, the National Commission on Criminal Justice Standards and Goals, and the Law Enforcement Assistance Administration Task Force on Juvenile Justice. She received a BA degree from Vassar College, an LLB degree from Harvard Law School, and an LLM degree from Georgetown University Law Center.

RICHARD A. BERK is professor of sociology at the University of California, Santa Barbara. His research is concerned with evaluation research, the sociology of law, and applied econometrics. He is coauthor of *A Measure of Justice* (1977), *Prison Reform and State Elites* (1977), and *Money, Work, and Crime: Experimental Evidence* (1981). He is a member of the American Sociological Association, the American Economics Association, and the American Statistical Association and of the editorial boards of several journals. He received a BA degree from Yale University and a PhD degree from Johns Hopkins University.

JONATHAN D. CASPER is professor of political science at the University of Illinois, Urbana. Previously he was associate professor of political science at Stanford University. His research involves civil and political rights in the United States; plea bargaining in criminal courts; and defendant attitudes toward defense attorneys, judges, and prosecutors. He is the author of *American Criminal Justice: The Defendant's Perspective* (1972) and *The Implementation of the California Determinate Sentencing Law* (1982). He is a member of the American Political Science Association and of the board of trustees of the Law & Society Association. He received a BA degree from Swarthmore College and MA and PhD degrees from Yale University.

JOHN C. COFFEE, JR., is professor of law at Columbia University Law School. Previously he was on the faculty of the Georgetown University Law Center. His research in criminal law concerns sentencing and parole and white-collar or organizational crime. He is vice-chair of the Committee on Sentencing, Parole and Pardon Procedures of the American Bar Association. He received a BA degree from Amherst College and an LLB degree from Yale University Law School.

SHARI SEIDMAN DIAMOND is associate professor of psychology and criminal justice at the University of Illinois, Chicago. Her research involves judicial and jury decision making and methodological problems in the study of law. She is a member of the American Psychological Association, the American Psychology-Law Society, the board of trustees of the Law & Society Association, and the editorial boards of several journals. She received a BA degree from the University of Michigan and an MA degree in psychology and a PhD degree in social psychology from Northwestern University.

FRANKLIN M. FISHER is professor of economics, Massachusetts Institute of Technology. His research concerns price theory, particularly stability theory, industrial organization, and econometrics. He is a fellow of the American Academy of Arts and Sciences; a fellow and past council member of the Econometric Society; and a member, past vice-president, and past president of the American Economic Association. He received AB, MA, and PhD degrees from Harvard University.

DON M. GOTTFREDSON is dean and professor of the School of Criminal Justice, Rutgers University. Previously he was director of the National Council on Crime and Delinquency. His research concerns decision making in criminal justice, prediction methods, and program evaluation. He is coauthor of *Classification for Parole Decision Policy* (1978), *Guidelines for Parole and Sentencing* (1978), *Decisionmaking in Criminal Justice* (1980), and *Screening for Risk: A Comparison of Methods* (1981). He is a member of the American Society of Criminology, the American Psychological Association, the Academy of Criminal Justice Sciences, the Advisory Council of the National Institute of Criminal Justice, and the New Jersey Corrections Advisory Council and a fellow of the National Center for Juvenile Justice. He received a BA degree from the University of California, Berkeley, and MA and PhD degrees in psychology from Claremont Graduate School.

JOSEPH B. KADANE is professor of statistics and social sciences at Carnegie-Mellon University, and he previously also served as head of the department of statistics. His teaching and research interests center on the use of quantitative methods in various social sciences and in statistical theory. He is an elected fellow of the American Statistical Association, the Institute of Mathematical Statistics, and the American Association for the Advancement of Science and an elected member of the International Statistical Institute. He received a BA degree in mathematics from Harvard University and a PhD degree in statistics from Stanford University.

NORVAL MORRIS is Julius Kreeger professor of law and criminology at the University of Chicago, and he previously served as dean of the Law School. His research concerns the criminal justice system. He is the author of *The Future of Imprisonment* (1974) and *Madness and the Criminal Law* (1982). He is a fellow of the American Bar Foundation, a member of the American Academy of Arts and Sciences and the Police Board of the City of Chicago, and a member of the Board of Governors of the Chicago Bar Foundation. He received LLB and LLM degrees from the University of Melbourne, Australia, and a PhD degree in law and criminology from the University of London.

DAVID J. ROTHMAN is director of the Center for the Study of Society and Medicine and Bernard Schoenberg professor of social medicine at Columbia University. His research focuses on the history of institutions for deviant and dependent people, particularly incarcerative institutions. He is coauthor of *Doing Good: The Limits of Benevolence* (1978) and the author of *The Discovery of the Asylum: Social Order and Disorder in the New Republic* (1971), *Conscience and Convenience: The Asylum and Its Alternatives in Progressive America* (1981), and *The Willowbrook Wars* (1983). He received a PhD degree in history from Harvard University.

RUTH L. RUSHEN is director of the California Department of Corrections. Previously she served as vice-chair and member of the California Board of Prison Terms. Her work involves corrections (probation, parole, and institutions), social welfare, human relations, and community development. She is a member of the American Correctional Association, the American Probation and Parole Association, the California Probation, Parole and Correctional Association, the Black Probation Officers Association, the California Black Corrections Coalition, the board of directors of the Southern California Alumni in Public Administration, and the National Association for the Advancement of Colored People. She received a BA degree in social studies from Clarke College and an MPA degree from the University of Southern California.

JAMES Q. WILSON is Henry Lee Shattuck professor of government at Harvard University. He is the author of *Varieties of Police Behavior* (1973), *Thinking About Crime* (1975), and *The Investigators: Managing the FBI and Narcotics Agents* (1978). He is a fellow of the American Academy of Arts and Sciences and a member of the board of directors of the Police Foundation. He received a BA degree from the University of Redlands and a PhD degree from the University of Chicago.

SUSAN E. MARTIN, who served as study director of the Panel on Sentencing Research, is senior research associate with the Committee on

Research on Law Enforcement and the Administration of Justice, and she previously served as study director of the Panel on Research on Rehabilitative Techniques and as research associate with the Panel on Legislative Impact on the Courts. She is the author of *"Breaking and Entering": Policewomen on Patrol* (1980). Her research interests include police, career criminals, and public policy. She is a member of the American Sociological Association, the Society for the Study of Social Problems, the American Society of Criminology, and the Law & Society Association. She received a BA degree from Swarthmore College, an MS degree in education from the University of Rochester, and a PhD degree in sociology from American University.

JACQUELINE COHEN is associate director of the Urban Systems Institute and research associate in the School of Urban and Public Affairs, Carnegie-Mellon University. Her research concerns quantitative methods (including econometrics and stochastic processes), criminal careers, and incapacitation). She is a member of the Law & Society Association, the Operations Research Society of America, the American Society of Criminology, and the American Sociological Association. She received BS and MA degrees from the University of Pittsburgh and a PhD degree in urban and public affairs from Carnegie-Mellon University.

MICHAEL H. TONRY is associate professor at the University of Maryland School of Law. Previously he was a visiting fellow at the University of Chicago Law School, director of the sentencing guidelines project in the Center for Studies in Criminal Justice at the University of Chicago Law School, and he practiced corporate financial law. His research focuses on criminal law, consumer protection, and commercial law. He is coeditor of *Crime and Justice—An Annual Review of Research*. He received a BA degree from the University of North Carolina and an LLB degree from Yale University Law School.